Barcode in Back

FOR REFERENCE ONLY
NOT TO BE TAKEN FROM THIS ROOM

D1689305

HUMBER LIBRARIES LAKESHORE CAMPUS
3199 Lakeshore Blvd West
TORONTO, ON. M8V 1K8

The Psychology of Teen Violence and Victimization

The Psychology of Teen Violence and Victimization

Volume 1: From Bullying to Cyberstalking to Assault and Sexual Violation

Michele A. Paludi, Editor

Foreword by Lisa Krenkel

 PRAEGER

AN IMPRINT OF ABC-CLIO, LLC
Santa Barbara, California • Denver, Colorado • Oxford, England

HUMBER LIBRARIES LAKESHORE CAMPUS
3199 Lakeshore Blvd West
TORONTO, ON.   M8V 1K8

Copyright 2011 by Michele A. Paludi

All rights reserved. No part of this publication may be reproduced, stored in a retrieval system, or transmitted, in any form or by any means, electronic, mechanical, photocopying, recording, or otherwise, except for the inclusion of brief quotations in a review, without prior permission in writing from the publisher.

Library of Congress Cataloging-in-Publication Data

The psychology of teen violence and victimization / Michele A. Paludi, editor ; foreword by Lisa Krenkel.
   p. cm.
Includes bibliographical references and index.
ISBN 978-0-313-39375-4 (hardback: acid-free paper) – ISBN 978-0-313-39376-1 (ebk)
1. Children and violence. 2. Violence in children. 3. Youth–Crimes against. I. Paludi, Michele Antoinette.
HQ784. V55P79   2011
303.60835–dc23   2011033276

ISBN: 978-0-313-39375-4
EISBN: 978-0-313-39376-1

15 14 13 12 11 1 2 3 4 5

This book is also available on the World Wide Web as an eBook.
Visit www.abc-clio.com for details.

Praeger
An Imprint of ABC-CLIO, LLC

ABC-CLIO, LLC
130 Cremona Drive, P.O. Box 1911
Santa Barbara, California 93116-1911

This book is printed on acid-free paper ∞

Manufactured in the United States of America

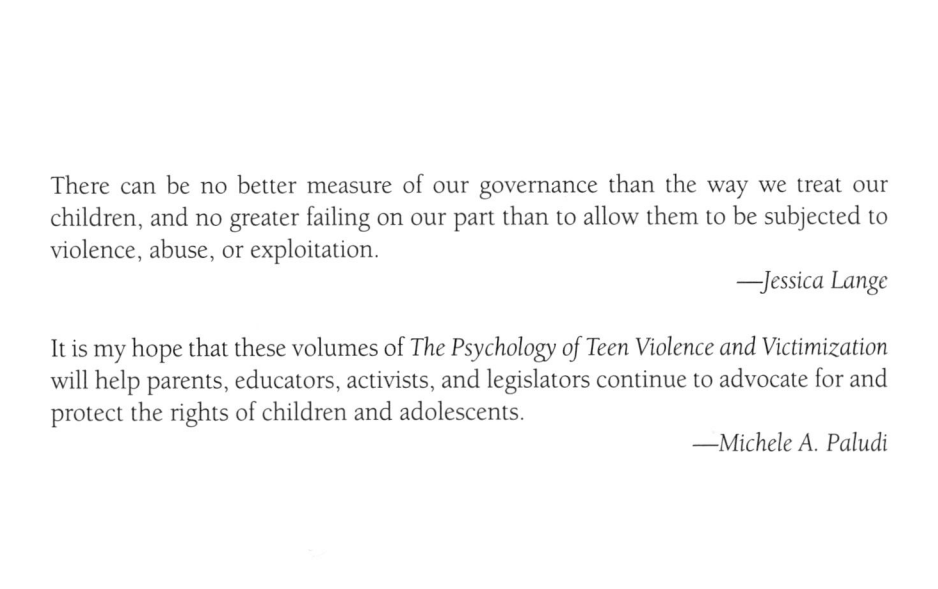

There can be no better measure of our governance than the way we treat our children, and no greater failing on our part than to allow them to be subjected to violence, abuse, or exploitation.
—*Jessica Lange*

It is my hope that these volumes of *The Psychology of Teen Violence and Victimization* will help parents, educators, activists, and legislators continue to advocate for and protect the rights of children and adolescents.
—*Michele A. Paludi*

Contents

Foreword by Lisa Krenkel — ix

Acknowledgments — xi

Introduction by Michele A. Paludi — xiii

PART I. DEVELOPMENTAL AND CULTURAL ISSUES IN TEEN VIOLENCE

Chapter One: Microaggressions: A Root of Bullying, Violence, and Victimization toward Lesbian, Gay, Bisexual, and Transgender Youths — 3
Kevin L. Nadal and Katie E. Griffin

Chapter Two: Violence in Emerging Adulthood: A Developmental Perspective — 23
Robert F. Marcus and Eric G. Jamison II

Chapter Three: "Mean Girls" in Real Life: The Media's Influence on Teen Violence and Victimization — 37
Jennifer L. Martin

Chapter Four: The Impact of Race on Perceptions of Adolescent Sex Offenders — 57
Margaret C. Stevenson, Katlyn M. Sorenson Farnum, Allison L. Skinner, and Rukudzo Amanda Dzwairo

PART II. TEEN VIOLENCE AT SCHOOL, ON THE INTERNET, AND AT WORK

Chapter Five: Schoolyard Violence — 83
Stuart C. Aitken and Donald E. Colley III

Chapter Six:	Bullying in Middle School: What Does It Look Like, Why Does It Happen, and Who Does It Hurt? *Christine M. Wienke Totura and Carol MacKinnon-Lewis*	105
Chapter Seven:	Teachers and Teen Bullying *Deborah James, Maria Lawlor, Niamh Murphy, and Ann Flynn*	127
Chapter Eight:	Sexual Harassment of Adolescent Girls by Peers, Teachers, Employers, and Internet Predators *Michele A. Paludi and Ashley Kravitz*	155

PART III. TEEN VIOLENCE BY FAMILY AND MATES

Chapter Nine:	No Safe Haven: Sexual Abuse of Teens by Family Members *Jeanette Krenek, Joanna L. Goodwin, Paula K. Lundberg-Love, Lindsay Marie Pantlin, and Britney Hilbun*	193
Chapter Ten:	Child Sexual Abuse and Adolescent Sexual Assault and Revictimization *Kate Walsh and David DiLillo*	203
Chapter Eleven:	Developing Teen Relationships: The Role of Violence *Andrea Poet, Catherine R. Swiderski, and Maureen C. McHugh*	221
Chapter Twelve:	Stalking of Adolescents *Thomas M. Evans and Todd Hendrix*	243
Appendix:	Organizations Concerned with Teen Violence and Victimization *Michele A. Paludi*	259

About the Editor and Contributors — 265

Index — 275

Foreword

Lisa Krenkel

> The solution of adult problems tomorrow depends in large measure upon the way our children grow up today. There is no greater insight into the future than recognizing that, when we save children, we save ourselves.
> Margaret Mead

The subject of teen violence in today's society is both volatile and controversial. Teenagers are the victims of violence, and the perpetrators are increasingly not only adults but also teens' own peers. As an attorney, I have seen the end result of this disturbing trend: a juvenile justice system that is overburdened, underfunded, outdated, and ill-equipped to deal with the onslaught of cases involving teenagers. Teenage victims are not often afforded the same resources as adult victims of physical abuse and sexual violence, and even when they are, the resources are designed to assist adult victims and are not tailored to the unique psychology of teens, who are often marginalized in our society. Ultimately this results in a resistance to treatment and assistance that can have life-threatening or lifelong consequences.

The statistics are staggering, and the solution is evasive. The violence is increasingly more violent in degree, and the age of the offender is younger and younger. Technology has quickly outpaced society's ability to codify many crimes such as sexting and child pornography. Sexual violence in schools and on school buses, bullying, and Internet crimes of harassment, humiliation, and intimidation are increasingly unmonitored, with devastating results.

Is the answer merely to treat these juvenile offenders as adults and absorb them into the adult criminal justice system? Should the adult laws of criminal intent and capacity be applied to teen offenders? Will adult concepts of punishment serve the same purpose when applied to teenagers? Can we help the teen victims in the same way that we try to help adult victims of violent crime?

In these two volumes, Dr. Paludi and her colleagues seek to examine the roots and causes of teen violence by exploring society's changing attitudes toward sex, gender, and violence and teenagers' precarious status within this paradigm. Dr. Paludi has dedicated her life to helping women and children. She is an educator, author, and expert witness and a psychological theoretician. In these volumes, she challenges us all to explore the difficult issues that affect children, specifically teenagers, in a time of technological advancement that is marked by social inequality and the marginalization of teenagers, who can neither defend nor empower themselves. As a litigator, I see the aftermath of the violence, its end result. Dr. Paludi and contributing authors explore the etiology of this violence as it manifests itself in an effort to change the pattern of violence and victimization that has besieged our nation's youths.

Acknowledgments

I have had the honor of knowing and working with individuals and organizations who have advocated for adolescents' rights, especially with respect to violence and victimization. I would like to acknowledge their work and the impact they have had in protecting our children and teens:

- The American Association of University Women
- Business and Professional Women's Club of Schenectady, New York
- Governor Mario Cuomo's Task Force on Sexual Harassment
- *Florence L. Denmark*
- *Susan Klein*
- *Lisa Krenkel*
- Donna Linder and Child Find of America
- *Paula K. Lundberg-Love*
- *Jennifer L. Martin*
- *Kevin L. Nadal*
- *Bernice Sandler*
- *Nan Stein*
- *Susan Strauss*
- *Brittany Tarabour*
- United States Department of Education's Subpanel on the Prevention of Violence, Sexual Harassment, Alcohol and Other Drug Abuse in Higher Education
- Women's Studies Program, Northeastern University

I also appreciate the caring and support of my sisters Rosalie Paludi and Lucille Paludi during the writing and editing of these volumes.

My sincere thanks to Debbie Carvalko and her colleagues at Praeger for knowing how much writing and editing books means to me. As Toni Morrison is quoted as saying, "If there's a book you really want to read but it hasn't been written yet, then you must write it." Debbie knows this about me!

Introduction

Michele A. Paludi

Adolescents and Hate Crimes

> Hate crimes are the scariest thing in the world because these people really believe what they're doing is right.
>
> Cher

During the writing of *The Psychology of Teen Violence and Victimization*, the following incidents received national attention:

March 2010: Massachusetts high school student Phoebe Prince committed suicide following bullying, verbal harassment, and physical abuse from peers at school.

May 2010: Cactus Grill Restaurant in Leawood, Kansas, was sued by the Equal Employment Opportunity Commission for sexually harassing an 18-year-old woman, including unwanted touching, sexual advances, and requests for sex.

July 2010: Cory Miller, a 16-year-old teen from Havana, Illinois, was attacked by bullies for the third time in two years. Cory was born with cerebral palsy and is confined to a wheelchair. The bullies had taunted and threatened him, violently kicked and beat him, spit on him, and broke his wheelchair and glasses. They left him lying in dirt.

August 2010: The Centers for Disease Control and Prevention High School Youth Risk Behavior Survey reported that Arkansas, Alaska, West Virginia, Kentucky, and Missouri were the five states with the highest percentages of girls being raped.

September 2010: Marco Gonzalez, a 15-year-old boy in Georgia, was abducted by individuals who stole his family car with him inside of it.

October 2010: Rutgers University student Tyler Clementi committed suicide after learning that his roommate and classmate had used a webcam to secretly broadcast Tyler's sexual relationship with another man.

> October 2010: Four teenagers in Staten Island, New York, were arrested for bullying a Muslim classmate, Kristian, for more than a year, which included spitting in his face, punching him in the groin, and calling him a terrorist.
>
> October 2010: Yale University fraternity Delta Kappa Epsilon paraded through the university campus shouting sexually offensive slogans against women, including "No Means Yes; Yes Means Anal."

Much violence against adolescents and committed by adolescents is a result of hate crimes (McConnell & Swain, 2000; Steinberg, Brooks, & Remtulla, 2003), as illustrated by the incidents listed above. A hate crime is a crime that in whole or in part is motivated by the offender's bias toward the victim's status. Hate crimes are intended to hurt and intimidate individuals because they are perceived to be different with respect to their sex, religion, race, color, national origin, sexual orientation, gender, or disability (Paludi, Ellens, & Paludi, 2010). While hate crimes are assaults against an individual, they are also assaults against everyone who shares the victim's status (e.g., Muslims, individuals with disabilities, African Americans, lesbians, gay males, females).

Legislation lists specific crimes that are identifiable as a hate crime, including murder; manslaughter; robbery; aggravated assault; burglary; motor vehicle theft; arson; forced and nonforced sex offenses; intimidation; destruction, damage, or vandalism of property; and other crimes involving injury to any person or property. When the behavior does not fall into one of the listed criminal categories identified above, hate offenses are referred to as bias-motivated incidents. These incidents may include cases of verbal slurs and may be precursors to more serious hate crimes (Paludi et al., 2010). Thus, violence against adolescents (as well as adults) exists along a continuum, from incivility and microaggressions to hate crimes, including assault and murder (Paludi, 2010; see also chapters 1 and 5, volume 1, and chapter 10, volume 2, of this book set).

A Closer Look at Gender-Based Hate Crimes

Gender-based hate crimes are the most prevalent type of hate crimes committed and experienced by teens. Gendered violence, or gender-based violence, has been defined as follows: "any act that results in, or is likely to result in, physical, sexual, or psychological harm or suffering to women, including threats of such acts, coercion or arbitrary deprivation of liberty, whether occurring in public or private life" (United Nations, 1995). This definition includes rape, stalking, intimate partner violence, and child

Introduction

sexual abuse. The terminology "gendered violence" is used, as highlighted by Russo and Pirlott (2006, p. 181), "because such violence is shaped by gender roles and status in society. . . . A complex mix of gender-related cultural values, beliefs, norms, and social institutions implicitly and even explicitly have supported intimate partner violence and provided little recourse for its victims."

Hate crimes against lesbians, gay men, and transgender individuals is gendered. Unlike other forms of hate crimes, however, gender-based hate crimes toward lesbian, gay, bisexual, and transgender youths are viewed as the most socially acceptable type of violence by adolescents (see chapter 1, volume 1, of this book set). Boys and men commit most of the violent crimes against gay males and lesbians (National Coalition of Anti-Violence Programs, 2009). The majority of murders of transgender individuals are perpetrated by nontransgender men; most victims are transgender women. Such violence has its roots in gender nonconformity (Schilt & Westbrook, 2009). The violence is fueled by anger as well as fear about gender nonconformity and feeling deceived by the individual's gender presentation (Schilt & Westbrook, 2009).

Adolescent girls are exposed to more violence than are adolescent boys (Flores, 2006; see also chapter 11, volume 2, of this book set). The National Survey on Drug Use and Health of the Substance Abuse and Mental Health Services Administration (2010) reported that from their sample of 33,091 girls aged 12 to 17, 18.6% got in a serious fight at school or work, 14.1% participated in a group-against-group fight, and 5.7% were violent toward others with an intent to hurt them. With respect to adolescent boys, this research found that 25.4% got into a serious fight at school or work, 17% participated in a group-against-group fight, and 9.3% attacked another person with the intent to harm that person.

Girls (and women) are most likely to be murdered by a romantic partner or ex-partner (Lundberg-Love & Wilkerson, 2006; McHugh, Livingston, & Frieze, 2008; Tan & Gregor, 2006). Ten percent of teen girls report that they have experienced physical violence in their own relationships, including hitting, shoving, throwing of objects, grabbing, and other physical force used with the intention to injure, harm, or kill another individual (McHugh et al., 2008; Ulloa, Castaneda, & Hokoda, 2010; see also chapter 2, volume 1, and chapter 4, volume 2, of this book set). A comparison of intimate partner violence rates in adolescents and adults indicates that teen girls are at a higher risk of intimate partner abuse (Silverman, Raj, Mucci, & Hathaway, 2001; see also chapter 11, volume 1, of this book set).

In addition, girls and women are more likely than males to experience stalking and sexual assault (see chapter 12, volume 1, of this book set).

In fact, adolescent girls aged 16 to 19 are almost four times more likely than the general population to be victims of rape, with the majority of these girls experiencing date rape, not stranger rape (Gerber & Cherneski, 2006; Maxwell, Robinson, & Post, 2003).

Approximately 71% of school-aged females report being bullied (Chisolm, 2010; Martin, 2010; Paludi, 2010; see also chapter 6, volume 1, and chapter 6, volume 2, of this book set). Eighty percent of adolescents have been sexually harassed by a peer, including name calling, graffiti written about them in school bathrooms, offensive drawings disseminated about them, unwanted touching, cyberbullying, sexual rumors, and pressure for sex (see chapter 8, volume 1, and chapter 8, volume 2, of this book set).

As another example of gendered violence, approximately 30% of adolescent girls are victims of child sexual abuse (Lundberg-Love & Marmion, 2006; see also chapters 9 and 10, volume 1, of this book set).

Placing Gendered Violence into an Adolescent Developmental Context: Power Issues

> American boys must be protected from a culture of violence that exploits their worst tendencies by reinforcing and amplifying the atavistic values of the masculine mystique. Our country was not created so that future generations could maximize profit at any cost. It was created with humanistic, egalitarian, altruistic goals. We must put our enormous resources and talents to the task of creating a children's culture that is consistent with these goals.
>
> *Myriam Miedzian*

In the life cycle, adolescence is a transitional stage between childhood and adulthood (Newman & Newman, 2008). According to theories of adolescent development, one of the most important developmental tasks of adolescence is establishing an identity (Erikson, 1963). During adolescence, individuals begin to integrate the opinions of influential others (e.g., parents, teachers, music idols, actors) into their own likes and dislikes. The eventual outcome is people who have a clear sense of their values and beliefs, occupational goals, and relationship expectations. This normative developmental task can be disrupted by individuals manipulating the adolescents (Kroger, 2000).

Adolescents are establishing intimacy and self-esteem during this stage as well (Chisholm, 2010). During adolescence, girls and boys want to be seen as popular with their peer group (Hartup & Stevens, 1999). The functions of a peer group for teens include social support, emotional intimacy, fun, and understanding. Adolescents are more likely to behave in ways that are gender-role stereotypic when with their peer group than when alone (Doyle & Paludi, 1998). Because of the importance placed on the peer group, behavior that is gender-role stereotypic is intensified during adolescence in order for teens to fit in with their peers.

Among boys, the pressure to be tough is intensified during adolescence; teen boys are likely to engage in fights with their peers. They do so in order to gain status and popularity among other teens in their peer group (American Association of University Women, 2001). Teen boys are likely to participate in a crowd, that is, a large group of boys recognized by a few characteristics, such as involvement in athletics (Way & Pahl, 1999). In addition, Paludi, Martin, and Paludi (2007) and Giladi (2005) noted that boys act out of extreme competitiveness or fear that they will lose their position of power. Since they don't want to be viewed as less masculine or weak by their male peers, they engage in sexual victimization of girls. Thus, girls are the objects of the game to impress other boys.

De-individuation is common among adolescent boys; they discontinue self-evaluation and instead adopt group norms and attitudes. De-individuation causes group members to behave more aggressively than they would as individuals (Paludi, 2010).

In addition, Doyle and Paludi (1998) and DeSouza (2004) noted that the male-as-aggressor theme is so central to many adolescent boys' self-concept that it spills over to their relationships with girls. The California Coalition Against Sexual Assault (2002) reported that among 1,600 juvenile sexual assault offenders, 23.5% perceived sex as a way to feel power and control, 9.4% perceived sex as a way to dissipate anger, and 8.4% perceived sex as a way to punish girls. In addition, both abusers and victims attribute the responsibility for violent dating behavior to victims; for example, the girl provoked the violence because of her personality, the girl had a need for affection, or the girl was influenced by her peer group (Lavoie, Hebert, Tremblay, Vitaro, & McDuff, 2002). Equally disconcerting is research by Jackson, Cram, and Seymour (2000) indicating that 77% of girls and 67% of boys in high school endorse sexual coercion, including unwanted genital contact and sexual intercourse.

Hate Crimes, Violence, and Stereotypic Beliefs

During adolescence, teens rely on stereotypes about individuals and, in the case of hate crimes, act on these stereotypes (Morrison, Morrison, Pope, & Zumbo, 1999; Otis & Loeffler, 2006). Stereotypes refer to individuals' cognitions that typically do not correspond with reality (Fiske & Lee, 2008). Stereotypes occur when individuals are classified by others as having something in common because they are members of a particular group or category or are perceived to be a member of this group (e.g., gay men, Latinos, disabled, female).

Social science research has identified that stereotypes have the following characteristics (Fiske, 1993):

> Groups that are targeted for stereotypes are easily identified and relatively powerless. This misperception is difficult to modify even though individuals who hold stereotypes have interacted with individuals of the group who disconfirm the stereotypes.
>
> There is little agreement between the composite picture of the group and the actual characteristics of that group. This is the product of a bias in individuals' information-processing mechanisms.

Race/color stereotyping is a psychological process that describes individuals' structured set of beliefs about the personal attributes of individuals because of their actual or perceived race or because it is believed that this individual has a particular racial background (Feinberg, 2000). Gender stereotyping is a psychological process describing individuals' structured set of beliefs about the personal attributes of men and women (Kite, Deaux, & Haines, 2008). Sexual orientation stereotyping is a psychological process describing individuals' structured set of beliefs about personal attributes of others because of their perceived or acknowledged sexual orientation (Herek & Garnets, 2007).

Psychologists have identified an emotional component to stereotypic cognitions: prejudice as well as a behavioral component to individuals' cognitions involving discrimination, harassment, and violence, including hate crimes (Fiske, 1993). Individuals' statements and nonverbal gestures toward women and men and individuals' race/color and sexual orientation provide insight into their structured set of beliefs about individuals of different sexes, races, and sexual orientations (Reskin, 2000).

Negative attitudes and feelings about individuals' sex, race, and sexual orientation develop as a consequence of cognitive, motivational, and sociocultural processes (Paludi et al., 2010). The cognitive aspect refers to placing individuals in categories that activate gender stereotypes, race stereotypes, and sexual orientation stereotypes. The motivational aspect refers to the need for individual power, control, and status. The sociocultural aspect refers to viewing as normal negative attitudes and behavior toward individuals because of their sex, race, or sexual orientation (Fiske & Lee, 2008).

Characteristics such as English fluency, skin color, and accents are salient features that individuals use to categorize a person. Consequently, individuals activate stereotypical traits about these characteristics

(Wigboldus, Dijksterhuis, & vanKnippenberg, 2003). Stereotypes are not labels but instead are assumptions about personality traits and behaviors that people in the labeled categories are thought to possess (Kite, Deaux, & Haines, 2008). Stereotypes have negative effects; the categorization process causes people to emphasize differences between groups and similarities within groups. Thus, for example, Latinos are seen as radically different from White individuals (Fiske & Lee, 2008).

Out-Group Homogeneity Bias

Related to stereotyping is the out-group homogeneity bias (Judd, Park, Yzerbyt, Gordijn, & Muller, 2005; Mulvey, Hitt, & Killen, 2010). This is a process by which individuals view groups in which they are not a part (e.g., a sexual orientation or race different from their own) as more homogeneous than their own group (e.g., their own sexual orientation or race). Thus, stereotypes concerning members of out-groups are stronger than those of in-group members. According to Judd (cited in DeAngelis, 2001, p. 3), "people are more willing to ignore individuating information about members of out-groups, lumping them all into a single disliked category." In actuality, focusing on differences among protected categories ignores in-group variability. The overemphasis on differences provides confirmation of the stereotype that religions are opposite and that one's own beliefs are normative while others are a deviation from the norm (Judd et al., 2005).

Adolescents hold stereotypes about victims, for example, victims of sexual assault (Maxwell et al., 2003). Adolescents typically blame the victim for the assault, including the style of dress and walking in certain neighborhoods. Kershner (1996) noted that most students aged 14 to 19 stated that forced sexual intercourse is acceptable under certain circumstances. Marciniak (1998) found that gender role attitudes, attitudes, and cognitive development are important factors in sexual aggression and in accepting rape myths. The continuation of stereotyping in adolescence is explained by the role that stereotyping plays in perpetuating group identity, group norms, and exclusion (Killen, Sinno, & Margie, 2007).

Gendered Violence in the Media

> We must also be careful to avoid ingesting toxins in the form of violent TV programs, video games, movies, magazines, and books. When we watch that kind of violence, we water our own negative seeds, or tendencies, and eventually we will think and act out of those seeds.
>
> *Thich Nhat Hanh*

Violence against adolescents has been explained by adhering to stereotypes about unequal power relations and patriarchal values. As Russo and Pirlott (2006, p. 181) summarized with respect to gender-based violence, "gender roles and expectations, male entitlement, sexual objectification, and discrepancies in power and status have legitimized, rendered invisible, sexualized, and helped to perpetuate violence against women." In addition, factors embedded in the adolescent culture that influence as well as support violence include alcohol and drug use, religious influences, devaluation of subordinated groups, the sexualization of violence, and video games (Maxwell et al., 2003; see also chapter 3, volume 2, of this book set). A major catalyst for the incidence of hate crimes, including gender-based hate crimes and other forms of violence in the United States, is the frequency with which violence is portrayed in media, especially media consumed by adolescents (see chapter 3, volume 1, of this book set).

The Parents Television Council (2003) noted that in 2002 compared to 1998, violence on television was 41% more frequent during the 8:00 p.m. time slot and 134% more frequent during the 9:00 p.m. time slot. Kaufman (2004) noted that in January 2004, three continuous hours of violent television programs were aired on one station on Thursday evenings: *Cold Case, CSI,* and *Without a Trace.* Kaufman (2004, p. 2) cited research from the National Cable Television Association's National Television Violence Study indicating that "across the three years of this study, a steady 60% of TV programs contain violence . . . [and] much of the violence is glamorized, sanitized, and trivialized" (p. 2).

Beresin (2010) reported that television programs offer 812 violent acts per hour, with children's cartoons displaying approximately 20 violent acts hourly. Violence in music videos has been observed in between 56% and 76% of the videos and include hitting, shootings, stabbings, punching, and kicking (Baxter, De Reimer, Landini, Leslie, & Singletary, 1985; Sherman & Dominick, 1986; Greeson & Williams, 1986). The most violent music videos are rap, followed by rock. These videos also included alcohol use and smoking as part of the violence.

Beresin (2010) noted that by the time children are 18 years old, they will have watched 28 hours of television per week, viewed 200,000 acts of violence in the television programs, and seen more than 16,000 murders in these shows. Seventy-five percent of children and teens watch music videos, with 60% of them indicating that they view these videos pretty much or a lot (Henry J. Kaiser Family Foundation, 2007; van den Bulck & Beullens, 2005). Klein and colleagues (1993) and the Council

Introduction xxi

on Communications and Media (2009) reported that teens aged 14 to 16 years old listen to music an average of 40 hours per week.

In violence portrayed in the media, girls and women are often portrayed as weak, objectified, submissive, and vulnerable (LaTouche, 2007). Pipher (1994) concluded that adolescent girls suffer psychologically from negative body image, lowered self-esteem, and achievement conflicts, all as a consequence of the culture's messages about young women's bodies needing to be protected, made more beautiful, and preserved. These messages are part of rock music videos, song lyrics, and television programs.

In contrast, the media portrays boys and men as aggressive and powerful. Violence is thus used to reinforce gender norms. Exposure to violence in media increases aggressive thoughts and a permanent hostility toward girls and women (Anderson & Bushman, 2002; Anderson, Carnagey, & Eubanks, 2003). Bretthauer, Zimmerman, and Banning (2007) noted that a review of "The Hot 100" list generated by Billboard Chart Research Services indicated that violence, especially violence against women, was prominent in music lyrics. They identified six themes in their review: men and power, sexual violence, objectification of women, sex as a main priority for men, women defined in terms of their relationships with men, and women not valuing themselves.

Armstrong (2001) found that gangsta rap music is identified with violent and misogynist lyric portrayals, including corporal punishment for women, hitting women with shoes, physically attacking women who refuse sex, rape, and murder. According to Armstrong (2001, p. 8), "the hegemonic dimension of gangsta rap music's narratives is immediate evidence of a rape culture. . . . In fact, gangsta rap music is a 'celebration' of rape culture and its most powerful contemporary voice."

Furthermore, exposure to violence in rock music videos has been linked to increased beliefs in stereotypes about sexuality, attractiveness, and violence. Adolescent boys who have been exposed to rock music videos have stated that they would engage in violence against women; boys who were not exposed to music videos did not endorse this view (Kaestle, Halpern, & Brown, 2007; Johnson, Adams, Ashburn, & Reed, 1995). Research by Malamuth and Check (1981) noted that when men who had never raped were exposed to depictions of sexual assault, they reported a heightened sexual arousal from the scenes and an increase in their rape fantasies. Thus, research suggests that most men find violence a stimulant to heighten or arouse their sexual feelings. Men find sexuality related at some level to an expression of aggression, and in turn aggression heightens their sexual fantasies or actual sexual behaviors (Doyle & Paludi, 1998).

Impact of Violence on Adolescents

The impact of violence has significant effects on adolescents. For example, teens (and children) who are exposed to violence on television will be provided with violent heroes to imitate and taught that violence is the way to resolve conflict with individuals, especially with dating partners (Beresin, 2010; Ward, 2002). Most of these adolescents have televisions in their own rooms, so they watch programs without parental supervision and editing (Beresin, 2010). Adolescents also use headphones, so their parents are not able to hear the lyrics to the music to which their teens are listening.

Bretthauer, Zimmerman, and Banning (2007) noted that music lyrics send relationship messages to listeners, who are predominantly adolescents. St. Lawrence and Joyner (1991) reported that adolescents' preference for heavy metal music is a significant marker for substance abuse, suicide risk, alienation, and risk-taking behaviors during adolescence (e.g., failure to use contraceptives, failure to use a seatbelt). Furthermore, according to Kaufman (2004, p. 3), "the hero of TV shows never gets in trouble for his/her violent actions. The hero is always 'justified' in one way or another when committing violent acts. . . . Television will never show a main character lose an arm, leg or get killed on screen. In reality, with as much gunplay that appears on TV, main characters should also get shot. . . . The hero can really be as violent as he/she wants."

Comstock and Paik (1991) identified four dimensions related to the way that violence is portrayed on television and that may heighten the likelihood of the influence of television: efficacy, normativeness, pertinence, and susceptibility. For example:

Violence is justified.

The perpetrator is similar to the viewer.

Violence is portrayed as real events, not events simulated for a television drama.

Violent acts leave the viewer in a state of unresolved excitement.

Research suggests a positive correlation between television violence and aggressive behavior (see chapter 7, volume 2, of this book set). Eron and Huesmann (1986) reported that there is a sensitive period between 8 and 12 years of age during which children are particularly susceptible to the impact of violence portrayed in the media. In addition, boys are more likely than girls to identify with a violent character and to subsequently model aggressive behavior.

Introduction xxiii

With respect to the impact of real-life violence on adolescents, including rape, intimate partner violence, sexual harassment, and bullying, several reports have documented the high cost of various forms of violence within three major perspectives: (1) psychological health, (2) physiological, and (3) education/work (e.g., Barron & Hebl, 2010; Contrada et al., 2000; Dansky & Kilpatrick, 1997; Katz, Joiner, & Kwon, 2002). Responses by adolescents to violence include headaches, sleep disturbances, disordered eating, gastrointestinal disorders, nausea, crying spells, scars, bruising, broken bones, absenteeism from school, decreased morale, decreased school satisfaction, performance decrements, damage to interpersonal relationships at school, and post-traumatic stress disorder (PTSD).

PTSD is a consequence of violence. Symptoms of PTSD include anxiety, physiological arousal, irritability, avoidance/denial, intrusion, repetitive nightmares, impaired concentration and memory, and acting-out behaviors. Immediately after the violent episode, individuals experience a sense of disbelief, shock, and psychological and physical numbing. A few days after the incident, individuals experience three different types of consequences:

1. Reexperiencing consequences (e.g., dreaming, flashbacks).
2. Withdrawal consequences (e.g., social withdrawal, absenteeism).
3. Other consequences (e.g., irritability, sleep disturbances, anger, exaggerated startle responses) (Avina & O'Donohue, 2002; see also chapters 1 and 2, volume 2, of this book set).

In addition, adolescents think about violence to themselves through self-injury (e.g., cutting) as well as suicide (see chapter 3, volume 1, of this book set). Furthermore, adolescents who have not had anyone intervene on their behalf to stop the violence learn to keep silent about future abuse because they believe that no one will ever help them (Paludi, 2010).

Present Volumes

Violence against adolescents has been recognized as a major public health and human rights issue that requires a coordinated response from parents, teachers, counselors, and providers (e.g., health care, mental health, rape crisis centers) in the teen's community (chapter 7, volume 1, and chapters 5, 9, and 12, volume 2). I wanted to edit these two volumes to highlight the following for parents, educators, guidance counselors, and adolescents themselves:

1. Implications of adolescence as a life stage for individuals learning to be violent and to accept violence.

2. Understanding the relationship among violence, powerlessness, and lack of access to resources with respect to adolescent victims of violence.
  3. Types of violence common to adolescence (e.g., bullying, harassment, intimate partner violence, gang violence, rape).
  4. Understanding the link between violence during adolescence and gender roles and gender-related life circumstances.
  5. Strategies for prevention for parents, teachers, counselors, and case workers.

This two-volume set on the psychology of teen violence and victimization features scholarly research about individual, institutional, and societal influences on violence against adolescents and perpetrated by adolescents. Contributors discuss the impact of race on perceptions of teen sex offenders (chapter 4, volume 1); the role of adolescent victimization in women's aggression in their relationships, violent behavior in girls, schoolyard violence, bullying, teen relationship violence, adolescent stalking, educating teens to discriminate abusive from nonabusive situations (chapter 5, volume 2); adolescents, firearms, and violent video games (chapter 3, volume 2); and teen violence prevention (chapter 13, volume 2). We take a multicultural approach to teen violence. In addition, I offer readers resources on teen violence, including organizations concerned with teen violence and victimization.

My goal is that these chapters and resources stimulate additional research agendas on teen violence and victimization that make Tyler, Phoebe, Cory, Marco, Kristian, and other victims of violence central, not marginal and visible, not invisible to our research and advocacy. Marion Wright Edelman's sentiment is expressed throughout these volumes: "If we don't stand up for children, then we don't stand for much."

References

American Association of University Women. (2001). *Hostile hallways: The annual survey on sexual harassment in America's schools.* Washington, DC: Author.

Anderson, C., & Bushman, B. (2002). The effects of media violence on society. *Science, 295,* 2377–2379.

Anderson, C., Carnagey, N., & Eubanks, J. (2003). Exposure to violent media: The effects of songs with violent lyrics in aggressive thoughts and feelings. *Journal of Personality and Social Psychology, 84,* 960–971.

Armstrong, E. (2001). Gangsta misogyny: A content analysis of the portrayals of violence against women in rap music, 1987–1993. *Journal of Criminal Justice and Popular Culture, 8,* 96–126.

Avina, C., & O'Donohue, W. (2002). Sexual harassment and PTSD: Is sexual harassment diagnosable trauma? *Journal of Traumatic Stress, 15,* 69–75.

Barron, L., & Hebl, M. (2010). Sexual orientation: A protected and unprotected class. In M. Paludi, C. Paludi, & E. DeSouza (Eds.), *Praeger handbook on understanding and preventing workplace discrimination: Vol. 1. Legal, management and social science perspectives* (pp. 251–273). Westport, CT: Praeger.

Baxter, L., De Riemer, C., Landini, A., Leslie, L., & Singletary, M. (1985). A content analysis of music videos. *Journal of Broadcasting and Electronic Media, 29,* 333–340.

Beresin, E. (2010). The impact of media violence on children and adolescents: Opportunities for clinical interventions. *American Academy of Child and Adolescent Psychiatry.* Retrieved on November 8, 2010, from http://www.aacap.org/cs/root/developmentor/the_impact_of_media_violence_on_children_and_adolescents_opportunities_for_clinical_interventions.

Bretthauer, B., Zimmerman, T., & Banning, J. (2007). A feminist analysis of popular music. *Journal of Feminist Family Therapy, 18,* 29–51.

California Coalition Against Sexual Assault. (2002). *Research on rape and violence.* Retrieved on November 11, 2010, from http://www.calcasa.org/stat/CALCASA_Stat_2008.pdf.

Chisholm, J. (2010). Perils in cyberspace: Current trends in cyberbullying. In M. Paludi & F. Denmark (Eds.), *Victims of sexual assault and abuse: Resources and responses for individuals and families: Vol. 1. Incidence and psychological dimensions* (pp. 59–88). Westport, CT: Praeger.

Comstock, G., & Paik, H. (1991). *Television and the American child.* San Diego, CA: Academic.

Contrada, R., Ashmore, R., Gary, M., Coups, E., Egeth, J., Sewell, A., Ewell, K., Goyal, T., & Chasse, V. (2000). Ethnicity-related sources of stress and their effects on well-being. *Current Directions in Psychological Science, 9,* 136–139.

Council on Communications and Media. (2009). Impact of music, music lyrics, and music videos on children and youth. *Pediatrics, 124,* 1488–1494.

Dansky, B., & Kilpatrick, D. (1997). Effects of sexual harassment. In W. O'Donohue (Ed.), *Sexual harassment: Theory, research and practice.* Boston: Allyn & Bacon.

DeAngelis, T. (2001). Understanding and preventing hate crimes. *Monitor on Psychology, 32,* 1–7.

DeSouza, E. (2004, July). *Intercultural and intracultural comparisons of bullying and sexual harassment in secondary schools.* Paper presented at the Association for Gender Equity Leadership in Education, Washington, DC.

Doyle, J., & Paludi, M. (1998). *Sex and gender: The human experience.* New York: McGraw-Hill.

Erikson, E. (1963). *Childhood and society.* New York: Norton.

Eron, L. D., & Huesmann, L. R. (1986). The role of television in the development of prosocial and antisocial behavior. In D. Olweus, J. Block, & M. Radke-Yarrow (Eds.), *The development of antisocial and prosocial behavior: Research, theories and issues* (pp. 285–314). New York: Academic Press.

Feinberg, M. (2000). *Racism: Why we dislike, stereotype and hate other groups and what to do about it.* Washington, DC: American Psychological Association.

Fiske, S. (1993). Controlling other people: The impact of power on stereotyping. *American Psychologist, 48,* 621–628.

Fiske, S., & Lee, T. (2008). Stereotypes and prejudice create workplace discrimination. In A. Brief (Ed.), *Diversity at work.* New York: Cambridge University Press.

Flores, R. (2006). Adolescent girls speak about violence in their community. In F. Denmark, H. Krauss, E. Halpern, & J. Sechzer (Eds.), *Violence and exploitation against women and girls* (pp. 47–55). Boston: Blackwell.

Gerber, G., & Cherneski, L. (2006). Sexual aggression toward women: Reducing the prevalence. In F. Denmark, H. Krauss, E. Halpern, & J. Sechzer (Eds.), *Violence and exploitation against women and girls* (pp. 35–46). Boston: Blackwell.

Giladi, A. (2005, August). *Sexual harassment or play? Perceptions and observations of young children's experiences in kindergarten and early schooling in Israel.* Paper presented at the Conference of the International Coalition Against Sexual Harassment, Philadelphia, PA.

Greeson, L. E., & Williams, R. A. (1986, December). Social implications of music videos for youth: An analysis of the content and effects of MTV. *Youth and Society, 18*(2), 177–189.

Hartup, W., & Stevens, N. (1999). Friendships and adaptation across the life span: Current directions. *Psychological Science, 8,* 76–79.

Henry J. Kaiser Family Foundation. (2007). *Parents, children and media: A Kaiser Family Foundation Survey.* Menlo Park, CA: Henry J. Kaiser Family Foundation.

Herek, G., & Garnets, L. (2007). Sexual orientation and mental health. *Annual Review of Clinical Psychology, 3,* 53–75.

Jackson, S., Cram, F., & Seymour, F. (2000). Violence and sexual coercion in high school students' dating relationships. *Journal of Family Violence, 1,* 23–36.

Johnson, J., Adams, M., Ashburn, L., & Reed, W. (1995). Differential gender effects of exposure to rap music on African American adolescents' acceptance of teen dating violence. *Sex Roles, 33,* 597–605.

Judd, C., Park, B., Yzerbyt, V., Gordijn, E., & Muller, D. (2005). Attributions of intergroup bias and outgroup homogeneity to ingroup and outgroup others. *European Journal of Social Psychology, 35,* 677–704.

Kaestle, C. E., Halpern, C. T., & Brown, J. (2007). Music videos, pro-wrestling, and acceptance of date rape among middle school males and females: An exploratory analysis. *Journal of Adolescent Health, 40,* 185–187.

Katz, J., Joiner, T., & Kwon, P. (2002). Membership on a devalued social group and emotional well-being: Developing a model of personal self-esteem, collective self-esteem and group socialization. *Sex Roles, 47,* 419–431.

Kaufman, R. (2004). *Filling their minds with death: TV violence and children.* Retrieved on November 8, 2010, from http://www.turnoffyourtv.com/healtheducation/violencechildren/violencechildren.html.

Kershner, R. (1996). Adolescent attitudes about rape. *Adolescence, 31,* 29–33.

Killen, M., Sinno, S., & Margie, N. (2007). Children's experiences and judgments about group exclusion and inclusion. In R. Kail (Ed.), *Advances in child development and behavior* (pp. 173–218). New York: Elsevier.

Kite, M., Deaux, K., & Haines, E. (2008). Gender stereotypes. In F. Denmark & M. Paludi (Eds.), *Psychology of women: A handbook of issues and theories* (2nd ed., pp. 205–236). Westport, CT: Praeger.

Klein, J., Brown, J., Childres, K., Oliveri, J., Porter, C., & Dykers, C. (1993). Adolescents' risky behavior and mass media use. *Pediatrics, 92,* 24–31.

Kroger, J. (2000). *Identity development: Adolescence through adulthood.* Thousand Oaks, CA: Sage.

LaTouche, K. (2007). *Gender representation in BET's 106 & Park and Sucker Free on MTV: A content analysis.* Thesis submitted to the College of Communication for the degree of master of science. Florida State University.

Lavoie, F., Hebert, M., Tremblay, R., Vitaro, L., & McDuff, D. (2002). History of family dysfunction and perpetration of dating violence by adolescent boys: A longitudinal study. *Journal of Adolescent Health, 30,* 375–383.

Lundberg-Love, P., & Marmion, S. (2006). *Intimate partner violence against women: When spouses, partners or lovers attack.* Westport, CT: Praeger.

Lundberg-Love, P., & Wilkerson, D. (2006). Battered women. In P. Lundberg-Love & S. Marmion (Eds.), *Intimate violence against women* (pp. 31–45). Westport, CT: Praeger.

Malamuth, N., & Check, J. (1981). The effects of mass media exposure on acceptance of violence against women: A field experiment. *Journal of Research in Personality, 15,* 436–446.

Marciniak, L. (1998). Adolescent attitudes toward victim precipitation of rape. *Violence and Victims, 13,* 287–300.

Martin, L. (2010). Bullying and peer sexual harassment: A prevention guide for students, parents and teachers. In M. Paludi & F. Denmark (Eds.), *Victims of sexual assault and abuse: Resources and responses for individuals and families: Vol. 1. Incidence and psychological dimensions* (pp. 89–109). Westport, CT: Praeger.

Maxwell, C., Robinson, A., & Post, L. (2003). The nature and predictors of sexual victimization and offending among adolescents. *Journal of Youth and Adolescence, 32,* 465–477.

McConnell, S., & Swain, J. (2000, August). *Victim-offender mediation with adolescents who commit hate crimes.* Paper presented at the 108th Annual Conference of the American Psychological Association, Washington, DC.

McHugh, M., Livingston, N., & Frieze, I. (2008). Intimate partner violence: Perspectives on research and intervention. In F. L. Denmark & M. Paludi (Eds.), *Psychology of women: A handbook of issues and theories* (pp. 555–589). Westport, CT: Praeger.

Morrison, M., Morrison, T., Pope, G., & Zumbo, B. (1999). An investigation of measures of modern and old-fashioned sexism. *Social Indicators Research, 48,* 39–50.

Mulvey, K., Hitti, A. & Killen, M. (2010). The development of stereotyping and exclusion. *Cognitive Science, 1,* 597–606.

National Coalition of Anti-Violence Programs. (2009). *Lesbian, gay, bisexual, transgender and queer domestic violence in the United States in 2008.* Retrieved on November 9, 2011, from http://www.avp.org/documents/2008NCAVPLGBTQDVReportFINAL.pdf.

Newman, B., & Newman, P. (2008). *Development through life: A psychosocial approach.* Belmont, CA: Wadsworth.

Otis, M., & Loeffler, D. (2006). Changing youths' attitudes toward difference: A community-based model that works. *Social Work with Groups, 28,* 41–64.

Paludi, M. (2010, October). *The continuum of campus violence: Applying "Broken Windows Theory" to prevent and deal with campus violence.* U.S. Department of Education National Meeting on Alcohol, Drug Abuse and Violence Prevention in Higher Education, National Harbor, MD.

Paludi, M., Ellens, H., & Paludi, C. (2010). Religious discrimination. In M. Paludi, C. Paludi, & E. DeSouza (Eds.), *Praeger handbook on understanding and preventing workplace discrimination: Vol. 1. Legal, management and social science perspectives* (pp. 157–182). Westport, CT: Praeger.

Paludi, M., Martin, J., & Paludi, C. (2007). Sexual harassment: The hidden gender equity problem. In S. Klein (Ed.), *Handbook for achieving gender equity through education* (2nd ed., pp. 215–229). Mahwah, NJ: Erlbaum.

Parents Television Council. (2003). *TV bloodbath: Violence on prime time broadcast TV.* Retrieved on November 11, 2010, from http://www.parentstv.org/ptc/publications/reports/stateindustryviolence/main.asp.

Pipher, M. (1994). *Reviving Ophelia: Saving the selves of adolescent girls.* New York: Ballantine.

Reskin, B. (2000). The proximate causes of employment discrimination. *Contemporary Sociology, 29,* 319–328.

Russo, N. F., & Pirlott, A. (2006). Gender-based violence: Concepts, methods, and findings. In F. Denmark, H. Krauss, E. Halpern, & J. Sechzer (Eds.), *Violence and exploitation against women and girls* (pp. 178–205). Boston: Blackwell.

Schilt, K., & Westbrook, L. (2009). Doing gender, doing heteronormativity: Gender normals, transgender people, and the social maintenance of heterosexuality. *Gender and Society 23*(4), 440–464.

Sherman, B., & Dominick, J. (1986). Violence and sex in music videos: TV and rock 'n' roll. *Journal of Communication, 36,* 79–93.

Silverman, J. G., Raj, A., Mucci, L. A., & Hathaway, J. E. (2001). Dating violence against adolescent girls and associated substance use, unhealthy weight control, sexual risk behavior, pregnancy, and suicidality. *Journal of the American Medical Association, 286,* 372–379.

St. Lawrence, J. S., & Joyner, D. J. (1991). The effects of sexually violent rock music on males' acceptance of violence against women. *Psychology of Women Quarterly, 15,* 49–63.

Steinberg, A., Brooks, J., & Remtulla, T. (2003). Youth hate crimes: Identification, prevention and intervention. *American Journal of Psychiatry, 160,* 878–989.

Substance Abuse and Mental Health Services Administration. (2010). *Factors affecting violent behavior in teen girls.* Retrieved on November 14, 2010, from http://www.teendrugabuse.org/mental-health/factors-affection-violent-behavior-in-teen-girls/.

Tan, J., & Gregor, K. (2006). Violence against pregnant women in northwestern Ontario. In F. Denmark, H. Krauss, E. Halpern, & J. Sechzer (Eds.), *Violence and exploitation against women and girls* (pp. 320–338). Boston: Blackwell.

Ulloa, E., Castaneda, D., & Hokoda, A. (2010). Teen relationship violence. In M. Paludi & F. Denmark (Eds.), *Victims of sexual assault and abuse: Resources and responses for individuals and families: Vol. 1. Incidence and psychological dimensions* (pp. 111–135). Westport, CT: Praeger.

United Nations. (1995). *Report of the Fourth World Conference on Women, Beijing, 4–5 September, 1995.* New York: United Nations.

van den Bulck, J., & Beullens, K. (2005). Television and music video exposure and adolescent alcohol use while going out. *Alcohol, 40,* 249–253.

Ward, R. (2002). Fan violence: Social problem or moral panic? *Aggression and Violent Behavior, 7,* 453–475.

Way, N., & Pahl, K. (1999). Friendship patterns among urban adolescent boys: A qualitative account. In M. Kopala & L. Suziki (Eds.), *Using qualitative methods in psychology* (pp. 145–161). Thousand Oaks, CA: Sage.

Wigboldus, D., Dijksterhuis, A., & vanKnippenberg, A. (2003). When stereotypes get in the way: Stereotypes obstruct stereotype-inconsistent trait inferences. *Journal of Personality and Social Psychology, 84,* 470–484.

PART I

Developmental and Cultural Issues in Teen Violence

CHAPTER ONE

Microaggressions: A Root of Bullying, Violence, and Victimization toward Lesbian, Gay, Bisexual, and Transgender Youths

Kevin L. Nadal and Katie E. Griffin

Introduction

In the fall of 2010, six young people in various regions of the United States committed suicide. While teen suicide in itself may not be a new phenomenon, these six individuals gained national attention because they were all reported to have committed suicide as a result of teen bullying. What was even more unique about these young people's stories was that they were all reported to have been bullied because they were (or were perceived to be) gay. One of these young people was Tyler Clementi, an 18-year-old college freshman at Rutgers University, whose classmates posted an Internet video of him having sex with another man. Clementi, who was allegedly a closeted gay man, was reportedly mortified and took his own life shortly after this cyberbullying had occurred. Immediately following this event, a nationwide campaign garnered attention when celebrities and laypeople alike began to create and post videos on the Internet with a message that "It Gets Better." These videos urged young lesbian, gay, bisexual, and transgender (LGBT) people to value their lives and not to view suicide as a viable option.

Following the course of these events, psychologists, educators, and other practitioners in the media began to hypothesize reasons why bullying exists and why bullying leads to potential suicide. Discussions ensued regarding the motivations of bullies and where bullies learn that such behavior is acceptable and tolerable. Others began to explore the psychological hardships of the victims of bullying, as well as the ways that educational systems were not protecting these LGBT children or creating a safe space for them. Regardless of the motivation of these discussions, all of these experts could agree that bullying needed to stop (or at least be minimized) in order to promote optimal physical safety and positive psychological health for our nation's youths. However, perhaps all of these questions would need to be examined further, in order to work toward a solution.

The purpose of this chapter is to explore how microaggressions, or subtle forms of discrimination, may potentially play a huge role in the bullying that occurs toward children and adolescents. Microaggressions are "brief and commonplace daily verbal, behavioral, or environmental indignities (whether intentional or unintentional) that communicate hostile, derogatory, or negative racial slights and insults toward members of oppressed groups" (Nadal, 2008, p. 23). Originally modeled from research on racial microaggressions (see Sue, Bucerri, Lin, Nadal, & Torino, 2007), this type of subtle discrimination is argued to exist toward all marginalized groups, including people of color, women, LGBT persons, persons with disabilities, and religious minorities (Nadal, 2008). The cumulative nature of microaggressions is suggested to detrimentally impact mental health, particularly depression, anxiety, mood, and self-esteem.

The current chapter will examine previous literature on microaggressions, in an attempt to understand the influences of such discrimination on the lives of bullies, victims, and all of society. First, we will examine how the microaggressions that bullies witness in their families, communities, and media may lead to the acceptance of hate toward various groups—particularly people who identify as (or are perceived to be) LGBT. Second, we will explore how microaggressions impact the lives of victims, and how victims learn to internalize or oppress discrimination and hate. Finally, we will examine the impacts that microaggressions have on more systemic and environmental levels, advocating for the changes that need to occur in media, government, and educational systems. This first section will define microaggressions—understanding the background behind the concept, the current research involving microaggressions, and the impacts that microaggressions may have on mental health.

Review of Microaggression Literature

The existence of discrimination and prejudice has been recorded throughout all of history. Thinking back to as recently as the 20th century, one can easily recall events like the Holocaust or the racial discrimination that led to the civil rights movement. The violence and cruelty that accompanied these historical events held their basis in racial and religious hatred, in conjunction with strongly held beliefs of inequality and inferiority. The teachings of groups like the Ku Klux Klan and the Nazis were more commonplace in families, communities, and even some school systems. Thus, people in American society were much more vocal and straightforward with their biases, making racism much easier to identify.

However, in present-day society, it may be less acceptable and "politically incorrect" to maintain the same sentiments as these aforementioned extremist groups. Nowadays, people tend to hide their biases and prejudices, while many try to be "color-blind" and not see or acknowledge others' races or ethnicities. As a result, explicit discrimination (such as race-based hate crimes and physical assaults) may have decreased in many parts of the United States, leading many people to believe discrimination to be extinct and a thing of the past. Despite this, blatant discrimination does still occur, albeit arguably at a lower frequency and magnitude. But many authors are now suggesting that racism manifests in a new form of subtle or covert discrimination, otherwise known as microaggressions (see Sue, 2010).

In 1970, Pierce first used the term "racial microaggressions" and later described it as "subtle, stunning, often automatic, and non-verbal exchanges which are 'put downs'" (Pierce, Carew, Pierce-Gonzalez, & Willis, 1978, p. 66). Sue, Capodilupo, and colleagues (2007) refined the term "microaggressions" to mean "brief, everyday exchanges that send denigrating messages to people of color because they belong to a racial minority group" (Sue, Capodilupo, et al., 2007, p. 273). Sue and colleagues (2007) proposed a taxonomy of racial microaggressions that included nine themes: (1) Alien in own land, (2) Ascription of intelligence, (3) Color blindness, (4) Criminality/assumption of criminal status, (5) Denial of individual racism, (6) Myth of meritocracy, (7) Pathologizing cultural values/communication styles, (8) Second-class citizen, and (9) Environmental microaggressions. An individual is a victim of a microaggression when asked where he or she is from (alien in own land) or when followed around in a store by an owner or a clerk (criminality/assumption of criminal status). In the first example, the individual is being sent the message that he or she is not American and doesn't belong, while the individual in the second example is being sent the message that she or he must be a criminal (Sue, Capodilupo, et al., 2007). In both instances the act may be unconscious or unintentional to the enactor but sends a hurtful message to the victim that she or he is different, unwelcome, or inferior in some way.

In this racial microaggression taxonomy, it was theorized that microaggressions can be categorized in three major ways: microassaults (direct, intentional statements or behaviors targeting people of color), microinsults (indirect, unintentional statements or behaviors that offend, upset, or hurt persons of color), and microinvalidations (indirect, unintentional statements or behaviors that disregard, discount, or ignore a person of color's experiences). A microassault would be most similar to "old-fashioned racism" and would reflect the types of discrimination that are often conscious and intentional. For example, someone making a racist joke or racial slur could be viewed as performing a conscious action that conveys his or her true intention and bias. Nadal, Rivera, & Corpus (2010) discussed how microassaults apply to microaggressions toward LGBT people (e.g., someone using homophobic insults or who blatantly conveys disgust or disapproval with nonheterosexual people). Microinsults are often unintentional, and the enactors are often unaware that their behaviors or statements may be hurtful to the people of color who experience them. For example, the aforementioned store owner who follows a person of color around in a store may not recognize that she or he only follows people of color. Moreover, if confronted, this individual may even become defensive and explain that he is simply trying to protect the store, or that he follows anyone who looks suspicious, regardless of race. However, for a person of color who experiences such discrimination regularly, it may be daunting and hurtful to feel these communications of fear or distrust. For LGBT people, microinsults can include everything from a person glaring at same-sex couples in curiosity or disgust to a person casually saying that something is "gay" as a synonym for "bad," "weird," or "awful" (Nadal, Rivera, & Corpus, 2010). Microinvalidations are usually statements that are demeaning; again, usually the enactor does not recognize the impact that such statements may have on people of marginalized groups. For example, when a White person tells a person of color that she or he is being paranoid and that racism doesn't exist anymore, the person of color's racial reality is challenged and dismissed. Similarly, when someone tells LGBT people to "get over it" or to "not be so sensitive," a message is communicated that there is something wrong with them, instead of acknowledging the heterosexism or discrimination that exists.

The taxonomy on racial microaggressions has been supported and extended by research on the experiences of Black/African Americans (Sue et al., 2008; Sue, Capodilupo, & Holder, 2008), Asian Americans (Sue, Bucceri, Lin, Nadal, & Torino, 2007), and Latino/a Americans (Rivera, Forquer, & Rangel, 2010). Both qualitative and quantitative studies have supported that experiencing microaggressions on a daily, consistent basis may have an accumulating affect on those who are victims of such discrimination. Furthermore, literature has purported that microaggressions can impact many other marginalized groups, including women (Nadal, 2010), religious minorities (Nadal, Issa, Griffin, Hamit, & Lyons, 2010), multiracial individuals, and LGBT people (Nadal, Rivera, & Corpus, 2010).

There has been an increase in the types of microaggressions that are experienced by LGBT individuals. Sexual orientation microaggressions can be defined as "brief and commonplace daily verbal, behavioral, and environmental indignities (whether intentional or unintentional) that communicate hostile, derogatory, or negative heterosexist and homophobic slights and insults toward gay, lesbian, and bisexual individuals, while transgender microaggressions are the verbal, behavioral, and environmental indignities that target transgender persons" (Nadal, Rivera, & Corpus, 2010, p. 218). Nadal, Rivera, and Corpus (2010) proposed a taxonomy for sexual orientation microaggressions based on relevant literature that included nine themes: (1) Use of heterosexist terminology, (2) Endorsement of heteronormative culture/behaviors, (3) Assumption of universal LGBT experiences, (4) Exoticization, (5) Discomfort/disapproval of LGBT experiences, (6) Denial of societal heterosexism/transphobia, (7) Assumption of sexual pathology/abnormality, (8) Denial of individual heterosexism/transphobia, and (9) Environmental microaggressions. LGBT individuals experience a sexual orientation microaggression when someone asks them to stop acting so gay (endorsement of heteronormative culture/behaviors) or when asked if they have HIV/AIDS (assumption of sexual pathology/abnormality) (Nadal, Rivera, and Corpus, 2010). A qualitative study regarding LGBT experiences with sexual orientation discrimination supported this taxonomy, revealing the same first five themes, grouping themes 6 and 8 together to form "Denial of the reality of heterosexism," and adding an additional theme of "Assaults and threatening behaviors" (Nadal et al., under review). (There were not enough examples given to support the environmental microaggressions theme.)

Just as research has revealed that racial microaggressions (Sue, Bucerri, et al., 2007; Sue, Capodilupo, et al., 2007; Sue, Nadal, et al., 2008) and gender microaggressions have an impact on the mental health of the victims of such recurring discrimination, research focusing on the experiences of LGBT individuals show similar results. Lesbian, gay, bisexual, and transgender individuals have shared the effect that their experiences of victimization have had on their daily functioning and their emotional and physical health (Nadal, Issa, et al., under review; Nadal, Wong, et al., under review; Nadal, Skolnik, & Wong, under review).

Similarly, the types of microaggressions that are related to teen bullying can fit into proposed categories of microassaults, microinsults, and microinvalidations. For example, the act of bullying itself (e.g., teasing, threatening, etc.) can be viewed as a microassault, in that the perpetrators are very aware of their actions and conscious of their biases and hatred. But, perhaps because they aren't physically assaulting the person, these individuals may believe their actions to be harmless or innocuous. The types of homophobic language that are used "jokingly" may be viewed as microinsults; these include words like "faggot" or "dyke," or phrases like "That's so gay" or "Stop being a sissy." When people use such words (either toward others or casually in conversation), a communication of intolerance or disapproval toward LGBT people can create a hostile environment for young people who identify as LGBT or who are questioning their sexual or gender identities. Finally, when young victims of bullying are told to "ignore" the problem or that they are "making a big deal" of the situation, their experiences are invalidated and they may feel dismissed. Such experiences are not only psychologically damaging to these young people but may send implicit messages that the bullying is tolerated and that bullying does not result in punishment.

Nadal, Skolnik, and Wong (under review) found that transgender participants reported feeling a variety of emotional reactions in response to victimization, including anger, frustration, and disappointment. Additionally, these participants reported that such experiences have negatively impacted their interpersonal relationships with their family, friends, and intimate partners and deemed these experiences as tiresome and wearing (Nadal, Skolnik, & Wong, under review). Coping mechanisms have also been found in the research on LGBT individuals, in that many LGBT people utilize various behavioral, emotional, and cognitive reactions to help them deal with discrimination (Nadal, Wong et al., under review). One type of behavioral response may be passive coping (e.g., the individual walks away from the perpetrator of the microaggression). A type of emotional response may be anger or frustration. Finally, examples of cognitive responses may include acceptance and conformity, which may be exemplified by an LGBT individual who may act more "straight" in a job interview so as to up his or her chances of being hired (Nadal, Wong, et al., under review). Victims of sexual orientation microaggressions, therefore, have necessarily found ways to cope with such experiences but still report feeling taxed and exhausted by these happenings and by their attempts to deal with them (Nadal, Wong, et al., under review).

Lesbian, Gay, Bisexual, and Transgender Teens' Experiences with Microaggressions

Now that we have examined the history of microaggressions and the various types of microaggressions that may manifest toward LGBT people, this next section will focus specifically on the microaggressions that are experienced by LGBT teens. As aforementioned, teen bullying may be a type of microaggression in itself, while the verbal and nonverbal microaggressions that create or maintain an unsafe environment may permit the bullying to continue. Thus, it is important to examine the types of bullying that may be considered microaggressive in nature, the various environments where LGBT teens may experience such bullying and other types of microaggressions, and the unintentional and unconscious behaviors that promote dangerous environments, thus allowing microaggressions to perpetuate and thrive.

While previous research on sexual orientation microaggressions has recruited adult participants to share their experiences, many of the examples given by these adults occurred when they were adolescents (Nadal, Issa, et al., under review). Because teenagers tend not to have reached their highest levels of emotional, psychological, and cognitive development, they can be particularly susceptible to the perpetration of microaggressions by their peers. Moreover, because adolescence is a time in which individuals may feel especially sensitive, the experience of microaggressions may be damaging to their self-esteem and mental health.

Furthermore, it is often during adolescence that LGBT individuals are in various stages of their sexual identity development in that they may be questioning, denying, hiding, or coming to terms with their sexual orientation, making this an often fragile period of their lives. Research has found that sexual minorities are more likely to report physical and sexual abuse than their heterosexual counterparts (Saewyc et al., 2006). Additionally, sexual minorities report more difficulties with their peers and families as well as increased levels of psychological distress (Ueno, 2005). Some of the protective factors that aid in combating against the effects of such discrimination are social connectedness and family connectedness; however, sexual minorities, and bisexual individuals specifically, report significantly less protective factors than heterosexual individuals (Saewyc et al., 2009). Adolescents, therefore, may be targets of all kinds of sexual orientation–based discrimination and microaggressions; these may occur at school, in their peer groups, and even in their family.

Microaggressions within Schools/Educational Systems

Teens spend about half their day in school, where they are immersed in a social as well as an educational atmosphere. As a result, adolescents may become victims of bullying or microaggressions in the hall between classes, in the lunchroom, and even in the classroom itself. While little research has been done on sexual orientation microaggressions experienced through classroom interactions, one study looked at the opinions of students regarding sexual orientation and the rights and safety of LGBT individuals (Horn, Szalacha, & Drill, 2008). These authors found that students could separate their own beliefs about homosexuality and their opinions regarding the rights of LGBT individuals. While these participants reported that LGBT individuals have a right to feel safe in school, students that endorsed conventional reasoning, or reasoning based on social norms, in addition to homosexuality as personal choice, were more likely to judge excluding and teasing others as acceptable behavior (Horn, Szalacha, & Drill, 2008). Thus, although students may report that everyone has the right to be protected and feel safe at school, they may still behave in such a way that has the opposite effect.

Another way in which LGBT teens may experience microaggressions at school is in the classroom as a result of student and teacher interactions. In a study on racial microaggressions, researchers found that such instances in the classroom can lead to a resultant dialogue on race (Sue, Lin, Torino, Capodilupo, & Rivera, 2009). While a discussion on race stemming from a racial microaggression has the potential to be constructive and have a positive impact on the whole class, the discussion, if handled poorly by the teacher, also has the potential of having detrimental consequences (Sue, Lin, et al., 2009). As research has shown that such an occurrence can happen in response to racial microaggressions, one would assume that the same could happen due to the commitment of a sexual orientation microaggression in the same setting. Therefore, LGBT teens may have these experiences in the school setting, which may lead to events that further exacerbate the issue.

Microaggressions from Peers

Another source of sexual orientation microaggressions for adolescents is their peers. Sexual minorities have reported more sexual harassment and bullying from their peers than have their heterosexual counterparts (Williams, Connolly, Pepler, & Craig, 2005). While both LGBT and heterosexual individuals experience dating violence, bisexual males are more likely to report all types of abuse more than heterosexual males, and bisexual females report more sexual abuse than heterosexual females (Freedner, Freed, Yang, & Austin, 2002). Furthermore, Freedner and colleagues (2002) found that lesbians reported feeling more scared about their own safety than did heterosexual females, and bisexuals experience more threats of outing than do gay males and lesbians. A study examining the basis for peer acceptance found that among 10th and 12th graders not only was sexual orientation taken into account, but so was gender conformity (Horn, 2007). This finding suggests that if sexual-minority teens do not conform to gender norms, they may be more susceptible to bullying, microaggressions, or other victimization from their peers.

Teens may have peer-related protective factors that help them to deal and cope with sexual orientation microaggressions; however, LGBT teens may lack the necessary protective factors to shield themselves from the effects of such discrimination. Williams and colleagues (2005) found that the relationship between social support and externalizing behaviors was mediated by peer victimization and that the relationship between sexual orientation and psychosocial symptoms was mediated by both peer victimization and social support. Furthermore, the results of the study revealed that sexual-minority adolescents reported less companionship with their best friends than did their heterosexual counterparts (Williams et al., 2005). Saewyc and colleagues (2009) reported that bisexual adolescents reported lower levels of school connectedness than heterosexual adolescents. Ueno (2005) suggests that bonding with other teens that have common social backgrounds is a protective factor for adolescents; however, while heterosexuals often form these bonds, this is less likely to happen for LGBT individuals. When these bonds do form, LGBT individuals report lower psychological distress than those without this protective factor (Ueno, 2005). Therefore, LGBT teens are likely to experience sexual orientation microaggressions from other peers and may lack a social support peer group to assist them in countering the negative effects of these events.

Microaggressions within the Family

Just as peer groups can serve as both a protective factor against and a source of sexual orientation microaggressions, so too can one's family. With family support, an LGBT teen may have a better coming out experience and may be better able to cope with other sources of such discrimination. Unfortunately, it is often the case that coming out to one's parents is a very stressful experience and leads to altered parent-child relationships (Saltzburg, 2004). Saewyc and colleagues (2009) found that bisexual individuals reported lower levels of family connectedness than their heterosexual counterparts, thereby reducing the existence of this protective factor. Additionally, Williams and colleagues (2005) found that sexual minorities reported less closeness with their mothers than did their heterosexual peers. In Saltzburg's (2004) study looking at the experience of parents after their child has come out to them, parents reported feeling various emotions, including disappointment, confusion, and fear of estrangement. Many of the parents in the study reported feeling as though they had lost their child and that all their hopes for what their child's life was to be were crushed (Saltzburg, 2004). Throughout this process, a child may lose connectedness with the parent, as both may feel that they are so different from each other as to not be able to relate to one another (Saltzburg, 2004). When this is the case or, worse, if the parent disowns the child, the LGBT teen loses a major protective factor and becomes more susceptible to the negative impact of discrimination.

In terms of microaggressions specifically, some studies found that unlike racial microaggressions, LGBT individuals often experience subtle discrimination within their own families (Nadal, Issa, et al., under review; Nadal, Skolnik, & Wong, under review). While the experience of outward rejection by one's family (particularly one's parents) can be distressing, so too can implicitly disapproving behaviors and statements. For example, lesbian, gay, and bisexual people are often told "not to act so gay" or to "tone it down," and parents of transgender people may have difficulty referring to their children by their preferred gender names or pronouns. Thus, even if family members may believe that they are accepting, their subtle behaviors may indicate unconscious desires for their children to be heterosexual. And because families may not be aware of their microaggressive statements or behaviors, they may not recognize the lack of support that they are conveying to their children.

Microaggressions Based on Intersectional Identities

When LGBT teens hold multiple identities, the experiences of microaggressions, bullying, and other forms of discrimination may be even more complex, damaging, or both. When LGBT teens of color (e.g., African

Americans, Latina/os, Asian Americans, etc.) are the victims of bullying or hate crimes, one may wonder if the experience is due to their sexual orientations (or perceived sexual orientations), because of their racial and ethnic backgrounds, or both. In 2003, Sakia Gunn, a 15-year-old African American woman, was murdered as a result of a hate crime in New Jersey (Smith, 2004). Some of her friends said that she identified as a lesbian, while others suggested that she may have identified as a transgender man. Regardless of her identity, the lack of media attention that was paid to Sakia's death demonstrates how the media often pay little attention to hate crimes that target LGBT people of color. Just a few years prior, the murder of Matthew Shepard, a young White male in Wyoming, became a national topic of interest that eventually led to greater awareness about hate crimes toward LGBT people. However, when a similar crime occurs toward an LGBT person of color, it did not (and still may not) have as much of an impact as a crime that targets a gay White man.

Similar experiences occur with LGBT people of color who may not necessarily be victims of overt racism, heterosexism, or hate crimes. Tyra Hunter, an African American transgender woman, died after she was struck by a car in Washington, D.C. When paramedics arrived on the scene, she was found to be seriously injured. While onlookers pleaded for them to help her, the paramedics who responded to the call stood back and ridiculed her. Some argue that it was because of her transgender identity, her gender presentation, her race, or some combination of all of these things. Although they eventually took her to the hospital, the delay in assistance eventually resulted in her death. Her injuries were serious, but they were not life threatening; therefore, her death was preventable. A jury later awarded her family 2.9 million dollars in an action against the District of Columbia Fire Department and the Dictrict of Columbia General Hospital for withholding treatment and for medical malpractice. Again, perhaps these paramedics were not the assailants of the hate crimes themselves. But because of their prejudices and discriminatory behaviors, they eventually caused the untimely death of a transgender woman who could have survived. It is unclear whether such an event was due to her race, gender identity, or both, but it is clear that discrimination (even such experiences that appear to be innocuous) can potentially result in detrimental or mortal consequences.

The Impacts of Microaggressions on LGBT Adolescents' Mental Health

Throughout this chapter so far, we have discussed some of the negative impacts that bullying, microaggressions, and other forms of discrimination may have on the lives of LGBT youths. Perhaps the most important reason for examining these experiences is that many studies have reported the numerous disparaging mental health experiences of LGBT youths, particularly in comparison to their heterosexual counterparts. Studies have revealed that LGBT youths tended to be much more depressed than their heterosexual counterparts, and they were more likely to report suicidal ideation and self-harm (Almeida, Johnson, Corliss, Molnar, & Azrael, 2009). Another study found that, in a sample with both urban and rural LGBT youths, 42% of the urban sample and 32% of the rural sample had attempted suicide at least once (Waldo, Hesson-McInnis, & D'Augelli, 1998). Literature has pointed out that LGBT individuals may be susceptible to developing social anxiety (Safren & Pantalone, 2005), and that LGBT individuals are more likely to develop substance abuse problems in comparison to their heterosexual counterparts (Marshal et al., 2008). Finally, one report revealed that LGBT persons are at higher risk of suffering from mental health problems (e.g., depression and substance abuse disorders) and from physical health problems like high blood pressure (Cochran, 2001; Meyer, 2003).

A substantial amount of research has reported that overt and covert discrimination has a significant impact on the mental health of LGBT individuals (Burn, Kadlec, & Rexer, 2005; Herek, 2000, 2007; Hill & Willoughby, 2005; Meyer, 1995, 2003; Walls, 2008). One study reported that LGBT youths who were victimized were more likely to hold suicidal thoughts, particularly if they were questioning or unsure of their sexual identities (Poteat, Aragon, Espelage, & Koenig, 2009). Some authors have cited that the harassment of gays during adolescence can be linked to the exceptionally high rate of suicide among LGBT youths (D'Augelli, 1992). Another study found that hate crimes toward LGBT individuals may result in more severe psychological consequences, such as depression, anxiety, post-traumatic stress disorder, and other mental health disparities in victims (Herek & Capitanio, 1999). Finally, studies have reported that experiences of discrimination and stigmatization may lead to lower self-esteem, fears of rejection, and/ or consistent hiding or concealing of identities (Burn et al., 2005; Rostosky, Riggle, Gray, & Hatton, 2007). Given all of these, it is important to recognize that all forms of discrimination, including bullying, hate crimes, assaults, and microaggressions, need to decrease in order to promote more favorable mental health outcomes for LGBT people, especially LGBT youths.

Recommendations for Addressing Teen Bullying and Microaggressions

Throughout this chapter, we have attempted to highlight the multitude of reasons for why it is important to reduce or eliminate microaggressions, in order to provide safer and more accepting environments for LGBT youths. Perhaps in creating these safer spaces, bullying toward LGBT youths will decrease and an environment of acceptance can be created. Because of this, Nadal, Hamit, and Issa (2010) discuss various ways that microaggressions can be prevented and/or dealt with, in order to create more welcoming and accepting spaces. These include the following:

1. Talking about microaggressions openly when they occur (e.g., confronting others when one observes a microaggression, or if appropriate or safe, confronting others when one is the victim of a microaggression).
2. Having dialogues in families, workplace environments, and other systems about discrimination, prejudice, and diversity, as well as the ways that race and culture impact various aspects of our lives.
3. Being a support system or resource for victims of microaggressions, particularly by validating others' experiences.
4. Educating others about the term "microaggressions" so that individuals are aware that discrimination may take more subtle forms, which may make some situations easier to identify or manage.

Because these suggestions focus on microaggressions in general, perhaps it may be beneficial to apply these suggestions and provide specific guidelines for addressing bullying toward LGBT youths.

First, it is important for individuals to acknowledge this bullying when it occurs. It is very easy for individuals to turn a "blind eye" to bullying because of our fears of dealing with conflict or because of our rationalization that "kids will be kids." However, when school systems, parents, and other individuals fail to address bullying, the levels of victimization may increase, which may lead to the multitude of psychosocial and mental health problems that have been discussed throughout the chapter. As a result, it is important for bullying to be tackled immediately, in order to convey the lack of tolerance toward victimizing others, as well as to prevent the victimization from becoming more painful or intolerable.

Second, it is necessary for dialogues to occur in various groups and systems, in order to prevent bullying from occurring. Perhaps parents need to discuss the importance of equality and respect with their children from an early age. And perhaps teachers and school systems need to emphasize the same. Sometimes children and adolescents are unaware that their behavior may be considered bullying; other times these young people may continue with their behaviors because they are not corrected, are not punished, or both. Perhaps one helpful approach may be to talk about the influx of teen suicides as a result of bullying. Adolescents who bully others may not recognize that their actions may lead to others' self-harm or even deaths. Perhaps in having these conversations, some adolescents may not want to live the rest of their lives knowing that they may have directly or indirectly caused someone to take his or her own life.

Third, being a support and resource for all adolescents, particularly LGBT teens who may be struggling with their identities, may be another approach to preventing the detrimental psychological consequences of bullying. Perhaps these teens may develop low self-esteem or social anxiety because they have not learned to accept or love themselves. And it is conceivable that the lack of role models or support systems may be one influence for this outcome. One simple way for showing this support is by talking with youths about their problems, instead of assuming that everything is okay. For example, it is very common for parents to avoid conversations with their children about adolescence and sexuality because they may feel awkward or uncomfortable in discussing such sensitive topics. Moreover, because many parents have developed heteronormative perspectives, oftentimes they may assume that their child is heterosexual. Therefore, they may not consider that their daughter or son may be struggling with sexual identity issues or victimization in schools. Because of this, it is important for open dialogues and communications to ensue (with parents, older siblings, grandparents, uncles, aunts, teachers, coaches, etc.), so that young people do not internalize their problems or turn to suicide as an option. It is also important for parents (and others) to be open to the possibility that their child may be LGBT. In doing so, they may be more alert to the potential symptoms of bullying and may be able to provide their children with the support and guidance they need.

Finally, identifying and acknowledging the spectrum of microaggressions that may lead to bullying is also an important step to creating safer environments for LGBT youths and for all youths in general. Disallowing anyone from using heterosexist or homophobic remarks (whether intentional or unintentional) is one step toward promoting equality and preventing discrimination or hatred. Not assuming that everyone is heterosexual and celebrating the various experiences of lesbians, gays, bisexuals, and transgender people can help to normalize those LGBT teens who may feel different, while teaching heterosexual teens about acceptance, open-mindedness, and social justice for all.

Furthermore, there are a myriad of ways that systemic changes can help to decrease microaggressions, which in turn can assist in decreasing the amount of bullying toward LGBT teens. First, perhaps all professional and governing organizations must take steps similar to those of the American Psychological Association or American Medical Association, which advocate that competently working with LGBT clients is an ethical responsibility in being an effective practitioner. Perhaps one reason that many practitioners do not perceive LGBT issues as being salient or relevant is because of the lack of emphasis in their professional training. Thus, incorporating LGBT issues into cultural competence guidelines may result in more positive outcomes for LGBT students, clients, and patients.

Changes in the media, government, and educational systems may also help to decrease microaggressions, which can then assist in decreasing LGBT teen bullying and victimization. An increase in positive LGBT images can potentially enhance the acceptance of LGBT people in American society. Perhaps hatred toward LGBT people exists because of their lack of visibility in the media, or because of the presence of disparaging and stereotypical images of them. Adolescents who are able to view LGBT people as normal and/or successful role models may help them to view LGBT individuals as human. Moreover, this greater exposure of LGBT individuals in the media should include all people in the LGBT community—ranging from LGBT people of color (e.g., African Americans, Asian Americans, Latina/os, Arab Americans, multiracial people, Pacific Islanders, etc.), as well as bisexual and transgender people. Because these groups are often invisible or marginalized in the LGBT community itself, LGBT youths who identify in these ways may feel a double burden, which may negatively influence their self-esteem and mental health. Thus, perhaps more media presence, visibility, and normalization can help to ameliorate some of these negative outcomes.

A series of amendments in the government and legal systems may also lead to a reduction in LGBT microaggressions, bullying, and victimization. When governments uphold laws that ban or prevent same-sex marriage or disallow LGBT people from serving in the military, a societal message is communicated that LGBT people are second-class citizens in this country. When LGBT people are not allowed to visit their partners in hospitals or when LGBT people are denied health care, their basic rights as humans are compromised. On the contrary, when LGBT people are protected and considered in laws, a societal message is communicated that they are valued human beings in our society. Thus, it is important for government to pass laws that promote equal rights and opportunities for LGBT people. In doing so, messages of acceptance will be transmitted throughout all of society, consequently resulting in a decrease in microaggressions and perhaps a decrease in teen bullying.

Finally, because bullying toward LGBT teens occurs most often in school systems, it is necessary for educational policies to promote the physical and psychological safety of LGBT youths. First, curriculum should include and implement diversity in all subjects—from the influences of LGBT people in world history to the inclusion of LGBT issues in psychology to the teaching of LGBT works in American literature. Second, harassment and bullying policies should be created and enforced, including special clauses that protect the rights of LGBT students. By developing an atmosphere that does not tolerate hateful behaviors, LGBT students will feel safer, and heterosexual students will learn about equality and social justice. Finally, promotion of egalitarianism and diversity should be incorporated into all aspects of student life—from the encouragements of gay-straight alliances to the hiring of LGBT teachers to the allowing of same-sex prom dates.

If school systems, the government, families, and the media really do care about the lives of LGBT youths, some or all of these recommendations can be implemented in many simple ways. Perhaps if these LGBT-affirmative environments had existed in the past, the number of LGBT teen suicides would not have been as substantial as it is (and has been). If we want to see our children survive and live healthy lives, we cannot just tell them that "It gets better." Rather, we have to show them that we are doing our parts to "Make it better" for them today.

References

Almeida, J., Johnson, R. M., Corliss, H. L., Molnar, B. E., & Azrael, D. (2009). Emotional distress among LGBT youth: The influence of perceived discrimination based on sexual orientation. *Journal of Youth Adolescence, 38,* 1001–1014.

Burn, S. M., Kadlec, K., & Rexer, R. (2005). Effects of subtle heterosexism on gays, lesbians, and bisexuals. *Journal of Homosexuality, 49,* 23–38.

Cochran, S. D. (2001). Emerging issues in research on lesbians' and gay men's mental health: Does sexual orientation really matter? *American Psychologist, 56,* 932–947.

D'Augelli, A. R. (1992). Lesbian and gay male undergraduates' experiences of harassment and fear on campus. *Journal of Interpersonal Violence, 7,* 383–395.

Freedner, N., Freed, L. H., Yang, Y. W., & Austin, B. (2002). Dating violence among gay, lesbian, and bisexual adolescents: Results from a community survey. *Journal of Adolescent Health, 31,* 469–474.

Herek, G. M. (2000). The psychology of sexual prejudice. *Current Directions in Psychological Science, 9,* 19–22.

Herek, G. M. (2007). Confronting sexual stigma and prejudice: Theory and practice. *Journal of Social Issues, 63,* 905–925.

Herek, G. M., & Capitanio, J. P. (1999). Sex Differences in how heterosexuals think about lesbians and gay men: Evidence from survey context effects. *Journal of Sex Research, 36,* 348–360.

Hill, D. B., & Willoughby, B. L. B. (2005). The development and validation of the genderism and transphobia scale. *Sex Roles, 53,* 531–544.

Horn, S. S. (2007). Adolescents' acceptance of same-sex peers based on sexual orientation and gender expression. *Journal of Youth and Adolescence, 36,* 363–371.

Horn, S. S., Szalacha, L. A., & Drill, K. (2008). Schooling, sexuality, and rights: An investigation of heterosexual students' social cognition regarding sexual orientation and the rights of gay and lesbian peers in school. *Journal of Social Issues, 64,* 791–813.

Marshal, M. P., Friedman, M. S., Stall, R., King, K. M., Miles, J., Gold, M. A., Bukstein, O. G., & Morse, J. Q. (2008). Sexual orientation and adolescent substance use: A meta-analysis and methodological review. *Addiction, 103,* 546–556.

Meyer, I. H. (1995). Minority stress and mental health in gay men. *Journal of Health and Social Behavior, 36,* 38–56.

Meyer, I. H. (2003). Prejudice, social stress, and mental health in lesbian, gay, and bisexual populations: Conceptual issues and research evidence. *Psychological Bulletin, 129,* 674–697.

Nadal, K. L. (2008). Preventing racial, ethnic, gender, sexual minority, disability, and religious microaggressions: Recommendations for promoting positive mental health. *Prevention in Counseling Psychology: Theory, Research, Practice and Training, 2,* 22–27.

Nadal, K. L. (2010). Gender microaggressions and women: Implications for mental health. In M. A. Paludi (Ed.), *Feminism and women's rights worldwide: Vol. 1. Mental and physical health* (pp. 155–175). Westport, CT: Praeger.

Nadal, K. L., Hamit, S., & Issa, M. A. (2010). Overcoming gender and sexual orientation microaggressions. In M. A. Paludi & F. M. Denmark (Eds.), *Victims of sexual assault and abuse: Resources and responses for individuals and families* (pp. 21–43). Westport, CT: Praeger.

Nadal, K. L., Issa, M. A., Griffin, K., Hamit, S., & Lyons, O. (2010). Religious microaggressions in the United States: Mental health implications for religious minority groups. In D. W. Sue (Ed.), *Microaggressions and marginality: Manifestation, dynamics, and impact* (pp. 287–310). New York: Wiley.

Nadal, K. L., Issa, M. A., Leon, J., Meterko, V., Wideman, M., & Wong, Y. (under review). Sexual orientation microaggressions: Perspectives of lesbian, gay, and bisexual people.

Nadal, K. L., Rivera, D. P., & Corpus, M. J. H. (2010). Sexual orientation and transgender microaggressions in everyday life: Experiences of lesbians, gays, bisexuals, and transgender individuals. In D. W. Sue (Ed.), *Microaggressions and marginality: Manifestation, dynamics, and impact* (pp. 217–240). New York: Wiley.

Nadal, K. L., Skolnik, A., & Wong, Y. (under review). Interpersonal and systemic microaggressions: Psychological impacts on transgender individuals and communities.

Nadal, K. L., Wong, Y., Issa, M. A., Meterko, V. M., Leon, J., & Wideman, M. (under review). Sexual orientation microaggressions: Processes and coping mechanisms for lesbian, gay, and bisexual individuals.

Pierce, C., Carew, J., Pierce-Gonzalez, D., & Willis, D. (1978). An experiment in racism: TV commercials. In C. Pierce (Ed.), *Television and education* (pp. 62–88). Beverly Hills, CA: Sage.

Poteat, V. P., Aragon, S. R., Espelage, D. L., & Koenig, B. W. (2009). Psychosocial concerns of sexual minority youth: Complexity and caution in group differences. *Journal of Counseling and Clinical Psychology, 77,* 196–201.

Rivera, D. P., Forquer, E. E., & Rangel, R. (2010). Microaggressions and the life experience of Latina/o Americans. In D. W. Sue (Ed.), *Microaggressions and marginality: Manifestation, dynamics, and impact* (pp. 59–83). New York: Wiley.

Rostosky, S. S., Riggle, E. D. B., Gray, B. E., & Hatton, R. L. (2007). Minority stress experiences in committed same-sex couple relationships. *Professional Psychology: Research and Practice, 38,* 392–400.

Saewyc, E. M., Homma, Y., Skay, C. L., Bearinger, L. H., Resnick, M. D., & Reis, E. (2009). Protective factors in the lives of bisexual adolescents in North America. *American Journal of Public Health, 99,* 110–117.

Saewyc, E. M., Skay, C. L., Pettingell, S. L., Reis, E. A., Bearinger, L., Resnick, M., Murphy, A., & Combs, L. (2006). Hazards of stigma: The sexual and physical abuse of gay, lesbian, and bisexual adolescents in the U.S. and Canada. *Child Welfare, 55,* 195–213.

Safren, S. A., & Pantalone, D. W. (2005). Social anxiety and barriers to resilience among lesbian, gay, and bisexual adolescents. In A. M. Omoto & H. S. Kurtzman (Eds.), *Sexual orientation and mental health: Examining identity and development in lesbian, gay, and bisexual people* (pp. 55–71). Washington, DC: American Psychological Association.

Saltzburg, S. (2004). Learning that an adolescent child is gay or lesbian: The parent experience. *Social Work, 49,* 109–118.

Smith, S. D. (2004). Sexually underrepresented youth: Understanding gay, lesbian, bisexual, transgendered, and questioning (glbt-q) youth. In J. L. Chin (Ed.), *Psychology of prejudice and discrimination: Bias based on gender and sexual orientation* (Vol. 3, pp. 151–199). Westport, CT: Praeger.

Sue, D. W. (2010). *Microaggressions in everyday life: Race, gender, and sexual orientation.* New York: Wiley.

Sue, D. W., Bucerri, J. M., Lin, A. I., Nadal, K. L., & Torino, G. C. (2007). Racial microaggressions and the Asian American experience. *Cultural Diversity and Ethnic Minority Psychology, 13,* 72–81.

Sue, D. W., Capodilupo, C. M., & Holder, A. M. B. (2008). Racial microaggressions in the life experience of Black Americans. *Professional Psychology: Research and Practice, 39,* 329–336.

Sue, D. W., Capodilupo, C. M., Torino, G. C., Bucceri, J. M., Holder, A. M. B., Nadal, K. L., et al. (2007). Racial microaggressions in everyday life: Implications for clinical practice. *The American Psychologist, 62,* 271–286.

Sue, D. W., Lin, A. I., Torino, G. C., Capodilupo, C. M., & Rivera, D. P. (2009). Racial microaggressions in the classroom. *Cultural Diversity and Ethnic Minority Psychology, 15,* 183–190.

Sue, D. W., Nadal, K. L., Capodilupo, C. M., Lin, A. I., Torino, G. C., & Rivera, D. P. (2008). Racial microaggressions against Black Americans: Implications for counseling. *Journal of Counseling and Development, 86,* 330–338.

Ueno, K. (2005). Sexual orientation and psychological distress in adolescence: Examining interpersonal stressors and social support processes. *Social Psychology Quarterly, 68*(3), 258–277.

Waldo, C. R., Hesson-McInnis, M. S., & D'Augelli, A. R. (1998). Antecedents and consequences of victimization of lesbian, gay, and bisexual young people: A structural model comparing rural university and urban samples. *American Journal of Community Psychology, 26*(2), 307–334.

Walls, N. E. (2008). Toward a multidimensional understanding of heterosexism: The changing nature of prejudice. *Journal of Homosexuality, 55*, 20–70.

Williams, T., Connolly, J., Pepler, D., & Craig, W. (2005). Peer victimization, social support, and psychosocial adjustment of sexual minority adolescents. *Journal of Youth and Adolescence, 24*, 471–482.

CHAPTER TWO

Violence in Emerging Adulthood: A Developmental Perspective

Robert F. Marcus and Eric G. Jamison II

Exploring the risk factors for serious violence across the years of early adulthood, which are some of the most dangerous years in the human lifespan, is a critical step toward understanding violence in early adulthood. In addition, exploring these risk factors, individually or collectively, can aid in predicting violent behavior. Greater research attention has focused on the dramatic increases in violent crime during adolescence and to its steady decline during the rest of the lifespan, than to the greater lethality of violence from the late teens through mid-20s. Research has shown a decline in the prevalence of serious violence after age 18 in such longitudinal studies as the National Youth Survey and the National Longitudinal Study of Adolescent Health (Marcus, 2009). The reduction in prevalence rates for violence in emerging adulthood can be explained using three complementary theoretical perspectives: the theory of emerging adulthood, the theory arising from developmental criminology, and evolutionary theory.

Public attention has been focused more on the rapid increase in serious violence during adolescence, but less so on the decline in violent behaviors among those in their 20s. Yet violence during the late teens to mid-20s remains a serious cause for public concern. Violence has consistently been the second-leading cause of death for those 15 through 24 years of age, and the dramatic increases for some seriously violent behaviors do not fade during mid- to late adolescence as quickly as they rise. For example, research compiled by the Centers for Disease Control and Prevention has shown that homicide fatalities for 19- to 25-year-olds for the year 2002 (i.e., 4,524) were 3.3 times greater than homicide fatalities for 12- to 18-year-olds (i.e., 1,391); the deadliest of violent acts actually increase after the years of adolescence. Moreover, beyond the threat to life, violence for those in their 20s can have enormous consequences as career, intimate partner choices, and other important decisions with lifelong significance are made.

Violence may have a serious impact on the entire course of adult development. The period between "emerging adulthood" (Arnett, 2000, 2004), roughly the late teens through mid-20s, and "young adulthood," roughly ages 28 through 36, have been referred to as a major transition stage in which "there is the potential for extensive changes in nearly all aspects of life within a few short years . . . (and research) emphasis has increased around issues related to achieving and not achieving developmental tasks and the path to individual identity" (Schulenberg, Sameroff, & Cicchetti, 2004, p. 804). Longitudinal research, for example, has begun to show that positive work and romantic involvement between the ages of 21 and 23 decreased involvement in antisocial behavior in emerging adulthood for those most impaired by childhood-onset and persistent antisocial behavior (Roisman, Aguilar, & Egeland, 2004). In addition, competence in the completion of developmental tasks of work and romantic involvement in emerging adulthood can predict successful adjustment to young adulthood (Masten et al., 2004). The developmental progression and the context of violence in the late teens and early to mid-20 is the focus of this chapter.

Violence in the Late Teens to Mid-20s

Research has generally found a decline in the prevalence of many serious, self-reported violent behaviors from late adolescence to the mid-20s, after which violence continues to decline as a cause of mortality and injury for the remainder of the lifespan. That is good news considering the lethality of violence at that stage. One of the first studies of developmental changes in self-reported violent behaviors from adolescence through the 20s, the well-known National Youth Survey (Elliott, Huizinga, & Morse, 1986), has offered valuable insight into the developmental course of violent behavior. The responses of a nationally representative cross section of adolescents, followed longitudinally for five years into their early 20s, relied on interviews of adolescents who were asked about their serious violent behaviors (such as aggravated assault, robbery, and gang fights) during the past year.

Those who had taken part in three or more of these behaviors were designated "serious violent offenders" (SVOs). Data for those between the ages of 12 and 21 showed that about 7% to 8% of males and 2% to 3% of females were SVOs during adolescence (about three times males versus females), but male SVOs were about 8 to 10 times as prevalent as females SVOs by ages 20 and 21. Age-related prevalence rates for males showed that the percentage of males in the SVO classification increased from 6.8% at age 12 to 7.8% at age 16, followed by a decline to 3.1% at age 21. Age-related prevalence rates for females at age 12 were 2.9%, and that prevalence rate declined to .3% by age 21. The findings of decline in rates of serious violent offending from the teen years to the early 20s was bolstered by longitudinal analysis of hazard rates, the percentage of individuals who were *first* classified as an SVO at various ages. The greatest hazard rate was 3.7% at age 17, and the rate had dropped to .4% by age 21. Thus, by the early 20s, individuals were not embarking on *new* violent careers, and those who were violent in their early 20s were most likely those who had started on that path by their late teens and very early 20s.

There is also good evidence from longitudinal research that most, but not all, individuals reduce their involvement in violence from late adolescence to their mid-20s, whereas some continue to perpetrate violent behavior. Studies tracking individual differences in violence from the late teens to the mid-20s have enabled greater understanding of the violent careers taken by individuals, and shown there to be many paths toward decline and one toward increase. Two studies of those trajectories will suffice, although the reader may wish to view the multiple paths found in a number of longitudinal studies (Piquero, 2004). First, a recent analysis of the National Youth Survey data (Nash & Kim, 2006) has found five distinct trajectories for those showing "any" violent behavior in adolescence and the mid-20s: (1) low/stable (67.6%); (2) adolescent onset (11.9%); (3) young adult onset (11.8%); (4) early onset/chronic (5.3%); and (5) early onset desister (3.4%). The four groups showing dramatic or moderate declines during mid-adolescence to age 24 were the early onset desisters, early onset/chronic, adolescent onset, and low/stable groups. The one group showing moderate *increase* in violent behavior from age 18 to 24 was the young adult onset (11.8%). Thus violent individuals cluster into heterogeneous subtypes, most of whom decline in their violent behavior, but some of whom remain violent into their mid-20s.

Other studies have illuminated both the nature of the violence as well as the unique paths or trajectories taken by individuals who continue or stop their violence. One such study of the seriousness of violent behavior itself was the Pittsburgh Youth Study (Loeber, Lacourse, & Homish, 2005).

The Pittsburgh study of violence and homicide among urban males was designed to assess both age-graded changes in violent behavior as well as different age trajectories for subgroups. Violent behavior (based on teacher, parent, and respondent reports) was classified as "0" for nonviolent; "1" as moderate in severity (e.g., gang fighting or carrying a weapon); or "2" as serious (e.g., attack to seriously hurt or kill someone). Results showed that violence seriousness for those who reported any violence (49% of the sample) declined between the ages of 20 and 24 to near zero. However, there were three subgroups showing different trajectories from mid-adolescence to the mid-20s. The first trajectory was named the "chronic group," 4.7% of the total sample who increased in their level of violence between 14 and 20, and slowly declined to age 24 (to below their level at age 14). A second, called the "late desister" group (22.4% of the sample), showed a steep decline in the seriousness of violence from age 14 to zero at age 24. A third, an "early desister" group (21.9% of the sample), whose initial level of violence seriousness was half of the chronic group, declined to near zero by age 24. The overall trend for violence seriousness was downward from mid-adolescence onward to age 24, as was shown by cross-sectional studies reviewed earlier, but examinations of trajectories showed both increases and decreases for different sets of individuals.

Based on the foregoing discussion of cross-sectional and longitudinal data, inspection of developmental trends for both men and women are likely to show a downward trend from age 18 onward, and that the trend downward may depend on the nature of the violent behavior itself. For some violent acts, and for some violent individuals, there may be no decline in violence at all.

The National Longitudinal Study of Adolescent Health

One ongoing cross-sectional and longitudinal study of a large, nationally representative sample of those ages 19 through 25 was Wave III of the National Longitudinal Study of Adolescent Health (Add Health). The methodology for Wave III of the Add Health study may be found elsewhere (e.g., Marcus, 2009). Important features of that study were that data were collected using a confidential recording by the respondent into a laptop computer, attempts were made to interview those who had been incarcerated, and the sample was large enough to detect developmental changes in violent behaviors that were relatively rare. The six questions asked about violent behaviors, which were later dichotomized to their presence or absence to denote their prevalence, can be found in Table 2.1.

Violence in Emerging Adulthood

Table 2.1 Violence interview questions: National Longitudinal Study of Adolescent Health, Wave III.

1	In the past 12 months, how often did you use or threaten to use a weapon to get something from someone? (0 = never to 3 = 5 or more times)
2	In the past 12 months, how often did you take part in a physical fight where a group of your friends was against another group? (0 = never to 3 = 5 or more times)
3	In the past 12 months, how often did you use a weapon in a fight? (0 = never to 3 = 5 or more times)
4	In the past 12 months, how often did you hurt someone badly enough in a physical fight that he or she needed care from a doctor or nurse? (number of times)
	Which of the following things happened in the past 12 months?
5	You pulled a knife or gun on someone? (0 = not marked to 1 = marked)
6	You shot or stabbed someone? (0 = not marked to 1 = marked)

The six behaviors (e.g., gang fighting, robbery, use of weapons, and injury to another) were all serious enough to lead to injury and to criminal penalty, should the perpetrator be caught. Figure 2.1 presents the prevalence of "any" of the six forms of violence by age. Consistent with

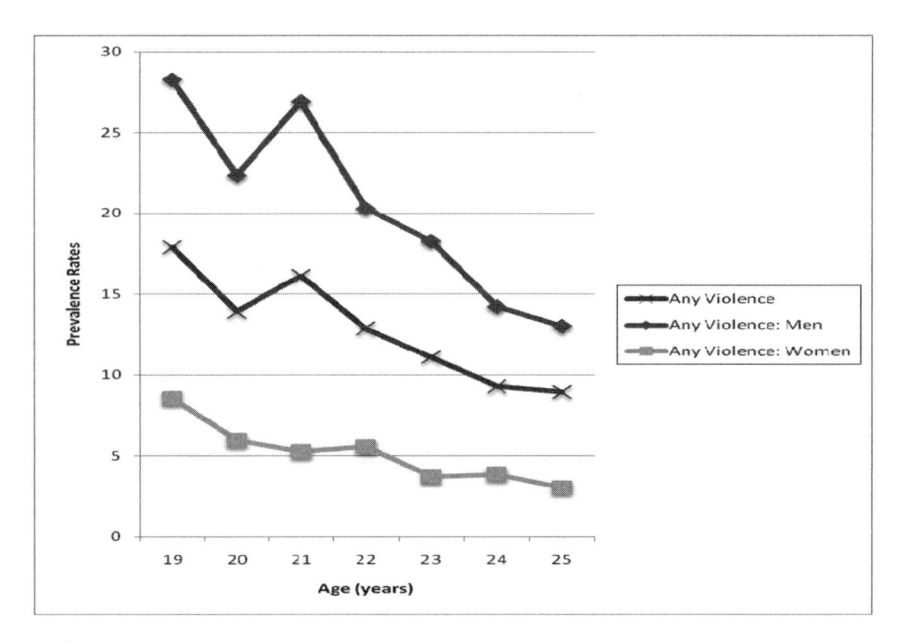

Figure 2.1 Prevalence of violence by age ($n = 13{,}764$; men: 6,453; women: 7,311). The lines represent violence irrespective of gender and by each gender.

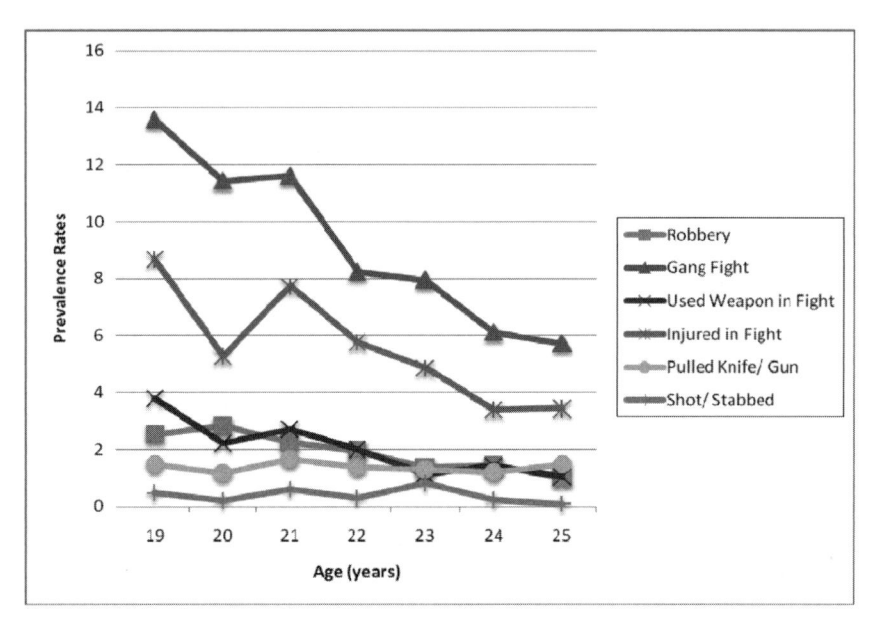

Figure 2.2 Prevalence of violence by age and type ($n = 13{,}978$). Each line represents a different form of violence.

cross-sectional and longitudinal research presented earlier, this cross-sectional study showed about a 50% decline in the prevalence rate for "any" violence, and a prevalence rate for men about three to four times that of women.

Since the declines in prevalence may not be the same for all types of violent behaviors, the six violent behaviors were separated out and presented by age. The cross-sectional data for each of the six behaviors are shown in Figure 2.2. The Add Health data showed dramatic declines of more than 50% for gang fighting and for injuring others in a fight, two violent behaviors that were highest in prevalence at age 19. Dramatic declines of similar magnitude, albeit starting from lower initial prevalence levels, also were found for the less common use of weapon in a fight and robbery. Interestingly, the prevalence of shooting or stabbing someone and pulling a knife or gun on someone do not fluctuate with age. The finding that some forms of weapon-related violence remained rather steady during this time period was consistent with the results from Wave I of Add Health, noting that teens in the 7th through 12th grades showed no age fluctuation in such violent behaviors as using a weapon in a fight, pulling a knife or gun on someone, or using a weapon to get something from someone (see Marcus, 2007, chap. 1). Analysis showing no developmental change for some serious violent behaviors and previous research showing no change for some of those who perpetrate these behaviors suggests an important focus for research. In addition, violence perpetration stability for this period suggests the importance of understanding the risk factors sustaining violence.

Sources of Violence in the Late Teens and Early 20s

There have been few attempts to analyze the theoretical basis and to organize risk factors based in theory specifically for violence perpetration, and then test a wide variety of possible risk factors for violence during the late teens and early 20s. One such study of the violent behaviors indicated above was undertaken using the responses of 19- through 25-year-olds from Wave III of Add Health (Marcus, 2009).

Given the developmental trends and unique trajectories for violence in subtypes of violent individuals in the later teens and early to mid-20s, research on a relatively large set of risk factors that may *increase* violence, and on protective factors that may *decrease* probability, is essential to understanding whether they operate individually or eclipse or cancel out one another, and which are the most potent predictors of violence. One such study of a home-interviewed, nationally representative, large (n = 14,098), and diverse sample of men and women has investigated the contribution of 14 risk and protective variables from Wave III of Add Health (Marcus, 2009). The results of the regression analysis for the sample as a whole identified four risk factors and three protective factors that contributed uniquely to the perpetration of "any" violence. Risk factors elevating the probability of "any" violence, with the interpretation of odds ratios in percentage terms reflecting the magnitude of that increase, were the following: (1) a history of three or more violent acts in adolescence (13.7% of the sample were in that group; increased 154%); (2) poverty, i.e., receipt of at least one of four forms of public assistance (11% of sample; increased 24%); (3) personality trait of high sensation seeking (increased 9%); and (4) symptoms of depression (increased 6%). These four (historical, demographic, and personality) risk factors were unique and additive, and in combination could increase the probability of violence by 193%. Since analyses completed separately for men and women sometimes reveal different risk factors, separate analyses by gender showed that women also were at greater risk if they did not complete high school (increased 138%).

The results of the study for protective factors showed the following unique variables to have lowered the probability of "any" violence: (1) female gender (lowered 77%); (2) being married (lowered 43%);

and (3) being older (lowered 13%). The joint effect of protective variables lowered the probability of "any" violence by a total of 133%. It is important to note that protective influences continued to moderate violence in this study despite the presence of risk factors, and that both risk and protective factors operated independently.

In sum, the risk for violence was found to be greater when individuals had a history of violence in adolescence, were poor, did not complete high school (girls only), and had significant sensation-seeking traits and depression symptoms. Conversely, individuals were less likely to engage in "any" violent behavior if they were female, married, or older. Explanations for these empirical findings, and their theoretical bases, now follow.

Theoretical Explanations for Risk and Protective Influences on Violence

There are three important theories with implications for antisocial and violent behavior during the late teens to mid-20s that help to explain the foregoing results. The three theories are the following: (1) the theory of "emerging adulthood" (Arnett, 2000); (2) the theory arising from developmental criminology and "turning points" (Sampson & Laub, 1993, 2005; Stouthamer-Loeber, Wei, Loeber, & Masten, 2004); and (3) the evolutionary perspective (Daly & Wilson, 1990, 2001; Campbell, 2006). Interestingly, these three theories do not offer diverging predictions about violence; they predict similar outcomes, often use similar constructs, and tend to converge and supplement one another, but the explanations for the changes found differed significantly in where the emphasis was placed.

Historically, our understanding of human development has come with an understanding of childhood, adolescence, and adulthood as periods in which major developmental milestones and challenges converge to shape the course of human development. One of the more recent conceptualizations pertains to a period between adolescence and early adulthood, roughly ages 18 through 30 years, as a period of "emerging adulthood" (Arnett, 2000). The theory proposes that, building on earlier development during adolescence, personal identity formation, explorations of romantic relationships, employment and career decisions, and education are revisited during emerging adulthood with greater seriousness and significance for later development (Arnett, 2000). By the mid-20s to the end of the 20s, and for most (but not all), personal identity crystallizes, careers are chosen, firm romantic attachments are established, and financial independence is achieved, and all these milestones occur with greater independence from family-of-origin approval and regulation than in earlier stages.

Emerging adults continue their personality evolution as well, which for most individuals proceeds in a positive direction, and such personality change reduces important, underlying risk factors for a variety of antisocial behaviors (e.g., drug use, violence, and illegal activities). Emerging adulthood is described generally as a stage of development in which the mood is more optimistic about life's possibilities than in adolescence, but it is also a stage in which some of life's major disappointments, rejections, and failures also may be present. Longitudinal research has found that from ages 18 to 25 individuals increase in self-esteem and decrease in depression and anger, particularly for those with greater family support, and the change is more dramatic for those who start with higher levels of those traits (Galambos, Barker, & Krahn, 2006). Other research shows that personality change usually continues to age 30 (McCrae et al., 1999), with reductions specifically in depression (Schulenberg & Zarrett, 2006), sensation seeking, and impulsivity (Sternberg, 2010). Reductions in depression, anger, sensation seeking, and impulsivity traits are particularly important because they have been positively associated with violent behavior and are likely to underlay decrement in violence for most adults. However, as suggested by the earlier discussions of the different trajectories taken by violent individuals and the research on 19- to 25-year-olds (Marcus, 2009), those adults who experience greater depression, higher impulsivity, and sensation seeking, or who less successfully negotiate romantic attachment and fail at educational and occupational achievement during emerging adulthood, appear to be at greater risk for violent behavior.

Before the 1980s, criminological research tended to focus on the factors that distinguished offenders from nonoffenders. More recently, research has focused on the onset, escalation, persistence, and desistance over the lifespan within the population of offenders. This theory most notably explains the hypothesis that crime declines with age, as Sampson and Laub (2005) demonstrate. Through this progression, the field of developmental criminology has enhanced our understanding of the life-course careers of criminals and has begun generating explanations for desistance from crime. Social control theory, for example, offers an explanation that an individual's emotional bonds are not only to family members but to society and its institutions as well (Marcus, 2009).

The second theoretical perspective, from developmental criminology, shifts focus toward the successful attachment to a romantic partner, as well as to attachments to the broader society in the form of investments in education, career, and financial security (Sampson & Laub, 1993, 2005; Stouthamer-Loeber et al., 2004). For example, Sampson and Laub (1993,

2005) found that being married provided a cutoff from past associations, increased social support, and furthered personal growth, which leads to identity transformations critical to desistance. Others have found that the best predictors of desistance from crime were a negative attitude toward delinquency and being either employed or in school (Stouthamer-Loeber et al., 2004).

Additionally, the greater the investment that individuals make in the conventional culture, the more anchored the individual will be and the less willing to jeopardize those bonds. Longitudinal research has found that making such an investment in marital commitment, and making better-quality educational and career choices, leads to desistance in criminal activity (Sampson & Laub, 1993, 2005; Stouthamer-Loeber et al., 2004). Investing in better relationship, educational, and financial endeavors yields "turning points" away from criminal activities (Sampson & Laub, 1993, 2005). As a result, individuals who make better choices have a greater investment to lose should they engage in antisocial behaviors that could jeopardize that capital investment. Conversely, it would follow that those who are unmarried, unemployed, and have poorer educational preparation would have less capital investment to risk losing through criminal or violent actions.

The third theoretical perspective, the evolutionary perspective, also pays close attention to the 18- to 30-year-old demographic, as the overarching goal of evolution is Darwinian fitness, and fitness variance is greatest among young men at this stage of life (Daly & Wilson, 1990, 2001). The idea of competition encompasses most of the criminal acts that are likely deemed "instrumental" or "rational," as well as those crimes deemed "expressive" or "irrational." For example, most lethal violence occurs not within the family but between unrelated acquaintances and strangers, and much of this violence arises in the context of competition for material goods (Daly & Wilson, 1988).

The evolutionary theory proposes that men during their late teens through late 20s compete intensively for women, and that sensation seeking and resultant risk-taking behavior motivates that competition (Daly & Wilson, 1990, 2001; Campbell, 2006). This theory has been applied to women, although the levels of violence and motivation would be less extreme than for men (Campbell, 2006). Furthermore, there is evidence that young women engage in lesser forms of physically violent behavior as a means by which to subdue female rivals as well as a means to attract male attention (Campbell, 2006).

In addition, this perspective hypothesizes that the potential for violence is greatest among men when competition for women is most intense, when fitness variance is greatest, and when sensation seeking and resultant risk-taking behavior is most intense (Marcus, 2009). As a corollary to this theory, those with fewer resources, in the sense of having less money, being unemployed, and having lower education levels, would compete more intensely with same-gender opponents for available partners, and competition for partners would be more fierce during the late teens and early 20s. Criminal violence and homicide in urban America can be considered an outcome of steep future discounting and escalation of risk in social competition (Daly & Wilson, 1997). Accordingly, Daly and Wilson (1990) have found that marriage and increasing age (beyond the mid-20s) were associated with a decline in homicide among men. There is also some evidence that homicide perpetration is more common among men who were unemployed in the United States (Daly & Wilson, 1990), and more common among Japanese men who had lower income and education attainment than the general Japanese population (Hirwaiwa-Hasegawa, 2005). Thus, evolutionary theory would predict that violence would be greater for men who possess such qualities.

Conclusion

Research has found declines in the prevalence of violent behavior for both men and women during emerging adulthood for a nationally representative sample of 19- through 25-year-olds. Not all forms of violence or violent career paths show moderation with age. Two forms of weapon-related violence did not show such developmental decline during this period. Theoretical explanations suggest that the failure to establish successful romantic relationships, personality traits of depression and sensation seeking, gender, and poverty continue to place individuals at risk for violence, and that violence may have lifelong significance for successful adjustment in early adulthood. Further understanding of violence and its consequences in the late teens to the mid-20s, and who does and who does not successfully negotiate the transition to adulthood, is an important area for study and one of the keys to successful transition to adulthood.

Note

This research uses data from Add Health, a program project designed by J. Richard Udry, Peter S. Bearman, and Kathleen Mullan Harris and funded by grant P01-HD31921 from the Eunice Kennedy Shriver National Institute of Child Health and Human Development, with cooperative funding from 17 other agencies. Special acknowledgement is due Ronald R. Rindfuss and Barbara Entwisle for assistance in the original design. Persons interested in obtaining data files from Add Health should contact Add Health, Carolina Population Center, 123 W. Franklin Street, Chapel Hill, NC 27516-2524 (addhealth@unc.edu). No direct support was received from grant P01-HD31921 for this analysis.

References

Arnett, J. (2000). Emerging adulthood: A theory of development from the late teens through the twenties. *American Psychologist, 55,* 469–480.

Arnett, J. (2004). *Emerging adulthood: The winding road from the late teens through the twenties.* New York: Oxford University Press.

Campbell, A. (1995). A few good men: Evolutionary psychology and female adolescent aggression. *Ethology and Sociobiology, 16,* 99–123.

Campbell, A. (2006). Sex differences in direction aggression: What are the psychological mediators? *Aggression and Violent Behavior, 11,* 237–264.

Daly, M., & Wilson, M. (1988). *Homicide.* New York: Aldine.

Daly, M., & Wilson, M. (1990). Killing the competition. *Human Nature, 1,* 83–109.

Daly, M., & Wilson, M. (1997). Crime and conflict: Homicide in evolutionary psychological perspective. *Crime and Justice, 22,* 51–100.

Daly, M., & Wilson, M. (2001). Risk-taking, intrasexual competition, and homicide. *Nebraska Symposium on Motivation, 47,* 1–36.

Elliott, D. S., Huizinga, D., & Morse, B. J. (1986). Self-reported violent offending: A descriptive analysis of juvenile violent offenders and their offending careers. *Journal of Interpersonal Violence, 1,* 472–514.

Galambos, N. L., Barker, E. T., & Krahn, H. J. (2006). Depression, anger, and self-esteem in emerging adulthood: Seven-year trajectories. *Developmental Psychology, 42,* 350–365.

Hirwaiwa-Hasegawa, M. (2005). Homicide by men in Japan, and its relationship to age, resources, and risk taking. *Evolution and Human Behavior, 26,* 332–343.

Loeber, R., Lacourse, E., & Homish, L. (2005). Homicide, violence, and developmental trajectories: Developmental origins of aggression. In R. Tremblay, W. Hartup, & J. Archer (Eds.), *Developmental origins of aggression* (pp. 202–219). New York: Guilford.

Marcus, R. F. (2007). *Aggression and violence in adolescence.* Cambridge, UK: Cambridge University Press.

Marcus, R. F. (2009). Cross-sectional study of violence in emerging adulthood. *Aggressive Behavior, 35,* 188–202.

Masten, A., Burt, K., Roisman, G., Obradovic, J., Long, J., & Tellegen, A. (2004). Resources and resilience in the transition to adulthood: Continuity and change. *Development and Psychopathology, 16,* 1071–1094.

McCrae, R., Costa, P., Ostendorf, F., Angleleitner, A., Caprara, G., Barbaranelli, C., De Lima, M., Simoes, A., Marusic, I., Bratko, D., Chae, J., & Piedmont, R. (1999).

Age differences in personality across the adult life span: Parallels in five cultures. *Developmental Psychology, 35,* 466–477.

Nash, J., & Kim, J. S. (2006). *Trajectories of violent offending and risk status in adolescence and early adulthood.* Washington, DC: U.S. Department of Justice National Criminal Justice Reference Service.

Piquero, A. R. (2004, October). *Taking stock of developmental trajectories of criminal activity over the life course.* Paper presented at the National Institute of Justice Conference on Longitudinal Studies, Washington, DC.

Roisman, G., Aguilar, B., & Egeland, B. (2004). Antisocial behavior in the transition to adulthood: The independent and interactive roles of developmental history and emerging developmental tasks. *Development and Psychopathology, 16,* 857–871.

Sampson, R. J., & Laub, J. H. (1993). *Crime in the making: Pathways and turning points through life.* Cambridge, MA: Harvard University Press.

Sampson, R., & Laub, J. (2005). A life-course view of the development of crime. *The Annals of the American Academy of Political and Social Science, 602,* 12–45.

Schulenberg, J. E., Sameroff, A., & Cicchetti, D. (2004). The transition to adulthood as a critical juncture in the course of psychopathology and mental health. *Development and Psychopathology, 16,* 799–806.

Schulenberg, J. E., & Zarrett, N. R. (2006). Mental health during emerging adulthood: Continuity and discontinuity in courses, causes, and functions. In J. J. Arnett & J. L. Tanner (Eds.), *Emerging adults in America: Coming of age in the 21st century* (pp. 135–172). Washington, DC: American Psychological Association.

Sternberg, L. (2010). A dual systems model of adolescent risk-taking. *Developmental Psychobiology, 52,* 216–224.

Stouthamer-Loeber, M., Wei, E., Loeber, R., & Masten, A. S. (2004). Desistance from persistent serious delinquency in the transition to adulthood. *Development and Psychopathology, 16,* 897–918.

CHAPTER THREE

"Mean Girls" in Real Life: The Media's Influence on Teen Violence and Victimization

Jennifer L. Martin

Introduction

Millennial girls have been provided with more opportunities for success than ever before, beginning with Title IX in the early 1970s; however, they are faced with new pressures that inhibit their potential. One half of girls indicate that they do not like their bodies, twice as many girls as boys commit suicide, and girls have a higher risk of abusing alcohol and drugs than do boys; additionally, the number of violent physical assaults committed by girls has increased 60% in the last two decades (Powderhouse Productions, 2009). The media contribute to these problems in a variety of ways. Girls are presented with a barrage of unrealistic expectations for their bodies and selves; simultaneously, the media seduces girls through the presentation of increasingly violent (yet still sexy) female characters in the name of strength and empowerment. These feminist ideals are co-opted and commodified in a damaging glorification of violence, while traditional stereotypes of appropriate feminine appearance and behavior are also sold back to girls, limiting them even more.

This juxtaposition has severe consequences for teenage girls. On the one hand, the media tell girls they should be empowered and strong, through images like Power Puff Girls and more violent characters like

Mrs. Smith (played by Angelina Jolie). These newer violent images are no longer incompatible with femininity. These violent images are also "avatarized" in video games, allowing girls to ape patriarchal dominance through violence, but without providing any tangible or sustainable sense of power. However, at the same time, we are bombarded with media images on television, on the Internet, and in magazines and movies portraying very traditional and stereotyped femininities: for example, the preoccupation with appearance, which demands that girls buy products in order to compete against other girls for the ultimate goal—to get and keep a boyfriend. These media images tell girls that they can never be good enough. There is always something they can change, improve, alter, which always comes with a price tag. The consequences of these new realities are that we have more violent teenage girls who are also still self-doubting. This can manifest itself in heightened harassment of girls at the hands of other girls, and this harassment is becoming ever more physical. Peer harassment has devastating effects on victims, such as social isolation, anxiety, and depression (Kopels & Dupper, 1999). To exacerbate this, teen culture is such that victims often do not tell teachers or parents when faced with harassment for fear of being labeled a snitch. Instead, victims attempt to deal with the harassment on their own, and bystanders remain silent.

Erikson (1968) has argued that adolescence is a period of self-exploration, of the analysis and evaluation of the self; ideally, adolescence culminates in the establishment of a cohesive and integrated identity. However, this process may be more complex for female adolescents because of the societal barriers that promote a fragmented female self, such as sexual objectification and patriarchal modes of discourse (Brown & Gilligan, 1992; van Roosmalen, 2000). Brown and Gilligan (1992) argue that girls are still taught to avoid conflict and to "be nice," to self-censor and suppress any desires that may be incompatible with what they perceive to be "appropriate" societal expectations for females. In others words, the stereotype of the self-sacrificing female is still largely reinforced today, and it has negative consequences for girls.

In the late 20th century, research on girls indicated that girls' innate, self-protective resistance has a tendency to be squashed; that is, females often become self-censored by a society (reinforced by the media) that does not value women's voices. The emerging body of girls' literature indicates that something happens to girls during their teenage years, causing a drop in self-esteem, confidence, and performance (American Association of University Women, 1991; Gilligan, Lyons, & Hanmer, 1990). Gilligan and colleagues (1990) discovered that between the ages of 11 and 15 or 16, it became "dangerous" for girls to give voice to what they knew or felt. As Stern (2002) states, "Some scholars contend that girls begin to practice self-censorship because they have learned that speaking up can get them in trouble with teachers, worry their parents, and endanger their friendships" (p. 226). Silence, loss of voice, or self-censorship thus became a focus of this emerging body of literature. Scholars also found a loss in articulateness in girls during those adolescent years (Brown & Gilligan, 1992; Stern, 2002). Girls who were once articulate began showing signs of verbal ambiguity in responses and in conversational patterns in general, using phrases such as "I don't know," "you know," etc. In essence, girls often cover up what they know.

This is still the case, to a large degree. However, we are witnessing a new problem with girls as well, a heightened sense of aggression. Historically, girls kept their bullying of other girls more covert than did their male counterparts (at least more hidden from teachers and adults). The tradition of silence that was instilled in girls, as well as their charge to behave and follow rules, was culturally conveyed in how they bullied and excluded other girls. New digital media have made bullying easier and more anonymous. The average American teen sends and receives approximately 2,000 texts per month, which is more than double the rate of one year ago (Powderhouse Productions, 2009). Some teens even sleep with their cell phone, which speaks to how integral social networking is to their lives, but it also increases the potential for cyber harassment, social shunning, and public humiliation. Again, most victims do not tell their parents when facing these problems; instead, they face them alone.

With images of women in the media becoming increasingly violent, it is more acceptable for girls to act out their anger within public view. Although the anger might be more overt, it is often misdirected and still speaks to the silencing of girls, which prevents girls from bonding in order to challenge existing forms of discourse and representations of femininity. Instead, anger pits girls against one another for the maintenance of the status quo, where "girl fighting" is acceptable, and even sexy, but girls' anger toward traditional forms of power is still unacceptable. This exacerbates the problem of bullying in general and adds to the charge with which educators and parents are already faced: to protect our children.

Alienation and Body Image

Carol Gilligan's *In a Different Voice* (1982) is still relevant to today's discussion of girls. In it, Gilligan argues that women and girls often have trouble expressing themselves because they experience a "divided judgment" that stems from their subject positions as both females and human beings.

Language helps to reinforce the division between the human (male) norm and that of the female; the latter is often described in terms of inferiority and subordination. As Gilligan states, "The difficulty women experience in finding or speaking publicly in their own voices emerges repeatedly in the form of qualification and self-doubt, but also in intimations of a divided judgment, a public assessment and private assessment which are fundamentally at odds" (p. 16). This divided judgment is also experienced by many girls today in the realm of the body. As Brumberg (1997) states, "By age thirteen, 53 percent of American girls are unhappy with their bodies; by age seventeen, 78 percent are dissatisfied" (p. xxiv). Girls receive an abundance of media messages—from television, literature, the Internet, music, and video games—that will them to conform to an unrealistic idea of what it means to be (and look like) a woman.

Younger (2003) conducted an analysis of young adult literature written between the years 1975 and 1999 and found a disturbing pattern: thin young women/girls were portrayed as in control, and larger girls were portrayed as passive and irresponsible with their sexuality. Male bodies are rarely described in young adult literature. Descriptions of female bodies proliferate as the male gaze is reappropriated upon characters, the image of the self, etc. (Younger, 2003). This gaze becomes internalized by characters, and as Younger states, it "encourages young women's self-surveillance of their bodies" (p. 48). Along with identity development, body image lies at the center of adolescence.

According to the American Association of University Women (1991), negative body image is correlated with the risk of suicide for girls. The same is untrue for boys. According to Younger (2003), "Using starvation to suspend the onset of sexual maturity complicates the meaning of being thin. For many girls controlling food intake provides a sense of power, but that sense of power is false, since deliberately reducing one's body size usually diminishes physical strength" (p. 53). This deliberate "project" of body reduction, essentially making one's self "disappear" or take up less physical space in the world, is a metaphor for female powerlessness and diminished subjectivity in the world. This speaks volumes about the absence of true empowerment for today's girls. Girls are receiving messages from a variety of sources that, in order to be "good" or "have value," they must be thin.

White Western standards of beauty contribute to girls feeling negatively about their bodies. Kalodner (1996) found that girls of color who do not identify with mainstream culture reported less concern regarding issues of physical image. However, eating disorders among girls of color are on the rise, especially among those girls who are acculturated to Western patriarchal values (Kalodner, 1996). According to Basow and

Rubin (1999), "As evident in the literature on minority girls, having strong female models and androgynous traits seems to help girls resist negative cultural messages regarding women" (p. 44).

Brumberg (1997) argues that female bodies have increasingly been commodified in modern culture such that they have become personal projects where women and girls on an individual level are continually in the process of surveying, altering, changing, and ultimately "improving" upon their bodies. Their bodies are their canvases. According to Harris (2004), "This trend toward a regulation of young women's interiority, whether the private space of their bedrooms, bodies, emotions, or personal conversations, suggests that the normal girl's life is one that is lived large. The normalization of the insertion of the public gaze into the private regulates young women by demanding a constant display of self. Young women become ever-available and ever-monitored" (p. 130). This sense of monitoring also comes from without in the realm of consumer monitoring through hygiene. Advertising teaches girls and women that their bodies are dirty: that they need products to clean, sanitize, and perfume themselves. It is hygiene, not sexuality, that is focused upon with menarche and menstruation.

As we know, media messages can be damaging for both women and men, girls and boys, but perhaps they are most damaging for female persons because some of the most prominent media images are those that keep women apart and direct them to compete against each other for the attention of men. These same images teach girls and women to constantly compare themselves to other girls and women and to adjust accordingly. This results in keeping women apart—women become alienated from one another, and thus from themselves. This sense of division contributes to the cultural animosity between women that creates the mean girl paradigm and sets the tone for the bully/victim dynamic. In sum, the alienation of American girls and women through media images ultimately prevents them from obtaining true power collectively. Collective power can bring empowerment and perhaps even the creation of alternatives to damaging patriarchal messages.

Alienation through Social Space

From an evolutionary and biological point of view, girls cannot *physically* afford to risk retaliation by attacking openly; culturally, physical aggression is not acceptable in girls and women. Also, girls seem to develop social intelligence before boys do—and, hence, are capable of engaging in effective social manipulation (Chesler, 2001, p. 93).

As Chesler's theory suggests, girls are still more likely to act in more covert ways when bullying. Starting in the late 1990s and continuing into the 2000s, there was much talk of "mean girls," and new terms were coined, such as female aggression or relational aggression, to explain how girls alienate other girls in decisive but covert ways that often involve the entire peer group at the instigation of the "alpha female." Many books were written on the subject, such as *Odd Girl Out: The Hidden Culture of Aggression in Girls* (Simmons, 2002) and *Queen Bees and Wannabes: Helping Your Daughter Survive Cliques, Gossip, Boyfriends, and other Realities of Adolescence* (Wiseman, 2002). These books, as does the organization *The Ophelia Project*, purport to explain how, beginning in middle school, many girls are forced into silence through regimented regulation at the hands of female bullies. However, in a study of women and girls across cultures, silence is one of the most prominent themes (Iglesias & Cormier, 2002). Female aggression attempts to regulate or punish female behavior (Brown, 2003); often the victim does not know what she did wrong. More specifically, if a girl is not acting in an appropriate manner according to the "proper" feminine codes of the peer culture of which she is a part, she may become shunned, ostracized, the subject of gossip, and subject to social terrorism. These interactions conjoined with the societal notion that girls are supposed to be interested in boys (through the romanticization of heterosexual romance as girls' ultimate goal) teach girls that "female friendship is dangerous, suspect, or unimportant" (Brown, 2003, p. 21).

Brown (2003) argues that not only do girls police other girls, but they also benefit in the short term from adhering to female sexist stereotypes: "Girls draw on readily available sexist stereotypes of girls and women as excuses to separate from other girls, to join boys, or privilege their relationships with boys" (p. 149). This is done in an attempt, whether consciously or not, to gain power through male approval, or to gain "male power" (Brown, 2003). The cultural messages women receive are the devaluation of all things female. Instead of identifying with what is perceived as negative, or female, women often choose to male identify, to strive to be "one of the boys," or an honorary man. Or, girls can achieve power and status within the peer culture through a romantic relationship with a powerful boy. This gives women a false sense of power because they can never truly be what they seek to imitate or to "put on." Moreover, power gained merely through association is not truly personal power.

Gilligan and colleagues (1990) argue that something happens in adolescence that causes girls to silence themselves; girls realize that their (relational) style is not valued and validated by society. Girls and women are often denied access to the emotions of anger and aggression by a culture that expects them to be caring, giving, and "nice." As Brown and Gilligan (1992) state, "Girls who fear speaking their anger readily become confused about whether anger really exists, whether they are really feeling angry" (p. 174). This causes a disconnection between thought, feeling, and action. These "severed connections" have serious implications in the lives of girls and are reinforced through many societal institutions, both formal and informal, such as female aggression, socialization, gender inequity in schools, sexual harassment and assault, etc. As Iglesias and Cormier (2002) state, "the implications of silence and speaking out may vary as gender, race, sexual orientation, and social class interact. Silence first becomes an issue for many latency-age girls as they move into early adolescence. With loss of voice also comes loss of self" (p. 259). When females are denied access to emotions such as anger, when they are not allowed to express anger, and/or when their anger has no outlet, it may turn inward. Girls then begin to devalue themselves and one another. What then becomes all important is to be accepted in a heterosexual dating relationship (van Roosmalen, 2000).

Girls must deal with societal and internalized sexism, which reinforces that girls and women are inferior in a variety of ways to boys and men. Basow and Rubin (1999) found internalized sexism in their study of girls, and that girls preferred to be considered "just one of the guys," as opposed to "one of the girls." Basow and Rubin warn that there is "danger for girls when they confront sexism through choosing to distance themselves from other girls instead of deconstructing and evaluating the negative images of women" (p. 43). This distancing will provide girls a retreat from the negative images of women in society in the short term, but in the long term it only serves to fragment and alienate women from themselves and from truly bonding with other women. In essence, this distancing also prohibits women from confronting the societal problem of sexism in general.

Some negative ideas about girls and women are passed down through the culture in nursery school jokes: for example, that "girls have cooties." As Brown (2003) states, "Girls are still seen by boys as pollutants, as contaminators, as carriers of a deadly strain of femininity. These seemingly innocent insults are given cultural weight by the media and socializing institutions like schools, and are engaged with and passed on by children themselves. It is still considered an insult of great magnitude to call a boy a girl; the reverse, of course, is not true" (p. 20). This dichotomous thinking is dangerous and detrimental to women and girls (Brown, 2003). It is not surprising that many girls give up their female friendships to engage in relationships with boys (which they see as the more important relationships) and/or to strive to become one of the boys.

As an educator, I have found a strong sense of alienation within the culture of girls. When attempting to start an empowerment workshop for at-risk high school girls, I heard comments such as "I hate females," "You can't trust females—they talk too much stuff," and "All of my friends are guys." Although many of these girls had devastating experiences with sexual harassment and assault at the hands of boys, they did not feel any sense of allegiance with other girls whatsoever. They indicated that phenomena such as sexual harassment were typical experiences for women, unpleasant, but normal nonetheless. They felt that there was nothing they could do about such issues. Moreover, they could not relate to their sex as a group when discussing such experiences. To be more specific, they took on a victim-blaming stance when hearing of other women's experiences with sexual harassment and assault. Their personal experiences were the only exceptions to this victim blaming. They shared similar experiences with other girls, but refused to see this. They saw other girls as obstacles. Because of this sense of separateness, one of the biggest challenges for them was that they would not be upfront with other girls when they were upset. If a girl did something to hurt another's feelings, instead of honestly communicating this hurt the offended girl would gossip, roll her eyes, make backhanded comments, etc. I attempted to teach the girls better ways to resolve such conflicts. We did many role-playing activities on how to honestly and openly communicate one's feelings in a positive manner both inside and outside of class. This seemed to lessen the amount of female conflict that occurred. But the fact remains that they had learned, somewhere along the line, *not* to value female friendship.

The 18-week workshop helped tremendously in girls identifying with other girls and with feminism, and in their ability to identify sexism within the culture. Thus, this type of analysis can be taught, and young girls can achieve a healthier sense of self, yet it takes time and effort on behalf of caring adults. (For more information on this intervention, see Martin, 2009a.)

Sexuality, Desire, and the Bad Reputation

Lack of sexual agency contributes to girls' lack of voice (Fine, 1988). Women are degraded in American culture while simultaneously being presented with standards of beauty that they can never attain. This combination of heightened and unattainable feminine beauty and a culture that sexualizes, degrades, and devalues women is a breeding ground for such phenomena as sexual harassment, sexual assault, and domestic violence

(Brumberg, 1997). The literature on sexual harassment suggests that more than 90% of the time males are the perpetrators of sexual harassment against females (Fineran & Bennett, 1999).

The devaluation of the voices of girls and women within American culture also carries over into the sexual arena. Many girls are not only unable to voice their sexual desires (or lack thereof), but they also may be unable to express their desire to say no to sexual advances because they do not know how. As Brumberg (1997) states, "In a world where men and women still have unequal power and resources, it is hard for many to overcome the gender imbalance, or even to assert themselves, in the domain of intimate relations with men" (p. 192). To a certain degree females are still taught to be deferential to males when they are being pursued (de Becker, 1997).

In addition to this gender imbalance, society implicitly pushes adolescent girls away from one another and toward heterosexual dating relationships through the media, traditional fairy tales and stories, toys, etc. When girls and women are pushed away from one another they are thus further alienated from themselves, for they are taught to value the male and their relationships with males more so than relationships with other females. Additionally, to the further detriment of girls, these heterosexual relationships to which they are taught to aspire are organized around male desire. As van Roosmalen (2000) states, "Having sex is stereotyped as a male goal and avoiding sex as a female goal among adolescents. . . . The underlying principle of heterosexuality in a patriarchal culture demands a sexuality organized around male desire" (p. 214). Thus, females are, again, disconnected from their own thoughts and desires, this time in the realm of sexuality.

Van Roosmalen (2000) and Fine (1988) both argue that adolescent girls are not taught to act on or even acknowledge their desires; this is often true of adult women as well. Instead, they are taught to suppress their desires. As van Roosmalen states, "Absent a language of female desire, boys and girls may end up interpreting silence and passivity as consent: Sometimes it may be that they intuit incorrectly, and sex becomes coercion" (p. 219). American culture does not provide adolescent girls with an adequate method of discourse through which to express their desires when it comes to sexuality, heterosexual or otherwise. As van Roosmalen states, "Girls look at the world through concepts of male sexuality so that even when they are not looking at male sexuality as such, they are looking at the world within its frame of reference" (p. 223). In other words, even when girls feel that they are in touch with their sexuality and their sexual desire, it is often the girls performing for males: through sexual display or in the performance of sexual acts. Girls are often not the sole receivers of sexual pleasure.

On the other hand, girls' alienation from sexual desire is maintained through instruction via the family, the media, and through peer networks: girls are taught only to remain silent or to abstain; if they do not, they are told only that they will become victims, become pregnant, or come to possess a "bad reputation." As Tolman (1999) states, "In a sense, young women have to be prepared to lose valued social relationships in order to assert control over their own sexuality. They are in a double bind because they need to take initiative in sexual situations, as well as to admit that they are being sexual, while they want to be conventionally feminine, which is by definition to be passive and sexually inexperienced" (p. 235). For some girls, then, to achieve sexual agency may mean to live a secret sexual life or to risk being shunned by peers who may fear developing a bad reputation by association. As Tolman, Striepe, and Harmon (2003) state:

> Even though alternative ways of being sexual are available, such as those embodied in superstars like Madonna, many girls do not feel they themselves have access to these constructions of female sexuality. Rather, their narratives suggest that they believe female role models who exhibit sexual agency have a status that protects them from being labeled as promiscuous. These girls continue to fear invoking a punitive response from others girls and boys, who enforce more conventional constructions of female sexuality. (p. 5)

The phenomenon of girls sexually policing other girls adds to the complications of young female sexuality and of female expression of sexual desire. The sexual arena is but another area where girls are vulnerable to bullying at the hands of their peers. Girls can damage the reputations of other girls by spreading sexual rumors and labeling a girl with the devastating and stigmatizing slut label. Sometimes boys and girls work together to isolate and stigmatize girls into social pariahs by using this label and corresponding sexual gossip. Being labeled a slut has severe consequences for girls, such as anxiety, depression, social withdrawal, lowered grades, increased rates of self-harm, etc. Many who are labeled as such are not even sexually active; they are simply being punished for some offense and in the process are saddled with a "bad reputation," of which many will never be able to shake. Possessing a bad reputation, to be seen as a slut, or as sexually promiscuous by one's peer group, still has negative consequences for girls; the sexual double standard is alive and well in the American high school. Words like "slut" and "whore" are common and contribute to the maintenance of a male hierarchy with boys at the top.

As with other feminine norms, girls are taught to regulate the sexual behavior of other girls around patriarchal, heterosexual, and monogamous norms. According to Basow and Rubin (1999), "Messages about female sexuality are contradictory: Females are supposed to be sexy and attract males' sexual interest, but sexually active females are often viewed negatively, especially among Whites, Hispanics, and Asian Americans" (p. 33). Social expectations for traditional feminine norms go hand in hand with traditional (read heterosexual) sexual expectations or compulsory heterosexuality. As Tolman, Striepe, and Harmon (2003) argue, "the meaning of gender is organized by patriarchy and, more specifically, by institutionalized heterosexuality" (p. 4). This occurs across the socioeconomic spectrum. According to Brumberg (1997), most studies on teenage female sexual behavior deem sexual decision making equivalent to risky behavior and study mainly heterosexual behavior. In other words, the phenomenon of compulsory heterosexuality is still reinforced; heterosexuality is seen as the norm. Phenomena such as asexuality, homosexuality, bisexuality, and transgendered youths are understudied.

Despite society's aversion to addressing teenage sexuality, particularly female sexuality and sexual desire, there are societal consequences for denying females the right to engage in discourse about their own desires in the realm of sexuality. As Fine (1988) states:

> Growing evidence suggests that women who lack a sense of social or sexual entitlement, who hold traditional notions of what it means to be female—self-sacrificing and relatively passive—and who undervalue themselves, are disproportionately likely to find themselves with an unwanted pregnancy and to maintain it through to motherhood. (p. 48)

Adolescent females who possess traditional gender-role orientations may be limiting themselves in terms of future goals, for they may be more likely to become pregnant in their teenage years.

A common theme in the sexual lives of girls across racial and socioeconomic lines is violence. When coming to terms with their sexuality, girls in America today must negotiate between their attempt to achieve sexual pleasure and the attempt to avoid real danger (Brumberg, 1997; Tolman, Striepe, & Harmon, 2003). According to Brumberg (1997), "Unfortunately, in this new disease environment, girls must also handle an increase in sexual pressure, often at a very early age. National data reveal that fourteen and fifteen are two of the peak ages for becoming a victim of sexual assault; approximately 50 percent of rape victims are between ten and nineteen, and half of this group are under sixteen" (p. 186). Implicit in the high incidence of sexual violence against women is the system of patriarchal control of women. As Tolman (1999) states, "the exception is among the few girls who had experienced some form of violence but who had also voiced a critique of patriarchal privileges associated with sexuality.

These findings offer empirical support for a feminist theoretical and political position that claims sexual violence is a way of controlling women by pushing them out of relationship with themselves, their power, and their pleasure" (p. 242). Education seems to be one way to assist in solving this problem. Positive gender instruction is necessary for both boys and girls, as is open, healthy, non–gender stereotyped sexuality instruction in schools (Wilcox, 1999).

Additionally, both girls and boys should be taught about the limitations of patriarchy and the negative consequences it has for both females and males. Educators must present more information to students about the entire spectrum of sexuality, rape culture, its effects on both women and men, and the limitations of traditional sex role expectations. As Brumberg (1997) states, "Although many people will not like it, American girls should be presented, as they mature, with the full range of sexual options that young women now experience, including lesbianism as well as heterosexuality, and also thoughtful discussions of female pleasure as well as danger" (p. 210). Specifically, girls must be taught both resistance strategies, in order to find their own voices to say no when it comes to sexual advances, and the ability to acknowledge their own desires. It is important for girls to come together as one to be taught counterhegemonic discourses. This can be done through education; it is important for girls to engage in critiques of patriarchal norms that are damaging to them and that keep them from identifying with other girls.

Anger and the "Bad" Girl

To some extent, studies suggest that men are *in control* when they use violence and that women are not (Chesler, 2001, p. 39).

It has been discussed that girls in American culture have, in a sense, been forced underground in terms of expressing their emotions. Since they are, in large part, still expected to be "nice," and to control their anger, these "negative" or "unfeminine" emotions do not simply disappear; they appear in other forms, such as female aggression. However, there are girls who resist such stereotypes, who reject traditional notions of femininity, who break those barriers that hold them in limiting spaces or categories: the aggressive girls. As previously indicated, the paradigm of the aggressive girl is becoming more and more acceptable. The aggressive girl is the girl who attempts to be heard; aggression can become an attempt at subjectivity or action. However, this girl creates a tension when she does not adhere to traditional notions of femininity. As Barron and Lacombe (2005) argue, "what troubles society most about the violent girl is that she has come to represent the excesses of the changed social, political, and economic status women have gained through their struggles for equality since the 1960s" (p. 64). According to White and Kowalski (1994), aggressive women are judged more critically by society than are aggressive males, for they push the boundaries of or deviate from social mores. In fact, girls are less likely to be arrested but receive harsher sentences than boys for the same offense. When femininity is defined by passivity, girls who do not fit this limiting binary are often viewed by others as social outcasts, as rejecting femininity (Adams, 1999).

In 1999, 670,800 girls were arrested, representing an 83% increase from the 1980s (Dohrn, 2004). This increase coincided with a nine-year drop in youth crime. As Dohrn argues, "Arrest and incarceration are different matters, yet the institutionalized confinement of girls has also escalated, despite the lesser severity of girls offending" (p. 305). So it seems that nontraditional girls and girls who acknowledge their anger may receive harsher consequences simply by virtue of being female (and not because of the nature of their "crime").

Programs for delinquent girls are not designed with gender in mind but are modeled on male institutions (Dohrn, 2004). Dohrn warns against essentialist programs that "assume a single racial, cultural, [heteronormative] and class understanding of what is appropriate or effective for girls" (p. 318). Additionally, incarceration is sometimes used to "protect" girls from themselves or from situations in which they find themselves. Such paternalistic practices are not found with such frequency in situations where boys are incarcerated. As Barron and Lacombe (2005) state, "Girl power, the source of social anxieties, is the real nasty here; the moral panic over the statistically insignificant Nasty Girl is a projection of a desire to retrieve a patriarchal social order characterized by gender conformity" (p. 65). The real societal problem is the patriarchy and its proponents attempting to maintain control over girls and women. This problem manifests itself in the societal panic over female anger.

As stated previously, girls and women who freely express anger and aggression, emotions that are deemed "natural" in men, are often seen as deviants; girls and women who do not freely express such emotions often suppress them—but they are revealed implicitly in such phenomena as relational aggression, alienation, or insanity. In other words, whether or not girls' anger is punishable is determined by where it is directed. If girls' anger is directed inward (girls are more often internalizers) or directed toward other girls, it is acceptable. Female anger toward self or anger toward other females through the policing of other females (based on patriarchal norms) or female aggression are perfectly nonthreatening, for they maintain the status quo. However, anger toward the patriarchy is never acceptable; we still see this with society's backlash against feminism and with people's hesitancy to embrace the term. Girls and women need real outlets for these emotions just like men do; denying them the right to express emotions such as anger will not make those emotions disappear. As Brown (2003) states:

> Anger, in fact, seems a legitimate response to a society that objectifies girls and women and too often offers them empty roles, roles that in effect say "in the real game of power, you don't matter." The answer in these cases is not to fix girls but to help them locate the legitimate sources of their anger and to provide them ways to understand and confront the pressures and limitations imposed on girls who do not comply with feminine ideals. (p. 208)

Anger can be a source of inspiration and a source of power for girls and women; it can be a tool for promoting social and political change for girls, who as Brown (2003) states, "want to feel powerful, to be visible, and to be respected" (p. 228). According to DeBlase (2003):

> For women within oppressed groups who have experienced so many feelings—despair, rage, anguish—who do not speak, out of fear, coming to voice, or telling stories, is an act of resistance. . . . girls do find spaces within which they resist cultural codes represented in classroom and popular texts. However, this resistance is often caught up within a web of social matrixes and competing ideologies that complicate and problematize girls' agency and developing sense of self. (p. 635)

This resistance, which can be realized through feminism, can be an outlet for this anger and a positive channel for promoting a more egalitarian society. When girls have a true outlet for their anger and venues through which to discuss gender norms and expectations, issues of power, etc., perhaps then they cease to view all others of their gender as competition and start seeing them as allies.

The Hope of Education

Foucault (1972) argues that education is viewed as a system whereby individuals can gain access to the discursive activity. However, in reality, there is a system of power at play that serves to maintain the traditional appropriation of discourse. Without a strong sense of self-esteem, girls are "less able to fulfill their potential, less willing to take on challenges, less willing to defy tradition in their career choice, which means sacrificing economic equity" (Orenstein, 1994, xxviii). Without a strong critique of patriarchal norms, many girls will grow up without a sense of their true potential. In today's educational system, which is driven by standards and high-stakes testing, concepts such as media literacy, feminist consciousness raising, and critiques of the status quo and of White, male hegemony are becoming less and less a focus. In the educational realm, girls continue to encounter stereotypes of appropriate feminine norms; girls are still channeled into careers that pay less and are more nurture oriented.

Research indicates that girls are still, to a certain extent, being funneled into traditional "feminine" careers; for example, girls are five times less likely than boys to study technology in college (Melymuka, 2001). Role models are necessary to inspire girls in science and technology (Thom, 2002). Today girls are just as likely as boys to complete high school courses in math. However, when they enter college, they have less definitive ideas than their male counterparts about potential math/science careers (Thom, 2002). Girls are five times less likely than boys to entertain technology-related careers (Melymuka, 2001). They are still channeling themselves into such traditional female arenas as teaching and nursing.

In today's political climate, Title IX, which has in the past provided programs and opportunities to increase the number of girls in math and science, was seriously limited by the Bush administration (Feminist Majority Foundation, 2006). The No Child Left Behind Act of 2001 (NCLB) contains a proposal limiting Title IX: a proposal that encourages the establishment of single-sex classes and schools in the public arena (Sadker & Zittleman, 2005). NCLB ignores every aspect of gender but to use it in order to segregate and separate. Some proponents of single-sex schools may argue that biology (read adolescent hormones) dictates that more success will be found educationally if the sexes are separated. However, adolescent hormonal development occurs regardless of the school facility the student attends. Sexism must be fought and eliminated rather than avoided. Sex equity can be transformative for men as well as women and can only occur in an integrated environment.

Proponents of single-sex initiatives cite the success of some private single-sex schools as a reason to allow public single-sex schools. However, such success has been found to be more related to selective admissions processes, smaller class sizes, parental involvement, and greater resources per pupil than the factor of gender segregation. Private co-ed schools with these same advantageous features are also quite successful. Legislators should work to provide public schools the funding needed to implement these proven methods of improving educational outcomes rather than hoping that separating boys and girls will substitute for them. This single-sex initiative has traded off women's rights to equal educational opportunity to give some parents the opportunity to segregate their children by sex. This is not the solution for the problems students are facing in public schools today, and it only perpetuates gender stratification, which reinforces traditional gender norms that benefit men and disadvantage women.

In the current era of standardization and testing, schools are becoming more regimented, and issues such as women and gender studies, feminism, and sex education are becoming obsolete. As Giroux (2001/1983) states:

> Public schools don't need standardized curriculum and testing. On the contrary, they need curricular justice—forms of teaching that are inclusive, caring, respectful, economically equitable, and whose aim, in part, is to undermine those repressive modes of education that produce social hierarchies and legitimate inequality while simultaneously providing students with the knowledge and skills needed to become well-rounded critical actors and social agents. (p. xxvi)

Schools should be sites for social transformation: where students learn the ideals of democracy and aversion to domination (Giroux 2001/1983). However, schools are increasingly becoming sites of regimentation where curricula is increasingly standardized despite students' interests, strengths, and needs, and despite the social, political, and intellectual importance of democratic participation on individuals (Torre & Fine, 2006).

Students are becoming less involved in their own education; thus, schools are becoming less the sites of social transformation and more the bastions of the status quo. Giroux (2001/1983) argues that social transformation is a goal of public education: "learning is not about processing received knowledge but actually transforming it as part of a more expansive struggle for individual rights and social justice" (p. xxvii). Unfortunately, this, to the detriment of our children and our society, is becoming less and less a priority.

In today's American public education system, students have less time to take electives and chosen areas of study in favor of additional required standards-based classes. This allows less time for self and social examination and critique. According to Lewis-Charp, Cao, and Soukamneuth (2006), "critical self-awareness not only helps an individual identify the seeds of her own problems, but also sheds light on dominant discourses that contribute to her marginalization and oppression of others. Education about the 'self' and identity is key to social transformation because it helps individuals identify and articulate what it is that needs to be changed" (p. 23). In other words, students need time to reflect on themselves, on their position within the world, and on the world in general, in order to determine what is wrong with the world and how they may take part in making changes around them in their own lives and in their own schools and communities. Such examinations can open up dialogue on school culture, where issues such as bullying, bystander responsibility, and the development of healthy peer relationships can be addressed.

Conclusions

In order to work for the cause of promoting healthy, self-reliant girls today, educators should provide girls with the tools necessary to combat patriarchy and the patriarchal structures that relegate them to places of vulnerability. Teaching girls about feminism, media literacy, and cultural critique can assist them in understanding what is wrong in the culture and how they can create their own safe places, places of resistance, where they can find other girls with whom to bond. As Brown (2003) states, "Women hold the power to perpetuate or to contest girlfighting in their own lives and among the next generation of girls" (p. 175).

The first step in this process is for girls to learn to value themselves. The second step is in finding their power or agency, and to use this power for social change. One of these changes should be to create safe spaces for girls to exist that stretch the boundaries of what is acceptable for them. Then stretch those boundaries into the larger culture to promote cultural transformation. In short, young girls and women can be empowered to channel their anger to combat the social prejudices that keep them from self-fulfillment, from one another, and ultimately from themselves. According to Basow and Rubin (1999), "*Truth telling,* the style of directly confronting negative cultural messages . . . appears to benefit all girls" (p. 43). It is this truth telling that will serve as a catalyst for social change—toward dismantling the status quo.

The question is how do we do this? Research suggests that if adolescents have one caring adult in their lives that they will be less likely to engage in risky behaviors (Lopez, 2009). Perhaps it is adults—educators, parents, mentors—who need to lead the way in initiating the difficult discourses about power, aggression, anger, and social norms based on gender. Other questions that remain include: How do we go about helping girls come to voice? How will we inspire them to challenge traditional forms of discourse, and to bring girls together instead of keeping them apart, with the goal of ending the pattern of female aggression? Educational interventions seem to be the only answer. The work will be difficult, but fruitful, and must involve feminism, media literacy, and cultural critique.

For more information on bullying and female empowerment, see Martin (2008, 2009a, 2009b, 2011).

References

Adams, N. G. (1999). Fighting to be somebody: Resisting erasure and the discursive practices of female adolescent fighting. *Educational Studies, 30,* 115–139.

American Association of University Women. (1991). *Shortchanging girls, shortchanging America.* Washington DC: American Association of University Women.

Barron, C., & Lacombe, D. (2005). Moral panic and the nasty girl. *Canadian Review of Sociology and Anthropology, 42,* 51–69.

Basow, S. A., & Rubin, L. R. (1999). Gender influences on adolescent development. In N. G. Johnson, M. C. Roberts, & J. Worell (Eds.), *Beyond appearance: A new look at adolescent girls* (pp. 25–52). Washington, DC: American Psychological Association.

Brown, L. M. (2003). *Girlfighting: Betrayal and rejection among girls.* New York: New York University Press.

Brown, L. M., & Gilligan, C. (1992). *Meeting at the crossroads: Women's psychology and girls' development.* New York: Ballantine Books.

Brumberg, J. J. (1997). *The body project: An intimate history of American girls.* New York: Random House.

Chesler, P. (2001). *Women's inhumanity to woman.* New York: Thunder's Mouth.

de Becker, G. (1997). *The gift of fear and other survival signals that protect us from violence.* New York: Dell.

DeBlase, G. (2003). Acknowledging agency while accommodating romance: Girls negotiating meaning in literacy transactions. *Journal of Adolescent and Adult Literacy, 46,* 624–635.

Dohrn, B. (2004). All Ellas: Girls locked up. *Feminist Studies, 30,* 302–324.

Erikson, E. (1968). *Identity: Youth and crisis.* New York: Norton.

Feminist Majority Foundation. (2006, October 27). Changes to Title IX weaken safeguards against sex discrimination in public ed. Retrieved from http://www.feminist.org/news/newsbyte/printnews.asp?id=9964.

Fine, M. (1988). Sexuality, schooling, and adolescent females: The missing discourse of desire. *Harvard Educational Review, 58,* 29–53.

Fineran, S., & Bennett, L. (1999). Gender and power issues of peer sexual harassment among teenagers. *Journal of Interpersonal Violence, 14,* 626–641.

Foucault, M. (1972). The discourse on language. In A. M. Sheridan Smith (Trans.), *The archaeology of knowledge* (pp. 215–238). New York: Pantheon Books.

Gilligan, C. (1982). *In a different voice: Psychological theory of women's development.* Cambridge, MA: Harvard University Press.

Gilligan, C., Lyons, N. P., & Hanmer, T. J. (Eds.). (1990). *Making connections: The relational worlds of adolescent girls at Emma Willard school.* Cambridge, MA: Harvard University Press.

Giroux, H. A. (2001/1983). *Theory and resistance in education: Towards a pedagogy for the opposition.* Westport, CT: Bergin and Garvey.

Harris, A. (2004). *Future girl: You women in the twenty-first century.* New York: Routledge.

Iglesias, E., & Cormier, S. (2002). The transformation of girls to women: Finding voice and developing strategies for liberation. *Journal of Multicultural Counseling and Development, 3,* 259–271.

Kalodner, C. R. (1996). Eating disorders from a multicultural perspective. In J. L. Delucia-Waack (Ed.), *Multicultural counseling competencies* (pp. 197–216). Alexandria, VA: Association of Counselor Education and Supervision.

Kopels, S., & Dupper, D. R. (1999). School-based peer sexual harassment. *Child Welfare, 78,* 435–460.

Lewis-Charp, H., Cao, Y. H., & Soukamneuth, S. (2006). Civic activist approaches for engaging youth in social justice. In S. Ginwright, P. Noguera, & J. Cammarota (Eds.), *Beyond resistance! Youth activism and community change: New Democratic possibilities for practice and policy for America's youth* (pp. 21–35). New York: Routledge.

Lopez, S. L. (2009). *Gallup student poll national report.* Washington, DC: Gallup.

Martin, J. L. (2008). Peer sexual harassment: Finding voice, changing culture, an intervention strategy for adolescent females. *Violence Against Women, 14,* 100–124.

Martin, J. L. (2009a). Reclaiming feminism: A qualitative investigation of language usage by girls in a high school women's studies course. *Girlhood Studies: An Interdisciplinary Journal, 2,* 54–72.

Martin, J. L. (2009b). "Talk to us": A study in student generated service-learning, mentoring middle school girls. *Information for Action: A Journal for Research on Service-Learning with Children and Youth, 2,* 1–25.

Martin, J. L. (2011). Bullying and sexual harassment of peers. In M. Paludi & F. Denmark (Eds.), *Victims of sexual assault and abuse: Resources and responses for individuals and families* (pp. 89–109). Westport, CT: Praeger.

Melymuka, K. (2001). If girls don't get IT, IT won't get girls. *Computerworld, 35,* 44.

Orenstein, P. (1994). *School girls: Young women, self-esteem, and the confidence gap.* New York: Doubleday.

Powderhouse Productions, Inc., & the Independent Television Service (ITVS). (2009). *A girl's life with Rachel Simmons* [video recording]. Available from PBS, http://www.pbs.org/parents/raisinggirls/girlslife/.

Sadker, D., & Zittleman, K. (2005, April). Gender bias lives, for both sexes. *Principal,* 27–30.

Simmons, R. (2002). *Odd girl out: The hidden culture of aggression in girls.* Orlando, FL: Harcourt Books.

Stern, S. R. (2002). Virtually speaking: Girls' self-disclosure on the WWW. *Women's Studies in Communication, 25,* 223–253.

Tanenbaum, L. (2000). *Slut! Growing up female with a bad reputation.* New York: Perennial.

Thom, M. (2002). Girls in science and technology: What's new, what's next? *Education Digest, 67,* 17–24.

Tolman, D. L. (1999). Female adolescent sexuality in relational context: Beyond sexual decision making. In N. G. Johnson, M. C. Roberts, & J. Worell (Eds.), *Beyond appearance: A new look at adolescent girls* (pp. 227–246). Washington, DC: American Psychological Association.

Tolman, D. L., Striepe, M. I., & Harmon, T. (2003). Gender matters: Constructing a model of adolescent sexual health. *The Journal of Sex Research, 40,* 4–12.

Torre, M., & Fine, M. (2006). Researching and resisting: Democratic policy research by and for youth. In S. Ginwright, P. Noguera, & J. Cammarota (Eds.), *Beyond resistance! Youth activism and community change: New Democratic possibilities for practice and policy for America's youth* (pp. 269–285). New York: Routledge.

van Roosmalen, E. (2000). Forces of patriarchy: Adolescent experiences of sexuality and conceptions of relationships. *Youth and Society, 32,* 202–227.

White, J., & Kowalski, R. (1994). Deconstructing the myth of the nonaggressive woman: A feminist analysis. *Psychology of Women 18,* 487–508.

Wilcox, B. L. (1999). Sexual obsessions: Public policy and adolescent girls. In N. G. Johnson, M. C. Roberts, & J. Worell (Eds.), *Beyond appearance: A new look at adolescent girls* (pp. 333–354). Washington, DC: American Psychological Association.

Wiseman, R. (2002). *Queen bees and wannabes: Helping your daughter survive cliques, gossip, boyfriends, and other realities of adolescence.* New York: Crown Publishers.

Younger, B. (2003). Pleasure, pain, and the power of being thin: Female sexuality in young adult literature. *NWSA Journal, 15,* 45–56.

CHAPTER FOUR

The Impact of Race on Perceptions of Adolescent Sex Offenders

Margaret C. Stevenson, Katlyn M. Sorenson Farnum, Allison L. Skinner, and Rukudzo Amanda Dzwairo

Societal fear of dangerous sex offenders has not only been the legal impetus for sex offender registration policies for adults, but also for recently extending registration policies to juveniles who commit sex offenses (Caldwell, Ziemke, & Vitacco, 2008; SORNA, 42 U.S.C. § 16911). Although registration policies were created to protect society from sex offenders, evidence suggests that these laws might not be effective. To date, research has revealed no evidence that registration policies successfully reduce sex offenses (e.g., Letourneau & Armstrong, 2008). Instead, substantial research shows that sex offender registration harms the lives of those registered in ways that, ironically, might lead to further offending (Levenson & Cotter, 2005; Levenson, D'Amora, & Hern, 2007; Tewksbury, 2005; Tewksbury & Lees, 2006, 2007; for reviews, see Chaffin, 2008; Trivits & Reppucci, 2002).

How does the public react toward juvenile sex offenders? Although there is strong public support for registration laws applied to adult sex offenders (Levenson, D'Amora, & Hern, 2007; Phillips, 1998), research on perceptions of juvenile sex offenders tells a more complex story. Salerno, Najdowski, and colleagues (2010) revealed strong public support for registering juvenile sex offenders, but only when participants were asked to consider juvenile registration laws in the abstract. When asked about specific, less serious juvenile sex offenses, such as harassment or nonforced sex (offenses for which juveniles are registered in several states), public support for registration was much lower. Even so, when asked to describe the typical juvenile sex offender, the majority of respondents described a juvenile who had committed a serious sex offense (e.g., forced rape), which might help explain why abstract support for juvenile sex offender registration policy is so high. Public support might explain why registration policies have been extended to juvenile offenders (Salerno, Stevenson, et al., 2010), even though juvenile sex offenders differ in important ways from adult sex offenders (e.g., juveniles are much less likely to recidivate). (For reviews, see Chaffin, 2008; Trivits & Reppucci, 2002.)

The trend toward increasingly severe treatment of juvenile sex offenders likely has serious ramifications for minority juvenile offenders, who are overrepresented in the juvenile justice system (Snyder & Sickmund, 2006). In fact, Black juveniles are more likely than White juveniles to be detained, transferred to criminal court, and given longer sentences, even when controlling for offense severity and prior offenses (Engen, Steen, & Bridges, 2002; Wordes, Bynum, & Corley, 1994).

Consider the case of Marcus Dixon, an 18-year-old African American high school senior with a college football scholarship (*Dixon v. State of Georgia,* 2004). Although Dixon claimed that he had consensual sex with a 15-year-old White girl from his high school, he was charged with sexual molestation and rape. The jury acquitted him of the rape charge due to a lack of evidence, yet found him guilty of aggravated child molestation—a crime that requires sex offender registration and a mandatory, minimum 10-year prison sentence (*Dixon v. State of Georgia,* 2004). Notably in this case, the issue of race was hotly contested: Dixon claimed that the victim's rape allegations stemmed from her fear that her extremely racist father would kill them both if he discovered that they had consensual sex. Articulating such sentiments, civil rights activist Dr. Joseph Lowery argued during a rally opposing Dixon's 10-year sentence that if "the young lady were Black and Marcus Dixon was White, I don't think we would be here" (Jacobs, 2004, p. 1).

Only a few years later, a strikingly similar case emerged involving another African American teen—Genarlow Wilson, a 17-year-old high school senior, honors student, and star of his football team (*Wilson v. State of Georgia,* 2006). Wilson was receiving recruitment letters from Ivy League colleges, but just short of graduation, he was charged with aggravated child molestation. A videotaped recording of a New Year's Eve party he attended had surfaced showing Wilson receiving consensual oral sex from a

15-year-old White girl. Because juveniles are automatically registered for adjudicated sex crimes in juvenile court, some juveniles attempt to avoid automatic registration by waiving their cases to adult criminal court, where they receive a trial by jury instead of a disposition rendered by a family court judge. A desire to avoid automatic registration (the standard juvenile court outcome) led Wilson to opt to waive his case from juvenile court to adult court, where he risked the possibility of a much harsher sentence—a possibility that came to fruition. In adult court, Wilson was convicted of aggravated child molestation, registered as a sex offender, and sentenced to 10 years in jail, the mandatory minimum sentence under Georgia law (*Wilson v. State of Georgia*, 2006). Again, the issue of race in this case was hard to ignore, and Wilson received support from several civil rights leaders. Former president Jimmy Carter even wrote a letter to the U.S. attorney general, requesting him to consider the possibility that race played a role in Wilson's harsh sentence (e.g., National Public Radio, 2007; Rome News Tribune, 2008).

Although Wilson served only 2 years and Dixon served 15 months in prison before their convictions and sentences were overturned on appeal, these cases inspire important questions about the role of ethnicity in the treatment of juvenile sex offenders and the fairness of these laws and judicial outcomes in general. These questions have been the topic of a good deal of journalistic debate. The Dixon case, for instance, was even featured by Oprah Winfrey on her television show (Rome News Tribune, 2004). Yet, the courts have continued to ignore social science evidence that sex offender registration policies are likely ineffective at best (e.g., Letourneau & Armstrong, 2008) and detrimental to society at worst (e.g., Chaffin, 2008). Indeed, policy aimed at increasingly punitive treatment of sex offenders has not slowed (Wright, 2009). Such trends have particularly unfortunate implications for juveniles because registration has been linked to various negative outcomes, including public harassment, social rejection, and depression (Levenson, Brannon, Fortney, & Baker, 2007; Levenson & Cotter, 2005; Tewskbury, 2005; Tewksbury & Lees, 2006)—all factors shown to increase the likelihood of suicide (Bridge, Goldstein, & Brent, 2006), the third-leading cause of death among adolescents (Xu, Kochanek, & Tejada-Vera, 2009). One particularly alarming case involved a 15-year-old boy who attempted suicide by walking into oncoming traffic because of constant harassment from high school students who had discovered that he was on the registry (Jones, 2007). Another adolescent, William Elliott, was placed on the sex offender registry at age 16 after engaging in consensual sex with his girlfriend, who was just weeks away from the legal age of consent (16).

Several years later, a vigilante who identified Elliott's name and address from the registry shot him to death in his home (Ahuja, 2006). Although there are certainly many more shocking instances of brutality perpetrated against registered juveniles, more commonly, adolescents suffer social rejection and harassment as a result of registration. For instance, after being registered at age 11, one girl became the target of lewd phone calls and sexual advances from older men (Jones, 2007).

Thus, it has become increasingly important to study perceptions of developmentally vulnerable adolescent sex offenders, particularly racial minority youths who are susceptible to discriminatory treatment. This chapter represents an exploration of the influence of juvenile offender and victim ethnicity on perceptions of juvenile sex offenders, focusing primarily on perceptions of African American adolescents. Although it is certainly important to study perceptions of other racial minority groups, doing so is simply beyond the scope of this chapter. Even so, we believe that exploring perceptions of African American adolescents represents an important first step, particularly given the unique sociopolitical history of racism against African Americans in the United States.

First, we review relevant social psychological theory and research, drawing largely from research exploring the influence of race on perceptions of adult offenders. We then turn to research illustrating the effects of race on perceptions of juvenile offenders, where we also review the only existing research in which the races of juvenile sex offenders and victims are experimentally manipulated. Finally, we present the results of preliminary data testing our theory and conclude with directions for future research and implications for policy and law.

Effects of Defendant and Victim Race

Although the literature on effects of defendant and victim race paints a complex picture, a thorough review reveals compelling evidence of racial bias, such that Whites generally render more pro-prosecution case judgments for Black than for White adult defendants and when the victim is White rather than Black. (For a review, see Sommers & Ellsworth, 2006.) For example, a meta-analysis exploring the effects of adult defendant race on sentencing in 14 mock juror studies revealed that Black defendants, on average, receive longer sentences than White defendants (Sweeney & Haney, 1992; see also Mitchel, Haw, Pfeifer, & Meissner, 2005). Mock jury studies involving adult defendants accused of rape also tell a cohesive story: White mock jurors tend to be most punitive in reactions to mock rape cases when a Black defendant rapes a White victim than in any other defendant-victim racial combination (e.g., Feild, 1979; Foley & Chamblin, 1982; Klein & Creech, 1982; Ugwuegbu, 1979). Using the adult mock jury literature as a guide, it appears likely that similar effects of racial bias will manifest for juvenile sex offenders.

Social Psychological Theory Explaining Effects of Race

Several social psychological theories help inform the issue of racial bias against minority offenders. First, well-documented negative stereotypes that African Americans are more violent, aggressive, and sexually deviant than Whites (e.g., Devine, 1989) likely drive discriminatory treatment. Myriad research reveals that people pay more attention to, and subsequently remember better, information that is consistent rather than inconsistent with their stereotypes (for a review, see Hilton & von Hippel, 1996). Stereotypes that Black men are more dangerous and criminal-like than White men likely cause mock jurors to perceive Black defendants as more likely to be guilty than White defendants accused of the same crime (for a review, see Sweeney & Haney, 1992). Similar stereotypes exist for minority juvenile defendants. Juvenile probation officers rated minority offenders as more criminal-like, dangerous, and likely to recidivate than similar White juvenile offenders (Bridges & Steen, 1998).

Although it is clear that stereotypes play a role in discriminatory treatment of minority offenders, stereotypes alone do not account for why some mock jury studies fail to find effects of defendant race on case outcomes (e.g., Conley, Turnier, & Rose, 2000; Mazzella & Feingold, 1994; Shaw & Skolnick, 1995; Skolnick & Shaw, 1997). To understand this mixed body of research on the effects of race, we next turn to the theory of aversive racism, which is the newer, modern form of racism that has replaced blatant old-fashioned racism (Gaertner & Dovidio, 1986). Although it is no longer socially acceptable to appear outwardly racist (in most social circles), according to aversive racism theory, individuals are still influenced by anti-Black attitudes, particularly when the motivation behind one's behavior is ambiguous and can be justified in non-racially motivated ways (Gaertner & Dovidio, 1986). Consistent with aversive racism theory, Sommers and Ellsworth (2001) argue that effects of defendant race can be eliminated simply by making the issue of race salient during a mock trial, or in other words, by highlighting the issue of race during the trial. Specifically, Sommers and Ellsworth experimentally manipulated race salience in the context of a mock trial through the presence or absence of a racially sensitive comment (i.e., the victim merely mentioned or did not mention the defendant's race during her testimony).

In support of their theory, White participants' sentence recommendations were unaffected by defendant race (Black or White) when race was made salient. But, when race was not made salient (i.e., when the victim did not mention the defendant's race), mock jurors convicted the Black defendant more frequently than the White defendant. The authors theorized that making jurors aware of the issue of race heightens their concern about being racist and, in turn, drives them to control their racial prejudice. Yet, when race is not made salient, participants let their guard down, and underlying racial biases manifest, resulting in more convictions for Black defendants than White defendants. Sommers and Ellsworth argue that these results help account for the mock trial studies that reveal null effects of defendant and victim race, suggesting that the methodology of those studies made race overly salient, which consequently eliminated race effects (see also Sommers & Ellsworth, 2003). Thus, aversive racism can, at least in part, drive discriminatory treatment of Black defendants, particularly when race is not salient throughout the course of the trial.

Another relevant psychological theory is the similarity-leniency bias: People simply like similar others more than nonsimilar others, and thus treat similar others preferentially (e.g., Davis, Bray, & Holt, 1977). Thus, because White jurors likely perceive themselves as more similar to White than Black defendants, they should therefore treat White defendants more leniently than Black defendants. Likewise, because Black jurors likely perceive themselves as more similar to Black than White defendants, they should, in turn, treat Black defendants more leniently than White defendants. In support, a meta-analysis by Mitchel and colleagues (2005) revealed that White people tend to treat White defendants more favorably than Black defendants, whereas Black people tend to treat Black defendants more favorably than White defendants.

The various theories reviewed thus far to explain bias against minority adult defendants can also be applied to understanding possible bias against minority juvenile defendants. Next, we review existing research examining this possibility.

Effects of Juvenile Defendant and Victim Race

Scott, Reppucci, Antonishak, and DeGennaro (2006) were the first to experimentally explore the effects of race on perceptions of juvenile offenders. Community member participants watched a video depicting a masked juvenile rob a convenience store at gunpoint (Scott et al., 2006). The race of the juvenile was experimentally manipulated by showing participants a photo of the juvenile's face (either Black or White). They found no effects of the juvenile's race on sentence judgments or ratings of the juvenile's culpability. Yet, it is possible that the method of manipulating race (the photo of a Black youth) enhanced suspicion that the study was about race and, in turn, increased participants' motivation to avoid racial prejudice. Such a possibility is consistent with Sommers and Ellsworth's (2001) research showing that participants tend to correct racial biases by treating White defendants no differently than Black defendants, but only when the issue of race is made salient.

In a similar study, Stevenson and Bottoms (2009) manipulated a juvenile defendant's race in a way that made it noticeable, yet not overly salient to participants. Their mock case transcript described a juvenile defendant (portrayed as Black or White) who was tried in adult court for the murder of an elderly man (Black or White). Although there were no main effects of defendant or victim race on guilt judgments, there were interactions of juror gender and defendant and victim race. Specifically, men, but not women, convicted more often when the juvenile defendant was Black than when he was White and when the victim was White rather than Black. These findings are consistent with research by Dovidio and colleagues (1997), who manipulated an adult defendant's race in a mock capital case. Again, men, but not women, recommended the death penalty more often for the Black adult defendant than for the White adult defendant. Perhaps partially explaining these results, men, compared to women, have higher levels of explicit racism and ethnocentrism (Carter, 1990; Kim, & Goldstein, 2005; for a review, see Ekehammar, Akrami, & Araya, 2003) and score lower in measures of general acceptance of others (Mills, McGrath, Sobkoviak, Stupec, & Welsch, 1995). Even so, controlling for participants' scores on the Modern Racism Scale did not change Stevenson and Bottoms's results, suggesting that men's racism alone might not fully explain why men (but not women) were more punitive toward the Black than the White defendant.

Alternatively, these results might be understood in the context of gender-related social categorization. Because the defendant and victim in this study were male, women may have classified them as out-group members more than men. Indeed, people generally pay more attention to in-group than out-group members (e.g., Bernstein, Young, & Hugenberg, 2007; MacLin & Malpass, 2001; for a review, see Meissner & Brigham, 2001). Thus, women might have simply paid less attention to the defendant's and victim's racial characteristics than did men. In turn, women might have been less influenced by defendant and victim race, primarily because they did not perceive a male defendant or male victim (Black or White) as part of their in-group. In support, women demonstrate strong positive implicit in-group associations toward women and negative implicit associations toward men (Rudman & Goodwin, 2004). Although men also demonstrate positive implicit in-group associations toward men over women, this bias is less pronounced for men (Rudman & Goodwin, 2004). Thus, because men likely attended more than women to the male defendant and victim, men might have been more influenced by the defendant's and victim's racial characteristics.

In summary, a review of literature exploring the influence of defendant and victim race on perceptions of adult and juvenile offenders provides the necessary theoretical background to understand the influence of race on perceptions of juvenile sex offenders. Using the adult mock trial literature as a guide, we have uncovered evidence of discrimination against Black defendants accused of rape—bias that might extend toward minority adolescent offenders. Yet, not all sex crimes involve violent rape. In fact, only a minority (15%) of juvenile sex offenders are rapists (*Uniform*, 2007). Contrary to sensationalized stranger rape cases that frequently receive media attention, most sex crimes (76%) occur in the context of existing intimate relationships, friendships, etc. (Tjaden & Thoennes, 1998). In fact, several rape-victim crisis support groups have openly criticized sex offender registration policies, arguing that they are motivated by and designed to prevent highly sensationalized stranger rape crimes—crimes that simply are not experienced by the vast majority of their clients (e.g., Coombs, 2006). To understand how race might influence perceptions of less sensationalized, yet more common sex crimes, we turn next to literature exploring the influence of race on perceptions of domestic violence.

Perceptions of Interracial Domestic Violence

Recall the case of Genarlow Wilson—a nonviolent, statutory offense consisting of mutually desired, yet technically illegal sexual activity between two similarly aged minors. This type of crime carries a unique set of issues relevant to understanding the complex influence of juvenile defendant and victim race. Specifically, the defendant and victim were close in age and were alleged to have engaged in consensual sexual activity. To explore how race influences perceptions of these types of sex crimes, we turn to research on attitudes toward interracial romantic relationships.

Despite the progress we have made since the 1960s, when interracial marriage was still illegal in some states (Porterfield, 1982), we are far from full societal acceptance of interracial relationships (e.g., Ross, 2005). For instance, even though interracial couples can now legally marry, many are reluctant to do so: Only 32% of individuals without prior interracial dating experience indicated a willingness to date someone of a different ethnicity (Knox, Zusman, Buffington, & Hemphill, 2000). Further, interracial couples continue to be viewed more negatively in general than same-race couples. For instance, as compared to same-race couples, interracial couples are perceived as less compatible and as less supported and accepted by family (Carrasco, 2007; Harrison & Esqueda 2000; Lewandowski & Jackson, 2001; Mills, Daly, Longmore, & Kilbride, 1995; Ross, 2005). Lewandowski and Jackson (2001) experimentally manipulated a married couple's racial composition and found that, relative to a White married man and woman, a White woman married to a Black man was perceived as less psychologically adjusted and less traditional, and a White man married to a Black woman was perceived as less professionally successful and less competent in general. Similarly, relative to a Black married couple, Black men or women married to Whites were considered less traditional and less compatible.

Societal lack of acceptance of interracial relationships might cause people to perceive sexual behavior between interracial teens as more dysfunctional and more deviant than if they were of the same race. In support, Harrison and Esqueda (2000) examined participants' perceptions of a vignette describing a case of domestic violence. The male batterer's race and the female victim's race (Black or White) were experimentally manipulated. Although they found no main effects of race, there was an interaction of defendant and victim race such that the batterer was rated guiltier when he was in an interracial relationship than when he was in a same-race relationship. Thus, it is possible that interracial juvenile sex offenses might be perceived as more criminal-like than same-race juvenile sex offenses, particularly when the offender is not a stranger, but rather someone who has a relationship with the victim (as do most sex offenders; Tjaden & Thoennes, 1998).

Next, we turn to the only published study designed to experimentally test the influence of juvenile offender and victim race on perceptions of a juvenile convicted of statutory rape, followed by preliminary data testing the influence of defendant and victim race on perceptions of a juvenile accused of forced rape.

Effects of Juvenile Defendant and Victim Race on Registration Support for Statutory Rape

Stevenson, Sorenson, Smith, Sekely, and Dzwairo (2009) recruited 158 community members and presented them with a short vignette depicting the case of a 15-year-old boy convicted of aggravated child molestation of a similarly aged girl. For ecological validity, the case was based on the *Wilson v. State of Georgia* (2006) case: The defendant received consensual, videotaped oral sex from a similarly aged girl victim. Victim and defendant race were fully experimentally manipulated (Black or White), resulting in four conditions of all possible victim-defendant race combinations. After reading the vignette, participants indicated their support for registering the juvenile as a sex offender and made several additional case judgments designed to explain registration support, including perceived likelihood that the defendant will reoffend (i.e., utilitarian concerns for society) and support for registration even if it is ineffective at reducing sex crimes (i.e., retributive goals of punishment).

Because the authors were interested in exploring possible participant gender by defendant and victim race interactions, the study conformed to a 2 (defendant race: Black, White) X 2 (victim race: Black, White) X 2 (participant gender) between-subjects design.

Although there were no main effects of any independent variables on registration support, there was a marginally significant interaction between defendant and victim race. The simple effects analyses did not reach statistical significance, yet a clear crossover trend emerged such that participants supported registration more when the juvenile offender and victim were of different races than when they were of the same race. Similarly, participants endorsed marginally greater retributive goals of punishment when the defendant and victim were of different races than of the same race. Further, mediation analyses revealed that retributive goals of punishment—not utilitarian goals to protect society—partially explained why participants supported registration more for the interracial than same-race crime (see Figure 4.1). This effect is in line with previous research revealing that retributive goals tend to be more influential than utilitarian goals in the context of legal decision making (Carlsmith, Darley, & Robinson, 2002; Darley, Carlsmith, & Robinson, 2000). Further, these results suggest that participants might have perceived an ambiguously serious sex act between two teens as more like a true crime when the teens were of different races. Such findings might reflect lingering societal lack of acceptance of interracial relationships and the belief that interracial couples are not compatible (Carrasco, 2007; Harrison & Esqueda, 2000; Lewandowski & Jackson, 2001; Mills, Daly, Longmore, & Kilbride, 1995; Ross, 2005). In other words, participants might have perceived teens of the same race as more likely to have been in a romantic relationship and, in turn, perceived the sex act to be more developmentally normative and consensual. In contrast, participants might have perceived teens of different races as less likely to have been in a romantic relationship and, in turn, perceived the sex act to be more like a true crime.

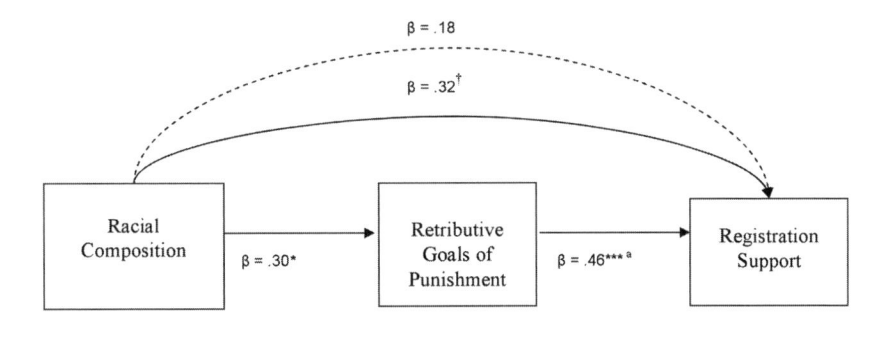

```
                          β = .18
                    ---------------------
                       β = .32†
                  ------------------
   ┌──────────────┐              ┌──────────────┐              ┌──────────────┐
   │   Racial     │              │  Retributive │              │ Registration │
   │ Composition  │──── β = .30* │   Goals of   │── β = .46***ᵃ│   Support    │
   │              │              │  Punishment  │              │              │
   └──────────────┘              └──────────────┘              └──────────────┘
```

Figure 4.1 Retributive goals of punishment as a mediator of the effect of racial composition on registration support.

Note. Racial composition was coded as 0 (*defendant and victim were the same race*) and 1 (*defendant and victim were different races*). Retributive goals of punishment were coded such that higher values indicate greater retributive desires to punish. Registration support was coded such that greater values indicate greater support for the full application of the registry.
ᵃ Sobel $z = 1.29, p < .10$
† $p < .10$, * $p < .05$, *** $p < .001$

There was also a marginally significant interaction of gender and victim race on registration support and retributive goals of punishment, and a statistically significant interaction for the belief that the juvenile will recidivate. Follow-up analyses revealed that women, but not men, were significantly more likely to support registration, believe that the defendant would recidivate, and endorse retributive goals of punishment when the victim was White rather than Black. Mediation analyses showed that retributive goals of punishment—not fear that the juvenile would recidivate—drove the effect of victim race on women's support for registration. In other words, a retributive desire to punish sex offenders, and not a utilitarian desire to protect society, explained registration support—an effect in line with previous research (Carlsmith et al., 2002; Darley et al., 2000).

These results support the hypothesis that gender-related social categorization (Rudman & Goodwin, 2004) might have caused women to pay attention to features of the female victim more than men did. In turn, women's greater attention toward the female victim might have caused them to be more influenced by her racial characteristics. Yet, men likely paid less attention to the female victim than women did because they categorized her as an out-group member, and consequently they were less influenced by her racial characteristics. Thus, at least for women, these results provide evidence that negative stereotypes about Black women drove them to devalue the worth of the Black victim by supporting sex offender registration less often when the victim was Black than when she was White. Well-documented stereotypes that Black women are more sexually experienced, promiscuous, and perverse than White women may, in part, explain this effect (Devine, 1989; Powell, Wyatt, & Bass, 1983; Weinberg & Williams, 1988; Wyatt, 1982). In other words, negative stereotypes about the sexual deviance of Black women might have caused non-Black women to label the sex act as a less serious sexual offense and, in turn, support registration less when the victim was Black rather than White.

Finally, contrary to hypotheses, there were no main effects of defendant race. Why? On the one hand, although there certainly are negative stereotypes associating criminality with Black men (e.g., Devine, 1989), such stereotypes might not encompass the specific crime of sex offending. In support, Jackson and Nuttall (1993) found that clinicians perceived child sex offenders as more likely to be White than Black or Hispanic. On the other hand, perhaps there were no effects of defendant race because the sexual offense in this study was a nonviolent sexual act described as consensual. As described above, these findings are likely driven by a lack of societal acceptance of interracial relationships (e.g., Lewandowski & Jackson, 2001; Mills et al., 1995; Ross, 2005), which drove people to perceive an ambiguously criminal sex act as more like a true crime when the defendant and victim were of different races than when they were of the same race. Yet, how will defendant and victim race shape perceptions of a juvenile who commits an unambiguously criminal sex act—forced rape? We have recently started testing this question, and next we present the preliminary results of this new line of research.

Effects of Juvenile Defendant and Victim Race on Registration Support for Forced Rape

Recall that studies reviewed earlier reveal that participants tend to react more punitively when an adult rapist is Black and the victim is White than with any other victim-defendant racial combination (e.g., Feild, 1979). Aversive racism (Gaertner & Dovidio, 1986) and well-documented negative stereotypes that Blacks are more violent, aggressive, and sexually deviant than Whites (e.g., Devine, 1989) likely drive discriminatory treatment. Thus, it is possible that aversive racism and anti-Black stereotypes might lead participants to support registration more when the juvenile defendant convicted of forced rape is Black and the victim is White than with any other victim-defendant racial combination.

Alternatively, the stereotype that Black women are physically dominant, powerful, and aggressive (e.g., Donovan, 2007; Donovan & Williams, 2002; Esqueda & Harrison, 2005; West, 1995) supports a competing hypothesis. To the extent that participants perceive Black women as particularly physically strong, they might also believe that Black women are either physically intimidating enough to deter a prospective rapist or strong enough to stop him. Thus, when a Black woman is raped, participants might perceive the rapist as especially dangerous and strong to have successfully raped her. In support, Willis (1992) experimentally manipulated victim race in a forced-rape case and found that participants were more confident in the defendant's guilt, perceived the defendant as more likely to reoffend, and found the victim to be less blameworthy when the victim was Black rather than White. These results support the possibility that participants perceived the rapist as particularly dangerous and strong to have raped a Black woman, compared to a White woman, possibly because they perceived the Black victim as physically powerful (e.g., Donovan, 2007; Donovan & Williams, 2002; Esqueda & Harrison, 2005; West, 1995).

We tested these competing theories by examining perceptions of a juvenile defendant (Black or White) convicted of forcibly raping a teenaged victim (Black or White).

Method

Participants were 250 community members (77% women; M age = 36) who participated in a computer-simulated survey. Participants volunteered to take the anonymous survey, which was posted on the www.craigslist.com volunteer section in various cities across the United States. African Americans were excluded from the data set because this was an examination of anti-Black bias. Eighty four percent of participants were White, 6% were Hispanic, 4% were Asian, 4% were from other racial groups, and 2% declined to state race.[1]

A brief vignette presented a case involving a 15-year-old boy convicted of forcibly raping a 15-year-old girl. Specifically, the defendant was described as attacking the victim in a park, pulling her into a wooded area, and raping her. This vignette was developed previously by Salerno, Najdowski, and colleagues (2010). Juvenile defendant and victim race were experimentally manipulated in a fully crossed between-subjects design. Demographic descriptors of "African American" or "Caucasian," and race-consistent names for the defendant (Jamal or David) and victim (Jennifer or Keisha) constituted the race manipulation.[2] Participants indicated their support for registering the juvenile as a sex offender by responding to the following question on a 5-point scale ranging from 1 (strongly disagree) to 5 (strongly agree): "Public registration laws are too severe for the defendant's case."

This variable was reverse coded such that higher numbers indicated greater registration support. On the same scale, we assessed perceived defendant recidivism (i.e., "David/Jamal is at high risk for reoffending") and the belief that the defendant is dangerous (i.e., "David/Jamal is a cold and calculating 'superpredator.'") Our item assessing defendant recidivism was previously developed and used by Salerno, Stevenson, and colleagues (2010) and Stevenson and colleagues (2009), and the item assessing the belief that the defendant is dangerous was developed by Haegerich (2002).

Preliminary Results

We conducted a series of 2 (defendant race: Black or White) X 2 (victim race: Black or White) analyses of covariance (ANCOVAs), including participant gender as a covariate. We controlled for gender because past research has revealed that gender interacts with defendant and victim ethnicity (Stevenson & Bottoms, 2009; Stevenson et al., 2009) and because our preliminary data did not have enough male participants ($n = 57$) to include participant gender as an independent variable.

There were no main effects of defendant race on registration support, perceived likelihood of defendant recidivism, and belief that the defendant is dangerous, all $Fs < .88$, #. Supporting our alternative hypothesis, participants were more supportive of registration when the victim was Black ($M = 3.79$, $SD = 1.14$) rather than White ($M = 3.46$, $SD = 1.25$), $F(1, 245) = 4.53$, $p < .05$. Participants were also significantly more likely to believe that the defendant was dangerous when the victim was Black ($M = 2.71$, $SD = 1.05$) rather than White ($M = 2.40$, $SD = 1.07$), $F(1, 244) = 5.28$, $p < .05$, and marginally more likely to believe that the defendant would recidivate when the victim was Black ($M = 3.99$, $SD = .92$) rather than White ($M = 3.75$, $SD = .90$), $F(1, 245) = 3.43$, $p = .07$. There were no significant defendant race by victim race interactions for any dependant variables, $Fs(1, 244 - 245) < 1.90$, all #.

Next, we conducted mediation analyses to understand the effects of victim race on registration support. In line with Baron and Kenny's (1986) recommendations, we first found that our potential mediators (i.e., perceived likelihood of recidivism and the belief that the defendant is dangerous) significantly predicted our primary dependant variable (i.e., registration support), $\beta s > .16$, $ps < .05$. When victim race and the two potential mediators were simultaneously entered into a regression predicting registration support, the effect of victim race was no longer statistically significant, $\beta = -.07$, # (see Figure 4.2). Perceived

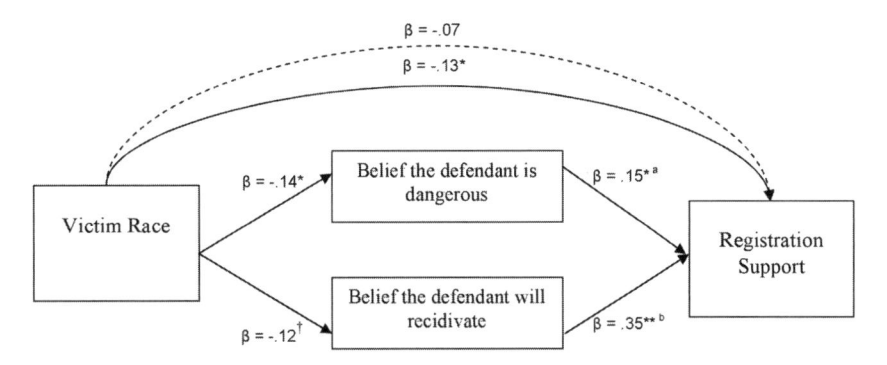

Figure 4.2 Belief that the defendant is dangerous and perceived likelihood of recidivism as mediators of victim race on registration support.

Note. Victim race was coded as 0 (Black victim) and 1 (White victim). Greater values indicated greater belief that the defendant is dangerous, greater belief that the defendant will reoffend, and greater support for registration laws.

[a] Sobel $z = -1.62$, $p = .05$, [b] Sobel $z = -1.86$, $p < .05$
† $p < .10$, * $p < .05$, ** $p < .001$

recidivism likelihood (Sobel $= -1.86$, $p < .05$) and the belief that the defendant is dangerous (Sobel $= -1.62$, $p = .05$) remained statistically significant, βs $> .16$, $ps < .05$. Thus, participants were more supportive of registration when the victim was Black rather than White because they believed that the defendant was more dangerous and likely to recidivate when he successfully raped a Black victim rather than a White victim.

Discussion of Preliminary Findings

The results of this research, although preliminary, provide a good first step toward understanding the influence of juvenile defendant and victim ethnicity on perceptions of juvenile sex offenders. Consistent with past research (Stevenson et al., 2009), we again found no effects of juvenile defendant race on registration support. Although it is possible that juvenile defendant ethnicity simply has no influence on registration support, we caution readers from endorsing this conclusion. This research constitutes preliminary data, and it included only 57 male participants. Thus, we simply did not have enough statistical power to include participant gender as a third independent variable in analyses. Because past research has shown that men, but not women, treat Black juvenile defendants more punitively than White juvenile defendants (Stevenson & Bottoms, 2009), it is possible that similar effects will emerge in this study as we increase the number of men in our sample.

We did, however, find support for a competing hypothesis regarding victim race: Participants were more supportive of registration when the victim was Black rather than White. This finding is contrary to effects of victim race found in several other studies, which reveal that Black victims often receive less retribution than White victims (e.g., Feild, 1979; Foley & Chamblin, 1982; Klein & Creech, 1982; Ugwuegbu, 1979). Yet, these findings support an alternative theory. To the extent that participants perceive Black women as more physically powerful than White women (Donovan, 2007; Donovan & Williams, 2002; Esqueda & Harrison, 2005; West, 1995), they might, in turn, have perceived a defendant who successfully raped a Black girl as more dangerous and likely to recidivate. In support, perceived defendant dangerousness and likelihood to recidivate drove effects of victim race on registration support. Further, Willis (1992) found similar effects: Participants perceived an adult rapist as more likely to recidivate and perceived the victim as less blameworthy when she was Black rather than White. Future research should continue to explore additional mediators of victim race effects, including perceived victim strength, to more fully test this theory.

Conclusions and Directions for Future Research

The theory and research reviewed in this chapter helps fill practical and theoretical gaps in the field of psychology and the law. This chapter also helps consolidate a complex body of research that highlights the various ways in which racial stereotypes influence marginalized groups of young sex offenders and their victims. Further, we presented novel preliminary data that extends the limited field of research on how race shapes perceptions of juvenile sex offenses—a topic that is particularly important and timely in light of the government's recent extension of sex offender registration laws to juveniles (Caldwell et al., 2008).

Yet, it is clear that much work remains to be done before we can fully understand the complex influence of defendant and victim race on perceptions of juvenile sex offenders. Future research should continue to test the impact of race on perceptions of juveniles accused of other types of sex crimes including, for instance, sexting, date rape, etc. As called for by professionals in the field of psychology and the law (e.g., Diamond, 1997), this research should also strive for greater ecological validity by employing more detailed and realistic case scenarios or even including videotaped simulated trials. In addition, research on perceptions of juvenile sex offenders has begun to uncover a variety of factors that influence registration support, including, for instance, age of offender (Salerno, Najdowski, et al., 2010), participant education level (Stevenson, Sekely, Smith, & Sorenson, 2010), and the juvenile's history of having been sexually abused as a child (Stevenson, Najdowski, Sorenson, 2010). Yet, it is possible that these factors might interact with juvenile offender and victim race—a possibility that deserves empirical research. For instance, a juvenile sex offender's history of having been sexually abused as a child might be used as a mitigating factor (e.g., reducing registration recommendations) only for White juvenile offenders and not for minority juvenile offenders. In support, Lynch and Haney (2000) found that jurors not only were more punitive toward a Black adult defendant than to a White adult defendant, but also that mitigating evidence of a history of child abuse elicited a lenient sentence more often for White defendants than for Black defendants.

Perhaps most importantly, although the research and theory reviewed in this article focuses on perceptions of African American defendants and victims, future research should explore perceptions of juvenile sex offenders of other racial minority groups, including Hispanic, Arabic, Asian, and Native American juvenile offenders and victims. Given our current sociopolitical climate and research revealing biases against Hispanic adult offenders (Demuth & Steffensmeier, 2004; Esqueda, 1997; Steffensmeier & Demuth, 2000), it is likely that racial biases against Hispanic juvenile sex offenders and victims will manifest. Consider, for instance, the case of Brandon Coronado, a 17-year-old Hispanic high school student with no prior criminal record (*Coronado v. State of Texas,* 2003). Although Coronado claimed he had consensual sex with a girl whom he believed was 16 years old, he was charged with aggravated child sexual assault because the girl was actually 12. Coronado waived his right to a trial by jury to avoid a possible life sentence, instead accepting a plea that resulted in 10 years of adjudicated probation and sex offender registration (*Coronado v. State of Texas,* 2003). Yet, his probation was soon revoked due to a violation, and he is currently serving a 60-year sentence (Crimes, 2010).

Understanding how defendant and victim race influence a juvenile's likelihood of being registered is important given that registering juveniles is not only ineffective at reducing sex offenses, but also negatively impacts the lives of those registered in ways that could contribute to future recidivism (e.g., Levenson, Brannon, et al., 2007). Understanding biases against racial minorities is one important step toward the development of future policy designed to combat discrimination against marginalized and vulnerable young offenders.

Notes

1. Because it is possible that the 2% ($n = 4$) of participants who failed to report their ethnicity were African American, we replicated all analyses excluding those 4 participants. Yet, there was only one difference in the results: The p-value of the victim race effect on registration support dropped from statistically significant ($p < .05$) to marginally significant ($p = .06$). Because there was just one difference in the results and the difference was such that our hypothesized effects were weaker when excluding these participants, we therefore present the analyses including participants who did not report ethnicity to preserve statistical power.

2. Victim and defendant socioeconomic status (SES) were also manipulated in this study. Yet, because we were uninterested in effects of SES for the purposes of this study, we do not report the SES effects. Instead, we have conducted all analyses collapsed across these independent variables.

References

Ahuja, G. (2006, April 18). Sex offender registries: Putting lives at risk? *ABC News.* Retrieved from http://abcnews.go.com/US/story?id=1855771&page=1.

Baron, R. M., & Kenny, D. A. (1986). The moderator-mediator variable distinction in social psychological research: Conceptual, strategic, and statistical considerations. *Journal of Personality and Social Psychology, 51,* 1173–1182. doi:10.1037/0022-3514.51.6.1173

Bernstein, M. J., Young, S. G., & Hugenberg, K. (2007). The cross-category effect: Mere social categorization is sufficient to elicit an own-group bias in face recognition. *Psychological Science, 18,* 706–712. doi:9280.2007.01964.x

Bridge, J. A., Goldstein, T. R., & Brent, D. A. (2006). Adolescent suicide and suicidal behavior. *Journal of Child Psychology and Psychiatry, 47,* 372–394. doi:10.1111/j.1469-7610.2006.01615.x

Bridges, G. S., & Steen, S. (1998). Racial disparities in official assessments of juvenile offenders: Attributional stereotypes as mediating mechanisms. *American Sociological Review, 63,* 554–570. Retrieved from http://www.asanet.org/journals/asr/.

Caldwell, M. F., Ziemke, M. H., & Vitacco, M. J. (2008). An examination of the sex offender registration and notification act as applied to juveniles: Evaluating the ability to predict sexual recidivism. *Psychology, Public Policy, and Law, 14,* 89–114. doi:10.1037/a0013241

Carlsmith, K. M., Darley, J. M., & Robinson, P. H. (2002). Why do we punish? Deterrence and just deserts as motives for punishment. *Journal of Personality and Social Psychology, 83,* 284–299. doi:10.1037/0022-3514.83.2.284

Carrasco, G. (2007). *Perceptions of same-race and interracial dating couples on sexuality and relationship variables.* Master's thesis. Available from Texas Tech University Electronic Theses and Dissertations (etd-04042007-182456).

Carter, R. T. (1990). The relationship between racism and racial identity among White Americans: An exploratory investigation. *Journal of Counseling and Development, 69,* 46–50. Retrieved from http://www.counseling.org/Publications/Journals.aspx.

Chaffin, M. (2008). Our minds are made up—don't confuse us with the facts: Commentary on policies concerning children with sexual behavior problems and juvenile sex offenders. *Child Maltreatment, 13,* 110–121. doi:10.1177/1077559508314510

Conley, J. M., Turnier, W. J., & Rose, M. R. (2000). The racial ecology of the courtroom: An experimental study of juror response to the race of criminal defendants. *Wisconsin Law Review,* 1185–1220. Retrieved from http://heinonline.org/HOL/Page?handle=hein.journals/wlr2000&div=52&g_sent=1&collection=journals#1203.

Coombs, R. (2006). Sexual assault coalition announces opposition to Jessica's Law. *California Coalition Against Sexual Assault: Public Affairs.* Retrieved from http://calcasa.org/publicaffairs/sexual-assault-coalition-announces-opposition-to-jessica%E2%80%99s-law/.

Coronado v. State of Texas. 119 S.W. 3d 844, 848 (Tex. App. Ct. 2003).

Crimes committed in Nueces County by current inmates. (2010, June 20). *Texas Tribune.* Retrieved from http://www.texastribune.org/library/data/texas-prisons/counties/nueces/crime/?page=11.

Darley, J. M., Carlsmith, K. M., & Robinson, P. H. (2000). Incapacitation and just deserts as motives for punishment. *Law and Human Behavior, 24,* 659–683. doi:10.1023/A:1005552203727

Davis, J. H., Bray, R. M., & Holt, R. W. (1977). The empirical study of social decision processes in juries. In J. Tapp & F. Levine (Eds.), *Law, Justice, and the Individual in Society: Psychological and Legal Issues* (pp. 326–361). New York: Holt, Rinehart.

Demuth, S., & Steffensmeier, D. (2004). Ethnicity effects on sentence outcomes in large urban courts: Comparisons among White, Black, and Hispanic defendants. *Social Science Quarterly, 85,* 994–1011. doi:10.1111/j.0038-4941.2004.00255.x

Devine, P. G. (1989). Stereotypes and prejudice: Their automatic and controlled components. *Journal of Personality and Social Psychology, 56,* 5–18. doi:10.1037/0022-3514.56.1.5

Diamond, S. S. (1997). Illuminations and shadows from jury simulation. *Law and Human Behavior, 21,* 561–571. doi:10.1023/A:1024831908377

Dixon v. State of Georgia, 278 Ga. 4 (2004).

Donovan, R. (2007). To blame or not to blame: Influences of target race and observer sex on rape blame attribution. *Journal of Interpersonal Violence, 22,* 722–736. doi:10.1177/0886260507300754

Donovan, R., & Williams, M. (2002). Living at the intersection: The effects of racism and sexism on Black rape survivors. *Women and Therapy, 25,* 95–105. doi:10.1300/J015v25n03_07

Dovidio, J. F., Smith, J. K., Donnella, A. G., & Gaertner, S. L. (1997). Racial attitudes and the death penalty. *Journal of Applied Social Psychology, 27,* 1468–1487. doi:10.1111/j.1559-1816.1997.tb01609.x

Ekehammar, B., Akrami, N., & Araya, T. (2003). Gender differences in implicit prejudice. *Personality and Individual Differences, 34,* 1509–1523. doi:10.1016/S0191-8869(02)00132-0

Engen, R. L., Steen, S., & Bridges, G. S. (2002). Racial disparities in the punishment of youth: A theoretical and empirical assessment of the literature. *Social Problems, 49,* 194–220. doi:10.1525/sp.2002.49.2.194

Esqueda, C. W. (1997). European American students' perceptions of crimes committed by five racial groups. *Journal of Applied Social Psychology, 27,* 1406–1420. doi:10.1111/j.1559-1816.1997.tb01605.x

Esqueda, C. W., & Harrison, L. A. (2005). The influence of gender role stereotypes, the woman's race, and level of provocation and resistance on domestic violence culpability attributions. *Sex Roles, 53,* 821–834. doi:10.1007/11199s-005-8295-1

Feild, H. S. (1979). Rape trials and jurors' decisions: A psycholegal analysis of the effects of victim, defendant, and case characteristics. *Law and Human Behavior, 3,* 261–284. doi:10.1007/BF01039806

Foley, L. A., & Chamblin, M. H. (1982). The effect of race and personality on mock jurors' decisions. *Journal of Psychology, 112,* 47–51.

Gaertner, S. L., & Dovidio, J. F. (1986). The aversive form of racism. In J. F. Dovidio & S. L. Gaertner (Eds.), *Prejudice, discrimination and racism* (pp. 61–90). Orlando, FL: Academic Press.

Haegerich, T. M. (2002). *Influences of stereotypes on individual and group decisions in a novel context: Juvenile offenders in court.* Ann Arbor, MI: UMI Dissertation Services.

Harrison, L. A., & Esqueda, C. W. (2000). Effects of race and victim drinking on domestic violence attributions. *Sex Roles, 42,* 1043–1057. doi:10.1023/A:1007040701889

Hilton, J. L., & von Hippel, W. (1996). Stereotypes. *Annual Review of Psychology, 47,* 237–271. Retrieved from http://www.annualreviews.org/doi/abs/10.1146/annurev.psych.47.1.237.

Jackson, H., & Nuttall, R. (1993). Clinical responses to sexual abuse allegations. *Child Abuse & Neglect, 17,* 127–143. doi:10.1016/0145-2134(93)90013-U

Jacobs, A. (2004). Student sex in Georgia stirs claims of old south justice. *New York Times,* January 22.

Jones, M. (2007, July 22). How can you distinguish a budding pedophile from a kid with real boundary problems? *New York Times.* Retrieved from http://www.nytimes.com/2007/07/22/magazine/22juvenilet.html?ei=5090&en=0daaac50edd79404&ex=1342756800&adxnnl=1&partner=rssuserland&emc=rss&adxnnlx=1197461353G8A0n8Cqb/wV9/fasi/wKA&pagewanted=all.

Kim, R. I., & Goldstein, S. B. (2005). Intercultural attitudes predict favorable study abroad expectations of U.S. college students. *Journal of Studies in International Education, 9,* 265–276. doi:10.1177/1028315305277684

Klein, K., & Creech, B. (1982). Race, rape, and bias: Distortion of prior odds and meaning changes. *Basic and Applied Social Psychology, 3,* 21–33. doi:10.1207/s15324834basp0301_2

Knox, D., Zusman, M. E., Buffington, C., & Hemphill, G. (2000, March). Interracial dating attitudes among college students. *College Student Journal.* Retrieved from http://findarticles.com/p/articles/mi_m0FCR/is_1_34/ai_62839403/pg_3/?tag=content;col1.

Letourneau, E. J., & Armstrong, K. S. (2008). Recidivism rates for registered and nonregistered juvenile sex offenders. *Sexual Abuse, 20,* 393–408. doi:10.1177/1079063208324661

Levenson, J. S., Brannon, Y. N., Fortney, T., & Baker, J. (2007). Public perceptions about sex offenders and community protection policies. *Analyses of Social Issues and Public Policy, 7,* 137–161. doi:10.1111/j.1530-2415.2007.00119.x

Levenson, J. S., & Cotter, L. P. (2005). The effect of Megan's Law on sex offender registration. *Journal of Contemporary Criminal Justice, 21,* 49–66. doi:10.1177/1043986204271676

Levenson, J. S., D'Amora, D. A., & Hern, A. (2007). Megan's Law and its impact on community re-entry for sex offenders. *Behavioral Sciences and the Law, 25,* 587–602. doi:10.1002/bsl.770

Lewandowski, D. A., & Jackson, L. A. (2001). Perceptions of interracial couples: Prejudice at the dyadic level. *Journal of Black Psychology, 27,* 288–303. doi:10.1177/0095798401027003003

Lynch, M., & Haney, C. (2000). Discrimination and instructional comprehension: Guided discretion, racial bias, and the death penalty. *Law and Human Behavior, 24,* 337–358. doi:10.1023/A:1005588221761

MacLin, O. H., & Malpass, R. S. (2001). Racial categorization of faces: The ambiguous race face effect. *Psychology, Public Policy, and Law, 7,* 98–118. doi:10.1037/1076-8971.7.1.98

Mazzella, R., & Feingold, A. (1994). The effects of physical attractiveness, race, socioeconomic status, and gender of defendants and victims on judgments of mock jurors: A meta-analysis. *Journal of Applied Social Psychology, 24,* 1315–1344. doi:10.1111/j.1559-1816.1994.tb01552.x

Meissner, C. A., & Brigham, J. C. (2001). Thirty years of investigating own-race bias in memory for faces: A meta-analytic review. *Psychology, Public Policy, and Law, 7,* 3–35. doi:10.1037/1076-8971.7.1.3

Mills, J. K., Daly, J., Longmore, A., & Kilbride, G. (1995). A note on family acceptance involving interracial friendships and romantic relationships. *Journal of Psychology, 129,* 349–351. Retrieved from http://www.questia.com/googleScholar.qst?docId=76922505.

Mills, J. K., McGrath, D., Sobkoviak, P., Stupec, S., & Welsch, S. (1995). Differences in expressed racial prejudice and acceptance of others. *Journal of Psychology, 129,* 357–359. Retrieved from http://www.questia.com/googleScholar.qst?docId=76922566.

Mitchel, T. L., Haw, R. M., Pfeifer, J. E., & Meissner, C. A. (2005). Racial bias in mock juror decision-making: A meta-analytic review of defendant treatment. *Law and Human Behavior, 29,* 621–637. doi:10.1007/s10979-005-8122-9

National Public Radio (2007, June 12). *Teens, sex and the law: Genarlow Wilson.* Retrieved from http://www.npr.org/templates/story/story.php?storyId=10972703.

Phillips, D. (1998). *Community notification as viewed by Washington's citizens.* Olympia, WA: Washington State Institute for Public Policy.

Porterfield, E. (1982). Black-American intermarriage in the United States. *Marriage and Family Review, 5,* 17–34. doi:10.1300/J002v05n01_03

Powell, G. J., Wyatt, G. E., & Bass, B. A. (1983). Mental health professionals' view of Afro-American family life and sexuality. *Journal of Sex and Marital Therapy, 9,* 51–66. doi:10.1080/00926238308405833

Rome News Tribune. (2004). Dixon is on Oprah's mind. Retrieved from http://rn-t.com/view/full_story/3401153/article-Dixon-case-back-on-%E2%80%98Oprah%E2%80%99-toda—Local-New.

Rome News Tribune. (2008, May 28). Genarlow Wilson, released after sex case, wants to attend college. *Georgia News.* Retrieved from http://romenews-tribune.com/view/full_story/3462861/article-Genarlow-Wilson-released-after-sex-case-wants-to-attend-colleg-Georgia-New.

Ross, W. (2005). The perceptions of college students about interracial relationships. *National Forum of Applied Educational Research Journal* [Electronic Version], *17E*(3), 1–16.

Rudman, L. A., & Goodwin, S. A. (2004). Gender differences in automatic in-group bias: Why do women like women more than men like men? *Journal of Personality and Social Psychology, 87,* 494–509. doi:10.1037/0022-3514.87.4.494

Salerno, J. M., Najdowski, C. J., Stevenson, M. C., Wiley, T. R. A., Bottoms, B. L., Vaca, R., Jr., & Pimental, P. S. (2010). Psychological mechanisms underlying support for juvenile sex offender registry laws: Prototypes, moral outrage, and perceived threat. *Behavioral Sciences and the Law, 28,* 58–83. doi:10.1002/bsl.921

Salerno, J. M., Stevenson, M. C., Wiley, T. R. A., Najdowski, C. J., Bottoms, B. L., & Schmillen, R. A. (2010). Public attitudes toward applying sex offender registry laws to juvenile offenders. In J. L. Lampinen & K. Sexton-Radek (Eds.), *Protecting children from violence: Evidence based interactions* (pp. 193–218). New York: Psychology Press.

Scott, E. S., Reppucci, N. D., Antonishak, J., & DeGennaro, J. T. (2006). Public attitudes about the culpability and punishment of young offenders. *Behavioral Sciences and the Law, 24,* 815–832. doi:10.1002/bsl.727

Sex Offender Registration and Notification Act (SORNA). (2011). 42 U.S.C. § 16911.

Shaw, J. I., & Skolnick, P. (1995). Effects of prohibitive and informative judicial instructions on jury decision making. *Social Behavior and Personality, 23,* 319–325. doi:10.2224/sbp.1995.23.4.319

Skolnick, P., & Shaw, J. I. (1997). The O. J. Simpson criminal trial verdict: Racism or status shield? *Journal of Social Issues, 53,* 503–516. doi:10.1111/j.1540-4560.1997.tb02125.x

Snyder, H. N., & Sickmund, M. (2006, March). Juvenile offenders and victims: 2006 national report. *Juvenile Justice Bulletin.* Washington, DC: Office of Juvenile Justice and Delinquency Prevention, US Department of Justice.

Sommers, S. R., & Ellsworth, P. C. (2001). White juror bias: An investigation of prejudice against Black defendants in the American courtroom. *Psychology, Public Policy and Law, 7,* 201–229. doi:10.1037/1076-8971.7.1.201

Sommers, S. R., & Ellsworth, P. C. (2003). How much do we really know about race and juries? A review of social science theory and research. *Chicago-Kent Law Review, 78,* 997–1031. Retrieved from http://cklawreview.com/.

Sommers, S. R., & Ellsworth, P. C. (2006). On racial diversity and group decision making: Identifying multiple effects of racial composition on jury deliberations. *Journal of Personality and Social Psychology, 90,* 597–612. doi:10.1037/0022-3514.90.4.597

Steffensmeier, D., & Demuth, S. (2000). Ethnicity and sentencing outcomes in U.S. federal courts: Who is punished more harshly? *American Sociological Review, 65,* 705–729. Retrieved from http://asr.sagepub.com/.

Stevenson, M. C., & Bottoms, B. L. (2009). Race shapes perceptions of juvenile offenders in criminal court. *Journal of Applied Social Psychology, 39,* 1660–1689. doi:10.1111/j.1559-1816.2009.00499.x

Stevenson, M. C., Najdowski, C. J., & Sorenson, K. M. (2010, March). *Effects of a defendant's history of being sexually abused on perceptions of juvenile sex offenders.* Paper presented at the meeting of the American Psychology Law Society, Vancouver, Canada.

Stevenson, M. C., Sekely, A., Smith, A., & Sorenson, K. M. (2010, March). *Individual differences as predictors of attitudes toward juvenile sex offenders: Level of education, political orientation, and gender.* Paper presented at the meeting of the American Psychology Law Society, Vancouver, Canada.

Stevenson, M. C., Sorenson, K. M., Smith, A. C., Sekely, A., & Dzwairo, R. A. (2009). Effects of defendant and victim race on perceptions of juvenile sex offenders. *Behavioral Sciences and the Law, 27,* 957–979. doi:10.1002/bsl.910

Sweeney, L. T., & Haney, C. (1992). The influence of race on sentencing: A meta-analytic review of experimental studies. *Behavioral Sciences and the Law, 10,* 179–195. doi:10.1002/bsl.2370100204

Tewksbury, R. (2005). Collateral consequences of sex offender registration. *Journal of Contemporary Criminal Justice, 21,* 67–81. doi:10.1177/1043986204271704

Tewksbury, R., & Lees, M. (2006). Perceptions of sex offender registration: Collateral consequences and community experiences. *Sociological Spectrum, 26,* 309–334. doi:10.1080/02732170500524246

Tewksbury, R., & Lees, M. (2007). Perceptions of punishment: How registered sex offenders view registries. *Crime and Delinquency, 53,* 380–407. doi:10.1177/0011128706286915

Tjaden, P., & Thoennes, N. (1998). Prevalence, incidence, and consequences of violence against women: Findings from national violence against women survey. *National Institute of Justice Centers for Disease Control and Prevention Research in Brief.* [Data File]. Washington, DC: U.S. Department of Justice. Retrieved from http://www.ncjrs.gov/pdffiles/172837.pdf.

Trivits, L., & Reppucci, N. (2002). Application of Megan's Law to juveniles. *American Psychologist, 57,* 690–704. doi:10.1037/0003-006X.57.9.690

Ugwuegbu, D. C. E. (1979). Racial and evidential factors in juror attribution of legal responsibility. *Journal of Experimental Social Psychology, 15,* 133–146. doi:10.1016/0022-1031(79)90025-8

Uniform crime report: Crimes in the United States. [Data File]. (2007). Washington, DC: U.S. Department of Justice—Federal Bureau of Investigations. Retrieved from http://www.fbi.gove/ucr/ucr.htm.

Weinberg, M. S., & Williams, C. J. (1988). Black sexuality: A test of two theories. *The Journal of Sex Research, 25,* 197–218. doi:10.1080/0024498809551455

West, C. M. (1995). Mammy, Sapphire, and Jezebel: Historical images of Black women and their implications for psychotherapy. *Psychotherapy: Theory, Research, Practice, Training, 32,* 458–466. doi:10.1037/0033-3204.32.3.458

Willis, C. E. (1992). The effect of sex role stereotype, victim and defendant race, and prior relationship on rape culpability attributions. *Sex Roles, 26,* 213–226. doi:10.1007/BF00289708

Wilson v. State of Georgia, 279 Ga. App. 459, 631 S.E.2d 391 (2006).

Wordes, M., Bynum, T. S., & Corley, C. J. (1994). Locking up youth: The impact of race on detention decisions. *Journal of Research in Crime and Delinquency, 31,* 149–165. doi:10.1177/0022427894031002004

Wright, R. G. (Ed.) (2009). *Sex offender laws: Failed policies, new directions.* New York: Springer Publishing.

Wyatt, G. (1982). Identifying stereotypes of Afro-American sexuality and their impact upon sexual behavior. In B. Bass, G. Wyatt, & G. Powell (Eds.), *The Afro-American family: Assessment treatment and research issues* (pp. 333–346). New York: Grune & Stratton.

Xu, J., Kochanek, K. D., & Tejada-Vera, B. (2009). Deaths: Preliminary data for 2007. [Data File]. *National Vital Statistics Reports, 58*(1), 1–51. Hattysville, MD: National Center for Heath Statistics. Retrieved from http://www.cdc.gov/nchs/data/nvsr/nvsr58/nvsr58_01.pdf.

PART II

Teen Violence at School, on the Internet, and at Work

CHAPTER FIVE

Schoolyard Violence

Stuart C. Aitken and Donald E. Colley III

August 17, 2010: A student is shot and killed in the schoolyard of Belleville Township High School East in Illinois.

April 30, 2009: 13 students and staff members are shot and killed at the Azerbaijan State Oil Academy in Baku School.

March 11, 2009: 16 students and staff members are shot and killed in a schoolyard at Winnenden School, Germany.

March 6, 2008: A lone Palestinian gunman shot multiple students in the schoolyard of Mercaz HaPav yeshiva, a religious school in Jerusalem, Israel.

October 2, 2006: Charles Carl Roberts, 32, takes 10 girls hostage in an Amish school in Nickel Mines Pennsylvania, killing 5.

September 29, 2006: Eric Heinstiock, 15, took guns to school in Cazenovia, Wisconsin, and fatally shot the principal.

Sept 27, 2006: Duane Morrison, 53, takes six girls hostage, fatally shooting one.

November 8, 2005: Assistant principal Ken Bruce was killed by 15-year-old student Kenny Bartley in Jacksboro, Tennessee.

May 21, 2005: Jeff Weise, 16, kills five students, a security guard, and a teacher in Red Lake, Minnesota.

November 24, 2004: James Lewerke, 15, stabs seven classmates at Valparaiso High School in northern Indiana.

February 2, 2004: 17-year-old James Richardson was shot to death at Ballou Senior High School in Washington, D.C.

April 24, 2003: James Sheets, 14, shot and killed his middle school principal in Red Lion, Pennsylvania.

April 26, 2002: 17-year-old Dragoslav Petkovis opened fire with a handgun at his high school in Vlasenica, Bosnia-Herzegovina, killing one teacher and wounding another.

April 26, 2002: Robert Steinhauser, 19, returned to school in Erfurt, Germany, after being expelled and shot to death 13 teachers, 2 students, and a police officer.

February 19, 2002: A 22-year-old gunman shot and killed his school's headmaster in Munich, Germany.

Jun 8, 2001: Mamoru Takuma forced his way into Ikeda Elementary School in Osaka, Japan, and stabbed to death eight students.

March 5, 2001: 15-year-old Andrew Williams killed 2 classmates and wounded 13 others at Santana High School in Santee, California.

February 29, 2000: A first-grade boy at Buell Elementary School in Michigan fatally shot Kayla Rolland, 6, after the two children had a verbal spat.

April 28, 1999: A 14-year-old boy who had been bullied by his classmates opened fire at W. R. Myers High School in Alberta, Canada, killing a 17-year-old student and wounding another.

April 20, 1999: Columbine High School students Dylan Klebold, 17, and Eric Harris, 18, shot and killed 12 classmates and a teacher.

April 28, 1998: Two teenage boys were shot to death in the schoolyard of a Pomona, California, elementary school.

February 19, 1997: 16-year-old Evan Ramsey opened fire with a shotgun in a high school common area in Bethel, Alaska, killing the principal and a student.

March 13, 1996: Thomas Hamilton, 43, entered an elementary schoolyard in Dunblane, Scotland, and killed 16 children, all 5 or 6 years old.

We begin this chapter with a long list of schoolyard violence, including shootings and stabbings that resulted in death, to make five initial points. First, serious violence in schoolyards and common areas is a matter of considerable public concern. Second, in reading details from below the headlines and synopses, it seems clear that in many cases of violent crime an undetected or ignored series of lesser events led to the ultimate tragedies. Third, although a large preponderance of shootings are in the United States, schoolyard violence is a problem affecting a number of countries, with reporting primarily from the Global North (see Akiba, LeTendre, Baker, & Gosling, 2002). Fourth, the list is generated from the Associated Press and other news media venues, which have considerable culpability in the propagation of what sociologist Barry Glassner (1999) calls a "culture of fear," where certain institutions, organizations, and politicians profit from societal anxieties and fears. Glassner points out that these institutions are adept at manipulating our perceptions of schoolyard violence and goes on to argue that Americans in particular are worried about the wrong things. As Small and Tetrick (2001, p. 1) note, "[t]he perception of risk is often greater than the reality, as schools have been largely successful in keeping students and staff safe from harm." Muschert (2007, p. 60) notes that compared with homes, schools are among the safest places for children, and less than 2 percent of homicides involving school-age youths occur at school.[1]

When school shootings occur, media hype is only part of the issue; the spectacle is propagated in large part by the idea of child safety and the creation of places that are presumed to be safe, but are not. In a recent book on space and violence, Jim Tyner (2011) notes that schoolyards are indeed violent places for children. This is our fifth initial point. Violence in schoolyards is an impression that resonates with many adult memories of childhood, not because of shootings and other violent tragedies but because of banal everyday violence. Emotionally upsetting taunting, stealing of lunch money, ostracizing, name calling, and bullying are constant features of the schoolyard. Tyner points out that there is a silence surrounding these forms of violence that is akin to the tacit condoning of intimate partner violence.[2]

What we want to argue here is, first, that the scale of schoolyard violence, whether real or illusory, is part of a larger demonization and criminalization of youths (cf. Aitken 2001; Aitken & Marchant, 2003; Tyner 2011). To do so, we construct a narrative suggesting that schoolyards are a spatialized part of society's moral integrity, and problematic moral issues foreground the content of lists like the one with which we started. Second, we note that there is another important story relating to playground violence, which is less about serious violence and how it is portrayed in the media and more about insidious, small-scale violent acts that may or may not presage more deadly violence. To make this second argument we construct a narrative of schoolyards that exceed their boundedness, and a narrative of violence that promotes its multiplicity. We assume that schoolyards are not containers of youth activities but are primarily a set of social and spatial relationships. The politics of the event of schoolyard violence begs the question of just how social relations turn up in schoolyards, how relations of power are solidified on the ground and made as real as the space that encapsulates them and gives them form. Schoolyard rules, prescribed activities, territories, dress codes, and buffer zones very much prescribe a normative description of how things ought to be under a neoliberal model of education rather than the way they are in actuality.

To help focus this notion of power and space, we bring to bear the weight of a relatively new understanding of geographies of violence. We outline in the next section a definition and conceptual understanding of violence that takes hold of the spatial aspects of the problem. In so doing, we weave perspectives from sociology, education, psychology, and anthropology, having each turn into, around, and through space and spatiality. Our argument is that there is nothing in our social, psychological, political, and cultural world that is not also spatial, and there is nothing in our spatial world that is not also social, psychological, political, and cultural. This premise enables us to look briefly at schoolyard violence from implicit, structural, and cultural perspectives before elaborating on how schoolyard violence can be understood from a relational perspective that is less likely to demonize students and that unties from identity politics the notion of violence as a monolithic event perpetrated by particular people and groups. We begin by considering the schoolyard as a moral space.

Schoolyards as Moral Spaces

The existence of playgrounds or schoolyards attached to a school building has been part of educational environments since at least the 18th century. In 1799, Robert Owen erected a "new educational institution" as part of New Lanark, his experiment for a planned industrial village. At this time, the village housed 2,500 people and hosted the biggest cotton mill in Scotland. Owen attracted worldwide attention by the gradual introduction of his Utopian moral, social, and spatial experiment. As part of that experiment, the educational institution was placed contiguous to the main mill, and an enclosed play area was laid out at its front:

> The area is intended for a playground for the children of the villagers, from the time they can walk alone until they enter the school. . . . As the happiness of man chiefly, if not altogether, depends on his own sentiments and habits, as well as those of individuals around him; and as any sentiments and habits may be given to all infants, it becomes of primary importance that those alone should be given to them which can contribute to their happiness. Each child therefore, on his entrance into the playground, is to be told in language which he can understand "he is never to injure his playfellows, but on the contrary he is to contribute all his power to make them happy." This simple precept, when comprehended in all its bearings, and the habits which will arise from its early adoption into practice, if no counteracting principles shall be forced on the young mind, will effectually supersede all the errors which have hitherto kept the world in ignorance and misery. (Owen, 1816/1972, 81)

Of course, much of Owen's perspective on education may be found, in more sophisticated form, with Jean-Jacques Rousseau's *Émile* (1762/1962), which depicts children as angels rather than demons and argues that they are a tabula rasa upon which society can write and instruct. Owen's writing, however, emanates from the practicalities of the new industrial system and is an important attempt to dissolve the emerging geographic separation of the public and the private that continues today unabated. These are compelling reasons to connect young people to adults and productive activities that are beyond the purview of this essay (cf. Aitken 2001; Aitken, Estrada, Jennings, & Aguirre, 2006; Jennings, Aitken, Estrada, & Fernandez, 2006), but it is also important to recognize in Owen's writing a set of beliefs about children's moral behavior that carries over to how the spaces of their play were designed at least through the 19th century (cf. Stow, 1839, cited in Thomson, 2005). Things began to change in the early 20th century, when the moral imperative also incorporated concerns about health and fitness, and playgrounds became spaces for drilling and marching exercises (Mero, 1908).

The spatial contiguity of Owen's cotton mill and his new educational institution is also worth considering in terms of the dissolution and segregation of public and private spaces. Tom Loveless (1998) argues that universal education began as a means of controlling young people who recently had been released from the world of adult work by a series of Factory Acts, which were put in place about 50 years after Owen's social experiment moved to the planned community of Harmony, Indiana, in the United States and ultimately failed. In addition to their exclusion from the factory floor, young people in North America and Europe were less likely at this time to be taken on as apprentices or child servants (Tyner 2011). With rapid industrialization, public schools were created as part of the sphere of reproduction, as means to producing a well-disciplined and educated labor force. The societal power to discipline is important here because otherwise there was the threat of masses of idle young people roaming wild in the streets. In opposition to the Rousseauvian ideas of children as angels, the ideas of wild and unruly children who require discipline go back in the United States to the puritanical ideas of Cotton Mather, who, through a series of pamphlets in the early 17th century, argued the need to whip the devil out of young people. Written 150 years before Owen's moral experiment with playgrounds and happy children, Mather's work was cited as cause for the obligatory schooling system established in Massachusetts in 1647. Specifically, universal education was seen as a means of destroying (thrashing out) that part of a child's personality that was afflicted by original sin, but it was also about separating children from the adult patriarchal world of work.

By the end of the 19th century, Jacob Riis's *How the Other Half Lives* (1890) added a class and racial dimension to an evolving story that demonizes and segregates youths. Whether crime and poverty existed in threatening proportions at this time is irrelevant to the fact that middle-class people were convinced by Riis's rhetoric and representations of inner-city youths to the extent that they felt that society's social fabric would unravel unless so-called delinquent adolescents (a recently coined term) from immigrant and the lower classes were disciplined more fully. Universal schooling provided a morally upstanding solution to the problem. The pioneering psychologist and educator G. Stanley Hall forwarded theories of recapitulation, which argued that children can be socialized out of their wild ways to better serve society. Tied to a belief that young people were by nature instinct driven, Hall argued that the individual is dissolved into a collective that exhibits all the traits of evolution, including, during the teenage years, being drawn into tribes or gangs. He characterized preadolescent children as savages, arguing that reasoning with them was a waste of time. Hall claimed that child development recapitulates the history of human evolutionary development, and that the wild and gang instincts could be civilized out of young people through educational institutions. As Tyner (2011) correctly noted, public schools were built on the belief that the schools could rehabilitate children and adolescents who were delinquent.

Following Hall and later Piaget, 20th-century public education was predicated on the notion that children must follow a normalized sequence of development. Valerie Walkerdine (1984, 1988) locates public education within a child-centered pedagogy and a set of social and spatial educational practices that constitute not only a mode of observation and surveillance but also the production of a certain kind of child (Aitken and Herman, 1997, p. 68). By looking, among other things, at the ways elementary classrooms and playground in the United Kingdom are laid out, Walkerdine notes a relation between spatial relations and educational practices. At the risk of oversimplifying the complex connections Walkerdine makes between theory and practice, her analysis suggests that the acceptance of developmental theories in educational institutions results in an inability to deal with the practical and complex contexts of children's lives on the one hand, and an inadequate understanding of the multiple ways that children learn on the other. The notion of the monolithic child, traversing a linear set of developmental stages, does violence to multiple and nonlinear modes of learning and creating identity. It also suggests that zero-tolerance policies and one-size-fits-all dictates constrict not only how we understand children but also how we understand violent events.

Sarah Thomson (2005, p. 64) argues that playgrounds today are more likely to be "segmented, delimited and customized according to teachers' and others' mandates about children's spatiality." Using insightful methods of auto-photography and records of perceived intervention, she demonstrates that although primary school children in the United Kingdom see their playgrounds as child focused, they are, in actuality, a space conceived by adults to contain children through prescriptive patterns of usage. An important insight from Thomson's work is that despite well-meaning intentions, rules and regulations set up problematic tensions. Contemporary school playgrounds localize and place students, and they "do nothing to encourage resourcefulness, risk competency and freedom of movement" (Thomson, 2005, p. 67). Space is used to mold compliant pupils by teaching them what is acceptable and what is deviant. Over the years, Owen's moral imperative to "make them happy" has dissolved into a larger concern for keeping young people safe and controlling potentially violent interactions.

Rethinking Spaces of Violence

Definitions of violence vary. For example, the term "violence" may refer to a number of different behaviors. Yet by speaking of violence as violence, we imply that it is one thing. Through that one word all the forms and manifestations of violence are said to represent the same social phenomenon.

Violence, as it actually becomes visible in real-life situations, is about the intertwining of the human emotions of fear, anger, and excitement in ways that run against the conventional morality of normal situations (Collins, 2008, p. 4).

Defining the scale of violent acts and the spaces through which they are perpetrated is central to our discussion. We take as a starting point the idea that violence, like childhood, is not a monolithic idea and can be viewed from different affective angles. Moreover and importantly for what we argue later, the multiplicities of violence are not reducible to particular identities or bodies, as their dimensionality constantly shifts (Aitken, 2006, p. 503). As a result of such movements, violence is decentered and enters into new relations with itself and others. It cannot be contained by schoolyard fences or zero-tolerance policies. That said, Dupper and Meyer-Adams (2002) come closest to situating a complex intertwining of space and scale when they suggest that violence, at least at the level of the schoolyard, is complicated by scale and intensity. They suggest, at a first instance, that violence is encountered and enacted at a high or a low level. The former, they suggest, is indicative of the most violent and intense acts, including murder, rape, sexual assault, and weapon possession. Low-level violence, on the other hand, is related to less overtly violent behaviors, "such as bullying, peer sexual harassment, victimization . . . and the psychological maltreatment of students" (Dupper and Meyer-Adams, 2002, p. 351). They argue appropriately that the underlying problems associated with low-level enactments are the most common forms of school violence today, despite the prevalence of media and policy attention on high-level violence and school security initiatives. Problematically, schoolyard shootings, and other dramatic and tragic events, evoke strong public outcries that push for policy solutions based on zero-tolerance and more space-related security.[3] While different theories engage with both high-level and low-level forms of violence, the priority of most school violence studies in recent years is low level, which is a reversal from previous years when gun violence took precedence.

In what follows, we suggest that most contemporary studies of schoolyard violence can be grouped into four broadly defined and mutually constitutive categories: (1) schoolyard violence as implicit, (2) schoolyard violence as cultural, (3) schoolyard violence as structural, and (4) schoolyard violence as relational. These ideas about violence also frame the complexities around which a discussion of who participates in violent activities, as well as where and why these activities occur, finds form. Approaches to understanding violence range from practical attempts to "stop bullying" to theoretical attempts to understand how to defuse violent interactions before they can develop.

In what follows, we look at each of these categories in turn with the admonition that they are not mutually exclusive and that understanding often flows from a simplistic view of aggression to one that is more complex in terms of space and scale, and that it considers the multiple conditions that enable violent interactions to take place.

Schoolyard Violence as Implicit

Some researchers studying violence in the context of young people and schoolyards do not attempt to explain why violent behavior occurs, but rather they set out to define a small part of violent behavior, like bullying, or they reify stereotypes and misconceptions about bullying and bullies (like terrorism and terrorists) by ascribing the identities of "bully" and "victim" to different individuals based on the so-called facts of particular situations. Profiling of potential perpetrators is problematic and often comes from surprising sources. After the 1999 Columbine shootings, for example, the U.S. surgeon general published a report based upon a logit regression analysis identifying predominant "risk factors," including as the first three variables general delinquency, substance abuse, and being male. Aitken and Marchant (2003) address the culture of fear around youth violence that unfairly targets boys from Middle America. They elaborate sexist, classist, and racist biases in reporting, and academic culpabilities in stereotyping perpetrators, victims, and the spaces of violence. Using the case of the murder by stabbing of a girl by another girl from a high school in Santa Monica, California, they show how certain forms of violence are dismissed or covered up, and how moral panics are often misplaced. That the murder occurred at a party in an affluent part of Westwood where students from the high school were gathered does not detract from the schoolyard events in Santa Monica that set the stage for the violence. Contrasting this event with the contemporaneous and highly publicized Santana schoolyard shootings in El Cajon, Aitken and Marchant (2003, p. 162) point out that the dual tendency to vilify and ignore speaks to a highly equivocal reaction to youth violence that greatly depends on where it occurs on the one hand, and on defining the perpetrators and the victims on the other.[4]

Another problematic geographic blindness is toward the often endemic violence in inner-city public schools. Unfortunately, high-profile shootings by boys in middle-class suburbia often hide a more insidious problem of violence in high-density public schools, such as beatings, stabbings, and gang- and class-related violence. African American, Asian, and Latino youth violence is usually gang- or class-related or caused by personal disputes at schools, but these mostly inner-city minority crimes rarely warrant front-page news.

Profiling around mass schoolyard shootings leaves little room for understanding why bullying occurs, and as a consequence this taken-for-granted context of violence can only be approached from the position of intervention (e.g., Benbenishty, Astor, & Estrada, 2008; Small & Tetrick, 2001). Intervention in this sense is problematic because prescriptions for solving violent activity are focused primarily on increasing security at schools and eliminating opportunities for violence. A weakness of strategies related to the zero-tolerance approach, for example, is that all violent acts are generally treated equally—there are few if any distinctions between people who are likely to commit school shootings and those who often fight with their classmates. While this approach can be beneficial because it addresses real-life situations, it is myopic and potentially harmful for coming to grips with the mysteries of violence in the long term. It fails to address the primary problems that relate to the complex forces that drive violent behaviors and circumstances. When this approach is related to studies that find violence to be associated with distinct populations or identity groups, then it begins to gain problematic racist tones.

Schoolyard Violence as Cultural

As suggested above, many studies of violence cite evidence that the most violent individuals are young males who, because of a particular set of circumstances (e.g., a broken home, poverty, living in Middle America, belonging to a certain ethnicity, growing up urban, etc.), are driven to join violent groups and/or engage in violent behavior. In this way, violence is explained as part of a cultural context, which can be expressed in terms of one identity group or another (see O'Connell, Pepler, & Craig, 1999). While this research may be relevant for elaborating a certain subsection of violent activity and is potent input to simplistic regression analyses, it suffers from the same inherent short-sightedness that bedevils research taking violence for granted. It may not label situations simply in terms of a bully/victim dynamic, but it does take a similar approach to solving problems of violence, which lies in a desire to intervene in the lives of troubled youths. Again, this type of intervention is problematic because it relies on profiling and identifying certain populations based on a set of assumptions, instead of looking more deeply into the social and spatial complexities that create the conditions for violence. In addition, although complexity sometimes shows up in, for example, the distinction between high-level and low-level violence, because of the way it attempts to identify problem cases, the intervention primarily focuses on violence, as if lower forms of violence like bullying are always a gateway to other types of assault. Approaches such as zero-tolerance once again seem appropriate. For example, Leary and colleagues (2003) focus on the likelihood of one-on-one schoolyard bullying resulting in higher-level forms of violence. While it is possible that this type of profiling may be successful, the danger lies in the reification of certain kinds of violence being stereotypically connected to certain kinds of individuals. Also, a successful intervention of this strategy at the local level (e.g., one particular school) has the potential to obscure the understanding of violence at a larger scale (e.g., at the city or national levels). This is also important to point out because school violence is often thought of as a phenomenon local to the United States, but in reality it is a societal feature of many countries across the world.

Schoolyard Violence as Structural

Discussion of schoolyards creates a particular environmental context. Violent-events research studying "schoolyards" focuses less on particular populations of students or on ideals of violence and more on the specific conditions leading to those events. Some of the issues considered when examining the structural nature of school violence include the relationships between students and teachers, and students and their peers; the classroom and schoolyard setting; the makeup of the socioeconomic conditions of the neighborhood; and the institutional functions of the school itself (e.g., the disciplining of youths). These myriad issues are also reflected in ecological models, which explore how violence is transmitted across different levels within a particular social structure from the community to the individual (Dresler-Hawke & Whitehead, 2009). While there is some overlap between cultural and structural studies of school violence, what primarily differentiates the two is the notion that the school already manifests the conditions for violent acts, given the inherent problems in the power structures in place. One of these problems, as Noguera (1995, p. 194) points out, is the "routinization of every aspect of life" similar to that of other controlling institutions like the asylum or prison. Tyner (2011) goes further, arguing that schools are effectively jails and militarized zones where children learn violence, while Thomson (2005, p. 77) notes that primary school children "perimeter walk" playgrounds and play games about "jails" and "gaolers."

LeFebvre (1991) famously notes that the production of space—how it is designed, manufactured, and imagined—is also about the production of rules. Young people learn rules in myriad ways: which chair to sit on, how to approach a teacher, which part of the playground is safe and which should be avoided, when and where to use a mobile phone. The production of space is about disciplining young minds and bodies (see Aitken & Jennings, 2004). The production of space, then, is about power relations. The dominant power in a school institution, wielded by faculty members, counselors, and custodial staff, set them apart from the students, and when punishment or attention is distributed unevenly among the students, certain problems can arise between different students. Although power is often linked to force or violence in a hierarchical sense, a Foucauldian perspective understands power "as something that circulates, or rather as something which only functions in the form of a chain. It is never localized here or there, never in anybody's hands, never appropriated as a commodity" (Foucault, 1980, p. 98). The important point that is the crux of our argument in this chapter is that questions of schoolyard violence do not revolve around the idea of who has power over people and places, but rather who has power to do certain things in certain places at certain times. This understanding requires us to think of violence as an event. The critical questions of violence as events are not about why violence occurs in schoolyards but are rather about why certain actors continue to perpetrate violent behaviors in, through, and around schoolyards. Questions of this kind refocus attention on dominant actors or institutions as a means of illustrating social practices and relations.

Because of unequal power relations in the hierarchy of faculty to students and the expectations for security and concerns of the community, schools are able to pass zero-tolerance policies and thereby treat all violence equally. Unlike implicit and cultural approaches, structural approaches to school violence critique zero-tolerance policies in cases where certain low-level violent activities and student misconducts are treated in the same way as more violent behaviors. Noguera (1995, pp. 200–201), for example, argues that a structural critique points to fear that an overreaction to school violence only perpetuates the problem and that "alternative ways of responding to violent, or potentially violent, behavior would necessarily require a fundamental change in how the institution . . . were conceptualized by those in authority."

It should be noted, however, that while structural approaches explain violence based on the environmental and institutional conditions that shape the schoolyard, they offer a simplistic conceptualization of why violence occurs. That is to say, instead of accepting violence as taken-for-granted or located within a specific culture, a structural critique of violence is still understood as a singular problem. Despite this, structural theories of school violence ultimately bring us to a more complex way of thinking through violent events. The key use of the word "event" here is important because, as we discuss below, relational approaches to violence take into consideration a fuller array of factors that create the opportunities for violence to occur.

Schoolyard Violence as a Relational Event

Rather than focusing on a particular population or an environment, a relational perspective is concerned with how a specific set of conditions arises where an individual or a group of individuals are thrown together in a context out of which violence emerges. Whether high-level or low-level violence occurs is a less important distinction because relational perspectives attempt to embrace the total complexity of a particular event. Doreen Massey (2005, pp. 149–152) describes thrown togetherness as "the politics of the event of place. . . . [Places] pose in particular form the question of our living together."

Schoolyards are, in many ways, primarily a set of relationships. The politics of the event of schoolyard violence begs the question of just how social relations turn up in schoolyards, how relations of power are solidified on the ground and made as real as the space that encapsulates them and gives them form. The question of violent schoolyard events rests, then, with how institutions (legislators, police, parks and recreation boards, school boards, custodial services, families) and individuals connect, given that they are thrown together with baggage (racism, sexism, substance abuse, and so forth) from elsewhere and a predisposition to act. Schoolyards also exist in relation to other properties: parks, classrooms, liquor stores, junkyards. Their influence goes beyond their boundaries, as students leave to enter classes or walk home. Violent events, then, are material, geographic, and comprised of myriad complex relations between youths, adults, institutions, and places.

A key figure in relational work on schoolyard violence is Randall Collins (2008, p. 3), who dismisses the notion of violent individuals by suggesting that "even people that we think of as very violent—because they have been violent in more than one situation, or spectacularly violent on some occasion—are violent only in very particular situations." This may be more indicative of cases of high-level violence because of infrequency in occurrence, but it can also explain low-level behaviors like harassment and bullying. While bullying can seem to be a more pervasive (read: inherent, cultural, or structural) problem, especially in light of the constant connections students have with their peers because of social networking, it is nonetheless necessarily prescribed by a set of relations that precipitate a violent event. For example, although there are cases where students have maintained a consistent "attack" on a classmate via mobile phones or through Internet chat, the primary form of bullying occurs somewhere at school. Because there is a certain geography—a social setting and a physical location—to bullying, it is necessarily a relational problem involving youths and a physical context, such as a schoolyard. That is, two or more people engage in a violent act in a particular place.

Collins (2008, p. 8) explains the relations that precipitate "violence [a]s a set of pathways around confrontational tension and fear." In other words, violence is a series of emotions and circumstances, which play out between different individuals or groups of individuals and ultimately result in a confrontation that is mutual or one-sided. Even if we ascribe the labels "bully" and "victim" to these individuals, both have equal parts in the violent event because "[s]uccessful violence battens on confrontational tension/fear as one side appropriates the emotional rhythm as dominator and the other gets caught in it as victim" (Collins, 2008, 19). Hence, while there is a buildup to (and a letdown from) violence, violent events as relational moments are usually very brief, taking the form of a physical altercation or verbal assault. This is an important distinction because the most commonly accepted definition of bullying as a form of violence states that it must be a continuous process of physical or psychological harassment over an extended period of time (Dresler-Hawke & Whitehead, 2009; Dupper & Meyer-Addams, 2002; O'Connell, Pepler, & Craig, 1999). If we understand violence as a relational and discontinuous set of events, then bullying is prescribed as less linear and cumulative. We make this argument not to ignore or demean the problems created by bullying behaviors, but because we think it is important to stop thinking of, and treating it, like other types of violence.

Schoolyard bullying as defined in the studies above comes across as either an inherent problem within a particular culture or within a school structure and thus can only be diagnosed as a "global" phenomenon within the school setting. In other words, bullying can only be treated like a disease in a system where only the most stringent and universal policies can eliminate it. Slogans like "stop bullying now" or zero-tolerance policies punish all misconduct and do little to solve the problems that perpetrate violent events because they ultimately ignore, as relational events, the situations and places where bullying first occurs. If we analyze bullying behaviors in terms of violent moments or events, we more effectively determine the nuanced relations that precipitate the problem, and we are less likely to stereotype the individual. For example, if a group of students is harassing an individual student, a policy that approaches each moment of harassment as a violent event may have a more likely chance of success than would labeling a particular student or group of students as violent. On the other hand, if we wait for a pattern to emerge where one group of students becomes bullies and another group of students becomes victims, then the problem can only be treated retroactively. Hence, we have resorted back to the original proposition where bullying is only violence once it has fulfilled the necessary conditions of a group enacting a violent act on an individual or group of individuals. By this point, it may be too late in the process to understand or defuse the problem. While bullying is only one example of school violence that must be reconsidered in terms of a relational approach, it is perhaps the most salient because it is the most commonly associated form of violence on the schoolyard or playground, whatever the age of the population of students. Certainly, bullying and other low-level violent behaviors like fighting occur everywhere within the context of the school, but the fundamental characteristics that bring children to the schoolyard (e.g., recess, physical education, after-school activity, etc.) necessarily precipitate an increased opportunity for violence. In this way, the schoolyard's sociospatial properties become intertwined with other places in and out of the school context, and a more explicit geographical approach to understanding violent interactions can perhaps facilitate the way we think about schoolyard violence.

The Complex Schoolyard Geographies of Violent Events

Violent events on schoolyards may result from complex relations presupposing seemingly endless numbers and types of activities that students engage in with peers, adults, and the nonhuman (computers, walls, gates, garbage bins, trees and other plants). This complexity notwithstanding, and in terms that resonate with Massey's politics of the event of place, Tyner (2011) argues that "power to violence" can be understood in terms of "place-as-disciplined" space, and as such, schoolyards provide a very important venue for understanding violence as a social and spatial practice. He points out that from a very early age we are socialized into a recognition and an understanding of the appropriate use of space, and who has access and rights within particular spaces. Tyner goes on to evoke David Sibley's (1995) rendering of geographies of exclusion, wherein with any given situation and at any given place, the presence of certain bodies (including nonhuman bodies), as well as specific behaviors and representations, are deemed acceptable or not. Shopping malls are appropriate places for most adult consumers, but people who tend to loiter and not spend money, like groups of teenagers and vagrants, have restricted or no access to them. Today's schoolyards are secured for enrolled students, teachers, and those who are registered with the school. In most U.S. schools, no unregistered person, including parents and siblings, are allowed on schoolyards, whether children are present or not. Many facilities, particularly in inner-city neighborhoods, are locked down at all times, while some are opened to community use after (and sometimes during) school hours. These security practices extend beyond the schoolyard with buffer zones that exclude liquor stores, pornographic representations, and registered sex-offenders.

The microgeography of schoolyard violence is perhaps most closely associated with the sociospatial practices of inclusion and exclusion. Inclusionary violence, while still a very negative consequence of schoolyard activity, is not always a dangerous or an unproductive form of violence. In many ways, inclusionary violence fosters the type of relationships understood by geographer Yi-fu Tuan as relationships of "dominance" and "affection." Exclusionary violence, on the other hand, is the type of low-level violence most commonly interpreted as bullying, which when paired with territory creates the possibilities for certain people and practices to be considered "out of place" (Cresswell, 1996). Although the words inclusion and violence do not invite similar connotations, they are nonetheless often linked with a certain tacit recognition. For example, if we think of boxing matches, hockey fights, fraternity hazing, or even political debates, the inclusionary nature of violent relational events is evident. In the case of the schoolyard, a basic example of this is seen in the occasional emotional overflow that leads to bickering, or mutual fighting, over the possession of something like a toy or a ball. The point is that inclusive violence can spontaneously erupt from sport, recreation, and other types of play. This is primarily because, in many of the interactions within the contexts of "play," a hierarchy emerges based on the capabilities of the individuals in a group, but for the interaction of the play to continue and the hierarchy to persist, all the members of the group must continue to participate. Take, for instance, the infamous notion of someone "picked last"; while this kind of bullying can be psychologically and emotionally damaging, the fact of being included in the game at all sets up a dynamic where an individual is both disempowered and shown affection. As Tuan (1984, p. 164) notes in the context of children's play, "This power to dominate another—including the power to inflict pain and humiliation on another—is vaguely pleasurable. And yet there is also deep attachment." This attachment, he notes, is because objects (like toys) and other subjects (e.g., peers) are extensions of the child: "They are his possessions; their worth reflects his worth; praise for them is praise for him." Many children's schoolyard experiences are forged within this dominant, and yet often affectionate, relationship. Other forms of this type of relationship include the archetypical example of the bully's lackey, the sycophantic relationship between members of a clique, or a spontaneous verbal argument about the rules of a game. Much inclusionary violence is benign, although there are certainly larger cultural issues of concern for the ways this violence is institutionalized into adulthood. Still, schoolyard violence by and large only becomes really problematic when it involves the control of space.

Tim Cresswell (1996, p. 3) argues that the word "place" turns up as part of the daily vernacular because we are socialized into understanding that "[s]omething or someone *belongs* in one place and not another." The idea of belonging to a particular place necessarily creates the potential for violent interaction. This is especially true in conceptualizing the schoolyard in terms of its many microgeographies. When a particular group occupies a certain place on the schoolyard, they may set the conditions for use of that space despite state and school regulations. When the individuals using that space come into conflict with the rules of that space, belonging can result in exclusionary practices, which may or may not result in violence. On the schoolyard, exclusionary violence can be as basic as verbal warnings or as dangerous as perpetual bullying to keep someone off a group's "turf." Bullying, in the context of exclusionary violence, is very different from the type of bullying that occurs during moments of inclusion. Inclusive bullying is the relationship between the bully and those within the hierarchy, which therefore puts them "in place," whereas exclusionary bullying occurs between a bully and an outside source. In this situation, exclusion from a place results in the objectification of an individual; he or she literally becomes an object of torment for the bully. This can perhaps be best understood if we look more closely at an example of the microgeographic politics of the schoolyard.

Mary Thomas (2009, 2011) focuses on what she calls "misplacement" in a Los Angeles high school schoolyard's segregated territories of racial-ethnic difference. The violent event that her 2011 book turns upon is a so-called race riot involving Latino and Armenian boys in the school, when several hundred students fought until police arrived in riot gear and locked down the school. Thomas's focus is on the school's teen girls and the ways in which their subjectivities surround the event of the riot but also exceed their bodies of difference. The girls who were part of her ethnography understood well the "borderline" that divided the "pretty people" (high-income groups) from "gangsters" (poorer Hispanic students) and Armenians. On the day of the riot, this was the line where students gathered to hurl whatever objects they could find or had (trash cans, milk cartons, golf balls).

Thomas followed 26 young women and their feelings and behaviors around the riot, school spaces, sexuality, shopping malls, immigration, families, and home spaces before returning to the riot and the ways it was implicated with and through campus space. The study is relational to the extent that it explores the complex and conflicting relations leading up to and in the aftermath of a violent event. On the schoolyard, the girls expressed discomfort and pain when their racialized bodies entered into the "wrong" segregated territory and were met with stares, racial epithets, or silence, each of which can be characterized as a violent act. In an important sense that echoes the performative work of Judith Butler (1990, 1993), these feelings of discomfort and pain, argues Thomas, indicate the girls' failure to be fully captured by the categories that mark them. On the schoolyard, she goes on to note, the spatiality of the social-racial body is experienced acutely: "as part of the pressures to conform and solidify identification in their teen years, the girls also reproduce racial-ethnic identification and segregation by accepting and often reproducing the same categorizations of difference that pain them" (Thomas, 2009, p. 8). Thomas's work is liberating in the sense that it relieves girls from the "impossible responsibility" (2011, p. 10) of undoing institutionalized and discursive political identities through empowerment and agency (e.g., "girl power"). She creates a psycho-geographic, postfeminist reading of racialized and sexualized urban spaces that pivot around the schoolyard. Drawing theoretically from psychology (Laplanche and Freud) and identity politics (Butler), Thomas challenges contemporary feminists, psychologists, and policy makers to unburden young women (and men) from the huge responsibility of creating a self that is empowered and engaged. Her point is that although academics interested in identity politics insist that the practices of young subjects are always embodied, these girls' narratives may also indicate the failure of embodiment to fully represent the subject: "The 'uncomfortable' awkwardness of being in the wrong racial territory," Thomas (2009, p. 17) argues, "marks how complexly the social body is taken up." Her work on, around, and beyond the schoolyard suggests that boundaries—of bodies or places—and violent events are fluid, intersubjective, and multispatial. This comes together on the schoolyard where the girls' depictions of their bodies in "other" territories "point to the intersubjective, spatial negotiations at the heart of coming to terms with social relations, norms and differences" (Thomas, 2009, p. 17). There is an inclusivity and exteriority to understanding political embodiment as a precursor to violent events.

Moreover, and importantly, Thomas's girls are not fully and fundamentally invested in social and spatial categories of difference: "They shrug and leave the territories of their 'friends,' they live segregated lives, and they claim ethnic-racial identities smoothly and without irony in their self-descriptions and through their casual marking of others' racial-ethnic identifiers" (Thomas, 2009, p. 18). Political identities always exceed the spaces of their demarcation.

A Concluding Comment

Contemporary geographers no longer think of space as merely a container of activities. Space, rather, is all around us. We occupy it, but we also move through it and are changed by, and simultaneously change, it. Indeed, space is not an "it" but an active participant in co-creating our world. As a consequence, we do not think of the schoolyard as a container of young people's activities for certain periods of time, but rather as a site of flows, intensities, and capacities that are hugely important for the relations between young people, adults, and the non-human (bricks, fences, bells, mobile phones).

Lefebvre (1991) famously argues that any social order or moral imperative "excretes" space. Space and social relations are produced out of the relations that comprise everyday life, and as such, space and social practices are mutually co-created. Iris Marion Young (1990, p. 62) connects violence to social practices, which Tyner (2011) interprets in terms of its routine and everyday occurrences. Importantly, he goes on to note, violence is a spatial as well as a social practice. It occurs in particular places at particular times to particular people. He argues that violent acts are naturalized and normalized in today's schoolyards to the extent that we pay them less attention than they deserve.

With this chapter, we describe the complex coproduction of social practices and schoolyard spaces that foments the possibility of violent events. Understanding schoolyards as moral spaces opens a critique of violence as inherent, cultural, or structural. It leads to rethinking schoolyards and violence as relational events comprising a multiplicity of affects rather than the acts of particular (disturbed) individuals or gangs. By looking at violent events this way, the politics of the schoolyard is not foreclosed upon, and solutions do not reside in spatial containment (lockdowns) or zero-tolerance, one-size-fits-all determinations. All societies and social orders excrete laws and regulations, which produce space. Laws and regulations are problematic when they become mechanistic and do not accommodate difference. When schoolyards epitomize mechanistic regulations designed to contain children, keep them safe, and avoid litigation, they foreclose upon creativity, innovation, and a politics of everyday living and growing into the world.

Notes

1. After the infamous 1999 Columbine shooting, Los Angeles journalist Mike Males (2001, p. M1) pointed out that "of the 150,000 Americans murdered by gunfire in the last decade, perhaps 150 were killed in or around a school, and only a fraction were White youths. If the U.S.'s overall murder rate was as low as that in high schools, America would be as safe as Sweden."

2. This perspective may be changing. On October 1, 2010, a series of lawsuits was filed by families in Owen Sound, Ontario, Canada, accusing the school board of failing to protect students from abuse, including bullying and taunting by other students and teachers (Nguyen 2010).

3. After the 1999 Columbine shooting, myriad entrepreneurial companies found niche markets for products such as metal detectors and threat-assessment systems.

4. In the wake of criticism about profiling, Dedman (2000) interviewed U.S. Secret Service investigators, who suggested that alienation or persecution drove children to violence. The Secret Service urged adults, instead of looking for traits, to ask about what children say, to understand their grievances and what their friends know, and to assess whether they are depressed.

References

Aitken, S. C. (2001). *Geographies of young people: The morally contested spaces of identity.* London and New York: Routledge.

Aitken, S. C. (2006). Leading men to violence and creating spaces for their emotions. *Gender, Place and Culture, 13,* 491–507.

Aitken, S., Estrada, S., Jennings, J., & Aguirre, L. (2006). Reproducing life and labor: Global processes and working children in Tijuana. *Childhood, 13,* 365–367.

Aitken, S. C., & Herman, T. (1997). Gender, power and crib geography: From transitional spaces to potential places. *Gender, Place and Culture: A Journal of Feminist Geography, 4,* 63–88.

Aitken, S. C., & Jennings, J. (2004). Clarity, rights and children's spaces of discipline. In R. Transit (Ed.), *Disciplining the child via the discourse of the professions* (pp. 130–155). Springfield, IL: Charles C. Thomas.

Aitken, S. C., & Marchant, R. (2003). Memories and miscreants: Tales of teenage terror in America. *Children's Geographies, 1,* 151–164.

Akiba, M., LeTendre, G., Baker, D., & Gosling, B. (2002). Student victimization: National and school system effects on school violence in 37 nations. *American Educational Research Journal, 39,* 829–853.

Benbenishty, R., Astor, R., & Estrada, J. (2008). School violence assessment: A conceptual framework, instruments, and methods. *Children and Schools, 30,* 71–81.

Butler, J. (1990). *Gender trouble: Feminism and the subversion of identity.* New York: Routledge.

Butler, J. (1993). *Bodies that matter: On the discursive limits of "sex".* New York: Routledge.

Collins, R. (2008). *Violence: A micro-sociological theory.* Princeton, NJ: Princeton University Press.

Cresswell, T. (1996). *In place/out of place: Geography, ideology, and transgression.* Minneapolis: University of Minnesota Press.

Dedman, B. (2000). Deadly lessons: School shooters tell why. *Chicago Sun-Times,* October 15–16.

Dresler-Hawke, E., & Whitehead, D. (2009). The behavior ecological model as a framework for school-based, anti-bullying health promotion interventions. *The Journal of School Nursing 25,* 195–204.

Dupper, D. R., & Meyer-Adams, N. (2002). Low-level violence: A neglected aspect of school culture. *Urban Education, 37,* 350–364.

Foucault, M. (1980). Two lectures. In C. Gordon (Ed.), *Power/knowledge: Selected interviews and other writings, 1972–1977* (pp. 78–108). Sussex, UK: Harvester.

Glassner, B. (1999). *The ecology of fear: Why Americans are afraid of the wrong things.* New York: Perseus Books.

Jennings, J., Aitken, S., Estrada, S., & Fernandez, A. (2006). Learning and earning: Relational scales of children's work, *Area, 38,* 231–240.

Leary, M. R., Kowalski, R., Smith, L., & Phillips, S. (2003). Teasing, rejection, and violence: Case studies of the school shootings. *Aggressive Behavior, 29,* 202–214.

LeFebvre, H. (1991). *The production of space* (Donald Nicholson Smith, Trans.). Oxford, UK: Blackwell.

Loveless, T. (1998). Uneasy allies: The evolving relationship of school and state. *Education Evaluation and Policy Analysis, 20,* 1–8.

Males, M. (2001, March 11). The real story left untold. *Los Angeles Times,* pp. M1, M6.

Massey, D. (2005). *For space.* London: Sage.

Mero, E. (1908). *American playgrounds: Their construction, equipment, maintenance and utility.* Boston: American Gymnasia Co.

Muschert, G. (2007). Research in school shootings. *Social Compass, 1,* 60–80.

Nguyen, L. (2010, October 2). Families seeking $35 million in bullying lawsuits. *Vancouver Sun,* p. B-2.

Noguera, P. A. (1995). Preventing and producing violence: A critical analysis of responses to school violence. *Harvard Educational Review, 65,* 189–212.

O'Connell, P., Pepler, D., & Craig, W. (1999). Peer involvement in bullying: Insights and challenges for intervention. *Journal of Adolescence, 22,* 437–452.

Owen, R. (1816/1972). *A new view of society.* London: Macmillan Press Ltd.

Reiss, A., & Roth, J. (Eds.). (1993). *Understanding and preventing violence.* Washington, DC: National Academy Press.

Riis, J. (1890). *How the other half lives.* New York: Charles Scribner and Sons.

Rousseau, J. (1762/1962). *The Émile of Jean-Jacques Rousseau: Selections.* (William Boyd, Ed. & Trans.). New York: Columbia University Press.

Sibley, D. (1995). *Geographies of exclusion.* New York: Routledge.

Small, M., & Tetrick, K. (2001). School violence: An overview. *Juvenile Justice Journal, VIII,* 1–10. Retrieved from http://www.ncjrs.gov/html/ojjdp/jjjournal_2001_6/jj1.html.

Stow, D. (1839). *National education. Supplement to moral training and the training system with plans for erecting and fitting up of training schools.* Glasgow: W. R. M'Phun.

Thomas, M. (2009). The identity politics of school life: Territoriality and the racial subjectivity of teen girls in LA. *Children's Geographies, 7,* 7–21.

Thomas, M. (2011). *Unheroic girlhood.* Philadelphia, PA: Temple University Press.

Thomson, S. (2005). Territorializing the primary school playground: Deconstructing the geography of playtime. *Children's Geographies, 3,* 63–79.

Tuan, Y. F. (1984). *Dominance and affection: The making of pets.* New Haven, CT: Yale University Press.

Tyner, J. (2011). *Space, place and violence.* New York: Routledge.

Walkerdine, V. (1984). Developmental psychology and the child-centered pedagogy: The insertion of Piaget into early education. In J. Enriques, W. Hollway, C. Urwin, C. Venn, & V. Walkerdine (Eds.), *Changing the subject: Psychology, social regulation and subjectivity* (pp. 153–202). New York: Methuen.

Walkerdine, V. (1988). *The mastery of reason: Cognitive development and the production of rationality.* New York: Routledge.

Weiner, N., Zahn, M., & Sagi, R. (1990). *Violence: Patterns, courses, public policy.* San Diego, CA: Harcourt Brace Jovanovich.

Widom, C. (1989). Does violence beget violence? A critical examination of the literature. *Psychological Bulletin, 106,* 3–28.

Young, I. M. (1990). *Justice and the politics of difference.* Princeton, NJ: Princeton University Press.

CHAPTER SIX

Bullying in Middle School: What Does It Look Like, Why Does It Happen, and Who Does It Hurt?

Christine M. Wienke Totura and Carol MacKinnon-Lewis

On a brisk Colorado morning in late April 1999, 2 young gunmen entered their school and opened fire, killing 13 people and then themselves. The reason for this massacre? In addition to reportedly suffering multiple emotional and psychological problems, the gunmen allegedly struggled for years in a school climate that condoned bullying and victimization (Block, 2007). Eric Harris and Dylan Klebold initiated one of America's most notorious and deadly mass shootings, blowing the research on school violence wide open and forever changing the way the world views bullying as a result. This infamous moment at Columbine High School has served as a marker for how cultures define, anticipate, and deal with the consequences of peer aggression.

Columbine is an extreme case of what could happen if bullying goes unchecked. Although most youths who either perpetrate bullying or are victims of it will not become violent, the pervasive and negative impact of bullying remains a critical issue for researchers, practitioners, and parents alike. Trends in estimates show that bullying occurs at all age levels but tends to peak during early adolescence, ages 11–13 (Scheithauer, Hayer, Petermann, & Jugert, 2006). Therefore, middle school is a particularly prominent time to focus on the emotional and social impact of bullying and victimization. Most studies conducted over the years have demonstrated that exposure to bullying is a significant risk factor to healthy psychological and physical development for youths, as well as to effective school climates (Haynie et al., 2001; Totura, MacKinnon-Lewis et al., 2009). Of particular importance for school districts, is the consistent finding that bullying disrupts the classroom learning environment—victimization has been linked to declines in student academic motivation, grades, and test scores (Schwartz & Gorman, 2003).

Multiple individual and environmental factors influence the frequency of bullying and victimization, as well as the likelihood of youths becoming a bully and/or victim of bullying (Nansel et al., 2001; Totura, MacKinnon-Lewis et al., 2009). This chapter focuses on providing an overview of the longstanding issues associated with how bullying is defined and classified, how boys and girls in middle school differentially experience bullying, the contexts and consequences of peer aggression, and finally suggestions for building upon existing prevention and intervention efforts. It is important to examine these variables and the relationships among them in order to provide schools with feasible approaches that can be used to improve their environments.

Bullying: A Far Reaching Problem

Bullying is a well-documented national and international problem. Estimates of bullying problems vary from study to study and place to place. Worldwide averages estimate that roughly 35% of adolescents age 11–15 report involvement in bullying, with percentages of regular bullying and victimization ranging from 2% in Sweden to almost 50% in Lithuania (Craig & Harel, 2004). Within the United States, researchers estimate that 30% of 6th- through 10th-grade students were involved in moderate to frequent bullying (Nansel et al., 2001). Of those students, 13% were classified as bullies, 11% as victims, and 6% as both bullies and victims. Other studies find higher estimates among rural youths, with 82% reportedly experiencing victimization (Dulmus, Theriot, Sowers, & Blackburn, 2004). When considering the rapid adoption of technology among youths, such as cell phones and social networking websites, national prevalence rates of cyberbullying show that 30% of adolescents report regular involvement (Raskauskas & Stoltz, 2007), with a dramatic increase in online victimization observed since 2000 (David-Ferdon & Hertz, 2007). Despite variability in estimates, it appears that bullying is more prevalent and more severe than many people think (Benbenishty &

Astor, 2005). The inconsistency in bullying and victimization estimates is likely attributable to how bullying is defined and observed.

What Is Bullying?

Researchers have spent years trying to find the best ways to identify bullying and victimization among adolescents. Despite so much focus, no single definition of bullying has emerged as the gold standard. One of the more recent and most widely recognized definitions used to guide identification and assessment of bullying was developed by Olweus (2003). This definition combines several concepts established in earlier bullying definitions and clearly outlines the common characteristics: bullying is (1) a social form of aggression that takes places among youths who encounter each other regularly; (2) physical, verbal, or psychological aggression intended to hurt others and cause distress in a victim; (3) aggression involving the existence of a power differential between the bully and victim; and (4) not a response to aggressive acts (Cook, Williams, Guerra, Kim, & Sadek, 2010). Olweus's current definition has been used to guide assessments for the model Blueprints Bullying Prevention Program (e.g., Olweus, 2005). To complicate matters further, bullying has also been categorized as either direct or indirect. This distinction between direct and indirect behaviors has had tremendous implications for estimates of bullying and victimization (e.g., Totura, Green, Karver, & Gesten, 2009).

The Many Types of Bullying Behavior

Based on definitions of bullying commonly used in the field, researchers have been able to categorize aggression into specific types of behavior: direct and indirect. Direct bullying is as it sounds—the victim has direct interaction with a bully. This mode of bullying generally comprises two types: physical and verbal. Physical forms of bullying include such behaviors as hitting, kicking, pushing, punching, slapping, and spitting on others. These are visibly aggressive behaviors that are universally recognized as bullying by both adults and youths (for a review, see Berger, 2007). Verbal bullying involves making negative and hurtful comments about another. This could include name calling, insults, hurtful teasing, or nasty remarks. As youths enter adolescence, this type of bullying becomes more prevalent than physical aggression (Berger, 2007; Tapper & Boulton, 2005).

Indirect bullying, on the other hand, is covert in nature. The victim is not fully aware of who their attacker is because these behaviors are hard to detect and do not occur face to face. This type of bullying takes on two forms: relational and cyberbullying. Relational aggression is a form of bullying that also becomes more frequent among early adolescents as they develop instrumental social skills and a reliance on peer approval. Relational aggression involves rumor spreading, manipulation of friendships, and purposeful social isolation of others (Crick & Grotpeter, 1995; Xie, Swift, Cairns, & Cairns, 2002).

Cyberbullying is a relatively new form of indirect aggression among youths in which electronics and technology (computers, web blogs, texts, social networking websites, etc.) are used as the medium for intentionally harming others through taunting, threatening, harassment, and intimidation (Berger, 2007; Williams & Guerra, 2007). The viral or rapid-spread nature of this type of aggression can make cyberbullying especially far-reaching and damaging for adolescents who rely heavily on their social networks for guidance and approval.

Bullying Roles: Profiling the Bullies, the Victims, and Those Caught in Between

Youths can experience bullying in a number of roles, each associated with unique emotional and behavioral profiles (e.g., Olweus, 2003). It is important to examine these profiles to get a picture of the context for bullying, and to unlock clues that could help parents and school personnel prevent problems, as well as intervene when problems arise.

Bullies. Adolescents who bully others tend to have a harder time overall in social situations (Haynie et al., 2001). Widespread theories affirm that bullies can be poor at reading social cues and accurately interpreting interactions with peers (Crick & Dodge, 1994). As a result, they are not as likely to identify prosocial solutions to what they misperceive as hostility or threats from others. Bullies, in addition to aggression, often display other problem behaviors, such as hyperactivity, attention difficulties, anger, and rule breaking (Haynie et al., 2001). Bullies also tend to associate with friends who are similar to them—they exhibit a greater frequency of problematic behaviors and greater acceptance of misconduct than other youths (Nansel et al., 2001). Interestingly, despite studies that suggest bullies do not express much emotionality, they tend to have more symptoms of anxiety and depression than students who are not involved in bullying (Haynie et al., 2001; Nansel et al., 2001). These levels, however, are not as high as that of victims. Finally, bullying has been associated with distraction from schoolwork and poorer academic outcomes, findings that are especially important for teachers who may find themselves spending a lot of energy on classroom management instead of instruction (Graham, Bellmore, & Mize, 2006).

Studies have shown that many bullies view their behavior as reasonable and use skilled methods to exert their control over others (Rose, Swenson, & Waller, 2004). Those who know how to use these skills avoid the peer rejection that less skilled bullies often experience. Indeed, middle school bullies can be popular among their classmates (Keisner & Pastore, 2005), though as they progress into high school, bullies become less popular compared to their more socially skilled peers.

Victims. Victims can be divided into two types: passive and reactive. Passive victims are those that receive bullying and tend to present as defenseless and submissive to aggressors (Berger, 2007). Conversely, reactive victims are not defenseless. These youths will respond to bullying with aggression, rather than becoming isolated and withdrawn. Victims often have individual characteristics that make them an easy target (Carney & Merrell, 2001). Psychologically, they are more anxious, depressed, withdrawn, and have lower self-esteem than those who are not bullied (Haynie et al., 2001). As they get older, adolescents are more often harassed and bullied for their suspected or known sexual orientation (Berlan, Corliss, Field, Goodman, & Austin, 2010). Victims, especially those who are withdrawn and shy, are generally less popular in school or bonded with classmates than are other students, even including bullies (Haynie et al., 2001). Victimization can be associated as well with school avoidance, potentially resulting in greater incidence of truancy, which can have a negative impact on academic performance (Kochenderfer & Ladd, 1996). Interestingly, victims can also display behavior problems, such as delinquency, substance use, and acceptance of misconduct, although often not to the same degree as bullies (Sullivan, Farrell, & Kliewer, 2006).

Bully/Victims. Recent studies have found that bully/victims (youths who both bully others and are bullied) represent a distinct group, although typically much smaller in size and frequency than the groups of bullies and victims (Haynie et al., 2001; Nansel et al., 2001). Bully/victims, also known as aggressive victims or provocative victims, are not to be mistaken for reactive victims. Their bullying behavior is not a reaction to an incident of victimization, but rather is a separate and purposeful bullying act (Pelligrini & Long, 2002). These youths are considered the most at-risk bullying group—they tend to have more overall behavioral and emotional problems and poorer social abilities than other youths (Totura, Green et al., 2009). Academically, bully/victims also have the poorest performance, likely a result of poor adjustment and lack of bonding with teachers and clasmates (Haynie et al., 2001; Nansel et al., 2001). Often at a greater rate than bullies, bully/victims display deviant and defiant behavior, including cigarette and alcohol use and truancy, as well as verbal and physical aggression (Nordhagen, Neisen, Stigum, & Kohler, 2005). Unlike bullies who tend to progress from physical to indirect forms of bullying as they age, bully/victims primarily engage in physical aggression throughout childhood and adolescence (Unnever, 2005).

The peer group-observers. Bystanders are peers who observe victimization and either pretend to ignore it or downplay it, inadvertently contributing to an environment that tolerates youth aggression. Demonstrated intervention efforts have worked toward transitioning bystanders from passive observers into active defenders of victims (Salmivalli, 2001). These efforts capitalize on environmental approaches to changing the context in which bullying occurs, rather than focusing solely on changing the behavior of bullies or victims' coping abilities. Henchmen/ contributors are peers who serve as contributors to bullies and also help to create an environment in which bullying is tolerated, but in a much more active manner. These youths are observers who engage in teasing, taunting, or other forms of indirect aggression alongside the primary bully. Henchmen are part of a network of peers that assist bullies in establishing dominance and power over others (for a review, see Berger, 2007; Olweus, 2003). Defenders, though rarer than other observer groups, are youths who buck the common trend of contributing to or passively observing bullying situations by stepping up to support and defend victims. These youths are instrumental in taking a stand to shift the peer culture that may tolerate bullying, and they can be key players in school prevention and intervention efforts (Salmivalli, 2001).

Cultural Differences in Expressions of Bullying

There is a range of bullying roles that adolescents may take and of peer contexts that are conducive to bullying; however, in order to better understand the experiences of bullying, it is important to consider cultural variations in the prevalence and expression of bullying. Research has identified a number of factors that can influence bullying roles and behaviors; notable among them are gender, race, and ethnicity.

Evidence on gender differences in bullying has evolved but is still somewhat inconclusive. Early research reported that more boys are bullies and victims than are girls and that bullying decreases with age (Berger, 2007). More recently, research confirmed that boys are more often bullies and that physical aggression decreases with age but that other forms of aggression (e.g., relational, social) reported to be more prevalent among girls increase during the middle school years (Malecki, 2003; Williams & Guerra, 2007). Physical and verbal aggression, as well as cyberbullying, tend to be more common among middle school boys, and relational aggression is more typical of girls (Crick & Werner, 1998; Giles & Heyman, 2005; Kowalski & Limber, 2007). Interestingly, even though boys and girls appear to be at equal risk of being bullied, middle school boys are more frequently victimized (Olweus, 2003). Both boys and girls tend to be crueler to their same-sex peers than to the opposite sex (Ladd, 2005). However, when there is gender crossover, boys tend to bully girls more than the reverse (Moffitt, Caspi, Rutter, & Silva, 2001).

Researchers both nationally and internationally have examined variations in bullying and victimization by race and ethnicity. For instance, African American youths are more often identified as bullies than victims, as compared to Caucasian and Hispanic youths (Graham & Juvonen, 2002). While ethnic bullying has become problematic in some communities among boys and girls, particularly if students have not been exposed to cultural diversity issues, evidence suggests that race or ethnicity does not necessarily put a youth at risk of peer aggression. Bullying appears to be more prevalent within ethnic/racial groups than between them (Bellmore, Witkow, Graham, & Juvonen, 2004; Berger, 2007). In fact, a large-scale study found that only a small proportion of adolescents felt that their race or ethnicity was a factor in bullying (Nansel et al., 2001).

While some cultural trends have emerged in the incidence of bullying, gaps in the research preclude definitive conclusions. Indeed, there is much to be learned about the gender, racial, and ethnic variants of bullying among adolescents. These effects need to be examined further to gain a better understanding of how culture impacts the significance, consequences, and prevention of bullying.

Consequences: What Happens to Bullies, Victims, and Bully/Victims?

By all counts, aggression in middle school has future negative outcomes. By high school, bullies find that their overtly aggressive behavior is less the norm among peers and that individuals whom they used to pick on often find friends (Laursen, Finkelstein, & Betts, 2001). Many bullies don't learn adaptive social skills for negotiating difficult peer interactions and thus become increasingly unpopular as they get older. At a minimum, bullying is associated with other disruptive behaviors, both in and out of school, such as delinquency, alcohol and drug use, and adjustment problems (Nansel, Overpeck, Saluja, & Ruan, 2004; Prinstein, Boergers, &

Vernberg, 2001). More seriously, bullying has also been linked to violent behaviors, including weapon carrying, frequent fighting, and violence-related injuries (Nansel et al., 2001). Given these behaviors, future criminal behavior in adulthood is a greater likelihood as well (Olweus, 1999). Aggressive girls suffer from unique problems, including dating violence and teenage pregnancy (Putallaz & Bierman, 2004). Perhaps most problematic among bullies is the potential for suicidal thoughts and intentions. Studies have found that older adolescents, especially boys, have a four-fold greater incidence of suicidal thoughts than do other youths (Kaltiala-Heino, Rimpela, Marttunen, Rimpela, & Rantanen, 1999).

Victims, as well, experience significant disruptions to their developmental course, especially if victimization is chronic and involves multiple types (e.g., "ploy-victimization"; Finkelhor, Ormrod, Turner, & Hamby, 2005). Victimized youths feel anxious about attending school and often try to avoid going, which has a negative impact on future educational achievement and job attainment (Macmillan & Hagan, 2004). Bullying, especially severe and chronic, has been a factor in several recent suicides among youths and young adults. Peer aggression appears to be doubly impactful for youths who are gay or lesbian (Rivers, 2001), or even perceived to be so by their peers, thereby contributing to ongoing trauma and potentially suicide (Friedman, Koeske, Silvestre, Korr, & Sites, 2006). When considering the rarity of homicide among youths, such as the Columbine tragedy, a common factor threading such incidents together has been a repetitive and longstanding bully-victim cycle. In many of the past two decades' school shootings, the perpetrators were often teenagers who had hit their limit of teasing, ridicule, and torment from classmates (Vossekuil, Fein, Reddy, Borum, & Modzeleski, 2002). For those who are not pushed to the fatal acts of suicide or homicide, victimization has long-term consequences. These adolescents grow up with progressively worsening anxiety and depression, along with fears of social interactions. These fears often lead to isolation from others and potentially future victimization into adulthood (Troop-Gordon & Ladd, 2005). Young adolescents who experience both bullying and victimization are by far the most troubled among their peers. These youths are likely to have the poorest trajectories into adulthood because even when they try to improve their social skills, they remain rejected by surrounding social supports among peers, at school, and at home (Bierman, 2004).

Given what is known about the long-term impact of bullying, it is easy to see why preventing it should be a priority among schools, parents, and teenagers. It is important to consider where the bully-victim cycle starts in order to identify early risk factors that make some youths vulnerable to bullying and/or victimization, as well as factors that can protect them.

Risk Factors: What Contributes to Bullying and Victimization?

Although not an exhaustive list, researchers have looked at risk factors such as physical appearance and demeanor, genetic predispositions, and certain contextual factors in homes and schools that increase the likelihood that youths will become a bully or be bullied. Interestingly, many consequences of bullying have also been found to be predictors of it, creating a sort of "chicken and egg" scenario of peer aggression that researchers and practitioners are still trying to disentangle.

Several studies examined the relationship between bullying and victimization and youth adjustment among adolescent boys and girls. In terms of physical appearance and presentation, bullies and victims are more often boys than girls (Olweus, 2003). However, with more and more research accumulating on the effective assessment of relational and indirect aggression, girls bully more than expected, but most research still finds that boys bully more than girls (Berger, 2007). Victims and bully/victims differ from other youths in that they are frequently younger adolescents, in the first year of middle school, with lower self-esteem. Additionally, youths with a physical or learning disability may be at risk for victimization, especially in school climates that tolerate bullying (de Monchy, Pijl, & Zandberg, 2004). A recent review concluded that physical size and perceived "power" are important risk factors, especially for boys—bigger kids victimize smaller kids, and stronger kids pick on kids they see as weaker (Berger, 2007). It is important to note that "power" can mean physical strength but also social stature, a characteristic particularly salient for adolescent girls (Casey-Cannon, Hayward, & Gowen, 2001). Expression of anger, while a consequence of bullying, is also a powerful predictor of it (Bosworth, Espelage, & Simon, 1999).

Researchers have recently begun looking at genetic precursors to bullying and victimization. Some characteristics, such as temperament and predispositions to anger, do have genetic components. However, these characteristics do not manifest and result in aggression in isolation (Van Goozen, 2005). Studies have shown that babies with difficult temperaments do not automatically become angry and aggressive or highly fearful youths (Kagan & Snidman, 2004). Whatever the genetic foundation, emotional and behavioral risk factors of bullying and victimization reach their potential when they are triggered by an environment that fosters aggression (Van Goozen, 2005).

Environments That Make a Difference

Adolescents come in contact with many environments on a daily basis. Naturally, it is important to examine the characteristics of these environments in combination with youths' individual characteristics to better identify what puts them at risk for bullying and victimization. For the purpose of this chapter, the focus will be on the two common contexts that youths experience: home and school.

Family context. Much work has been done on the relationship between parenting and peer aggression. Parents can influence their children's social development both directly (e.g., modeling and social reinforcement for aggression) and indirectly (e.g., shaping of perceptions and attitudes about aggression). Ambivalent family connections, harsh discipline practices, and inconsistent and demanding parenting styles are associated with bullying, while overprotective or coercive parenting is associated with victimization. Additionally, many parents of bullies usually provide minimal supervision and typically lack empathy and effective problem-solving skills (Curtner-Smith, 2000; Duncan, 2004). Simply put, these parents are not good role models for learning how to get along with others and solve problems (Walden & Beran, 2010). Conversely, some victimized youths have parents who are rather involved in their daily lives, but this involvement may not be emotionally supportive (Haynie et al., 2001).

Much work has shown that negative family environments can be detrimental to youths' social development. On the other hand, good parenting has a protective effect—it can prevent future problem-solving difficulties among at-risk youths (Simons-Morton, Hartos, & Haynie, 2004). When parents are able to model prosocial behavior and effective solutions to social difficulties, they decrease the likelihood that their children will engage in bullying or become bullied.

School climate. The prevalence of bullying is an important consideration for school administrators—bullying and group norms favoring bullying contribute to a lack of engagement in academic activities and lower overall achievement (Brody, Kim, Murry, & Brown, 2005). Early adolescents experience unique environmental changes as they move from elementary to middle schools. Middle school student bodies tend to be larger and more diverse than in elementary school, and students transition frequently throughout the day among multiple classrooms and teachers. A school's social-emotional climate can facilitate or deter bullying (Espelage, Holt, & Henkel, 2003). Teachers play a critical role in shaping the structure and values of school ecologies (Rodkin & Hodges, 2003). Schools in which aggressive behavior is tolerated by teachers and students can cultivate a climate that is associated with higher rates of bullying (Espelage, Holt, & Henkel, 2003).

In contrast, the protective effect of a positive school climate can assuage bullying and victimization for middle school students (Kuperminc, Leadbeater, & Blatt, 2001). Quality friendships and supportive relationships at school go a long way toward protecting adolescents from the negative outcomes of bullying and victimization (Schwartz, Dodge, Pettit, Bates, & The Conduct Problems Prevention Group, 2000). Also, students who are engaged, and in a sense "fit," with their school environment are less likely to experience aggression and bullying (Nansel, Haynie, & Simons-Morton, 2003). These findings highlight the pivotal role that a supportive school environment plays on adolescents' socioemotional development.

Prevention and Intervention: What Can Be Done?

It is clear that bullying is a big problem for youths, parents, and schools—now what? Research over the last couple of decades has laid the groundwork for figuring out what works to prevent bullying and what doesn't. Many theories have guided the development and evaluation of programs designed to reduce aggressive behavior. One of the most well-founded theories, social-information processing (SIP), indicates that programs should target children's attributional (beliefs about intent) and affective (emotional) deficits (Crick & Dodge, 1994). These theories suggest that how youths process social cues impacts whether they will respond to situations in an aggressive or nonaggressive manner (MacKinnon-Lewis, Lamb, Hattie, & Baradaran, 2001). One aspect of SIP shown to be particularly important for understanding aggression is the "hostile attribution bias" (Crick & Dodge, 1994). Researchers have shown that in situations where a peer's intent is vague, youths with a hostile attribution bias are inclined to believe that the peer intended harm and will respond aggressively (Orobio de Castro, Merk, Koops, Veerman, & Bosch, 2005). Early research focused on looking at attributional biases and physical aggression, but more recent work demonstrates the applicability of the SIP model with relational aggression as well (Crick, Grotpeter, & Bigbee, 2002). Affective, or emotional, aspects of the SIP model are also important for decreasing aggression, by focusing on the ability to accurately interpret emotional cues, especially anger, and regulate (or control) emotional responses (Crick & Dodge, 1994). As such, emotion regulation techniques, in addition to addressing attributional biases, are important components included in interventions aimed at reducing physical (e.g., Anger Coping Program; Lochman, 1992) and relational aggression (Crick et al., 2002).

It is important to note that not all youths who bully others suffer from attributional biases or emotional regulation difficulties. Some youths use aggressive means instrumentally to control others because they (1) lack more effective social skills for negotiating relationships, or (2) are rewarded for using aggression to manipulate peers in seeking approval or popularity (e.g., Rose et al., 2004). This is where bystanders of bullying can play a key role in either reinforcing or dissuading aggression (Salmivalli, 2001), an important consideration for schools since they play a critical role in modeling appropriate interactions and creating an environment that rewards positive behavior rather than bullying.

What works and what doesn't work? Scores of programming and techniques, some well researched and some not, have been devoted to reducing bullying and victimization among adolescents. A few select evidence-based programs will be described in this section, followed by recommendations for program enhancement. Starting with early prevention among youths, the Roots of Empathy program has been shown to have a dramatic effect in reducing aggression by developing empathy for others' experiences (Gordon & Green, 2008). Designed for kindergarten to grade 8, a neighborhood infant (accompanied by a parent) serves as the "lever" to teach children perspective-taking skills as well as fostering the development of empathy. The program, which began in Canada, has expanded to other countries, including the United States, United Kingdom, and New Zealand. Among first- to third-grade program participants, proactive aggression was found to be reduced by 88%, with similar reductions in both proactive and relational aggression among fourth through seventh graders (Schonert-Reichl, 2007).

Incredible Years is another early prevention program with demonstrated effects in reducing the cycle of youth aggression, a contributor to later bullying behavior (Webster-Stratton et al., 2001). By working with families of preschool and early elementary children, both parents and at-risk youths learn prosocial problem-solving skills. This successful program has been extended to schools in which teachers are taught effective behavior management skills to be applied universally within classrooms.

Several programs have also been employed with older children and adolescents to intervene with existing bullying problems in schools. Using a variety of intervention strategies, Second Step Violence Prevention has been successful in reducing the incidence and tolerance for both relational and physical aggression and for improving youths' social skills (Frey, Nolen, Van Schoiack Edstrom, Hirschstein, 2005). The program focuses on changing maladaptive attitudes about aggression by increasing empathy, perspective taking, problem-solving skills, and anger management abilities among elementary and middle school students. Further, the Anger Coping (Lochman, 1992) and BrainPower (Hudley, 1994) programs have successfully taught physically aggressive youths emotional regulation and to more accurately evaluate the intentions of others in social situations. Moreover, Leff and colleagues' (Leff et al., 2009) Friend to Friend program, an adaptation of the Anger Coping and BrainPower programs, specifically targets relational aggression and has been shown to be effective at reducing hostile attributional biases, as well as relational and physical aggression among highly relationally aggressive girls (Leff et al., 2009).

One of the most effective programs developed to date is the Olweus Bullying Prevention Program (Olweus, 2005). This Blueprints for Violence Prevention model program uses a whole-school approach to decrease bullying and victimization by improving awareness of these behaviors among teachers, students, and parents. Core components of the program are directed toward restructuring the existing school environment to reduce opportunities and rewards for bullying at the school, classroom, and individual-student levels. Longitudinal data from students and teachers have shown the program to be remarkably effective in substantially reducing by almost 50% the incidences of bullying and victimization (Olweus, 2005). Although the Bullying Prevention Program primarily targets physical forms of aggression, its emphasis on promoting awareness among teachers, students, and parents, along with strategies for behavior management, may be effective in reducing other forms of aggression and victimization.

Despite the promising outcomes described above, preventions and interventions are less effective in environments in which aggression is tolerated (Aber, Jones, Brown, Chaundry, & Samples, 1998). Effective structure and monitoring of student behavior by school staff has positive implications for how adolescents learn to get along and form peer relationships. Accordingly, one of the first goals of any school-based program should be to educate students, teachers, and other school staff about the negative consequences of aggression with the goal of creating a more positive school climate. Broadly applying zero-tolerance policies or peer mediation or simply suggesting that victimized youths take a stand against bullying are ineffective prevention strategies (Fox, Elliott, Kerlikowske, Newman, & Christeson, 2003). Zero-tolerance policies typically result in bullies receiving suspensions and unsupervised time at home, rather than providing an opportunity to truly understand the causes of bullying. Encouraging victims to stand up to bullies may actually put them at greater risk of future bullying. Finally, peer mediation does nothing to address the power that bullies have over victims and could lead to further emotional damage by assuming that victims have accountability in the aggression perpetrated against them.

Lessons learned. As a result of developmental research, much is known about bullies and victims, though intervention strategies have met with somewhat limited success (Rigby, 2005). However, researchers have continued to develop and refine preventive interventions to address bullying behavior, many of which are school based. Unfortunately, few school interventions have undergone scientific evaluation (Berger, 2007), a shortcoming that must be rectified. Moreover, much of the field's past prevention and intervention research focused on boys' physical aggression (Crick & Zahn-Waxler, 2003). Since research shows that both boys and girls can be physically and relationally aggressive, attention to how gender differences translate into the expression of aggression will lead to more sensitive and effective interventions (Ostrov et al., 2009). While much progress is left to be realized, effective programming has demonstrated common elements: (1) programs targeting youths' social-information processes and the connections between thoughts, feelings, and behaviors are the most promising; (2) effective programs work on both the individual and environmental levels and involve multiple components (e.g., teacher training, parent consultation, youth social-skill training); (3) programs that are successful across genders are specifically addressing female culture and relational aggression; (4) well-implemented school-based programs deal with school systemic issues that can pose challenges, such as leadership buy-in, demands on teacher time, teacher perceptions of student bullying, and available resources.

Despite some universal emphasis on these common elements across programs with empirical evidence, outcomes from many prevention and intervention efforts have been less than promising. Bullying is a multifactor, complex problem that involves effectively intervening with tightly intertwined developmental and social processes—doing this well is very difficult. The resulting lack of robust change in rates of bullying and victimization underscores the need to be sure that programs are firmly planted in sound behavior change theory and are embraced by all key players who have a stake in their success. By utilizing a social-ecological framework, in which efforts are targeted at youths and take into account the contextual factors that shape their lives, program developers adopt a holistic approach to involving the people and environments that impact youth behavior (Swearer, Espelage, Vaillancourt, & Hymel, 2010).

Future Directions for Research and Practice: Where Do We Go from Here?

With youths becoming increasingly tech savvy and with more and more bullying occurring in virtual formats, prevention and intervention programming must remain as innovative as the technologies adolescents are using to victimize their peers (Berger, 2007; Raskauskas & Stoltz, 2007). Over the years, studies have increasingly incorporated technology into assessments and observations of youth behavior as it occurs, including use of such devices such as pagers, cell phones, video cameras, and digital recorders (e.g., Tapper & Boulton, 2005). Not only does this provide a wealth of information about peer relationships, but the information is collected in real time without reliance on traditional observation, nomination, or survey techniques. This is a natural phenomenon—as time goes on, technology becomes more advanced and available, and youths are inherently the first market to be fully dialed into these advances. Thus, it seems a logical progression that technology would come to the forefront of prevention and intervention as well, in addition to its successful utility in the assessment of youth behaviors.

As it happens, the limited success of many behavior-change intervention programs has prompted some to question whether new strategies are needed to effectively reach youths (Baranowski, Buday, Thompson, & Baranowski, 2008). Initial evidence, though rare, suggests that computer-based applications hold great promise as an effective channel for targeting youth behavior change, primarily because adolescents find them to be engaging and they are already being used for social, entertainment, and educational purposes (Bers, 2006). Wilkinson, Ang, and Goh (2008), in their comprehensive review of the history and emergence of the Internet and video game literature, explore how recent technological and cultural innovations can be used to treat a host of mental health challenges. Despite an initial backlash by some scholars with concerns about the possible harmful effects of video games for therapeutic purposes, several program developers are identifying methods for harnessing youth attraction to video games and the communicative possibilities of the Internet in treating aggression (Bosworth, Espelage, DuBay, Daytner, & Karageorge, 2000). These pioneering efforts are opening new doors for innovative preventive interventions that have not previously been considered. Future researchers should consider how innovative technological approaches might be used in the dissemination and implementation of preventive interventions targeting bullying behavior.

References

Aber, J. L., Jones, S. M., Brown, J. L., Chaundry, N., & Samples, F. (1998). Resolving conflict creatively: Evaluating the developmental effects of a school-based violence prevention program in neighborhood and classroom context. *Development and Psychopathology, 10,* 187–213.

Baranowski, T., Buday, R., Thompson, D., & Baranowski, J. (2008). Playing for real: Video games and stories for health-related behavior change. *American Journal of Preventive Medicine, 34,* 74–82.

Bellmore, A. D., Witkow, M. R., Graham, S., & Juvonen, J. (2004). Beyond the individual: The impact of ethnic context and classroom behavioral norms on victim's adjustment. *Developmental Psychology, 40,* 1159–1172.

Benbenishty, R., & Astor, R. A. (2005). *School violence in context.* New York: Oxford University Press.

Berger, K. (2007). Update on school bullying at school: Science forgotten? *Development Review, 27,* 90–126.

Berlan, E. D., Corliss, H. L., Field, A. E., Goodman, E., & Austin, S. B. (2010). Sexual orientation and bullying among adolescents in the Growing Up Today Study. *Journal of Adolescent Health, 46,* 366–371.

Bers, M. (2006). The role of new technologies to foster positive youth development. *Applied Developmental Science, 10,* 200–219.

Bierman, K. L. (2004). *Peer rejection.* New York: Guilford.

Block, J. J. (2007). Lessons from Columbine: Virtual and real rage. *American Journal of Forensic Psychiatry, 28,* 1–27.

Bosworth, K., Espelage, D., DuBay, T., Daytner, G., & Karageorge, K. (2000) Preliminary evaluation of a multimedia violence prevention program for adolescents. *American Journal of Health Behavior, 24,* 268–280.

Bosworth, K., Espelage, D. L., & Simon, T. R. (1999). Factors associated with bullying behavior in middle school students. *Journal of Early Adolescence, 19,* 341–362.

Brody, G. H., Kim, S., Murry, V. M., & Brown, A. C. (2005). Longitudinal links among parenting, self-presentations to peers, and the development of externalizing and internalizing symptoms in African American siblings. *Development and Psychopathology, 17,* 185–205.

Carney, A. G., & Merrell, K. W. (2001). Bullying in schools: Perspectives on understanding and preventing an international problem. *School Psychology International, 22,* 364–382.

Casey-Cannon, S., Hayward, C., & Gowen, K. (2001). Middle-school girls' reports of peer victimization: Concerns, consequences, and implications. *Professional School Counseling, 5,* 135–147.

Cook, C. R., Williams, K. R., Guerra, N. G., Kim, T. E., & Sadek, S. (2010). Predictors of bullying and victimization in childhood and adolescence: A meta-analytic investigation. *School Psychology Quarterly, 25,* 65–83.

Craig, W. M., & Harel, Y. (2004). Bullying, physical fighting, and victimization. In C. Currie, C. Roberts, A. Morgan, R. Smith, W. Settertobulte, & O. Samdal (Eds.), *Young people's health in context* (pp. 133–144). Geneva, Switzerland: World Health Organization.

Crick, N. R., & Dodge, K. A. (1994). A review and reformulation of social information-processing mechanisms in children's social adjustment. *Psychological Bulletin, 115,* 74–101.

Crick, N. R., & Grotpeter, J. K. (1995). Relational aggression, gender, and social-psychological adjustment. *Child Development, 66,* 710–722.

Crick, N. R., Grotpeter, J. K., & Bigbee, M. A. (2002). Relationally and physically aggressive children's intent attributions and feelings of distress for relational and instrumental peer provocations. *Child Development, 73,* 1134–1142.

Crick, N. R., & Werner, N. E. (1998). Response decision processes in relational and overt aggression. *Child Development, 69,* 1630–1639.

Crick, N. R., & Zahn-Waxler, C. (2003). The development of psychopathology in females and males: Current progress and future challenges. *Development and Psychopathology, 15,* 719–742.

Curtner-Smith, M. E. (2000). Mechanisms by which family processes contribute to school-age boys' bullying. *Child Study Journal, 30,* 169–186.

David-Ferdon, C., & Hertz, M. F. (2007). Electronic media, violence, and adolescents: An emerging public health problem. *Journal of Adolescent Health, 41,* S1–S5.

de Monchy, M., Pijl, S. J., & Zandberg, T. (2004). Discrepancies in judging social inclusion and bullying of pupils with behavior problems. *European Journal of Special Needs Education, 19,* 317–330.

Dulmus, C. M., Theriot, M. T., Sowers, K. M., & Blackburn, J. A. (2004). Students' reports of peer bullying victimization in a rural school. *Stress, Trauma, and Crisis: An International Journal, 7,* 1–16.

Duncan, R. D. (2004). The impact of family relationships on school bullies and victims. In D. L. Espelage & S. M. Swearer (Eds.), *Bullying in American schools: A social-ecological perspective on prevention and intervention* (pp. 227–244). Mahwah, NJ: Lawrence Erlbaum Associates.

Espelage, D. L., Holt, M. K., & Henkel, R. R. (2003). Examination of peer-group contextual effects on aggression during early adolescence. *Child Development, 74,* 205–220.

Finkelhor, D., Ormrod, R. K., Turner, H. A., & Hamby, S. L. (2005). Measuring poly-victimization using the Juvenile Victimization Questionnaire. *Child Abuse and Neglect, 29,* 1297–1312.

Fox, J. A., Elliott, D. S., Kerlikowske, R. G., Newman, S. A., & Christeson, W. (2003). *Bullying prevention is crime prevention: A report by Fight Crime: Invest in Kids.* Retrieved from Fight Crime website: www.fightcrime.org/sites/default/files/reports/BullyingReport.pdf.

Frey, K. S., Nolen, S. B., Van Schoiack Edstrom, L., & Hirschstein, M. K. (2005). Effects of a school-based social-emotional competent program: Linking children's goals, attributions, and behavior. *Applied Developmental Psychology, 26,* 171–200.

Friedman, M. S., Koeske, G. F., Silvestre, A. J., Korr, W. S., & Sites, E. W. (2006). The impact of gender-role nonconforming behavior, bulling, and social support on suicidality among gay male youth. *Journal of Adolescent Health, 38,* 621–623.

Giles, J. W., & Heyman, G. D. (2005). Young children's beliefs about the relationship between gender and aggressive behavior, *Child Development, 76,* 107–121.

Gordon, M., & Green, J. (2008). Roots of Empathy: Changing the world child by child. *Education Canada, 48,* 34–36.

Graham, S., Bellmore, A. D., & Mize, J. (2006). Peer victimization, aggression, and their co-occurrence in middle school: Pathways to adjustment problems. *Journal of Abnormal Child Psychology, 34,* 363–378.

Graham, S., & Juvonen, J. (2002). Ethnicity, peer harassment, and adjustment in middle school: An exploratory study. *Journal of Early Adolescence, 22,* 173–199.

Haynie, D. L., Nansel, T., Eitel, P., Crump, A. D., Saylor, K., Yu, K., et al. (2001). Bullies, victims, and bully/victims: Distinct groups of at-risk youth. *Journal of Early Adolescence, 21,* 29–49.

Hudley, C. (1994). The reduction of childhood aggression using the BrainPower Program. In M. Furlong & D. Smith (Eds.), *Anger, hostility and aggression: Assessment, prevention, and intervention strategies for youth* (pp. 313–344). Brandon, VT: Clinical Psychology Publishing Co.

Kagan, J., & Snidman, N. C. (2004). *The long shadow of temperament.* Cambridge, MA: Belknap.

Kaltiala-Heino, R., Rimpela, M., Marttunen, M., Rimpela, A., & Rantanen, P. (1999). Bullying, depression, and suicidal ideation in Finnish adolescents: School survey. *British Medical Journal, 319,* 348–351.

Keisner, J., & Pastore, M. (2005). Difference in the relations between antisocial behavior and peer acceptance across contexts and across adolescence. *Child Development, 76,* 1278–1293.

Kochenderfer, B. J., & Ladd, G. W. (1996). Peer victimization: Cause of consequence of school maladjustment. *Child Development, 67,* 1305–1317.

Kowalski, R. M., & Limber, S. P. (2007). Electronic bullying among middle school students. *Journal of Adolescent Health, 41,* 22–30.

Kuperminc, G. P., Leadbeater, B. J., & Blatt, S. J. (2001). School social climate and individual differences in vulnerability to psychopathology among middle school students. *Journal of School Psychology, 39,* 141–159.

Ladd, G. W. (2005). *Children's peer relations and social competence.* New Haven, CT: Yale University Press.

Laursen, B., Finkelstein, B. D., & Betts, N. T. (2001). A developmental meta-analysis of peer conflict resolution. *Developmental Review, 21,* 423–449.

Leff, S. S., Gullan, R. L., Paskewich, B. S., Abdul-Kabir, S., Jawad, A. F., Grossman, M., Munro, M. A., & Power, T. J. (2009). An initial evaluation of a culturally-adapted social problem solving and relational aggression prevention program for urban African American relationally aggressive girls. *Journal of Prevention and Intervention in the Community, 37,* 1–15.

Lochman, J. E. (1992). Cognitive-behavioral intervention with aggressive boys: Three-year follow-up and preventive effects. *Journal of Consulting and Clinical Psychology, 60,* 426–432.

MacKinnon-Lewis, C., Lamb, M., Hattie, J., & Baradaran, L. P. (2001). A longitudinal examination of the associations between mothers' and sons' attributions and their aggression. *Development and Psychopathology, 13,* 69–81.

Macmillan, R., & Hagan, J. (2004). Violence in the transition to adulthood: Adolescent victimization, education, and socioeconomic attainment in later life. *Journal of Research on Adolescence, 14,* 127–158.

Malecki, C. K. (2003). Perceptions of the frequency and importance of social support by students classified as victims, bullies, and bully/victims in an urban middle school. *School Psychology Review, 32,* 471–489.

Moffitt, T. E., Caspi, A., Rutter, M., & Silva, P. A. (2001). *Sex differences in antisocial behavior: Conduct disorder, delinquency, and violence in the Dunedin longitudinal study.* Cambridge, UK: Cambridge University Press.

Nansel, T. R., Haynie, D. L., & Simons-Morton, B. G. (2003). The association of bullying and victimization with middle school adjustment. *Journal of Applied School Psychology, 19,* 45–61.

Nansel, T. R., Overpeck, M. D., Pilla, R. S., Ruan, W. J., Simons-Morton, B., & Scheidt, P. (2001). Bullying behavior among U.S. youth: Prevalence and association with psychosocial adjustment. *Journal of the American Medical Association, 285,* 2094–2100.

Nansel, T. R., Overpeck, M. D., Saluja, G., & Ruan, W. J. (2004). Cross-national consistency in the relationship between bullying behaviors and psychosocial adjustment. *Archives of Pediatrics and Adolescent Medicine, 158,* 730–736.

Nordhagen, R., Neisen, A., Stigun, H., & Kohler, L. (2005). Parental reported bullying among Nordic children. *Child: Care, Health, and Development, 31,* 693–701.

Olweus, D. (1999). Sweden. In P. K. Smith, Y. Morita, J. Junger-Tas, D. Olweus, R. F. Catalano, & P. T. Slee (Eds.), *The nature of school bullying* (pp. 8–27). London: Routledge.

Olweus. D. (2003, March). The profile of bullying at school. *Educational Leadership, 12*–17.

Olweus, D. (2005). A useful evaluation design, and effects of the Olweus Bullying Prevention Program. *Psychology, Crime, and Law, 11,* 389–402.

Orobio de Castro, B., Merk, W., Koops, W., Veerman, J. W., & Bosch, J. D. (2005). Emotions in social information processing and their relations with reactive and proactive aggression in referred aggressive boys. *Journal of Clinical Child and Adolescent Psychology, 34,* 105–116.

Ostrov, J. M., Massetti, G. M., Stauffacher, K., Godleski, S. A., Hart, K. C., Karch, K. M., et al. (2009). An intervention for relational and physical aggression in early childhood: A preliminary study. *Early Childhood Research Quarterly, 24,* 15–28.

Pellegrini, A. D., & Long, J. D. (2002). A longitudinal study of bullying, dominance, and victimization, during the transition from primary through secondary school. *British Journal of Developmental Psychology, 20, 259*–280.

Prinstein, M. J., Boergers, J., & Vernberg, E. M. (2001). Overt and relational aggression in adolescents: Social-psychological functioning of aggressors and victims. *Journal of Clinical Child Psychology, 30,* 477–489.

Putallaz, M., & Bierman, K. L. (Eds.). (2004). *Aggression, antisocial behavior, and violence among girls: A developmental perspective.* New York: Guilford.

Raskauskas, J., & Stoltz, A. D. (2007). Involvement in traditional and electronic bullying among adolescents. *Developmental Psychology, 43,* 564–575.

Rigby, K. (2005). The method of shared concern as an intervention technique to address bullying in schools: An overview and appraisal. *Australian Journal of Guidance and Counseling, 15,* 27–34.

Rivers, I. (2001). The bullying of sexual minorities at school: Its nature and long-term consequences. *Educational and Child Psychology, 18,* 32–46.

Rodkin, P. C., & Hodges, E. V. E. (2003). Bullies and victims in the peer ecology: Four questions for psychologists and school professionals. *School Psychology Review, 32,* 384–400.

Rose, A. J., Swenson, L. P., & Waller, E. M. (2004). Over and relational aggression and perceived popularity: Development differences in concurrent and prospective relations. *Developmental Psychology, 40,* 378–387.

Salmivalli, C. (2001). Peer-led intervention campaign against school bullying: Who considered it useful, who benefited? *Educational Research, 43,* 263–278.

Scheithauer, H., Hayer, T., Petermann, F., & Jugert, G. (2006). Physical, verbal, and relational forms of bullying among German students: Age trends, gender differences, and correlates. *Aggressive Behavior, 32,* 261–275.

Schonert-Reichl, K. A. (2007, March). *Middle childhood inside and out: The psychological and social world of children 9–12.* Research highlights: A University of British Columbia/United Way of the Lower Mainland Report. Burnaby, B.C.: The United Way of the Lower Mainland.

Schwartz, D., Dodge, K. A., Pettit, G. S., Bates, J. E., & The Conduct Problems Prevention Group. (2000). Friendship as a moderating factor in the pathway between early harsh home environment and later victimization in the peer group. *Developmental Psychology, 36,* 646–662.

Schwartz, D., & Gorman, A. H. (2003). Community violence exposure and children's academic functioning. *Journal of Educational Psychology, 95,* 163–173.

Simons-Morton, B. G., Hartos, J. L., Haynie, D. L. (2004). Prospective analysis of peer and parent influences on minor aggression among early adolescents. *Health Education Behavior, 31,* 22–33.

Sullivan, T. N., Farrell, A. D., & Kliewer, W. (2006). Peer victimization in early adolescence: Association between physical and relational victimization and drug use, aggression, and delinquent behaviors among urban middle school students. *Development and Psychopathology, 18,* 119–137.

Swearer, S. M., Espelage, D. L., Vaillancourt, T., & Hymel, S. (2010). What can be done about school bullying? Linking research to educational practice. *Educational Researcher, 39,* 38–47.

Tapper, K., & Boulton, M. J. (2005). Victim and peer responses to different forms of aggression among primary school children. *Aggressive Behavior, 31,* 238–253.

Totura, C. M. Wienke, Green, A., Karver, M. S., & Gesten, E. L. (2009). Multiple informants in the assessment of psychological, behavioral, and academic correlates of bullying and victimization. *Journal of Adolescence, 32,* 193–211.

Totura, C. M. Wienke, MacKinnon-Lewis, C., Gesten, E. L., Gadd, R., Divine, K. P., Dunham, S., & Kamboukos, D. (2009). Bullying and victimization among boys and girls in middle school: The influence of perceived family and school contexts. *Journal of Early Adolescence, 29,* 571–609.

Troop-Gordon, W., & Ladd, G. W. (2005). Trajectories of peer victimization and perceptions of the self and schoolmates: Precursors to internalizing and externalizing problems. *Child Development, 76,* 1072–1091.

Unnever, J. D. (2005). Bullies, aggressive victims, and victims: Are they distinct groups? *Aggressive Behavior, 31,* 153–171.

Van Goozen, S. H. M. (2005). Hormones and the developmental origins of aggression. In R. E. Tremblay, W. W. Hartup, & J. Archer (Eds.), *Developmental origins of aggression* (pp. 281–306). New York: Guilford.

Vossekuil, B., Fein, R. A., Reddy, M., Borum, R., & Modzeleski, W. (2002). *The final report and findings of the safe school initiative: Implications for the prevention of school attacks in the United States.* Washington, DC: U.S. Secret Service and U.S. Department of Education.

Walden, L. M., & Beran, T. N. (2010). Attachment quality and bullying behavior in school-aged youth. *Canadian Journal of School Psychology, 25,* 5–18.

Webster-Stratton, C., Mihalic, S., Fagan, A., Arnold, D., Taylor, T. K., & Tingley, C. (2001). *The incredible years: Parent, teacher, and child training series.* Blueprints for Violence Prevention Series, Book Eleven, BP-011. Boulder, CO: Center for the Study and Prevention of Violence.

Wilkinson, N., Ang, R., & Goh, D. (2008). Online video game therapy for mental health concerns: A review. *International Journal of Social Psychiatry, 54,* 370–382.

Williams, K. R., & Guerra, N. G. (2007). Prevalence and predictors of Internet bullying. *Journal of Adolescent Health, 41,* 14–21.

Xie, H., Swift, D. J., Cairns, B. D., & Cairns, R. B. (2002). Aggressive behavior in social interaction: A narrative analysis of interpersonal conflicts during early adolescence. *Social Development, 11,* 205–224.

CHAPTER SEVEN

Teachers and Teen Bullying

Deborah James, Maria Lawlor, Niamh Murphy, and Ann Flynn

Introduction

This chapter examines the ways that teachers influence school bullying. The first section outlines how teachers can influence the levels of bullying in schools in both a positive and negative manner. The second section outlines strategies and techniques that teachers can apply to prevent and respond to bullying. It covers general bullying and relational aggression and provides a rationale for why they should be dealt with in slightly separate ways.

Why Do Schools Vary in Their Levels of Bullying?

School bullying has been found to have diverse and negative effects on those victimized (James, Sofroniou, & Lawlor, 2003; Kim, Koh, & Leventhal, 2005; Skues, Cunningham, & Pokharel, 2005). Many countries have developed and introduced programs to combat bullying with mixed results (Olweus, 1993; Ortega, Del Rey, & Mora-Merchain, 2004; Stevens, De Bourdeaudhuij, & Van Oost, 2000). Research shows that interventions that focus on whole school antibullying efforts are more effective than curriculum-based approaches or social-skills training on their own (Swearer, Espelage, Vaillancourt, & Hymel, 2010). Efforts to understand differences in why interventions produce differing results have examined factors such as social climate, urbanization, catchments area, and school and class size (Galloway & Roland, 2004; Olweus, 1993; Swearer et al., 2010). Some researchers have advocated that bullying in schools should be tacked in a more holistic manner by examining the social climate (Siann, Callaghan, & Lockhart, 1993; Swearer et al., 2010). Studies examining effective schools have found that they are characterized by effective leadership, high expectations of students, students feeling supported and respected, consensus and cohesion among staff, a sense of community, staff modeling appropriate behavior, and members knowing, caring, and supporting one another (Ma, Stewin, & Mah, 2001; Swearer & Doll, 2001). "Successful" schools are associated with declines in bullying-related problems (Kasen, Berenson, Cohen, & Johnson, 2004), students liking school, more student empathy, greater academic motivation, and more altruistic behavior (Battisitch & Hom, 1997; Solomon, Watson, Battisitch, Schaps, & Deiucchi, 1992). Schools characterized by high conflict and poor student/teacher morale had higher levels of bullying (Kasen et al., 2004; Roland & Galloway, 2004). Research shows that teachers are central to the development and maintenance of school climate.

Teacher Attitudes toward Bullying

Studies have also shown that when teachers provide social support, students show better academic achievement, school adjustment, and mental health (Colarossi & Eccles, 2003; Flaspohler, Elfstrom, Vanderzee, & Sink, 2009). When students believe that teachers care about them, bullying was found to be lower (Lee, Buckthorpe, Craighead, & McCormack, 2008); they were less likely to engage in sex, alcohol, or drugs; and they were more likely to hold higher life satisfaction (Huebner, Funk, & Gilman, 2000). Support from teachers is protective, particularly when there is low parental support (Connors-Burrow, Johnson, Whiteside-Mansell, Mckelvey, & Gargus, 2009). When students feel that teachers are fair and caring, students feel that they have a stake in making the school safe (Hyman & Perrone, 1998), and they trust teachers to protect them from victimization (Doll, Song, & Siemers, 2004).

In terms of managing bullying in the school, children observe how the teacher responds (Aceves, Hinshaw, Mendoza-Denton, & Page-Gould, 2010), and this reinforces their beliefs as to whether teachers are people they can turn to and whether bullying is taken seriously in the school. Responding early is necessary to help students to feel safe (Doll et al., 2004; Meese, 1997). When teachers tolerate or dismiss bullying, it sends a message to all students (regardless of their involvement) that bullying is condoned (Hoover & Hazler, 1994). If bullies believe that their behavior is condoned or supported, it may escalate (Plaford, 2006; Salmivalli, 2001).

Although many antibullying programs advocate a "whole school" approach to the management of bullying, they tend to focus on behaviors between students and rarely focus on the quality of other relationships in the school, namely student to teacher, teacher to student, and teacher to teacher. If teachers bully students or are victimized by them, this is likely to influence the underlying culture of the school and may make antibullying strategies that concentrate solely on students ineffective.

Do Teachers Bully Students?

In one study (James et al., 2008) 30% of students reported being bullied by a teacher. The behaviors cited included being ignored, called names, threatened, physically hurt, and sexual harassment. While this sounds alarming, taking all reports of teacher bullying at face value may be too simplistic. It is possible that what teachers perceive as acceptable disciplinary measures may be seen by students as bullying behavior. For example, ignoring a student who is attention seeking may be an effective method for managing class discipline, but is it bullying? Ignoring a student for no reason or "picking on them" because they are disliked by the teacher is not appropriate. Stating the consequences of not completing work or of misbehavior, while appropriate, may be perceived by students as threatening behavior. Students may also perceive confiscation of their belongings as bullying, thus inflating the numbers reporting bullying by teachers. On the other hand, some of the behaviors described by students, such as name calling, physical abuse, and put downs are unequivocally bullying behaviors and fall within the category of "psychological maltreatment" (Hyman & Perrone, 1998; Sarno, 1992). This has huge implications for the well-being of students, in particular their emotional state and educational attainment, and affects the way in which they respond to teachers. To reduce misunderstanding in relation to this issue, it is important that bullying is discussed openly in the school, that all parties are aware of their actions, and that standards of acceptable behavior are met. This sounds simple, but in discussions with teachers, it appears that there is no clear-cut line between bullying and discipline. Some teachers view such behaviors as shouting at students and sarcasm as necessary classroom-management strategies. Often there is a difference of opinion among teachers as to whether these behaviors are acceptable. There is no way of knowing how many teachers engaged in bullying students in these studies. It is likely that extreme behaviors were perpetrated by a few individuals, but many of the behaviors mentioned are unequivocally bullying and need to stop. (See section on managing bullying in the school for ways to prevent misunderstandings.)

The power/authority that teachers have may make the effects of bullying worse for the individual. Most researchers agree than an incident of bullying involves an imbalance of power between the people involved (Olweus, 1997). In a classroom setting, teachers have an automatic power in the relationship (McEvoy, 2005) that does not apply when bullying is between two peers. Between students there is a theoretical possibility for the power to shift from one individual to another. Teachers may claim that their behavior is justified, either as a necessary classroom strategy or because they were provoked by their targets (McEvoy, 2005), thus drawing attention away from the unacceptable behavior. Bystanders are also less empowered to intervene in bullying between a teacher and students without involving another adult. Indeed, abusive behaviors by teachers send a message of fear to the others in the class, which enhances their vulnerability (McEvoy, 2005). If a teacher is bullying a student in a classroom, it is likely that there is an audience. This may make the situation more difficult for the person bullied in a number of ways: it increases the humiliation through its public nature and also sends a message to the others in the class that this person is unworthy of better treatment. This has the potential to set up the person for other forms of bullying. On the other hand, it may be possible to shrug off a put-down from a teacher more easily because his or her opinion may be less important than those of friends, but on the whole, it appears that being bullied by a teacher may have greater implications for young people than bullying by their peers.

Do Students Bully Teachers?

Students are also culpable of engaging in bullying teachers. Behaviors directed toward teachers include ignoring them, insolence, name calling, noncooperation, physical threats and theft of belongings, lack of preparation for or attention in class, verbal abuse, threats, insolence, sexual harassment, damage to their property, and rumors (James et al., 2008; Terry, 1998; TUI, 2006). Research shows that student misbehavior constitutes one of the major sources of stress for teachers (Borg & Falzon, 1989; Boulton, 1997; Smilansky, 1984), leaving them feeling drained and stressed, and lowering their morale (TUI, 2006). Some may simply shrug it off, but others may internalize or externalize the effects, which in turn may provoke a maladaptive response. Either way, it is unacceptable that teachers have to endure such behavior from their students. The high level of aggression and low level of respect for teachers is likely to substantially affect the level of discipline and subsequently the standard of teaching in the classes of teachers where these conditions prevail. In the TUI study, teachers estimated that dealing with threatening or intimidating behavior took more than 10 minutes of class time to deal with. Considering that teachers experienced disruptive behavior on a weekly and often daily basis, this adds up to a considerable amount of time that is not being used for teaching. In classes where these situations are common, such behavior must impact educational attainment. It also has implications for the effectiveness of antibullying programs. If students witness, or engage in, bullying teachers, then they are unlikely to respect that teacher or believe in that teachers' ability to mange bullying or help them with a bullying problem. It is difficult for anyone to admit that they are being bullied, and for teachers it is particularly difficult as they are alone in the classroom and are expected to deal with it. Admitting to being bullied to a colleague or management could be seen as failure.

Teachers Managing Bullying

There is no doubt that teachers are under increasing stress from disruption and harassment by students. However, teachers are the adults in the dynamic and, acting in loco parentis, have a role in directing the development of young people (Hart, 1987). They should be striving to create an environment that treats students with firmness, respect, and understanding. Without this, teachers may be seen as adversaries rather than positive role models (Twemlow, Fonagey, Sacco, & Brethour, 2006). Managing bullying is a difficult task, and as research shows, many teachers are unable to deal with it. There is a need for increased training at both preservice and in-service levels. Without the awareness and willingness to deal with bullying, it will continue to flourish. The role that teachers can play in the management of bullying is also highly dependent on the level of practical support provided by senior management. Without the support of the principal, antibullying programs will not work. Parents also have an important role in supporting teachers. If they have an understanding of bullying and are supportive of antibullying and disciplinary procedures, this aids teachers in managing bullying (Plaford, 2006).

Can Bullying Be Eradicated?

Smith & Brain (2000) state that "bully/victim problems are normative in the strictly limited sense that they are likely to be found in any relatively enduring human group, bullying is found in many societies, and although normative does not mean that they are socially acceptable." If this is true, it may be unrealistic to expect that bullying can be totally eradicated from our society and therefore must be managed. If we accept that bullying cannot be totally eradicated from our society, that it is difficult to encourage teenagers to tell someone about bullying, and that increased awareness results in more reporting (or realization that what is happening really is bullying), then program interventions need to focus on how bullying is dealt with in the school environment as well as aiming to reduce the frequency of bullying behaviors.

In general, initiatives designed for primary schools show more positive results than those aimed at adolescents (Rigby, 2002; Smith & Sharp, 1994). Cognitive development may have an impact. Younger children are more amenable to obeying directives from adults, and many stop bullying behaviors when asked to do so. They are also more likely to tell an adult if another child hits them, takes their belongings, or excludes them from games. Management of bullying is easier at the elementary level. Teachers are usually responsible for one class and can concentrate their efforts. Implementation of programs is more difficult at the middle/high school level, as there are more complex timetables and more complicated organizational structures, such as more students, student groups varying by subject, and more teachers (Weissberg, Caplan, & Harwood, 1991; Weissberg, Caplan, & Sivo, 1989). Teenagers are also less likely to seek adult help (Boulton & Underwood, 1992). A culture of secrecy surrounds bullying and, coupled with the reluctance to be thought of as a snitch, makes it difficult to encourage adolescents to tell about bullying (Boulton & Underwood, 1992; Melton et al., 1998; O'Moore, Kirkham, & Smith, 1997; Rigby & Barnes, 2002; Rivers & Smith, 1994; Whitney & Smith, 1993). Ortega & Lera (2000) suggest that older children, especially those involved in bullying or other antisocial behavior, may reject teacher influences and the values advocated by the school and therefore continue to bully, even though it goes against the rules of the school. Therefore, it is imperative that schools implement a planned and consistent approach to the management of bullying.

Studies show that many teachers do not have a good understanding of bullying and how to manage it (Bauman & Del Rio, 2005; Boulton, 1997). This is reflected in the views of students who indicate that they are skeptical about their teachers' ability to identify or respond appropriately to bullying (Hanish & Guerra, 2000; Houndoumadi & Pataeraki, 2001). In one study (Charach, Pepler, & Zieler, 1995) 70% of teachers thought they intervened "almost always" while only 25% of the students agreed. In another study (Harris, Petrie, & Willoughby, 2002), it was found that only 35% of students thought that their teachers were interested in stopping bullying, and only 25% thought that school administrators were interested in stopping bullying. Students are also skeptical of teachers' abilities to respond appropriately or to make a difference (Harris et al., 2002; Hoover, Oliver, & Hazler, 1992).

Telling about Bullying Is Not So Easy

The reluctance of teenagers to tell a teacher is unsurprising given their skepticism of teachers' abilities to deal with bullying effectively. Telling someone that you are being victimized is difficult to do. Many do not tell because they are ashamed to admit (to themselves as well as others) that it is happening. Others believe that the situation will get worse if they tell or that nothing will be done. Rigby & Barnes (2002) concluded that interventions by teachers could make matters worse unless handled in a competent and sensitive way. If students are to be encouraged to tell about bullying, then teachers need to be seen as people who are interested in finding out about bullying and who deal with it confidentially, sensitively, and competently. As Galloway & Roland (2004) suggest, the manner and effectiveness of interventions that show a teacher's ability to create a climate of security and to maintain constructive social relationships is crucial. For discipline and antibullying strategies to be effective in schools, there needs to be agreed-upon standards of behavior for both staff and students. If a standardized approach is taken across the school, then this lessens the opportunity for getting away with inappropriate behavior.

Managing Bullying in Schools

As mentioned earlier, antibullying strategies that encompass the whole school are generally found to be more effective. In successful schools, the staff have bought into the idea that they can play a constructive role in managing bullying. This involves proactive and reactive interventions by teachers. Even in the best-run schools, bullying will continue to occur, and staff have to consistently and continually demonstrate to students that they take it seriously and are prepared to deal with it.

Experience in working with schools has demonstrated that antibullying strategies will never reach optimal success without the support of principals and others in a management role. Schools where the principals have invested time and effort into managing bullying have been shown to increase results (Limber, Nation, Tracy, Melton, & Flerex, 2004). School management has an important task not only in setting the agenda that bullying is unacceptable and initiating responses that demonstrate that they are prepared to deal with it, but also in enabling staff to deal with it effectively. This involves:

- Providing on-going in-service training for teachers, especially new staff.
- Providing the time and resources for staff to investigate and respond to incidents.
- Scheduling regular antibullying-awareness weeks/days.
- Monitoring effectiveness of strategies and procedures.
- Developing and reviewing antibullying and code-of-discipline policies in conjunction with staff.
- Provision of parents' awareness nights.
- Providing/accessing support for victims of bullying.
- Providing/accessing support for those involved in bullying others.

As mentioned earlier, in order to prevent the types of misunderstandings associated with acceptable/unacceptable disciplinary strategies, it is advisable to hold staff meetings or in-service training days where acceptable/unacceptable behaviors are discussed and agreed upon by all staff. These should cover student-to-student, student-to-teacher, teacher-to-student, teacher-to-parent, and parent-to-teacher behaviors.

It can also be useful to set up a personal safety committee (ideally made up of management and interested staff members), whose function is to oversee the antibullying strategies and responses within the school. Ideally, schools should aim to hold an antibullying/friendship week at least once a year to reinforce the message that bullying is unacceptable and will be dealt with, and to remind students of the ways to support one another and to seek support from staff. This is an ideal time to teach antibullying curricula on both general and relational bullying (James, Flynn, Lawlor, & Murphy, 2010).

A Conceptual Model for Managing Bullying

A useful model for dealing with bullying behavior is offered by the concept of restorative versus retributive justice. Restorative justice provides a holistic view that seeks to restore the balance of relationships between students in the school. In addition to supporting the victim, a restorative approach also takes into account the needs of the person who is bullying (Morrison, 2002). Table 7.1 compares the framework for restorative justice versus retributive justice.

Table 7.1 Retributive versus restorative justice.

Retributive Justice	Restorative Justice
Misdemeanors defined as violation of school rules	Misdemeanor defined as violation of a person's right by another
Focus on establishing blame	Focusing on problem solving by expressing feelings and needs first, and then how to meet those needs
Adversarial relationship	Dialogue and negotiation—everyone involved, listening to each other
Punishment to deter/prevent	Restitution, reconciliation, and restoration as a goal
Accountability defined as taking punishment	Accountability defined as understanding the impact of the action, deciding to put things right, and making reparation
Conflict seen as individual versus the school	Misdemeanors recognized as interpersonal conflicts; value of conflict as potential opportunity for learning is recognized

Teenagers are often afraid and reluctant to tell an adult that they are being bullied; therefore, to manage bullying effectively within a school, teachers have to take a proactive role. There are many opportunities to address bullying, both formally and informally. Informal networking between teachers on a day-to-day basis provides opportunities for preempting and monitoring. Where a specific technique is being used to respond to a particular situation in class, it is important that all teachers involved with the class be informed of the approach being taken and be given appropriate feedback. In any approach to resolving bullying, care should be taken to ensure that information supplied to or by a teacher is not used to further torment a victim. The following three strategies can be used as preventative measures as well as for investigating incidents.

Confidential Questionnaires

Confidential questionnaires are the simplest way of discovering who needs help in dealing with bullying. A short questionnaire can be completed in class time. Table 7.2 provides a template for a class questionnaire.

A more confidential method would be to allow the same question to be answered at home, signed by parents, and returned in a sealed envelope. Some schools do this on a regular basis.

Table 7.2 Template for class questionnaire.

Name:

Class:

Would you like to talk to someone about bullying?

        No   Yes

Class Observation

Class observation involves all subject teachers recording behavior over an agreed-upon time period, pooling the information, and deciding on a course of action. This observation is carried out unobtrusively. Class observation is a useful tool for discovering the dynamics at work in the group. (Note that in relational aggression the dynamics may be too subtle to be observed using class observation alone.) Teachers may find class observation useful when bullying is suspected, but more evidence is required to determine its source. In cases where bullying has been reported and there is a risk of retaliation, this strategy protects confidentiality and enables evidence to be gathered through direct teacher observation. It may also be used to gather information when a teacher is being bullied, especially by a group of students.

Aims of Class Observation
- To improve class atmosphere, by protecting the rights of students and teachers.
- To coordinate teachers' responses to bullying behavior.
- To identify and encourage constructive influences in the class.
- To record problematic behavior systematically.
- To identify students who need support, including those engaged in questionable behavior.
- To provide management and parents with accurate information on bullying.
- To enable teachers to establish standards of what is acceptable and unacceptable, and to implement these.

Class observations are best carried out discreetly and confidentially with the support of the principal, who can facilitate teachers meetings to pool information and ensure follow-up (see table 7.3).

Steps for Implementation
- Convene an initial meeting of teachers and outline the nature of the problem.
- Explain the procedure and how you propose to use it.

Teachers and Teen Bullying　　　　　　　　　　　　　　　　　　　　137

Table 7.3 Sample class observation form.

Time	Name	Behavior	Directed toward
2:15	John	Sniggered when Harry asked a question	Harry
	Phillip	Joined in and made more comments	Harry
	Ann	Rolled her eyes and made sighing noises	Harry
3:30	Sarah	Defended Mary who was being teased	

- Emphasize confidentiality.
- Fix a date for returning completed forms. Two weeks should suffice, but urgent issues should be dealt with immediately under school procedures.
- Gather evidence and record on observation forms.
- Convene follow-up meeting of teachers and pool information.
- Decide on appropriate response in line with the school's policies and procedures.
- Interview students concerned. (See guidelines on conducting interviews.)
- Review progress with class teachers.

Behavior in the corridors, playgrounds, toilets, changing rooms, etc., should also be included. Ancillary staff may be aware and knowledgeable about what is going on, and their observations and comments should be included.

Bullying Sociogram

A sociogram is a useful strategy for exploring relationships in a class or group. The method employed is to ask each individual a series of questions designed to uncover the social dynamic in a class, thus identifying positive and negative influences in the group.

Aims of the Sociogram
Preventative
- To prevent bullying by adopting a pastoral approach. The direct intervention of an individual teacher will build trust and confidence in the school's antibullying policy and inspire better relationships among the students themselves. Awareness of the unacceptability of bullying will be raised even if there are no problems in the group.
- To provide a safe structure that encourages disclosure of bullying situations, thereby uncovering emerging or previously undetected cases.
- To establish a clear picture of the social dynamic operating within the class by identifying:

- The power structure among students
- Levels of bullying and victimization
- Students involved
- Students at risk

To identify strengths within the group. To empower bystanders, and to encourage mutual support between students.

This will give the teacher firsthand information and a better understanding of the hidden subculture of the group.

Reactive
- To investigate reported incidents of bullying. This includes one-to-one bullying or incidents involving a group.
- To stop bullying by providing an immediate response, and to reduce the possibility of retaliation.

Procedural
- To embed antibullying measures into teachers' classroom practice. Information may also be used as an early warning system to form the basis of a team response by other subject teachers.
- To fit in with the school's discipline structure by allowing teachers to establish standards of acceptable behavior.
- To facilitate the noting, recording, and investigating of bullying.

When to Use the Sociogram
The sociogram can be used as a powerful preventative measure in the first grade, before serious patterns of negative behavior take hold and when students are beginning to form relationships. Students will be reassured by the experience of a teacher who is supportive and is encouraging a safe and friendly atmosphere, and who is prepared to act with authority when necessary.

The sociogram can be used at regular intervals as part of the pastoral element of the school. It can be used in cases where bullying has occurred as a nonconfrontational intervention.

Steps for Implementation
Consult with school management, antibullying support team, or pastoral care team. Decide who should administer the sociogram.

Seek the cooperation of the subject teacher and arrange for a double class period if possible.

At the appointed time, explain the purpose of the sociogram to students. Inform the whole class that you are going to talk to everyone about their experience of the class atmosphere and whether it needs to be improved. Explain that this measure is part of the school's antibullying measures. Tell the class that you will give them feedback.

The subject teacher continues to work with the class, thus ensuring minimum disruption. Individual students are interviewed privately (see sample form for key questions). Each student is informed of the confidential nature of the interview, reassuring them that they will not be identified as providing the information. Be clear that all students will be asked the same questions. This protects victims from retaliation on the basis that the picture you have formed comes from the contributions of the whole class. Have the class list on hand to record information. You may find it useful to make a visual representation of the information on a chart, especially where there is a recurring problem. Record the details.

A clear picture of the class dynamic will emerge. Discuss general findings with the whole class. Identify ways in which the class is working well in terms of cooperation and friendships. If this is overwhelmingly positive, the preventative aspect of the strategy will still have come into play. Praise the class for their cooperative spirit and reward them if possible.

If problems have been identified, deal with the problem behavior immediately after interviewing all students. Discuss evidence privately with students who were identified as behaving in a bullying manner using the restorative approach.

Be specific about the problem behavior, explain why it is wrong, and challenge the inappropriateness of it. Be clear that it is totally unacceptable in the school. Seek agreement on facts and future behavior, and arrange a follow-up meeting. It may be useful to have a tutor or year head witness the agreement.

Inform the young person that this will be monitored and that other teachers will be made aware of the situation. Arrange a time to review progress. Mention the rights of others. Explain to the student that being popular in class is more likely to arise from being admired by others, rather than being feared. Emphasize that you have formed an opinion on his or her behavior by talking to everyone in the class. No one should be singled out for revenge or retaliation. This also applies to friends of the offending student. Make it clear that you will be checking up on this. Make a record of the interview.

Negotiate a whole-class agreement regarding future acceptable behavior.

Provide the results of the sociogram to teachers and decide on a strategy for supervision and monitoring.

Arrange to review progress with the class and class teachers.

Table 7.4 presents sample questions for the sociogram, and table 7.5 provides a template for the sociogram.

Table 7.4 Sample questions for the sociogram.

- Are you happy with the atmosphere in the class?
- Who are your friends?
- Are you being bullied in any way? (If the answer is yes, get the details and reassure the student that the problem will be addressed.)
- Is there anyone in the class who is being picked on or having a hard time?
- Is there anyone being left out or ignored?
- Is there anyone spreading rumors or gossip? Or using notes, phone calls, texts, emails, etc. to make others feel bad about themselves?
- Is anyone being unfair to others?
- Is there a group of students making life difficult for others?
- Are students from other classes giving anyone in this class a hard time?
- Can you give examples?
- What do you think is causing the problem?
- What can you do to help students who are having a hard time?
- Have you been bullying anyone?

What Can You Do When Young People Are Being Bullied?

Listen. Listening is therapeutic in itself. Being available to listen is the first step in supporting the victims. Allow victims to tell their stories in their own words.

Take notes. These form the basis of the report for dealing with the incident. Include such details as the nature of the incident, date, time, location, names of those involved, names of witnesses, and other relevant information.

Reassure. Affirm that they have done the right thing by coming forward and assure them that help is available and action will be taken. Reassure them that nothing is wrong with them and that they don't have to face it alone.

Table 7.5 Sample bullying sociogram form.

Who is bullying?	What is the behavior?	Who is it directed toward?
John	Kicking, calling names Mentioned Keith and Sam	Tom
Niamh, Orla	Used to be friends with Mary, now excluding her from the group Mentioned by Mary and Liz	Mary

Ensure students' safety. Ensure that students are not in any immediate danger. If there is a risk, ask the parents to collect them from the school, or make arrangements to keep the potential assailant from carrying out the attack. The school should also ensure that there is adequate supervision if the young person's safety has been compromised.

Negotiate confidentiality. Discuss with students the limits of confidentiality. Explain that while you will endeavor to maintain confidentiality, there are times when you have to discuss the matter with other staff to ensure the safety of all students. For example, in certain circumstances you may need to talk to the alleged bullies, parents, witnesses, other teachers, and school management as appropriate. Explain that you will only tell those who need to know and give a reason for why they have to be told. Clearly outline how you will build safeguards for the victims' safety and privacy. For example, the young people can be told that the perpetrators will be warned not to retaliate and that you will be checking up on this.

Tell the students that you will keep them informed. Let them know how you are going to proceed and how you will keep them informed.

Making the Intervention

Decide who to consult. Be clear about the school's policies and procedures, as these will vary from school to school.

Information and advice may be available from the following:

- Class tutor
- Year head
- Antibullying coordinator/team
- Management
- School counselor
- Parent/s of victim
- Parent/s of bully
- Outside agencies

Decide Whom to Interview

On the basis of the information you have, decide whom to interview. This will most likely include the victim, witnesses (either students or staff), and the alleged bully. It is advisable to interview the person with the most power in the group last. It may also be useful to interview students who are not involved. This may provide you with an unbiased perspective. Take a calm, problem-solving approach. Deal with conflict in a nonaggressive, nonconfrontational manner.

Conducting an Interview within a Restorative Justice Approach

There are a number of points to keep in mind when working within a restorative justice framework.

- Make sure all participants have an opportunity to tell their story. Ensure that the victim's experiences, needs, and feelings are respected and that they are given space to acknowledge their harm/loss.
- Focus on rebuilding relationships. Give the perpetrators an opportunity to hear in a safe and respectful forum how their behavior affected the victim.
- Success requires exploration of the complexities of the issue, a common understanding being reached, acceptance of responsibility, and acknowledgement of effort and compromise.
- Confront and disapprove of wrongdoing. Hold the bullies accountable for their actions while still supporting and valuing their inherent worth.
- Offer the perpetrators the opportunity to repair the harm they have caused. Reparation should be appropriate and within their capacity to fulfill. All participants should be encouraged to learn from the experience and move on.

Other important points to keep in mind include:

Privacy. Students usually disclose more in private because they feel safer. Dealing with incidents in public may cause unnecessary embarrassment for the victim, increase his or her vulnerability, and encourage confrontation and denial on the offender's side. Privacy is also important for witnesses and other members of the class; threats may have been made, or they may be under pressure to support one side or the other. It might be useful to enlist the support of a colleague to help with interviewing the members of the group individually.

Nonconfrontational approach. Welcome the students, thank them for their cooperation, and let them know that you see yourself as facilitating a problem-solving approach rather dishing out punishment. Refer to the behavior as being unacceptable, as opposed to labeling the person as a bully. Be calm and constructive, and allow enough time for the interview. Most young people respond to patience and the opportunity to talk, rather than to pressure, anger, or impatience.

What Not to Do!

Don't blame or finger-wag!

Don't lose your cool.

Don't accuse—ask for details.

Don't come to conclusions without hearing all sides of the story from all sources. Don't be afraid to ask for help from colleagues.

Examples of possible opening statements are the following:

- There seems to be difficulty between yourself and Mary. I am here to help resolve the situation. I need your cooperation to get it sorted. I feel your contribution to the problem is extremely important; your help is going to make all the difference. (Allow time to respond.)
- If you have made a mistake in your behavior, even if it is a serious one, I want to help you work things out. The most important thing from everyone's point of view is that it never happens again. I think it is very important that it is settled here and now. (Allow time to respond.)
- This talk is between the two of us at the moment, and I don't want to involve the principal or parents at this point. (Note that serious cases may need to be dealt with immediately.)
- We have dealt with a lot of different kinds of situations, and we usually manage to sort things out, even serious problems. (Allow time to respond.)

At this point, it should be clear to the teacher whether the student is responding to the approach. Check that the student understands what you are saying and what your approach is. Ask whether you need to clarify or repeat anything. Give the student time to think over what you have said.

Some questions you might like to use when seeking further information include:

- How do you get along with the other student/s?
- Did you know one another before the incident took place?
- How long have you known each other?
- Is there a history to the problem, or did it come out of the blue?
- Do you think it will be easy to get back on good terms with the other person?

Offer a choice between talking about what happened or writing it down. Writing can be less confrontational, especially for young people who might regard a one-to-one interaction with a teacher as adversarial.

Let's have a look at the incident now. I need to understand your involvement. Can you help me fill in the details from your point of view? This is what I need to be clear about.

- What happened?
- When and where did it take place?

- Who was involved?
- What part did you play?
- Was there more than one person involved on either side?
- Were there any witnesses?
- Did this take place more than once?
- Have you been involved in anything like this before?

Encourage the young person to focus on taking responsibility for his or her own actions, rather than assigning blame to others in the group. Don't accept standard techniques for saving face, such as "I was only messing" or "We were all doing it." Ask the young person to talk about his or her specific role at the time. For example:

- What did you actually say or do?
- How would someone who witnessed the incident describe your actions?
- Would you do the same thing again or act differently?
- What did you do wrong?
- Do you understand what was wrong about it?
- What was the problem with what you did?

When you have the information recorded, the conversation needs to focus on making restitution in the spirit of the restorative approach. Some questions to consider include:

- How do you feel about the situation?
- Are you worried about what is going to happen?
- What do you think is fair in this situation?
- This is what I think is fair. (Outline a fair outcome, such as apologizing, agreeing to mediation, signing an agreement with a parent present, agreeing to meet with a counselor, paying for damage, returning money or the equivalent value of property, serving time in detention or suspension.)

Invite a comment from the young person. A cooperative attitude should be praised. If the solution to the problem is agreed by all concerned, the matter may be concluded.

What If There Is Complete Denial?

Cases will arise from time to time where there is complete denial of involvement. Repeat the evidence as you see it and try again. It may be necessary to protect the confidentiality of your information. Stay focused on what you believe actually took place. Do not accuse the young person of lying:

- This is the situation as I see it. (Give details.)
- Anybody who examined it would think the same about your responsibility.
- I do not accept that I am hearing the full story from what has been said so far.

Explain your role again (as above) and let the young person know that this is an opportunity for him or her to be forthright and honest. If there is still denial, explain that you are not going to let the matter rest until it has been resolved, and outline what the next steps are according to school policy, for example:

- Reporting to the principal
- Initiating a wider investigation
- Contacting parents
- Contacting outside agencies, such as the juvenile liaison officer of the police. Psychology service may have a role if there appears to be psychological difficulties.

Where there is an admission of responsibility, it is crucially important to be unequivocal about the immediate and future behavior of the young person.

- The behavior should cease immediately.
- The young person is aware that disciplinary implications already apply in the situation.
- Agreement should be sought about not taking revenge against the victim or others who the bully suspects may have provided information for teachers.
- If agreement is not forthcoming, a warning should be made that also extends to the friends of the bully.
- Measures need to be taken by the school to ensure the safety of the victim and to supervise the behavior of the others involved. A case discussion involving school management and other relevant personnel will decide on possible sanctions.
- If bullying continues, management have to choose between suspension/expulsion or referral of the offender for psychological assessment. An assessment will point to whether the young person has psychological or psychiatric difficulties contributing to the behavior and whether anger management training might be a useful next step.
- Discuss with the parents the possibility for counseling for their son/daughter.
- Keep a record of the interview.

In cases where the bullying requires the imposition of sanctions, the cooperation of parents is crucial. Agreement should be sought from parents and the student involved in relation to future behavior. If the incident remains unsolved at the school level, the matter should be referred to the school's board of management. Failing this, it should be referred to the appropriate educational authority.

Management of Relational Aggression

Over the last several years, researchers have examined more subtle forms of aggression known as relational aggression (James, Flynn, Lawlor, & Murphy, 2010). They describe behaviors that harm others through damage or threat of damage to friendships or group inclusion. These can include manipulative, controlling, belittling, demeaning, rejecting, and exclusionary behaviors in a social context. They also include damage or threat of damage to reputation. Behaviors many be verbal or nonverbal, direct or indirect. They are often subtle and have a profound effect on the victim but may be less easy for an outsider to identify. Although relational aggression in girls comes to the attention of parents and teachers, it is known that boys also engage in this form of aggression, particularly in late adolescence and adulthood (James, Flynn, Lawlor, & Murphy, 2010).

Although not all incidents of relational aggression are bullying, we contend that when done in a systematic, repeated way it becomes bullying. There are many reasons suggested for why young people engage in relational aggression (retaliation, popularity, control, fear of being targeted, power, inadequate conflict resolution skills) (James, Flynn, Lawlor, Courtney, et al., 2010; James, Flynn, Lawlor, & Murphy, 2010). However, these reasons may be the symptoms of more complex behaviors, which may be conscious or unconscious. Relational aggression is modeled by parents, peers, and the media and is often portrayed as being a useful tool "for getting what you want" (James, Flynn, Lawlor, & Murphy, 2010). Parents may be relationally aggressive, using threats to the security of the parent-child relationship to force children to cooperate. Children may learn to use this type of behavior to force peers to comply with them. Children also experience and learn negative conflict-resolution skills from parents (Grynch & Fincham, 1990). Secure parental attachment is associated with social competence and subjective well-being. Poor attachment may lead children to feel insecure in their relationships with others. They may use socially aggressive strategies to protect personal status and may have learned that manipulating a relationship is a good way of achieving their needs. Children with attachment difficulties are often hyper-vigilant to signs of unavailability and become clingy to ensure proximity. They may also be sensitive to threats of rejection and may use withdrawal and the silent treatment to express anger (James, Flynn, Lawlor, & Murphy, 2010). We believe that relational aggression is not as straightforward as general bullying. While some of the behaviors may be deliberate, others may be an unconscious reaction to dynamics in the relationship. Young people may perceive an action as a threat to their sense of self and react aggressively to protect their sense of self. They may also remain in unhealthy relationships in the mistaken belief that these behaviors are part of normal friendships or because they are afraid to lose the friendships.

As teachers, it can be more difficult to determine when an individual needs help and support around relational aggression. Many of the behaviors are subtle and hard to distinguish from normal adolescent behavior. It is hard for a teenager to admit to general bullying, but it is even more difficult for them to discuss relational aggression. Many young people do not understand the dynamics involved in relational aggression and blame themselves. They are often ashamed and embarrassed to admit that their friendships are not working well.

There are a number of symptoms that teachers can be aware of:

- Changes in appearance
- Changes in engagement in class activities
- Changes in academic performance
- Social withdrawal
- Sitting apart from friends that used to be close
- School absence
- Reluctance to attend certain classes or places
- Frequent illnesses
- Fearfulness
- Anxiety
- Panic attacks
- Dropping of usual hobbies and interests
- Uncharacteristic outbursts of anger
- Excessive sensitivity to criticism

As a teacher, if you see any of these changes in a student, it may be worth checking in with the student.

Relational aggression is complex and often involves circular escalating patterns, where individuals alternate between being bully and victim. The "who did what and when" model of investigation may not be a particularly useful strategy in resolving the issue. Getting to the root of the problem may not be possible. In many cases, those involved are unable to pinpoint the beginning, and the behaviors have developed as a response to the situations that they find themselves in. Some responses may be a deliberate effort to exercise control, dominance, or manipulation; others may occur as a defense against feeling threatened (James, Flynn, Lawlor, Courtney, et al., 2010). As an outsider with limited knowledge of the individuals concerned, it may be impossible to tell why an individual is behaving in this way. That said, if an incident of relational aggression presents itself to you, you still have a duty to investigate and try to resolve it. (Note that not all incidents can be resolved, and the best-case scenario might be that individuals agree to have nothing more to do with each other.) The principles of restorative justice apply, and many of the interviewing techniques described above are useful, but there are a number of additional points you may wish to take into consideration. Working with the perpetrators:

- Start by stating that there seems to be a problem—someone is very hurt—can you throw any light on what is going on?
- Adopt a problem-solving approach. State that you are not here to apportion blame, but rather to reach a resolution.
- Refer to the power of a group and how it can be used or abused, and explore with the individuals their use of power and whether they are using it effectively.
- Refer to what it might *feel* like to be a victim of exclusion or isolation. Explore whether they have experienced this and how they may have coped. Explore whether this is how they want to make others feel.
- Focus on the leadership qualities that the perpetrators may have—how they can get others to do their bidding and how this gives them great responsibility. Ask them to consider how they can use these skills to help the situation.
- If there is clear evidence of bullying, get it stopped.
- Ask for their cooperation to ensure there is no more bullying in the group, and ask for their ideas as to how they may do this.
- Explain to them that you will be checking in regularly with the group to monitor progress and changes.
- Praise prosocial behavior.

Working with the people excluded:

- Listen to the story and be particularly empathic, as it is very difficult for a young person to admit to or talk about relational aggression. Admitting that you cannot solve problems in a relationship, or that you have been rejected by your friends, is shameful and embarrassing.
- Ask what led up to the exclusion, but do not get too caught up in "who did what." Make your judgment based on the stories of all involved.
- Explain that friendships change and that people have a right to make new friends. (This may be an important albeit painful point for some to accept.)
- Explain that you need to establish if the behavior is bullying, as everyone has the right not to be bullied.

- Ascertain if bullying is happening. (It may not; it may simply be a case of friendships ending.)
- If there is bullying behavior, ensure that it is stopped.
- Discuss options—what does he/she really want? "If you could wave a magic wand . . ."
- Explain that parting is painful but not life-threatening!
- Discuss the possibility of the victim making new friends. Encourage her/him to make the first move toward possible new friends. If appropriate, partner the individual with students who are likely to be supportive. This may be done during class/project work or through extracurricular activities. (You may need to enlist the support of other staff in this.)
- Check in with the student on a regular basis.

In some cases you may have to talk to the parents concerned and make a referral to appropriate services, if this is warranted.

Conclusion

Although dealing with bullying may seem like a daunting task, there is evidence to show that making the effort to ensure that students feel safe and cared for by the school can reap benefits in terms of a more positive school atmosphere, better academic performance, and better student/teacher relationships. There are many strategies that can be utilized to prevent and respond to bullying. Teachers play a range of important roles in the way bullying is dealt with in the school. Their behavior can act as a positive or a negative role model for students. If students believe that their teachers are bullies, are seen to condone bullying, or are ineffective in dealing with it, then they are unlikely to feel safe in school and will have no faith in the school's response to bullying. On the other hand, teachers are ideally placed to inspire confidence in students by developing and demonstrating codes of acceptable behavior, by implementing prevention strategies, and by intervening appropriately. In order for antibullying strategies to be effective, they have to fully encompass the concept of a whole-school approach and evaluate the role of schools in the dynamics. As teachers are central to the workings of the school, it makes sense that antibullying strategies should start by examining the roles that teachers play.

References

Aceves, M. J., Hinshaw, S. P., Mendoza-Denton, R., & Page-Gould, E. (2010). Seek help from teachers or fight back? Student perceptions of teachers' actions during conflicts and response to peer victimisation. *Journal of Youth Adolescence, 39,* 658–669.

Battisitch, D. K., & Hom, A. (1997). The relationship between students' sense of their school as a community and their involvement in problem behavior. *American Journal of Public Health, 87,* 1997–2001.

Bauman, S., & Del Rio, A. (2005). Knowledge and beliefs about bullying in schools. *School Psychology International, 26,* 428–442.

Borg, M. G., & Falzon, J. M. (1989). Primary school teachers' perception of pupils' undesirable behaviors. *Educational Studies, 15,* 251–260.

Boulton, M. J. (1997). Teachers' views on bullying: Definitions, attitudes and ability to cope. *British Journal of Educational Psychology, 67,* 223–233.

Boulton, M. J., & Underwood, K. (1992). Bully victim problems among middle school children. *British Journal of Educational Psychology, 62,* 73–87.

Charach, A., Pepler, D. J., & Zieler, S. (1995). Bullying at school: A Canadian perspective. *Education Canada, 35,* 12–18.

Colarossi, L. G., & Eccles, J. S. (2003). Differential effects of support providers on adolescents' mental health. *Social Work Research, 27,* 19–30.

Connors-Burrow, N. A., Johnson, D. A., Whiteside-Mansell, L., Mckelvey, L., & Gargus, R. A. (2009). Adults matter: Protecting children from the negative impacts of bullying. *Psychology in the Schools, 46,* 593–604.

Doll, B., Song, S., & Siemers, E. (2004). Classroom ecologies that support or discourage bullying. In D. L. Espelage & S. M. Swearer (Eds.), *Bullying in American schools: A social-ecological perspective on prevention and intervention* (pp. 161–184). Mahwah: NJ: Lawrence Erlbaum Associates.

Flaspohler, P. D., Elfstrom, J. L., Vanderzee, K. L., & Sink, H. E. (2009). Stand by me: The effects of peer and teacher support in mitigating the impact of bullying on quality of life. *Psychology in the Schools, 46,* 636–649.

Galloway, D., & Roland, E. (2004). Is the direct approach to reducing bullying always the best? In P. K. Smith, D. J. Pepler, & K. Rigby (Eds.), *Bullying in schools. How successful can interventions be?* Cambridge, UK: Cambridge University Press.

Grynch, J. H., & Fincham, F. D. (1990). Marital conflict and children's adjustment: A cognitive-contextual framework. *Psychological Bulletin, 108,* 267–290.

Hanish, L. D., & Guerra, N. G. (2000). Children who get victimised at school. What is known? What can be done? *Professional School Counselling, 4,* 113–119.

Harris, S., Petrie, G., & Willoughby, W. (2002). Bullying among 9th graders: An exploratory study. *NASSP Bulletin, 86,* 630.

Hart, S. N. (1987). Psychological maltreatment in schooling. *School Psychology Review, 16,* 169–180.

Hoover, J. H., & Hazler, R. J. (1994). Bullies and victims. *Elementary School Guidance and Counseling, 25,* 212–220.

Hoover, J. H., Oliver, R., & Hazler, R. J. (1992). Bullying: Perceptions of adolescent victims in the midwestern USA. *School Psychology International, 13,* 5–16.

Houndoumadi, A., & Pataeraki, L. (2001). Bullying and bullies in Greek elementary schools: Pupils' attitudes and teachers' and parents' awareness. *Educational Review, 53,* 19–27.

Huebner, E. S., Funk, B. A., & Gilman, R. (2000). Cross-sectional longitudinal psychosocial correlates of adolescent life satisfaction. *Canadian Journal of School Psychology, 16,* 53–64.

Hyman, I. A., & Perrone, D. C. (1998). The other side of school violence. Educator policies and practices that might contribute to student misbehavior. *Journal of School Psychology, 36,* 7–27.

James, D. J., Flynn, A., Lawlor, M., Courtney, P., Murphy, N., & Henry, B. (2010). A friend in deed? Can adolescents be taught to cope with relational aggression? *Child Abuse Review.* doi:10.10021.car.1120

James, D. J., Flynn, A., Lawlor, M., & Murphy, N. (2010). Relevance of relational aggression to boys. Submitted for publication.

James, D. J., Lawlor, M., Courtney, P., Flynn, A., Henry, B., & Murphy, N. (2008). Bullying behavior in secondary schools: What roles do teachers play? *Child Abuse Review, 17,* 160–173.

James, D. J., Sofroniou, N., & Lawlor, M. (2003). The response of Irish adolescents to bullying. *Irish Journal of Psychology, 24,* 22–34.

Kasen, S., Berenson, K., Cohen, P., & Johnson, J. G. (2004). The effects of school climate on changes in aggressive and other behaviors related to bullying. In D. L. Espelage & S. M. Swearer (Eds.), *Bullying in American schools: A social-ecological perspective on prevention and intervention* (pp. 187–210). Mahwah, NJ: Lawrence Erlbaum Associates.

Kim, Y. S., Koh, Y., & Leventhal, B. (2005). School bullying and suicidal risk in Korean middle school students. *Pediatrics, 115,* 357–363.

Lee, C., Buckthorpe, S., Craighead, T., & McCormack, G. (2008). The relationship between the level of bullying in primary schools and children's views of their teachers' attitudes to pupil behavior. *Pastoral Care in Education, 26,* 171–180.

Limber, S. P., Nation, M., Tracy, G. B., Melton, G. B., & Flerex, V. (2004). Implementation of the Olweus Bullying Prevention Programme in the south eastern United States. In P. K. Smith, D. Pepler, & J. K. Rigby (Eds.), *Bullying in schools: How successful can interventions be?* (pp. 55–80). Cambridge, UK: Cambridge University Press.

Ma, X., Stewin, L. L., & Mah, D. L. (2001). Bullying in school: Nature, effects and remedies. *Research Papers in Education, 16,* 247–270.

McEvoy, A. (2005, September). *Teachers who bully students: Patterns and policy implications.* Paper presented at the Hamilton Fish Institute's Persistently Safe Schools Conference, Philadelphia, PA.

Meese, R. L. (1997). Student fights: Proactive strategies for preventing and managing student conflict. *Intervention in School and Clinic, 33,* 26–33.

Melton, G. B., Limber, S. P., Cunningham, P., Osgood, D. W., Chambers, J., Flerex, V., et al. (1998). *Violence among rural youth.* Washington, DC: Office of Juvenile Justice and Delinquency Prevention.

Morrison, B. (2002). Bullying and victimisation in schools: A restorative justice approach. *Australian Institute of Criminology: Trends and Issues in Crime and Criminal Justice, 219,* 1–6.

Olweus, D. (1993). *Bullying at school: What we know and what we can do about it.* Oxford, UK: Blackwell.

Olweus, D. (1997). Bully/victim problems at school: Knowledge base and an effective intervention programme. *Irish Journal of Psychology, 18,* 170–190.

O'Moore, M., Kirkham, C., & Smith, M. (1997). Bullying behavior in Irish schools. A nationwide study. *Irish Journal of Psychology, 18,* 141–169.

Ortega, R., Del Rey, R., & Mora-Merchain, J. A. (2004). SAVE Model: An anti-bullying intervention in Spain. In P. K. Smith, D. Pepler, & J. K. Rigby (Eds.), *Bullying in schools: How successful can interventions be?* (pp. 167–186). Cambridge, UK: Cambridge University Press.

Ortega, R., & Lera, M. J. (2000). The Seville Anti-Bullying School Project. *Aggressive Behavior, 26,* 113–123.

Plaford, G. (2006). *Bullying and the brain.* Lanham, MD: Rowman & Littlefield Publishing Group.

Rigby, K. (2002). *New perspectives on bullying.* London: Jessica Kingsley.

Rigby, K., & Barnes, A. (2002). The victimised student's dilemma: To tell or not to tell. *Youth Studies Australia, 21,* 33–36.

Rivers, I., & Smith, P. K. (1994). Types of bullying and their correlates. *Aggressive Behavior, 20,* 359–368.

Roland, E., & Galloway, D. (2004). Professional cultures in schools with high and low rates of bullying. *School Effectiveness and School Improvement, 15,* 241–260.

Salmivalli, C. (2001). Group views on victimisation: Empirical findings and their implications. In J. Juvonen & S. Graham (Eds.), *Peer harassment in schools: The plight of the vulnerable and the victimised* (pp. 398–420). New York: Guilford.

Sarno, G. (1992). Emotional distress by school teacher or administrator. *American Journal of Proof of Fact, 18,* 103.

Siann, G., Callaghan, M., & Lockhart, R. (1993). Bullying: Teachers views and school effects. *Educational Studies, 19,* 307–321.

Skues, J. L., Cunningham, E. G., & Pokharel, T. (2005). The influence of bullying behaviors on sense of school connectedness, motivation, and self esteem. *Australian Journal of Guidance and Counselling, 15,* 17–26.

Smilansky, J. (1984). External and internal correlates of teachers' satisfaction and willingness to report stress. *British Journal of Educational Psychology, 54,* 84–92.

Smith, P. K., & Brain, P. (2000). Bullying in schools: Lessons from two decades of research. *Aggressive Behavior, 26,* 1–9.

Smith, P. K., & Sharp, S. (1994). *School bullying: Insights and perspectives.* London: Routledge.

Solomon, D., Watson, M., Battisitch, D. K., Schaps, E., & Deiucchi, K. (1992). Creating a caring community: Educational practices that promote childrens' pro-social development. In F. K. Oser, A. Dick, & J. L. Patry (Eds.), *Effective and responsible teaching: The new synthesis* (pp. 383–396). San Francisco: Jossey-Bass.

Stevens, V., De Bourdeaudhuij, L., & Van Oost, P. (2000). Bullying in Flemish schools: An evaluation of anti-bullying intervention in primary and secondary schools. *British Journal of Educational Psychology, 70,* 195–210.

Swearer, S. M., & Doll, B. (2001). Bullying in schools: An ecological framework. *Journal of Emotional Abuse, 2,* 7–23.

Swearer, S. M., Espelage, D. L., Vaillancourt, T., & Hymel, S. (2010). What can be done about school bullying? Linking research to educational practice. *Educational Researcher, 39,* 38–47.

Terry, A. (1998). Teachers as targets of bullying by their pupils: A study to investigate incidence. *British Journal of Educational Psychology, 68,* 255–268.

TUI. (2006). *Survey examining teacher perception of student disruption in their schools.* Dublin: Teachers Union of Ireland.

Twemlow, S. W., Fonagey, P., Sacco, F., & Brethour, J. R. (2006). Teachers who bully students: A hidden trauma. *International Journal of Social Psychiatry, 52,* 187–198.

Weissberg, R. P., Caplan, M. Z., & Harwood, R. L. (1991). Promoting competent young people in competence enhancing environments: A systems-based perspective on primary prevention. *Journal of Consulting and Clinical Psychology, 59,* 830–841.

Weissberg, R. P., Caplan, M. Z., & Sivo, P. J. (1989). A new conceptual framework for establishing school based social competence programmes. In L. Bond & B. E. Compas (Eds.), *Primary prevention of psychopathology: Primary prevention and promotion within the schools* (Vol. 12, pp. 255–296). London: Sage.

Whitney, I., & Smith, P. K. (1993). A survey of the nature and extent of bullying in junior/middle and secondary schools. *Educational Research, 35,* 3–25.

CHAPTER EIGHT

Sexual Harassment of Adolescent Girls by Peers, Teachers, Employers, and Internet Predators

Michele A. Paludi and Ashley Kravitz

Introduction: Sexual Harassment of Adolescent Girls Reaches Epidemic Proportions

In 2002, Girls Scouts of the United States of America released a research study entitled: "The Net Effect: Girls and New Media." This study surveyed 1,000 adolescent girls aged 13 to 18 to examine three major issues: (a) trends in adolescent girls' Internet habits; (b) adolescent girls' skills in dealing with difficult or emotional situations online; and (c) advice on how parents can empower adolescent girls to have online experiences that are safe. Girls Scouts reported that 30% of the teens indicated they have been sexually harassed in an Internet chat room. Examples of harassment included demands for bra size, requests for cyber sex, and receipt of unsolicited photos of naked men. Of these teens who reported they had experienced sexual harassment:

a. Seven percent indicated that they told their parents about the incidents;
b. Thirty percent said they kept quiet about the harassment;
c. Twenty-one percent indicated that they experience sexual harassment "all the time, and it is no big deal";
d. Four percent said, "Nothing is that bad online because it is not really real."

In addition to experiencing sexual harassment in chat rooms, adolescent girls experience this form of victimization in schools from peers, teachers, and other school employees. The American Association of University Women (AAUW) (1992, 2001) conducted the first scientific national studies of academic sexual harassment of children and adolescents by their peers. Their 1993 study included 1,632 girls and boys in grades 8 through 11 from 79 schools across the United States. The 2001 study was based on 2,064 students in grades 8 through 11.

Both AAUW studies reported a high incidence of sexual harassment of girls in schools. For example, the 2001 study found that 85% of girls reported experiencing some form of sexual harassment during their school lives. Girls experienced more sexual harassment than boys and were also more afraid of being sexually harassed. Furthermore, boys perpetrated more than twice as much sexual harassment than girls. Sexual harassment reported by girls included name calling, graffiti written about them in school bathrooms, the dissemination of offensive drawings, unwanted touching, sexual rumors, and pressure for sex.

Allen, Young, Ashbaker, Heaton, and Parkinson (2003) reported that, based on their study with 58 school bus drivers, 67% stated that they observed students engaging in sexual harassment of girls, with 46% of the bus drivers reporting the victimization to the school's principal or assistant principal. Behaviors reported included sexual joking, mooning, flashing, and sexual comments.

In the 2001 AAUW study, 38% of girls reported being harassed by a teacher or other school employee. Research subsequent to this study by the U.S. Department of Education (2004) found approximately 10% of public school students were targeted with unwanted sexual attention by teachers and other school employees. Timmerman (2002) reported that 27% of sexual harassment of students was perpetrated by school employees, with teachers comprising 81% of the offenders.

Research has also been conducted on adolescents' experiences with sexual harassment in the workplace. Research by Strauss and Espeland (1992) reported that 30% of female vocational students had been sexually harassed at work. Most adolescents work in movie theaters, fast-food chains, and construction companies. Fineran (2002) found that 35% of part-time employed adolescents experienced sexual harassment. More recently, Fineran and Gruber (2009) reported that more than half of the 260 adolescent employees experienced sexual harassment at their workplace. Compared to adult women employees, adolescents in Fineran and Gruber's study experienced more harassment and experienced it in a shorter time frame.

The Equal Employment Opportunity Commission (EEOC) received sexual harassment complaints from 268 adolescents in 2003, constituting 2% of the total number of complaints received. This incidence quadrupled in 2004 to 8%. Drobac (2007) noted that these incidence rates have continued to rise. Types of sexual harassment reported to the EEOC by employed adolescents include verbal harassment, unwanted touching, requests for sex, and repeated groping.

The statistics are alarming, as are incidence rates for other forms of gendered violence against adolescent girls (Paludi, 2011). Violence against adolescent girls, including sexual harassment, has been recognized as a major public health (Fineran & Bolen, 2006) and human rights issue (Paludi, Martin, & Paludi, 2007) that requires a coordinated response from parents, teachers, counselors, and providers in the teen's community. This violence has been explained by unequal power relations and patriarchal values. In addition, factors embedded in the adolescent culture that influence as well as support violence include alcohol and drug use, religious influences, media portrayal of violence, devaluation of subordinated groups, and the sexualization of violence (Paludi, 2011). Furthermore, research has identified that violence against adolescent girls exists along a continuum, from incivility and microaggressions to hate crimes, including assault and murder (Nadal, 2010; Paludi, 2010).

The present chapter addresses sexual harassment of adolescent girls, including its impact on girls' emotional and physical health, interpersonal relationships, self-concept, and career development. We will address sexual harassment by peers, teachers, employers, and Internet predators. We begin with an overview of the legal definitions and behavioral examples of sexual harassment to which we will refer throughout this chapter.

Legal Definition of Sexual Harassment

> A girl should not expect special privileges because of her sex but neither should she adjust to prejudice and discrimination.
>
> Betty Friedan

Sexual harassment is legally defined as "unwelcome sexual advances, requests for sexual favors, and other verbal or physical conduct of a sexual nature" when any one of the following criterion is met (Equal Employment Opportunity Commission, 1990):

a. Submission to such conduct is made either explicitly or implicitly a term or condition of the individual's employment or academic standing.

b. Submission to or rejection of such conduct by an individual is used as the basis for employment or academic decisions affecting the individual.
c. Such conduct has the purpose or effect of unreasonably interfering with an individual's work or learning performance or creating an intimidating, hostile, or offensive work or learning environment.

The Office for Civil Rights (OCR), U.S. Department of Education defined sexual harassment similarly:

> Unwelcome sexual advances, request for sexual favors, and other verbal, nonverbal, or physical conduct of a sexual nature by an employee, by another student, or by a third party, which is sufficiently severe, persistent, or pervasive to limit a student's ability to participate in or benefit from an education program or activity, or to create a hostile or abusive educational environment.

These legal definitions describe two types of sexual harassment: quid pro quo sexual harassment and hostile environment sexual harassment. Quid pro quo sexual harassment refers to an individual with organizational power who either expressly or implicitly ties an academic or employment decision or action to the response of an individual to unwelcome sexual advances. For example, a high school teacher may promise an adolescent student a reward for complying with a sexual request, such as an A for the course or a letter of recommendation for college. Another example of quid pro quo sexual harassment would be a teacher who threatened a student for failing to comply with the sexual requests, such as threatening to fail the student.

Hostile environment sexual harassment involves a situation where an atmosphere or climate is set up by teachers, staff, or other students in the school or school-sponsored event that makes it difficult or impossible for a student to study and learn because the student perceives the climate to be hostile, offensive, and/or intimidating.

Both quid pro quo and hostile environment sexual harassment of students is prohibited by Title IX of the 1972 Education Amendments, which states:

> No person in the United States shall, on the basis of sex, be excluded from participation in, or denied the benefits of, or be subjected to discrimination under any educational program or activity receiving federal assistance.

Title IX is an antidiscrimination statute prohibiting discrimination on the basis of sex in any educational program or activity receiving financial assistance. Title IX extends to recruiting of students, admissions, educational activities and programs, course offerings, counseling, financial aid, health and insurance benefits, scholarships, and athletics.

Employed students, as are adults, are protected from quid pro quo and hostile environment sexual harassment from Title VII of the 1964 Civil Rights Act. According to the Equal Employment Opportunity Commission (1999), sexual harassment of employees includes the following:

a. The victim as well as the harasser may be a woman or a man. The victim does not have to be of the opposite sex.
b. The harasser can be the victim's supervisor, an agent of the employer, a supervisor in another area, a coworker, or a non-employee.
c. The victim does not have to be the person harassed but could be anyone affected by the offensive conduct.
d. Unlawful sexual harassment may occur without economic injury to or discharge of the victim.
e. The harasser's conduct must be unwelcome.

Furthermore, sexual harassment may be physical, verbal, written, or visual. Sexual harassment may occur between individuals of the same sex or opposite sex.

Behavioral Examples of Sexual Harassment

Sexual harassment includes but is not limited to:

Unwelcome sexual advances
Sexual innuendos, comments, and sexual remarks
Suggestive, insulting, or obscene sounds
Implied or expressed threat of reprisal for refusal to comply with a sexual request
Pinching, patting, brushing up against another's body
Sexually suggestive books, magazines, objects, email, photographs, screen savers displayed in the school/work area
Actual denial of an academic- or employment-related benefit for refusal to comply with sexual requests (Paludi et al., 2007)

Sexual Harassment of Adolescent Girls by Peers and Teachers: Schools Are Not Safe Havens

> The solution of adult problems tomorrow depends in large measure upon the way our children grow up today. There is no greater insight into the future than recognizing that, when we save children, we save ourselves.
> *Margaret Mead*

Peer Sexual Harassment

As we discussed earlier in this chapter, the AAUW reported results of the first national study of adolescents' experiences with peer sexual harassment. In this study, students were asked the following questions, based on the legal definition of sexual harassment presented above:

> During your whole school life, how often, if at all, has anyone (this includes students, teachers, other school employees, or anyone else) done the following things to you when you did not want them to?
>
> Made sexual comments, jokes, gestures, or looks.
> Showed, gave, or left you sexual pictures, photographs, illustrations, messages, or notes.
> Wrote sexual messages/graffiti about you on bathroom walls, in locker rooms, etc.
> Spread sexual rumors about you.
> Said you were gay or lesbian.
> Spied on you as you dressed or showered at school.
> Flashed or "mooned" you.
> Touched, grabbed, or pinched you in a sexual way.
> Pulled at your clothing in a sexual way.
> Intentionally brushed against you in a sexual way.
> Pulled your clothing off or down.
> Blocked your way or cornered you in a sexual way.
> Forced you to kiss him/her.
> Forced you to do something sexual, other than kissing.

Eighty-one percent of students reported that they experienced one or more of these examples of sexual harassment during their school lives. Gender comparisons revealed that 85% of girls and 76% of boys reported experiencing sexual harassment. In addition, African American boys (81%) were more likely to have experienced sexual harassment than White boys (75%) and Latinos (69%). For girls, 87% of Whites reported experiencing sexual harassment compared with 84% of African American girls and 82% of Latinas. Thus, girls were more likely to report experiencing sexual harassment, regardless of race. The types of sexual harassment most reported by girls in this research were:

> Sexual comments, jokes, gestures, or looks. (76%)
> Touched, grabbed, or pinched in a sexual way. (65%)

Intentionally brushed against in a sexual way. (57%)

Flashed or "mooned." (49%)

Had sexual rumors spread about them. (43%)

Had clothing pulled at in a sexual way. (38%)

Sexual pictures, photographs, illustrations, messages, or notes were shown, given, or left for them to find. (31%)

Adolescents in this research reported experiencing behaviors that constitute hostile environment sexual harassment, especially in the hallways as they were going to class. The AAUW study also found that adolescents' experiences with sexual harassment were most likely to occur in the middle school or junior high school years of sixth to ninth grade.

Similar results were obtained by AAUW in its 2001 study. Furthermore, smaller, independent studies of peer sexual harassment of adolescents have confirmed the incidence rate initially reported by the AAUW. For example, Roscoe (1994) reported a significant percentage of early adolescents' experiences with peer sexual harassment. They reported that 50% of adolescent girls had been victimized, significantly more than the percentage of boys (37%). Fineran and Bennett (1999) reported that 87% of girls in their study were sexually harassed by their male peers. Research by Murnen and Smolak (2000) found adolescent girls at school commonly experienced having an entrance blocked and being stared at. Other studies indicate between 50% and 90% of adolescent girls are victims of sexual harassment by peers (e.g., Brown & Leaper, 2008; Fineran & Bennett, 1999; Fineran & Bolen, 2006; Roscoe, Strouse & Goodwin, 1994; Stratton & Backes, 1997). Similar to the AAUW findings, all of these studies indicate that girls report experiencing sexual harassment more frequently than boys and that boys perpetrate more sexual harassment than girls. Walsh, Duffy, & Gallagher-Duffy (2007) noted that comparable results to the AAUW study were obtained in their study with Canadian students in grades 7–12. They found that 70% of students reported being sexually harassed in school more commonly by a current or former student.

When schools fail to intervene in peer sexual harassment, students get the message that sexual harassment is accepted at the school. Strauss (2010) noted that this acceptance can be a "catalyst for increased sexual violence within the school and the community" (p. 189). Data supportive of Strauss's contention was obtained by Pellegrini (2002): students who bullied their peers in sixth grade engaged in sexual harassment in seventh grade. Furthermore, Klein (2006) noted that in school shootings in the United States over a six-year period, 11 out of 13 of the victims were girls.

Klein highlighted that sexual harassment was instrumental in instigating the shootings. According to Klein (2006, p. 148):

> Violence against girls is easy to render invisible because the behavior that precedes actual incidents is often perceived as normal; even after fatalities have occurred, the gendered components of crimes do not seem to register. . . . '[N]ormal' violence against girls—indeed, social acceptance of male hostility towards girls—tends to aid in concealing even the most dramatic incidents.

Stein (cited in Bogart, Simmons, Stein, and Tomaszewski, 1992, p. 208) reported girls' experiences with sexual harassment. For example:

> One female in diesel shop refused to go to lunch during her last two years of shop because she was the only young woman in the lunchroom at that time. When she went to the cafeteria, she was pinched and slapped on the way in, and had to endure explicit propositions made to her while she ate lunch.
>
> A particular shop's predominantly male population designated one shop day as National Sexual Harassment Day, in honor of their only female student. They gave her non-stop harassment throughout the day, and found it to be so successful (the female student was forced to be dismissed during the day), that they later held a National Sexual Harassment Week.

Girls' responses to the *Seventeen* magazine survey (Stein, Marshall, & Tropp, 1993) reported the following responses:

> Being harassed myself—I did not realize it at the time. I knew it was wrong and I know I felt horrible. Me? I would be trapped under tables and bothered by at least four guys. They thought it was all fun and games. It wasn't. These guys would grab my breasts and touch my butt. It always happened in Industrial Arts. (16-year-old)

> I had four boys harassing me. . . . I felt like they thought I was a slut. I even thought the whole bus thought I was a slut, because they would give me dirty looks. I hated it! I told the harassers to stop, but they wouldn't. So, I wrote them a note saying it was sexual harassment, and if they didn't stop I would report them. They started saying "It isn't sexual harassment, we didn't lay a hand on you." (14-year-old)

It is significant to note that only 15% of the girls (as opposed to 31% of the boys) in the AAUW study reported that their lives were untouched by sexual harassment (i.e., never been harassed and never harassed others).

Psychological Dimensions of Peer Sexual Harassment

Hill and Silva (2005, p. 22) offered reasons that boys identified for why they engage in sexual harassment of girls:

I thought it was funny.
I thought the person liked it.
My friends encouraged/pushed me into doing it.
I wanted something from that person.
I wanted that person to think I had some sort of power over them.

Stein (1996) argued that peer sexual harassment is tolerated and characterized as "normal" by school administrators. Phinney (1994) also noted that sexual harassment is a "dynamic element" in the lives of adolescent girls since schools perpetuate this male dominance through pedagogical techniques and sports. We return to this issue subsequently in this chapter.

Sexual Harassment of Adolescent Girls by Teachers

> The schools play an important role when it comes down to protecting children against violence. Violence is one of the principal reasons why children don't go to school. It's also one of the causes of the alarming school dropout rates.
> *Shakira*

In 1992, Bogart, Simmons, Stein, and Tomaszewski reported their review of sexual harassment complaints brought by students against teachers that were filed with the Massachusetts Department of Education. The following are two complaints they included in their report (p. 197):

> A science teacher measured the craniums of the boys in the class and the chests of the girls. The lesson in skeleton frame measurements were conducted one by one, at the front of the class, by the teacher.

The print shop teacher, who was in the habit of putting his arms around the shoulders of the young women, insisted, when one young woman asked to be excused to go to the nurse to fix her broken pants' zipper, that she first show him her broken zipper. She was forced to lift her shirt to reveal her broken pants' zipper.

Several studies have been conducted concerning the incidence of sexual harassment of adolescents by teachers. For example, Wishnietsky (1991) reported that 14% of high school students indicated that they had been coerced into sexual intercourse with a teacher. Strauss and Espeland (1992) found that 30% of high school students were sexually harassed by a teacher. Sexual harassment included sexually related remarks, staring, touching, gestures, and propositions. In their 2001 research, the AAUW reported that, of students who had been harassed, 38% identified teachers or other school employees as perpetrators. As another example, the U.S. Department of Education (2004) found approximately 10% of high school students have been targeted with unwanted sexual attention by school employees, including teachers.

While sexual harassment of adolescents by peers is more common than by teachers, incidence data may be difficult to obtain. Criminal rape laws and child abuse statutes may be filed against the teacher if the teen is younger than 18 years (Shakeshaft & Cohen, 1995). Behavioral examples of sexual harassment by teachers include a variety of forms (Strauss, 2010), including discussing girls' legs, commenting on their sex lives, touching a girl's breasts, fondling, and tickling.

Sexual Harassment of Adolescent Girls on the Internet

> If you believe email, blogs, and instant messaging are a completely harmless way for teens to communicate, think again!
>
> *Kate Fogarty*

There are a variety of behaviors that constitute online sexual harassment of adolescents, including unwelcome physical, verbal, or nonverbal behavior. For example, online sexual solicitation includes asking adolescents to discuss sex practices and requesting that the teen engage in a sexual act. Similar to child abductors who use a "confidence assault" (see Paludi & Kelly, 2010), online harassers engage in an organized plot to lure the teen into sexual solicitation. For example, online harassers initially try to gain the trust and confidence of the teen who is the targeted victim. This trust is then used to manipulate the teen into physical and psychological vulnerability. Then, by the time the teen realizes the individual is violent, her attempts at stopping the behavior are limited. The harasser continues the confidence assault by convincing the teen that she is a participant in the crime and/or caused the crime.

Sexual Harassment of Adolescent Girls

L. Dewey (2002, cited in Fogarty, 2009) and the Polly Klaas Foundation (2006, cited in Fogarty, 2009) noted, with respect to online sexual solicitation of adolescent girls:

a. Thirty percent had been sexually harassed while they were in a chat room.
b. Thirty-seven percent received links to sexually explicit content online.
c. Thirty percent have discussed meeting someone they met online.
d. Thirty-three percent had been asked about sexual topics online.

Research commissioned by Cox Communications and the National Center For Missing and Exploited Children (2005) reported:

a. Fifty-one percent of parents do not have or are unaware of computer software that monitors their adolescents' online behavior.
b. Forty-two percent of parents did not review the content of email sent to their adolescents, nor their chat room discussions or instant messaging.

Online sexual harassment of adolescent girls has indicated the following with respect to the most vulnerable targets of the victimization:

a. Girls between the ages of 14 and 17.
b. Girls with major depressive symptoms.
c. Girls who have experienced life transitions, including changing schools, not having many friends, or worrying about parents divorcing.
d. Girls who have close online relationships.
e. Girls with high Internet use.
f. Girls with emotional problems are more likely to have formed online sexual relationships, been asked for face-to-face encounters, and attended such encounters.
g. Girls whose Internet safety awareness is low.

The Girls Scouts of America's (2002) study discussed earlier in this chapter has noted that "internet communication technology is a pervasive part of girls' lives. On average, girls report going online two to three times a week, with dedicated users going online several times a day. . . . Girls appear to spend the majority of their time online socializing" (p. 9). According to the girls in their study (p. 15, 16):

> A guy threatened to come to my town if I didn't have cyber sex with him. (13-year-old girl)

> Some guy kept asking me if we could have cyber sex and I kept saying no but he kept asking. I got really scared and blocked him. He was so persistent

and scary that he wouldn't go away. If it wasn't for the blocking feature, I probably wouldn't feel that safe. (15-year-old girl)

I was chatting with two people who were friends (with each other) and after talking to them for like an hour, one of the guys (I didn't know them) told me that his friend had hacked into my computer and knew where I lived, and he told me that he was incredibly horny and was going to come find me. (16-year-old girl)

Berson, Berson, and Ferron (2005) reported that 74% of adolescent girls spend the majority of time online in chat rooms, sending emails, and/or sending instant messages.

Similar to research findings with school harassment of girls, girls who experience online sexual harassment are reluctant to tell their parents. This reluctance stems from fearing retaliation from their parents, including banning them from online socializing. Adolescent girls as well as boys want opportunities to vent about problems they experience, which is a normative part of this stage of the life cycle (Paludi, 2002). Banning them from using the Internet is thus perceived by adolescents as blocking them from having friends.

Online sexual harassment is not identical to cyberstalking (Chisholm, 2006). Stalking involves being persistently watched or followed. Cyberstalkers bombard their targets with emails at work, on mobile devices, or at school. Because the online stalker remains anonymous, adolescents feel threatened. Online harassers and stalkers may engage in both forms of victimization against teen girls.

Adolescent Employment and Sexual Harassment

> My character is fictional, but she is based on all the women who fought the sexual harassment case, and everything you see in the film actually happened.
> *Charlize Theron*

In 2009, PBS broadcasted the program *Is Your Daughter Safe at Work*. In this program, adolescent girls who experienced sexual harassment and other forms of gendered violence shared their experiences. This program announced that approximately 200,000 adolescents are assaulted at their jobs annually. One of these incidents took place in the early 2000s. The EEOC had received a complaint from a 16-year-old girl who alleged sexual harassment at her job at Pennsylvania Mexican Restaurant (Equal Employment Opportunity Commission, 2010a). In her complaint, this young woman said that her shift supervisor asked her to come to work even though she was not scheduled to do so. At the restaurant, she noticed that she and this supervisor were the sole employees present. She claimed that the supervisor sexually assaulted her.

The young woman reported this incident to the general manager of the restaurant on the following day. Her report was met with laughter and accusations of her fabricating the sexual assault. When the general manager asked the supervisor to respond to this complaint, the supervisor denied that he had sexually assaulted or sexually harassed the new employee. The general manager did suspend this supervisor the following day. The young woman never returned to work at the restaurant.

In addition, she reported the assault to local law enforcement. The supervisor admitted to the police that he had "sexual contact" with the girl. He pled guilty to "corruption of a minor." Consequently, he was fired from his job at the restaurant. The EEOC filed a lawsuit against the restaurant indicating that the restaurant had violated federal law because it did not fire the supervisor after the assault. This case was resolved in 2003. The EEOC required the restaurant to train all employees on sexual harassment. In addition, the EEOC received $1,500 to facilitate educational programs for adolescent employees in the food industry about sexual harassment. The young woman received payment of $150,000.

As another example, three adolescent girls, who were employed as servers and bussers at a yacht and golf club restaurant in northern California, filed formal employment discrimination complaints with the EEOC (2010b), which subsequently filed a lawsuit against the employer after investigating the adolescents' reports. The girls' complaints included male coworkers making inappropriate sexual jokes, requests for lap dances, and solicitation for sex. In addition, the girls stated that these men grabbed their breasts and buttocks. When reporting these incidents to older women servers, the girls were met with responses that were dismissive, indicating that they should expect such behavior to occur when working in restaurants. Managers failed at their attempts to cease the sexual harassment of these girls.

The lawsuit filed by the EEOC settled in 2004. It resulted in:

Termination of the two alleged harassers.

A $75,000 payment to the adolescents.

Training of all employees of the restaurant on sexual harassment.

Sexual harassment training for club board members.

Posting of the settlement of the lawsuit at the restaurant.

When asked about the results of the settlement, one of the girls stated:

> Some people might be afraid if they report sexual harassment, that they will be asked what they did to deserve it—"blaming the victim." But I'm glad we filed our complaint with the EEOC, and I hope this will encourage other women to step forward if they face a similar situation. (Equal Employment Opportunity Commission, 2010b, p. 1)

Mortimer (2005) reported that approximately 80–90% of adolescents are employed during high school, especially in fast-food restaurants, retail sales, grocery stores, and health care. Strauss and Espeland (1992) found that 30% of 250 female vocational students surveyed from four Minnesota school districts had reported experiencing sexual harassment at their jobs. Fineran (2002) found that 35% of 332 part-time employed adolescents experienced sexual harassment, with girls being more likely to be victimized than boys (63% vs. 37%).

Fineran and Gruber (2009) indicated that out of 260 adolescents in a New England private high school, 52% of girls stated that they experienced sexual harassment at work, with the majority of perpetrators being coworkers. The types of sexual harassment reported by these girls included unwanted sexual attention and sexual and sexist comments. Fineran and Gruber (2009) further noted that adolescent girls experienced more sexual harassment than did adult employed women and college women.

Mental Health Impact of Sexual Harassment on Adolescents

> There is an ancient Indian saying: "We do not inherit the earth from our ancestors; we borrow it from our children." If we use this ethic as a moral compass, then our rendezvous with reality can also become a rendezvous with opportunity.
>
> Patricia Schroeder

Research has indicated a significant impact on adolescent girls' mental health following experiencing quid pro quo and/or hostile environment sexual harassment by peers, employers, teachers, or individuals in online chat rooms.

For example, students in the AAUW study (1992) reported the following experiences:

Embarrassment

Self-consciousness

Being less sure of themselves or less confident

Feeling afraid or scared

Doubting whether they could have a happy romantic relationship

Feeling confused about who they are

Feeling less popular

Larkin (1994) pointed out that adolescent girls' decline in self-esteem may be attributable to the sexual harassment they frequently experience. In addition, Murnen and Smolak (2000) reported that adolescent girls were more likely than boys to perceive sexual harassment as frightening. Timmerman (2002) and Duffy, Wareham, and Walsh (2004) also found that sexual harassment of adolescent girls contributed to their lower self-esteem and poorer psychological health. Girls in their research reported embarrassment, fear, and self-consciousness, all of which prevented them from fully participating in class.

Fineran and Gruber (2004) noted that adolescents who were sexually harassed experienced depression, sadness, anxiety, anger, helplessness, nightmares or disturbed sleep, isolation from family, and loss of friends. Fineran and Gruber (2004) further found that adolescents who experienced sexual harassment had increased post-traumatic stress as a result of their diminished emotional well-being. Sheffield (1993) argued that sexual harassment and other forms of gendered violence encourage adolescent girls to feel fearful, what she described as "sexual terrorism."

In addition, the Massachusetts Youth Risk Behavior Survey (Massachusetts Department of Elementary and Secondary Education, 2007) reported that sexual-minority adolescents who experienced sexual harassment had higher suicide rates than did heterosexual adolescents. Stein (1986, cited in Bogart, Simmons, Stein, & Tomaszewski, 1992) noted that sexual harassment victims often experience a second victimization while seeking resolution for the sexual harassment. Girls are frequently blamed for their own victimization as a consequence of individuals defining sexual harassment as seduction.

Furthermore, stereotypes abound that girls do not tell the truth. In addition, Paludi and Barickman (1998) summarized research that indicates that adolescents do not label their mental health impact responses as being caused or contributed to by sexual harassment. Their responses are often attributed by their family, friends, and school administrators to other events in their lives, especially those related to hormonal changes and adolescent mood swings.

In addition to the mental health impacts of sexual harassment on adolescent girls, research indicates that girls withdraw from school and from friends. In addition, girls experience lowered grades, lost educational opportunities, and more limited career choices (Paludi et al., 2007).

Furthermore, compared to adolescent girls who have not reported experiencing sexual harassment, adolescent victims of sexual harassment report nightmares, disturbed sleep, eating disorders, lower self-esteem, poor body esteem, and lower life satisfaction (e.g., Lindberg, Grabe, & Hyde, 2007).

Stein (1993) also indicated that another impact of sexual harassment for adolescent girls is that it teaches them to accept sexual assault and other forms of gendered violence. According to Stein (1996):

> If school authorities do not intervene and sanction students who sexually harass, the schools may be encouraging a continued pattern of violence in relationships: Schools may be the training grounds for the insidious cycle of domestic violence. (p. 22)

This is especially true when students' voices are not heard by school personnel, an issue to which we now turn.

Responsibilities of Schools and Workplaces in Preventing and Dealing with Sexual Harassment of Adolescents

Sexual, racial, gender violence and other forms of discrimination and violence in a culture cannot be eliminated without changing culture.

Charlotte Bunch

Sexual harassment demands that schools intervene since, under Title IX, sexual harassment is an organizational responsibility with respect to prevention and reactive measures.

"Reasonable Care" in Preventing and Dealing with Sexual Harassment of Adolescent Girls

Paludi and Paludi (2003) recommended that schools should exercise "reasonable care" to ensure a sexual harassment–free environment and retaliatory-free environment for students. This "reasonable care," adapted from the Supreme Court ruling in *Faragher v. City of Boca Raton* (1998), includes the following. School districts should:

a. Establish and disseminate an effective antisexual harassment policy.
b. Establish and disseminate an effective investigatory procedure.
c. Offer training in sexual harassment in general and in the school's policy and procedures specifically.

Reasonable care is required of employers as well. With respect to sexual harassment, the EEOC has maintained:

> It is unlawful to harass a person (an applicant or employee) because of that person's sex. Harassment can include "sexual harassment" or unwelcome sexual advances, requests for sexual favors, and other verbal or physical harassment of a sexual nature.

Each of these components of reasonable care will be addressed below. The focus of this section will be on schools' responsibilities for preventing sexual harassment. The recommendations we offer are for employers of adolescents as well. We recommend consulting the following for additional information regarding school districts' responsibility to students for creating and maintaining a sexual harassment–free and retaliatory-free environment: Sandler & Stonehill (2005), Stein (2003), and the Office for Civil Rights, U.S. Department of Education (1997). We also recommend the following for preventing sexual harassment of employed adolescents: Fineran (2002) and Fineran & Gruber (2009).

Sexual Harassment Policy

In order to promote effective and equitable resolution of sexual harassment complaints, it is necessary to have an explicit policy adopted by the school in compliance with the provision of Title IX. According to the OCR (1997), Title IX does not require a school to adopt a policy specifically prohibiting sexual harassment or to provide separate grievance procedures for sexual harassment complaints. However, its nondiscrimination policy and grievance procedures for handling discrimination complaints must provide effective means for preventing and responding to sexual harassment. Thus, if, because of the lack of a policy or procedure specifically addressing sexual harassment, students are unaware of what kind of conduct constitutes sexual harassment or that such conduct is prohibited sex discrimination, a school's general policy and procedures relating to sex discrimination complaints will not be considered effective.

A grievance procedure applicable to sexual harassment complaints cannot be prompt or equitable unless students know it exists, how it works, and how to file a complaint. Thus, the procedures should be written in language appropriate to the age of the school's students, easily understood, and widely disseminated. Distributing the procedures to administrators, or including them in the school's administrative or policy manual, may not by itself be an effective way of providing notice, as these publications are usually not widely circulated to and understood by all members of the school community. Many schools ensure adequate notice to students by having copies of the procedures available at various locations throughout the school or campus; publishing the procedures as a separate document; including a summary of the procedures in major publications issued by the school, such as handbooks and catalogs for students.

In addition, the OCR (1997) stated the following:

> A policy specifically prohibiting sexual harassment and separate grievance procedures for violations of that policy can help ensure that all students and employees understand the nature of sexual harassment and that the school will not tolerate it. Indeed, they might even bring conduct of a sexual nature to the school's attention so that the school can address it before it becomes sufficiently serious as to create a hostile environment.

Recommendations identified as effective policies by the OCR have been translated by attorneys, human resource management specialists, and social scientists (see Paludi et al., 2007). The components of effective policy statements for students are the following:

a. Statement of Purpose
b. Legal Definition
c. Behavioral Examples
d. Statement Concerning Impact of Discrimination on Individuals and Organization
e. Statement of Individual's Responsibility in Filing Complaint
f. Statement of Organization's Responsibility in Investigating Complaint
g. Statement Concerning Confidentiality of Complaint Procedures
h. Statement Concerning Sanctions Available
i. Statement Concerning Retaliation
j. Statement of Sanctions for Retaliation
k. Statement Concerning False Complaints
l. Identification and Background of Individual(s) Responsible for Hearing Complaints

In addition, Paludi and Barickman (1998) offered a series of questions for school districts to address when reviewing their policy statement for effectiveness. Examples of checklist questions include:

a. Is there a policy statement for dealing with sexual harassment?
b. Does the policy forbid peer harassment or is it limited to harassment by individuals who hold organizational power over the victim?

c. Is the policy statement well publicized? Is it circulated periodically among all members of the institution?
d. How do individuals in the school district/organization learn whom they should see to discuss sexual harassment?
e. Are there specific individuals to whom individuals can go for help with sexual harassment issues?
f. Are remedies clear and commensurate with the level of sexual harassment?
g. What services are available at the school/organization to individuals who have experienced sexual harassment?
h. Does the school/organization foster an atmosphere of prevention by sensitizing individuals to the topic of sexual harassment?
i. Is the policy drafted in sex neutral terms?

Investigatory Procedures

The sexual harassment literature has also identified components for effective complaint procedures. These include all of the following at a minimum:

a. Informing students that the organization will not ignore any complaint of harassment.
b. Informing students that the investigator of complaints will not make determinations about the complaint based on the reputations or organizational status of the individuals involved.
c. Informing students that investigations of complaints will be completed promptly.
d. Informing students that witnesses to incidents and/or to changes in the parties' behavior will be interviewed.
e. Informing students that all documents presented by the complainant, alleged harasser, and witnesses will be reviewed.
f. Informing students that the complainant and the accused will be interviewed in detail.

Victims of sexual harassment must be guaranteed effective protection (Paludi et al., 2007). Monitoring of all parties to a complaint needs to be followed until the danger of new attempts at sexual harassment has passed. School administrators and teachers have an important responsibility to safeguard the victim at school. Student victims must be able to trust that their school administrators and teachers will protect them and provide help to them (Paludi & Barickman, 1998). If student victims are not taken seriously by school personnel, the situation will become worse.

The names and contact information for Title IX coordinators and sexual harassment counselors should be publicized and easy to find on the school's website.

Training Programs

Schools are legally required to facilitate training programs on sexual harassment awareness. Goals of effective training programs include (Paludi & Barickman, 1998; Paludi et al., 2007; Paludi & Paludi, 2003):

a. Defining quid pro quo and hostile environment sexual harassment.
b. Discussing the physical and emotional reactions to being sexually harassed.
c. Discussing peer sexual harassment.
d. Discussing means of resolving complaints of sexual harassment.

At the conclusion of training programs, students should be able to:

a. Assess their own perceptions of sexual harassment.
b. Label adequately behaviors as illustrative of sexual harassment, or not illustrative of sexual harassment.
c. Identify peer sexual harassment.
d. Describe the effects of sexual harassment on students.
e. State components of the school's policy statement on sexual harassment.
f. State the proper procedure to follow if sexual harassment occurs.

Research has indicated the following with respect to training programs on sexual harassment awareness for adolescents:

a. Training increases their tendency to perceive sexual harassment (Moyer & Nath, 1998).
b. Training increases students' knowledge acquisition and attitude change (Roscoe, 1994).
c. Training increases the reporting of sexual harassment (Roscoe, 1994).

Paludi and Barickman (1998) noted that adolescents' level of cognitive development must be taken into account when schools are designing training programs (as well as policies and procedures). Thus, teens may need to be provided with concrete examples rather than hypothetical, theoretical situations in order for them to understand the legal and psychological issues involved in sexual harassment.

Additional Educational Programs

Additional educational programs for adolescents have been identified in the sexual harassment literature (e.g., AAUW, 2001; Paludi & Paludi, 2003):

a. Include training on sexual harassment in new student/teacher orientation programs.
b. Report annually on sexual harassment cases.
c. Encourage teachers to incorporate discussions of sexual harassment in their classrooms.
d. Encourage students to start an organization with the purpose of preventing sexual harassment.
e. Facilitate a "sexual harassment awareness week" and schedule programs for students and teachers, including guided video discussions, guest lecturers, and plays.
f. Provide educational sessions for parents about sexual harassment and the school district's policy and procedures.

Reactive Measures

In order to be legally adequate, an investigation of a school and workplace sexual harassment complaint requires much more than a cursory look at events that may have taken place and an informal settlement of problems identified. As Levy and Paludi (2002) stated: "Specifics must be adhered to if the employer is going to be able to use the affirmative defense provided by the Supreme Court in hostile environment cases. Proper training and preparation for the investigation are invaluable in carrying out a process that will handle the situation appropriately and that will adequately remedy any problems that are uncovered" (p. 117).

Characteristics of Investigators

Schools and workplaces select the individual(s) who will be charged with investigating complaints of discrimination (e.g., Title IX coordinator, ombudsperson, human resource director). Several researchers and attorneys (e.g., Levy & Paludi, 2002; McQueen, 1997; Paludi & Paludi, 2003) have identified characteristics of effective investigators, including:

a. Have credibility in sexual harassment, including knowledge and formal training in legal and psychological aspects of sexual harassment.
b. Be accessible for individuals seeking assistance.
c. Have skill in verbal and nonverbal communication.
d. Have skill in eliciting information from individuals.
e. Be at ease with discussing matters of sexual harassment and power, including issues involving sexuality and sexual assault.
f. Report directly to the individual who will determine the organization's response (e.g., principal or president).
g. Not permit any party in the investigation procedure to pressure him/her to reveal confidential information or to become one party's advocate.

h. Not allow any personal feelings to interfere with effectiveness.
i. Be sensitive to collective bargaining agreements.
j. Maintain a distance from individuals involved in the investigation in order to be viewed as objective.
k. Be prepared for discussions to become emotional and be a calming force for these discussions.
l. Know that the organization has a legal as well as ethical obligation to make the school/workplace an environment free of sexual harassment and free of the fear of retaliation for speaking about sexual harassment.

Women or Men as Investigators

Research has indicated that investigators report gender comparisons in individuals discussing workplace discrimination, especially with respect to sexual harassment and sexual orientation (see Levy & Paludi, 2002; Paludi & Paludi, 2003). Males may be more comfortable, for example, having a woman investigator when they are reporting sexual harassment by other men. Girls and women may also be reluctant to discuss their experiences with a man because of the explicit sexual nature of complaints of sexual harassment. Paludi and Paludi (2003) recommended including both a woman and man as coinvestigators for complaints of sexual harassment. According to Paludi and Paludi (2003): "The team of investigators can rely on each other for support. . . . It is also important to have a second investigator should a complaint be filed against the other. Without two investigators, the complainant has no option. Of course, if the complainant files against one member of the investigation team, the accused must exclude herself or himself from the investigatory process" (p. 190).

Thus, the comfort of the complainant must be paramount. An organization should not want its process to be a problem in and of itself, either in creating a hostile environment or in taking away the opportunity to use the affirmative defense (Levy & Paludi, 2002). In addition, according to the EEOC (1999), an investigatory process that is reasonably believed to be ineffective or unnecessarily intimidating or burdensome will negate the ability of the employer to claim the affirmative defense if an employee fails to use internal report mechanisms.

Mediation

Some organizations have built into their grievance procedures a mediation technique whereby complaints may be resolved informally between the individuals involved (Stockdale & Sagrestano, 2011). In mediation, the complainant and accused typically meet together with a mediator to attempt to resolve the discrimination/harassment. Some students and employees may prefer mediation to a formal complaint process for several reasons, such as the perception of faster resolution, preservation of confidentiality, and avoidance of the stress of a formal investigation. We note, however, that mediation may become volatile. Individuals have powerful emotions associated with the situation. In addition, mediation assumes that both individuals are of equal power in the organization. However, most victims of sexual harassment hold less organizational and/or cultural power than their perceived harassers. Furthermore, research indicates that employees who believe that they have experienced sexual harassment want to flee the perceived harasser, not sit face to face with them. They fear that the mediation will become an extension of the sexual harassment. We recommend Stockdale and Sagrestano (2011) for further information about alternative dispute methods.

Legal Requirements for Investigating Discrimination and Harassment Complaints

Once a school district or employer is made aware of an alleged incident of sexual harassment, an investigation must be undertaken and completed as quickly as possible (Dowling, 2011; Levy & Paludi, 2002; Paludi et al., 2007). In addition, a school or employer is required to investigate when a teacher or manager is told of sexual harassment, even if this individual is not the official designated complaint officer and even if the complaint is not made in an "official" manner. Thus, once the school or employer knows, the requirement of responsive action begins.

The EEOC (1990) has identified three fundamentals in investigating complaints of harassment and discrimination: promptness, confidentiality, and impartiality. We also recommend these for investigating complaints of academic sexual harassment.

Promptness

Unless there are extenuating circumstances, the investigation process should begin as soon as the complaint is received. The investigation should be completed within two weeks. During the course of an investigation, the potential for further problems is great, and the stress levels of the parties involved in the complaint are high. It is therefore in the best interests of the employer as well as the employees that the "immediate corrective action" (EEOC, 1990) be followed.

Confidentiality

Investigations into complaints of harassment should be kept as confidential as possible. This includes having a separate filing system for investigation files. All personnel must be continually trained and monitored about their responsibilities in maintaining the confidentiality of investigations. According to the EEOC (1999):

> An employer should make clear to employees that it will protect the confidentiality of harassment allegations to the extent possible. An employer cannot guarantee complete confidentiality, since it cannot conduct an effective investigation without revealing certain information to the alleged harasser and potential witnesses. However, information about the allegation of harassment should be shared only with those who need to know about it.

Impartiality

It has been recommended in the literature on sexual harassment that a neutral party conduct investigations (Levy & Paludi, 2002; Smith & Mazin, 2004). In addition, investigators should be trained in the legal and psychological aspects of sexual harassment and determining credibility. Part of harassment training for investigators includes the following components if it is to be effective (Levy & Paludi, 2002; McQueen, 1997; Paludi & Paludi, 2003):

a. Psychological issues involved in dealing with harassment
b. Physical and emotional reactions to being harassed
c. The complainant's perspective
d. Psychology of the victimization process
e. Internally and externally focused strategies
f. The accused's perspective
g. Differential evaluations of identical behavior
h. Interviewing techniques
i. Determining credibility

According to the EEOC (1990), an investigative process that is reasonably believed to be ineffective or is unnecessarily intimidating or burdensome will negate the ability of an employer to claim the affirmative defense if an employee fails to report internally.

Retaliation

Victims of sexual harassment worry about retaliatory behavior taken toward them as a result of filing a complaint of harassment, such as receiving a failing grade or not receiving a letter of recommendation from teachers or school administrators (Sammons, in press). The failure to provide complainants with a complete and accurate description of an employer's/school's investigatory procedures will contribute to increased concerns of retaliation. As stated by the EEOC (1999):

> An employer should make clear that it will not tolerate adverse treatment of employees because they report harassment or provide information related to such complaints. An anti-harassment policy and complaint procedure will not be effective without such an assurance.

Resources for investigating complaints of sexual harassment, including questions to ask of complainants, accused individuals, and witnesses and how to determine credibility, may be found in Levy and Paludi (2002), Paludi and Barickman (1998), and Paludi and Paludi (2003).

Office for Civil Rights and Resolution of Sexual Harassment Complaints

The OCR conducts investigations of complaints of sexual harassment brought by students who have initially sought resolution through their school or who seek resolution first through the OCR (Herskowitz & Kallem, 2003). When its investigations indicate that a violation of Title IX has occurred, the OCR offers the school district an opportunity to voluntarily correct the problem. If the school refuses, the OCR initiates enforcement action. Such remedies include:

a. Psychological counseling
b. Compensatory education to make up for time lost from the educational program as a result of the sexual harassment
c. Adjustment of grades impacted by the sexual harassment and/or the opportunity for a student to repeat a course with a different teacher
d. Discipline of the harasser
e. Individualized training programs

Other Issues

> But the issue of sexual harassment is not the end of it. There are other issues—political issues, gender issues—that people need to be educated about.
> *Anita Hill*

Bullying versus Sexual Harassment in Schools

School districts have increasingly been focusing their attention on bullying (Stein, 2005a). Bullying prevention is important, given findings by

Espelage and Holt (2001) and Lund, Ertesvag, and Roland (2010), among others, that suggest at least 30% of adolescents are involved in bullying as bullies, victims, or both. In addition, victims score within the clinical range on standard depression and anxiety measures (Sandler & Stonehill, 2005). Focusing on bullying prevention is also important given findings by Lund, Ertesvag, and Roland (2010) indicating that adolescents identify nonsupportive school personnel to be the major explanation for why bullying occurs. A third reason to focus on bullying prevention concerns recent research that links workplace bullying to childhood and adolescent bullying that was never addressed properly (Daniel, 2009).

Almost 30 years after the project on the Status of Education of Women used the term "hidden issue" to describe sexual harassment, we have a backlash again because schools are focusing on bullying instead of sexual harassment. Despite the high incidence of various forms of sexual harassment and other forms of gendered violence against adolescent girls in schools, sexual harassment of girls is once again being "hidden" because it is being overshadowed by bullying (Paludi et al., 2007). In some school districts, sexual harassment is subsumed under bullying, which, according to Stein (2005a), further degenders peer aggression.

Sandler and Stonehill (2005) noted that while sexual harassment may be seen as a form of sexual bullying, when schools focus on bullying prevention, they are not likely to remember to deal with sexual harassment since they consider bullying and sexual harassment to be independent of each other. Stein (2003) noted that focusing on bullying ignores the fact that most victims of sexual harassment are girls and instead deals primarily with boys' experiences of being bullied. According to Stein (2005b):

> state legislators have been passing laws on school bullying which may serve to placate the general public. Concurrently, however, there has been an increase of incidents of sexual harassment and sexual violence in schools, along with greater frequency of violence in teen dating relationships. Unfortunately, the bullying focus may serve to both degender the problem of sexual harassment and sexual violence and to take attention away from the increasing severity of these problems. (p. 7)

Furthermore, attention to bullying rather than sexual harassment helps remove the school's responsibility in preventing and dealing with this form of violence against girls. Bullying is seen as an interpersonal problem that involves helping a pathological bully or group of bullies. Sexual harassment, on the other hand, is illegal and requires schools to both prevent and deal with sexual harassment when it occurs

(Paludi et al., 2007). It is paramount to deal with sexual harassment from an institutional level of analysis, not an individual level (Paludi & Barickman, 1998; Stein, 1996).

While the U.S. Department of Education has offered a definition of sexual harassment (as we discussed earlier in this chapter), it has not defined bullying but provides definitions of bullying from researchers. While sexual harassment is illegal, bullying is not. This fact has implications for adolescents seeking resolution to their complaints. If they define their experiences as sexual harassment, they can use the OCR's resolution procedures (see above). If, on the other hand, adolescents define their experiences as bullying, they do not have the same federal recourse. Stein (2003) has noted that state antibullying laws do not offer protection to adolescents that is identical to federal laws.

During the completion of the writing of this chapter, the OCR issued a statement identifying the need to deal with sexual harassment as well as bullying. This statement may be obtained by reviewing the following link: http://www2.ed.gov/ocr/letters/colleague-201010.html.

Cognitive Maturity of Adolescent Girls

> When the lives and the rights of children are at stake, there must be no silent witnesses.
>
> *Carol Bellamy*

Girls Scouts of America (2002) concluded its report as follows:

> All too often, these computer-savvy teenage girls are still naïve and emotionally vulnerable, as they grapple with issues such as how to react to sexual online content they unwittingly encounter. (p. 2)

The cognitive maturity of adolescent girls must be acknowledged in designing training programs, as we addressed earlier in this chapter. Part of sexual harassment prevention for adolescents also includes school personnel recognizing and addressing Elkind's (1967) components of egocentrism that are characteristic of adolescence: imaginary audience and personal fable. The imaginary audience refers to adolescents feeling that they are the focus of attention; it is imaginary in that peers are actually not that concerned with the adolescent's thoughts, as they are focused on their own.

This concept has been used to explain why adolescent girls are self-conscious about their clothing and body image, spend many hours primping in front of mirrors, and feel that they are on "display" and thus engage in eating disorders (Halpern, Udry, Campbell, & Suchindran, 1999; Pipher, 1994). Ferron (1997) noted that approximately 75% of American adolescent girls in her sample believed that they would be happier in their lives if they had a "flawless" body. Happiness was defined by these girls as having more friends, having an easier life, being accepted by a peer group, and finding love.

As a consequence of being absorbed with their own feelings, adolescents believe that their emotions are unique. Their belief in their uniqueness is expressed in a subjective story that they tell themselves about their "special qualities." This subjective story is referred to as the personal fable. Evidence of the personal fable is evident in diaries kept by adolescents; it includes stories about how they are immune from dangers suffered by others, so they can dispense with using seat belts and contraceptives and allow themselves to binge and purge. This is done because they are cognitively convinced that they are special, that nothing bad will happen to them.

Elkind (1967) noted that adolescent egocentrism disappears when girls have the role-taking opportunities that will help replace the imaginary audience with a real one and a subjective fable with an objective story. Egocentrism has been hypothesized to be declining by the time adolescents are 16 or 17 years old. However, adolescent girls may not be given the role-taking opportunities at home or in school or encouraged to speak up about abuse, including their own and peers' victimization, because of stereotypic beliefs about becoming argumentative, assertive, and, therefore, unattractive as dates and potential mates (Leaper & Brown, 2008; Paludi, 2002). Thus, adolescent girls seriously harm themselves and others in their struggle to "fit in" with a peer group that demands silence about violence, including sexual harassment.

Sexual harassment prevention programs for adolescents must address these issues if the goal is to intervene before, during, and after incidents. We recommend a variation of the bystander education program developed for rape prevention by Banyard, Plante, and Moynihan (2005). Such a program can assist adolescents in understanding the importance of assisting themselves and others who are experiencing sexual harassment and other types of violence, including intimate partner violence.

Research on egalitarian and traditional gender role orientations and intervening in sexual harassment is promising. Leaper and Brown (2008) found in their study of 600 adolescent girls aged 12 to 18 that those who learned about feminism from their teachers, their parents, or the media were more likely to recognize sexism, including sexual harassment, than those who did not. Furthermore, according to Leaper and Brown (2008):

> Exposure to feminism did not lead to increased reports of sexism for all girls equally. Feminist messages appeared to be most powerful for girls who either held moderately egalitarian attitudes or who were at least moderately discontent with gender norms. Thus, girls may need to be somewhat responsive to questioning the status quo for feminist messages to be most influential. (p. 699)

These results support in-class training programs for secondary students that utilize pedagogy that will provide the skills necessary for them to make connections among sexism, sexual harassment, illegal behavior, and reporting their experiences to school administrators. Such pedagogy includes case studies/scenarios to encourage adolescents to learn through guided discovery and teach them to think critically about discrimination (Carter, 2002). The major objective of the training modules and pedagogical techniques is to facilitate transference to the classroom, other school-sponsored activities, and the workplace. Transference can be accomplished by:

a. Association: having participants associate the new information with something with which they are already knowledgeable;
b. Similarity: presenting information that is similar to material that participants already know; i.e., it revisits a logical framework or pattern;
c. Degree of original learning: the degree of original learning for the participants was high;
d. Critical attribute element: the information learned by the participants contains elements that are extremely beneficial and/or critical at school and/or on the job (Paludi et al., in press).

Paludi, Martin, and Paludi (2007) noted that part of this training must deal with confronting hidden biases and stereotypes about females, males, sex, and power. Without these issues being discussed, they will remain unchallenged by adolescents.

Finally, we recommend including adolescents in designing training programs and in revising policies and procedures to promote their own empowerment as well as positive interaction among students. Adolescents experience sexual harassment. They want to be part of the solution. Girls in the AAUW study (2001), when asked "What could your school do to address sexual harassment," stated:

> "Maybe if they had an assembly about sexual harassment and expulsion for those who violate rules."

> "I'd just like them to, if the matter comes up, deal with it swiftly and fairly; taking in all considerations."

"Make aware what exactly it is and what to do about it if you are offended."

"Seminars, a definite policy in the handbook."

"Have the same no-tolerance policy as knives or guns and make an example of anyone who does commit sexual harassment, so maybe it will stop others." (p. 17)

We need to listen to adolescent girls and address what they ask of us in order to protect them and nurture their healthy emotional development throughout adolescence and into their adulthood.

References

Allen, M., Young, E., Ashbaker, B., Heaton, E., & Parkinson, M. (2003). Sexual harassment on the school bus: Supporting and preparing bus drivers to respond appropriately. *Journal of School Violence, 2,* 101–109.

American Association of University Women. (1992). *The AAUW Report: How schools shortchange girls.* Washington, DC: Author.

American Association of University Women (AAUW). (2001). *Hostile hallways: The annual survey on sexual harassment in America's schools.* Washington, DC: Author.

Banyard, V., Plante, E., & Moynihan, M. (2005). *Rape prevention through bystander education: Bringing a broader community perspective to sexual violence prevention.* Report to the U.S. Department of Justice. Retrieved on October 7, 2010, from http://www.ncjrs.gov/pdffiles1/nij/grants/208701.pdf.

Berson, L., Berson, M., Ferron, J. (2005). *Emergency risks of violence in the digital age: Lessons for educators from an online study of adolescent girls in the United States. North Carolina.* Retrieved October 9, 2010, from http://www.ncsu.edu/meridian/sum2002/cyberviolence/.

Bogart, K., Simmons, S., Stein, S., & Tomaszewski, E. (1992). Breaking the silence: Sexual and gender-based harassment in elementary, secondary, and postsecondary education. In S. Klein (Ed.), *Sex equity and sexuality in education* (pp. 191–221). Albany, NY: State University of New York Press.

Brown, C., & Leaper, C. (2008, April). *Adolescent girls' reactions to academic sexism: Cognitive appraisals, coping strategies and academic outcomes.* Paper presented at Third Gender Development Research Conference, San Francisco, CA.

Carter, S. (2002). Matching training methods and factors of cognitive ability: A means to improve training outcomes. *Human Resource Development Quarterly, 13,* 71–87.

Chisolm, J. (2006). Cyberspace violence against girls and adolescent females. *Annuals, New York Academy of Sciences, 1087,* 74–89.

Cox Communications and the National Center for Missing and Exploited Children (2005). *Parents' Internet monitoring study.* Retrieved on October 10, 2010, from http://www.cox.com/TakeCharge/includes/docs/results.pdf.

Daniel, T. (2009). *Stop bullying at work: Strategies and tools for HR and legal professionals.* Alexandria, VA: Society for Human Resource Management.

DeSouza, E. (2004, July). *Intercultural and intracultural comparisons of bullying and sexual harassment in secondary schools.* Paper presented at the meeting of the Association for Gender Equity Leadership in Education, Washington, DC.

Dowling, J. (2011). Conducting workplace investigations. In M. Paludi, C. Paludi, & E. DeSouza (Eds.), *Praeger handbook on workplace discrimination.* Westport, CT: Praeger.

Doyle, J., & Paludi, M. (1995). *Sex and gender: The human experience.* New York: McGraw Hill.

Drobac, J. (2007). I can't to I Kant: The sexual harassment of working adolescents, competing theories, and ethical dilemmas. *Albany Law Review, 70,* 675.

Duffy, J., Wareham, S., & Walsh, M. (2004). Psychological consequences for high school students of having been sexually harassed. *Sex Roles, 50,* 811–821.

Elkind, D. (1967). Egocentrism in adolescence. *Child Development, 38,* 1025–1034.

Equal Employment Opportunity Commission (EEOC). (1990). *Policy guidance on sexual harassment.* Washington, DC: U.S. Government Printing Office.

Equal Employment Opportunity Commission (EEOC). (1999). *Enforcement guidance: Vicarious employer liability for unlawful harassment by supervisors.* Washington, DC: U.S. Government Printing Office.

Equal Employment Opportunity Commission (EEOC). (2010a). *Sixteen-year-old claims she was harassed at Pennsylvania Mexican Restaurant.* Retrieved on October 8, 2010, from http://www.eeo.gov/youth//case2.html.

Equal Employment Opportunity Commission (EEOC). (2010b). *Teenagers report sexual harassment at California golf club.* Retrieved on October 8, 2010, from http://www.eeoc.gov/youth//case6.html.

Espelage, D., & Holt, M. (2001). Bullying and victimization during early adolescence. *Journal of Emotional Abuse, 2,* 123–142.

Faragher v. City of Boca Raton, 524 U.S. 725 (1998).

Ferron, C. (1997). Body image in adolescence: Cross-cultural research-results of the preliminary phase of a quantitative survey. *Adolescence, 32,* 735–744.

Fineran, S. (2002). Adolescents at work: Gender issues and sexual harassment. *Violence Against Women, 8,* 953–967.

Fineran, S., & Bennett, L. (1999). Gender and power issues of peer sexual harassment among teenagers. *Journal of Interpersonal Violence, 15,* 626–641.

Fineran, S., & Bolen, R. (2006). Risk factors for peer sexual harassment in schools. *Journal of Interpersonal Violence, 21,* 1169–1190.

Fineran, S., & Gruber, J. (2004, July). *Research on bullying and sexual harassment in secondary schools: Incidence, interrelationships and psychological implications.* Paper presented at the meeting of the Association for Gender Equity Leadership in Education, Washington, DC.

Fineran, S., & Gruber, J. (2009). Youth at work: Adolescent employment and sexual harassment. *Child Abuse and Neglect, 33,* 550–559.

Fogarty, K. (2009). *Teens and Internet safety.* Retrieved on October 9, 2010, from http://edis.ifas.ufl.edu/fy848.

Giladi, A. (2005, August). *Sexual harassment or play? Perceptions and observations of young children's experiences in kindergarten and early schooling in Israel.* Paper presented at the Conference of the International Coalition Against Sexual Harassment, Philadelphia, PA.

Girl Scouts of the United States of America (2002). *The net effect: Girls and new media.* Retrieved on October 9, 2010, from http://www.girlscouts.org/research/pdf/net_effect.pdf.

Halpern, C., Udry, J., Campbell, B., & Suchindran, C. (1999). Effects of body fat on weight concerns, dating, and sexual activity: A longitudinal analysis of Black and White adolescent girls. *Developmental Psychology, 35,* 721–736.

Herskowitz, E., & Kallem, H. (2003). The role of the Equal Employment Opportunity Commission and Human Rights Commission in dealing with sexual harassment. In M. Paludi & C. Paludi (Eds.), *Academic and workplace sexual harassment: A handbook of cultural, social science, management and legal perspectives* (pp. 200–215). Westport, CT: Praeger.

Hill, C., & Silva, E. (2005). *Drawing the line: Sexual harassment on campus.* Washington, DC: American Association of University Women Educational Foundation.

Klein, J. (2006). An invisible problem: Daily violence against girls in school. *Theoretical Criminology, 10,* 147–177.

Larkin, J. (1994). Walking through walls: The sexual harassment of high school girls. *Gender and Education, 6*(3), 263–280.

Leaper, C., & Brown, C. (2008). Perceived experiences with sexism among adolescent girls. *Child Development, 79,* 685–704.

Levy, A., & Paludi, M. (2002). *Workplace sexual harassment* (2nd ed.). Englewood Cliffs, NJ: Prentice Hall.

Lindberg, S., Grabe, S., & Hyde, J. (2007). Gender, pubertal development and peer sexual harassment predict objectified body consciousness in early adolescence. *Journal of Research on Adolescence, 17,* 723–742.

Lund, I., Ertesvag, S., & Roland, E. (2010). Listening to shy voices: Shy adolescents' experiences with being bullied at school. *Journal of Child and Adolescent Trauma, 3,* 205–223.

Massachusetts Department of Elementary and Secondary Education. (2007). *Health and risk behaviors of Massachusetts youth, 2007: The report.* Retrieved on October 9, 2010, from http://www.doe.mass.edu/cnp/hprograms/yrbs/.

McQueen, I. (1997). Investigating sexual harassment allegations: The employer's challenge. In W. O'Donohue (Ed.), *Sexual harassment: Theory, research, and treatment.* Boston: Allyn & Bacon.

Mortimer, J. (2005). *Working and growing up on America.* Cambridge, MA: Harvard University Press.

Moyer, R., & Nath, A. (1998). Some effects of brief training interventions on perceptions of sexual harassment. *Journal of Applied Social Psychology, 28,* 333–356.

Murnen, S., & Smolak, L. (2000). The experience of sexual harassment among grade-school students: Early socialization of female subordination? *Sex Roles, 24,* 319–327.

Nadal, K. L. (2010). Gender microaggressions: Implications for mental health. In M. Paludi (Ed.), *Feminism and women's rights worldwide: Vol. 2. Mental and physical health* (pp. 155–175). Westport, CT: Praeger.

Office for Civil Rights, U.S. Department of Education. (1997). *Sexual harassment guidance: Harassment of students by school employees, other students, or third parties.* Retrieved on October 9, 2010, from http://www2.ed.gov/about/offices/list/ocr/docs/sexhar00.html.

Paludi, C., et al. (in press). Exercising "reasonable care": Policies, procedures and training programs. In M. Paludi, C. Paludi, & E. DeSouza (Eds.), *Praeger handbook on workplace discrimination: Legal, management and social science perspectives.* Westport, CT: Praeger.

Paludi, C., & Paludi, M. (2003). Developing and enforcing effective policies, procedures, and training programs for educational institutions and businesses. In M. Paludi & C. Paludi (Eds.), *Academic and workplace sexual harassment: A handbook of cultural, social science, management, and legal perspectives* (pp. 176–198). Westport, CT: Praeger.

Paludi, M. (2002). *The psychology of women.* Upper Saddle River, NJ: Prentice Hall.

Paludi, M. (2010, October). *The continuum of campus violence: Applying "Broken Windows Theory" to prevent and deal with campus violence.* Paper presented at the U.S. Department of Education National Meeting on Alcohol, Drug Abuse and Violence Prevention in Higher Education, National Harbor, MD.

Paludi, M. (2011). Introduction. In M. Paludi (Ed.), *The psychology of teen violence and victimization.* Westport, CT: Praeger.

Paludi, M., & Barickman, R. (1998). *Sexual harassment, work, and education: A resource manual for prevention.* Albany: State University of New York Press.

Paludi, M., & Kelly, K. (2010). Missing children and child abductions: An international human rights issue. In M. Paludi (Ed.), *Feminism and women's rights worldwide* (pp. 47–80). Westport, CT: Praeger.

Paludi, M., Martin, J., & Paludi, C. (2007). Sexual harassment: The hidden gender equity problem. In S. Klein (Ed.), *Handbook for achieving gender equity through education* (2nd ed.) (pp. 215–229). Mahwah, NJ: Lawrence Erlbaum Associates.

PBS. (2009). *Is your daughter safe at work?* Retrieved on October 9, 2010, from http://www.pbs.org/now/shows/508/index.html.

Pellegrini, A. (2002). Bullying, victimization, and sexual harassment during the transition to middle school. *Educational Psychologist, 37,* 151–163.

Phinney, G. (1994). Sexual harassment: A dynamic element in the lives of middle school girls and teachers. *Equity and Excellence in Education, 27,* 5–10.

Pipher, M. (1994). *Reviving Ophelia: Saving the selves of adolescent girls.* New York: Ballantine.

Roscoe, B. (1994). Sexual harassment: An educational program for middle school students. *Elementary School Guidance and Counseling, 29,* 110–120.

Roscoe, B., Strouse, J., & Goodwin, M. (1994). Sexual harassment: Early adolescents' self reports of experiences and acceptance. *Adolescence, 29,* 515–523.

Sammons, D. (in press). Retaliation. In M. Paludi, C. Paludi, & E. DeSouza (Eds.), *Praeger handbook on understanding and preventing workplace discrimination.* Westport, CT: Praeger.

Sandler, B., & Stonehill, H. (2005). *Student to student sexual harassment in K–12: Strategies and solutions for educators to use in the classroom, school and community.* Lanham, MD: Rowman & Littlefield Education.

Shakeshaft, C., & Cohen, A. (1995). Sexual abuse of students by school personnel. *Phi Delta Kappan, 76,* 512–520.

Sheffield, C. (1993). The invisible intruder: Women's experiences of obscene phone calls. In P. Bart & E. Moran (Eds.), *Violence against women: The bloody footprints* (pp. 73–78). Newbury Park, CA: Sage.

Smith, S., & Mazin, R. (2004). *The HR answer book.* New York: AMACOM.

Stein, N. (1993, August). *Secrets in full view: Sexual harassment in our K–12 schools.* Paper presented at the American Psychological Association, Toronto, Canada.

Stein, N. (1996). From the margins to the mainstream: Sexual harassment in K–12 schools. *Initiatives, 57,* 19–26.

Stein, N. (2003). Bullying or sexual harassment? The missing discourse of rights in an era of zero tolerance. *University of Arizona Law Review, 45,* 783–799.

Stein, N. (2005a, August). *Gender safety in U.S. schools.* Paper presented at the Conference of the International Coalition Against Sexual Harassment, Philadelphia, PA.

Stein, N. (2005b). A rising pandemic of sexual violence in elementary and secondary schools: Locating a secret problem. *Duke Journal of Gender Law and Policy, 12,* 1–19.

Stein, N., Marshall, N., & Tropp, L. (1993). *Secrets in public: Sexual harassment in our schools—A report on the results of a Seventeen Magazine Survey.* Wellesley, MA: Wellesley College Center for Research on Women.

Stockdale, M., & Sagrestano, L. (2011). Resources for targets of sexual harassment. In M. Paludi (Ed.), *Praeger handbook on understanding and preventing workplace discrimination* (Vol. 2). Westport, CT: Praeger.

Stratton, S., & Backes, J. (1997, February/March). Sexual harassment in North Dakota public schools: A study of eight high schools. *High School Journal, 80,* 163–172.

Strauss, S. (2010). Sexual violence to girls and women in schools around the world. In M. Paludi (Ed.), *Feminism and women's rights worldwide: Vol. 1. Heritage, roles and issues* (pp. 187–231). Westport, CT: Praeger.

Strauss, S., & Espeland, P. (1992). *Sexual harassment and teens.* Minneapolis, MN: Free Spirit Publishing, Inc.

Timmerman, G. (2002). A comparison between unwanted sexual behavior by teachers and by peers in secondary schools. *Journal of Youth and Adolescence, 31,* 397–404.

U.S. Department of Education. (2004). *Educator sexual misconduct: A synthesis of existing literature.* Doc. No. 2004–09. Retrieved on October 9, 2010, from www2.ed.gov/rschstat/research/pubs/misconductreview/report.

Walsh, M., Duffy, J., & Gallagher-Duffy, J. (2007). A more accurate approach to measuring the prevalence of sexual harassment among high school students. *Canadian Journal of Behavioural Science, 39,* 110–118.

Wishnietsky, D. (1991). Reported and unreported teacher-student sexual harassment. *Journal of Education Research, 3,* 164–169.

PART III

Teen Violence by Family and Mates

CHAPTER NINE

No Safe Haven: Sexual Abuse of Teens by Family Members

Jeanette Krenek, Joanna L. Goodwin, Paula K. Lundberg-Love, Lindsay Marie Pantlin, and Britney Hilbun

Child sexual abuse is a pervasive and underreported social tragedy. Intrafamilial abuse, or incest, is a particularly insidious crime against children and adolescents because of the violation of trust in an intimate family relationship. While once considered an unspeakable problem on the fringe of society, the 2009 movie *Precious,* based on the novel *Push* by Sapphire, brought the experience of incest to national attention when it won two Academy Awards. *Precious* chronicles the resilience of an illiterate teenager, and survivor of incest, impregnated twice by her father. Many similar stories of adolescent incest survivors go unreported every year. Unlike victims of extrafamilial abuse, a teenage victim of incest cannot seek the support of caregivers at home, where sexual abuse is typically endured. Perpetrators of incest include any adult relative as well as siblings. While the legal definition of child abuse is a function of state law, usually it includes children and teenagers under 18 or sometimes 16 years of age. However, teenage victims experience unique and often unrecognized challenges as incest survivors due to their developmental stage.

What Is Incest?

The experience of incest differs from other experiences of childhood sexual abuse. Victims of incest tend to be younger when the abuse first occurs, and the abuse is more likely to be of longer duration (Gannon, Gilchrist, & Wade, 2008; Kristensen & Lau, 2007). Despite an increasing awareness of female perpetrators, researchers agree that most victims of incest are female and most perpetrators are male. However, other research findings are complicated by differences in defining incest. While there is no universal definition of incest in research literature, the most common definition of incest is "all sexual behavior whose purpose is the sexual gratification of the adult" (Carlson, Maciol, & Schneider, 2006). However, research definitions of incest offenders range from only including blood relatives, including relatives by adoption or marriage, to individuals who have a parental role in a child's life, such as a foster parent (Gannon et al., 2008). This wide array of definitions complicates the process of deriving meaningful conclusions and comparisons based upon the current research data. Courtois's (1997) definition of incest includes sexual contact occurring between related individuals, especially when the initiator is more powerful vis-à-vis the victim (e.g., size, age, money). Acts of incest may be grouped based upon the level of bodily contact. Acts of contact incest range in severity and include fondling, digital penetration, attempted or completed oral sex, anal sex, or rape (Burns Loeb et al., 2002). Noncontact incest includes voyeurism, the unwanted viewing of a child's private parts, and exhibitionism, the unwanted viewing of an offender's private parts (Finkelhor, Hammer, & Sedlak, 2008). Incest does not occur in a vacuum. Often it accompanies other family dysfunctions, such as spousal violence, physical and emotional abuse, substance abuse, and mental illness (Courtois, 1997).

How Common Is Incest?

There is a consensus in the literature that 1 in 3 women and 1 in 10 men in America are sexually abused prior to the age of 18 (Anderson, 2006). However, the stigma involved in sexual abuse, and particularly incest, results in substantial underreporting. No statistics can illuminate the full extent of the problem. In a 2008 report by the U.S. Department of Justice, 285,400 children under the age of 17 were sexually assaulted in 1999. Of these assaults, 10% were perpetrated by a family member, with 4% perpetrated by the father and 5% by a brother. Of the total assault victims, 81% were adolescents, between the ages of 12 and 17 (Finkelhor et al., 2008). In a 2000 report, with data provided by the National Incident-Based Report System (NIBRS), 33% of all sexual-assault victims were between the ages of 12 and 17 (Snyder, 2000). Among adolescent sexual assault victims between the ages of 12 and 18, 90.9% were female. Fourteen-year-old females were at the greatest risk of forcible rape. In 24.3% of the cases, a family member was the perpetrator of adolescent females, and the same was true for 23.7% of cases for adolescent males. Perpetrators of adolescents were five times more likely to be family members when the assault occurred in a residence (Snyder, 2000).

Sibling Incest

Definition

While father-daughter incest is the most common focus of research, sibling incest is now thought to be more common, despite the current lack of comprehensive available research (Carlson et al., 2006; Haskins, 2003). There is no universally accepted definition of sexual abuse by a sibling due to the difficulty in differentiating between sexual abuse and normal sexual exploration. According to the Office of Juvenile Justice and Delinquency Prevention, sibling incest is defined as "sexual acts initiated by one sibling toward another without the other's consent, by use of force or coercion, or where there was a power differential between the siblings" (Righthand & Welch, 2004). To discriminate normal sexual play from sibling incest, the minimum age difference between a sibling perpetrator and the victim is usually defined as between two to five years difference (Carlson et al., 2006). Despite research showing that some sexual exploration between siblings is a part of normal development, some researchers simply define sibling incest as any form of sexual activity between siblings without taking into account age differences or the use of coercion (Brennan, 2006). However, more commonly, sibling incest can be described as traumatic sexual contact that may include "physical touching, fondling, indecent exposure, attempted penetration, intercourse by coercion or force, or oral and anal sex" (Haskins, 2003).

Sibling Incest in Context

Sibling incest tends to be a manifestation of a severely dysfunctional family (Haskins, 2003). Individuals in abusive families often have "low self-esteem, high impulsivity, low frustration tolerance, an inability to identify or meet needs, a lack of problem-solving skills, affective and expressive problems, communication deficits, feelings of helplessness and futility, frequent and unresolved losses, and isolation" (Haskins, 2003, p. 341). In a comparison study of 32 adolescent sibling and nonfamilial sex offenders, Worling (1995) found that sibling offenders "reported significantly more parental physical punishment, a more negative and argumentative family environment, greater feelings of parental rejection, heightened marital discord, and less overall satisfaction with their family relationships" (p. 639). In violent families, sibling incest often develops out of a mutual need for nurturance. However, in this circumstance, the experience may become traumatic as an adolescent develops a sexual identity and a sense of shame about the sexual relationship (Brennan, 2006). In an exploratory study of 41 survivors of sibling incest, 46.3% reported that the experience began consensually and later involved coercion or force, particularly during adolescence (Carlson et al., 2006). While there is a need for more research on sibling incest, many researchers suggest that the experience of sibling incest may be more severe than that of incest by a father. In a study by M. O'Brien, comparing 170 juvenile sibling offenders to a control group of nonfamilial offenders, sibling perpetrators committed a greater amount of total sexual offenses, abused their victims for longer periods of time, and abused multiple victims (as cited in Righthand & Welch, 2004). In this sample, 46% of sibling offenders vaginally or anally penetrated their victims, as compared to 24% of extrafamilial offenders. Despite their more significant history of abuse, only one-third of sibling perpetrators had court-ordered treatment, while three-quarters of extrafamilial perpetrators received such treatment (Righthand & Welch, 2004). Similarly, in a study of 72 incest victims, 70.5% of incest cases perpetrated by a brother involved intercourse, as compared to 34.8% of abuse involving intercourse by fathers (Cyr, Wright, McDuff, & Perron, 2002).

Because most sexual abuse is committed by men or boys against girls or women, most of the research literature is based upon data involving male-perpetrated abuse. With the recent increase in research on child sexual abuse, a need for research on mother-child perpetrated sexual abuse has been discovered. Prevalence for mother-child abuse is uncertain but estimated at approximately 20% for male children and approximately 5% for female children, with mother-daughter incest being more commonly reported (Courtois, 1997). In some cases, it is the mother who actually reports herself.

The aftereffects of mother-child sexual abuse are, for the most part, similar to those of other forms of incest. It has been found, however, that there is often greater confusion with regard to identity formation in girls abused by their mothers. Women abused by their mothers reported chronic problems with poor self-esteem and having experienced during adolescence debilitating bouts of depression, suicidal behavior, self-mutilation, substance abuse, and sexual acting out (Ogilvie & Daniluk, 1995). People abused by their mothers tended to have difficulty trusting others. Kim Etherington (1997), of the University of Bristol, says, "Our capacity to form a durable bond with a member of the opposite sex later in life is largely dependent on the success or failure of the primal bond between a mother and her child." Sexual abuse of a child by his or her mother affects every aspect of the person's life, even down to whether or not he or she is able to have fulfilling relationships. The knowledge that a mother who is usually the protector of her children is capable of harming them in this way is incomprehensible.

What Are the Effects of Incest?

Developmental Effects

Adolescence is a challenging time of physical, emotional, and social development for all teenagers. While incest occurring at any age may have a devastating developmental impact, adolescent incest victims experience particularly challenging developmental consequences (Burns Loeb et al., 2002). Teenagers with a history of sexual abuse may experience abnormal hormone levels associated with earlier onset of puberty and hyperarousal. These biochemical abnormalities may lead to high-risk sexual behaviors during adolescence and the possibility of sexual revictimization (Burns Loeb et al., 2002). The trauma of incest can impact the still-developing adolescent brain. The frontal lobes of the brain are responsible for advanced logical thinking and impulse control. The adolescent brain does not have fully developed frontal lobes. Immaturity of the frontal lobes results in the tendency of adolescents to be impulsive and rely on emotional thinking rather than logical thinking. Abused adolescents tend to have less cortical development. Their ability to survive trauma typically occurs at the cost of cortical development, which results in more impulsive behavior and lack of emotional regulation (Child Welfare Information Gateway, 2009).

Typical female adolescent development includes sexual development, learning to make appropriate sexual decisions, and developing satisfying romantic relationships. The physical changes beginning at puberty require adequate psychological and social adjustments for males and females (Cole & Putnam, 1992). Adolescents whose first incestuous experience occurs after puberty may have a lower risk of psychopathology in adulthood than those abused before puberty. However, for many adolescents the incest experience begins in childhood and continues through adolescence (Cole & Putnam, 1992). The trauma of incest may result in an adolescent who does not develop a stable identity and uses self-destructive coping strategies, such as substance abuse. Lindberg and Distad (1985) concluded that the self-destructive behaviors of adolescent incest survivors, such as substance abuse, suicide attempts, perfectionism, isolation, and depression, are "logical and predictable survival responses" (p. 523). However, these behaviors become maladaptive when the adolescent is no longer in an incestuous situation.

Dissociation and Post-Traumatic Stress Disorder (PTSD)

The DSM-IV-TR defines dissociation as "a disruption of normally integrated function of consciousness, memory, identity or perception of environment or one's body." Individuals who experience long-term, uninterrupted abuse are at an increased risk of dissociative symptoms. To survive ongoing incest, individuals dissociate in order to distance themselves from reality (Courtois, 1997). Research has shown that women who experience incest as compared to extrafamilial sexual abuse tend to experience a greater degree of psychopathology. In a study of Turkish university students, incest was reported by 6.3% of 535 students. Students who reported incest also had significantly higher scores on the Dissociative Experiences Scale. In a study of 45 female incest victims from ages 13 to 18, Johnson and Kenkel (1991) found girls with the greatest level of psychopathology tended to cope by dissociation. Incest severity, which includes the duration, level of violence, degree of coercion, escalation, and penetration, as well as the experiences of multiple perpetrators, and disclosure without intervention, are related to a higher degree of dissociation. Cyr, Wright, McDuff, & Perron (2002) found that girls abused by their fathers and brothers reported more dissociative symptoms than girls abused by stepfathers.

In a survey study of college students, Ullman, Townsend, Filipas, and Starzynski (2007) found that students abused by a family member experienced significantly more post-traumatic stress disorder (PTSD) symptoms than did individuals abused by a stranger or acquaintance. Students abused by a family member who delayed disclosure had higher rates of PTSD symptoms than did individuals abused by a nonfamily member who also delayed disclosure. The traumatic betrayal of incest may be one reason for higher occurrences of PTSD and dissociative symptoms as compared to those who experience extrafamilial sexual assaults (Ullman et al., 2007).

Obesity and Eating Disorders

A prospective study of 84 female victims of childhood sexual abuse showed that they were more than twice as likely to be obese by the time they reached young adulthood when compared to a group of nonabused females (Noll, Zeller, Trickett, & Putnam, 2007). However, there was no difference in weight gain prior to young adulthood. Weight gain starts occurring in adolescence when teens may start dating and being sexually active. Researchers speculate that the manners in which incest victims cope with associated conditions, such as depression, may mediate their higher rates of obesity (Noll et al., 2007). Researchers in Australia conducted a birth cohort study of 2,461 young adults who experienced childhood sexual abuse by the age of 16. Despite controlling for "maternal education and income, marital circumstances, maternal lifestyle and mental health, childhood and adolescent behavioral problems, and family dysfunction," women who experienced penetrative sexual abuse had significantly higher body mass index (BMI) measurements at age 21 than did women who experienced nonpenetrative abuse and men who experienced penetrative and nonpenetrative abuse (Mamun et al., 2007).

Miller, McClusky-Fawcett, and Irving (1993) identified 72 women using the Bulimic Investigatory Test who had a high likelihood of having bulimia nervosa. The sexual-abuse histories of these women were compared to 72 control subjects. Women who were abused during adolescence by an adult relative were significantly more likely to be bulimic. This higher likelihood of adolescent incest survivors to be bulimic may be related to negative feelings regarding their bodies (Miller et al., 1993).

Psychological Effects

While not every victim of incest will experience adverse long-term effects, the trauma of incest is a significant risk factor for many adverse psychological outcomes. Factors that increase the risk of adverse outcomes include incest beginning at puberty, duration of abuse lasting longer than four years, the use of violence or coercion, blaming the victim, physical penetration, the existence of more than one perpetrator, and a traumatic intervention (Courtois, 1997).

According to the cognitive model of therapy, the psychological well-being of an individual who experiences a traumatic event is related to the way that he or she perceives and processes that event. Internal attributions consist of "self-blame" attributions that relate the cause of an event to something about oneself, while external attributions attribute the cause of the abuse to an outside source, such as a perpetrator. Some cognitive therapists also believe an individual who can find meaning in a traumatic event, or answer the question of "why," may also have better psychological outcomes. Morrow (1991) compared female adolescent incest victims' internal attributions, external attributions, and ability to find meaning in the abuse to their levels of self-esteem and depression. Of the 87 participants, 16.7% made internal attributions such as "It was my fault," "I was dressed inappropriately," and "I was being punished" (p. 479). Thirty-three and one-third of the participants made external attributions, such as "Because he was drinking," "My stepfather has a problem," and "I guess he was sick" (p. 479). There was no significant difference in the self-esteem and depression scores of girls who found meaning in their abuse and those who did not. However, girls who had internal attributions about their incest experience had lower self-esteem scores and high levels of depression compared to girls who had external attributions or who found no meaning in their abuse. There was a significant association between girls whose abuse involved intercourse and those who made internal attributions. Internal attributions may be an adaptive way of coping with the incest experience by distorting what really happened and allowing a child or adolescent to feel in control of the abuse. However, such self-blame is a common factor in future psychological maladjustment, the possibility for sexual revictimization, and the potential for self-harm (Morrow, 1991).

Conclusion

The trauma of incest is damaging at any point in life, but its occurrence during adolescence is particularly developmentally disruptive. While all sexual abuse during adolescence is damaging, incest involves intimate betrayal and a loss of safety at home. Incest is a significant risk factor for many future psychological problems. Adolescence is a turbulent and defining time in an individual's life. The challenges of adolescence are much more difficult to successfully navigate after experiencing the trauma of incest. Despite increasing public awareness, the majority of incest cases are underreported and perpetrators unpunished. It is impossible to determine the social cost to each survivor of incest. The majority of current research on incest does not take into account the unique situation of adolescents. More research is needed to determine appropriate interventions for adolescent survivors of incest. Adolescents, particularly males, are more likely to experience shame about incest. Through increased societal education, victims of incest are more likely to speak out and receive appropriate treatment.

References

Anderson, K. M. (2006). Surviving incest: The art of resistance. *Families in Society: The Journal of Contemporary Social Services, 87,* 409–416.

Brennan, S. (2006). Sibling incest within violent families: Children under 12 seeking nurture. *Health Sociology Review, 15,* 287–292.

Burns Loeb, T., Williams, J., Vargas Carmona, J., Rivkin, I., Wyatt, G. E., Chin, D., & Asuan-O'Brien, A. (2002). Child sexual abuse: Associations with the sexual functioning of adolescents and adults. *Annual Review of Sex Research, 13,* 307–348.

Carlson, B. E., Maciol, K., & Schneider, J. (2006). Sibling incest: Reports from 41 survivors. *Journal of Child Sexual Abuse, 15,* 19–34.

Child Welfare Information Gateway. (2009). *Understanding the effects of maltreatment on brain development.* Retrieved August 16, 2010, from www.childwelfare.gov/pubs/issue_briefs/brain_development.

Cole, P. M., & Putnam, F. W. (1992). Effect of incest on self and social functioning: A developmental psychopathology perspective. *Journal of Consulting and Clinical Psychology, 60,* 174–184.

Courtois, C. A. (1997). Healing the incest wound: A treatment update with attention to recovered memory issues. *American Journal of Psychotherapy, 51,* 464–496.

Cyr, M., Wright, J., McDuff, P., & Perron, A. (2002). Intrafamilial sexual abuse: Brother-sister incest does not differ from father-daughter and stepfather-stepdaughter incest. *Child Abuse and Neglect, 26,* 957–973.

Etherington, K. (1997). Maternal sexual abuse of males. *Child Abuse Review, 6,* 107–117.

Finkelhor, D., Hammer, H., & Sedlak, A. J. (2008). Sexually assaulted children: National estimates and characteristics. *National Incidence Studies of Missing, Abducted, Runaway and Thrownaway Children.* Retrieved from www.ojp.usdoj.gov/ojjdp.

Gannon, T. A., Gilchrist, E., & Wade, K. A. (2008). *Handbook of social work in child and adolescent sexual abuse* (pp. 71–101). New York: The Haworth Press.

Haskins, C. (2003). Treating sibling incest using family systems approach. *Journal of Mental Health Counseling, 25,* 337–350.

Johnson, B. & Kenkel, M. (1991). Stress, coping and adjustment in female adolescent incest victims. *Child Abuse and Neglect, 15,* 293–305.

Kristensen, E., & Lau, M. (2007). Women with a history of childhood sexual abuse: Long-term social and psychiatric aspects. *Nord Journal of Psychiatry, 61,* 115–120.

Lindberg, F. H., & Distad, L. J. (1985). Survival responses to incest: Adolescents in crisis. *Child Abuse and Neglect, 9,* 521–526.

Mamun, A. A., Lawlor, D. A., O'Callaghan, M. J., Bor, W., Williams, G. M., & Najman, J. M. (2007). Does childhood sexual abuse predict young adults BMI? A birth cohort study. *OBESITY, 15,* 2103–2110.

Miller, D. A., McCluskey-Fawcett, K., & Irving, L. M. (1993). The relationship between childhood sexual abuse and subsequent onset of bulimia nervosa. *Child Abuse and Neglect, 17,* 305–314.

Morrow, K. (1991). Attributions of female adolescent incest victims regarding their molestation. *Child Abuse and Neglect, 15,* 477–483.

Noll, J., Zeller, M., Trickett, P. & Putnam, F. (2007). Obesity risk for female victims of childhood sexual abuse: A prospective study. *Pediatrics, 120,* 61–67.

Ogilvie, B., & Daniluk, J. (1995). Common themes in the experiences of mother-daughter incest survivors: Implications for counseling. *Journal of Counseling and Development, 73,* 598–602.

Righthand, S., & Welch, C. (2004). Characteristics of youth who sexually offend. *Journal of Child Sexual Abuse, 13,* 15–32.

Synder, H. N. (2000, July). Sexual assault of young children as reported to law enforcement: Victim, incident, and offender characteristics. *U.S. Deptartment of Justice, Bureau of Justice Statistics,* 1–17.

Ullman, S. E., Townsend, S. M., Filipas, H. H., & Starzynski, L. L. (2007). Structural models of the relations of assault severity, social support, avoidance coping, self-blame, and PTSD among sexual assault survivors. *Psychology of Women Quarterly, 31,* 23–37.

Worling, J. R. (1995). Adolescent sibling-incest offenders: Differences in family and individual functioning when compared to adolescent nonsibling sex offenders. *Child Abuse and Neglect, 19,* 633–643.

CHAPTER TEN

Child Sexual Abuse and Adolescent Sexual Assault and Revictimization

Kate Walsh and David DiLillo

Child sexual abuse and adolescent sexual assault are significant societal problems that can result in a host of negative outcomes for victims. From a public health perspective, child and adolescent sexual abuse not only engender immediate costs in terms of police and child-welfare agency involvement, medical examinations and treatment, and mental health assessments and intervention, but also result in long-term costs associated with early sexual abuse. For instance, sexual abuse victims tend to have greater difficulty maintaining employment as adults, and mental and physical health barriers appear to account for associations between sexual abuse and adult employment problems (Lee & Tolman, 2006). Although the focus of the present chapter is exclusively on the risk factors for and consequences of sexual abuse during childhood or adolescence, it is important to recognize that the adverse outcomes of these experiences are potentially far-reaching, in many cases lasting into adulthood. Here, we review definitions of sexual victimization during both childhood and adolescence, the contexts in which child and adolescent victimization experiences most commonly occur, prevalence rates for victimization, risk factors for and outcomes of victimization, theories relating risk factors and outcomes to victimization, and treatment and prevention of victimization.

Definitions of Child Sexual Abuse, Adolescent Sexual Assault, and Child-to-Adolescent Revictimization

There are no universally used definitions of child or adolescent sexual abuse (CASA). Rather, different definitions can be found in the legal, research, and advocacy communities. Moreover, cultural context is important to consider when definining victimization. Most generally, however, CASA can be conceptualized as unwanted sexual contact under the age of 18. Researchers and clinicians have developed more specific parameters regarding the features that distinguish childhood and adolescent victimizations. Child sexual abuse (CSA) often is operationalized as sexual contact (ranging from kissing/fondling to penetration) occurring when the victim is under the age of 14 that is either (a) against the child's will; (b) with a family member; or (c) with a perpetrator at least 5 years older (DiLillo et al., 2010; for a summary of definitional criteria, see Rind, Tromovitch, & Bauserman, 1998). Adolescent sexual assault (ASA), in contrast, involves sexual contact occurring between the ages of 14 and 17 either against the adolescent's will or with a perpetrator 5 or more years older (regardless of consent). If the victim is between the ages of 14 and 17, but the perpetrator is 10 or more years older or a family member, the abuse is classified as CSA.

Although researchers have defined sexual revictimization using varied criteria (e.g., Daigle, Fisher, & Cullen, 2008), the most common definition refers to the experience of two or more sexual victimizations by different perpetrators, usually across two or more developmental time periods (typically CSA and ASA; Arata, 2002). Studies often have collapsed ASA into CSA by querying about unwanted sexual experiences that occurred "while growing up" or "before the age of 18." However, researchers have recently highlighted a need to consider ASA separately from either CSA or adult sexual assault, as the mechanisms and risk factors for each may differ across developmental time periods (Arata, 2002).

Socioemotional Context of Victimization

The social contexts in which childhood and adolescent victimization occur can vary considerably. Although not all perpetrators of CSA are family members or relatives, a substantial proportion of sexual abuse occurring during childhood is perpetrated by an older "trusted" individual or caregiver, which has been linked to more severe distress (Browne & Finkelhor, 1986; Ullman, 2007). Among adolescents, however, a large proportion of the victimization experiences involve a similar age perpetrator who is familiar to the victim, and thus can be classified as date or acquaintance rape (Wolitsky-Taylor et al., 2008). Coercion in the context of dating relationships can be extremely confusing for adolescents, who may be making novel attempts to develop intimacy with dating partners while attempting to establish and maintain personal boundaries (see Moore & Rosenthal, 2006). Thus, although CSA and ASA both involve lack of consent on the part of a victim, the contexts in which each occurs is often quite different. Despite these differences, the early experience of CSA is associated with increased likelihood of being revictimized during adolescence and beyond (Arata, 2002), perhaps by negatively affecting the development of a healthy sexual self-concept and appropriate personal boundaries.

Prevalence of Childhood and Adolescent Victimization and Revictimization

Sexual victimization during childhood or adolescence is an unfortunately prevalent experience in the United States. In fact, studies suggest that 20% to 25% of females and 5% to 15% of males experience sexual abuse as children (Finkelhor, 1994; Finkelhor, Hammer, & Sedlak, 2004). Further, 7% to 18% of adolescent females report forced sexual victimization, whereas 5–14% of adolescent males report forced sexual victimization (Howard & Wang, 2005). In nationally representative samples, 11.8% of adolescent girls reported sexual assault, and 2.1% of the sample reported incapacitated or drug-facilitated assault (McCauley, Ruggiero, Resnick, Conoscenti, & Kilpatrick, 2009), while 2.7% of female adolescents reported sexual assault occurring in the context of dating relationships (Wolitsky-Taylor et al., 2008). Among older adolescent samples, estimates suggest that 15–20% of college women report experiencing a rape or attempted rape during their lives (Brener, McMahon, Warren, & Douglas, 2003). Furthermore, there appears to be a strong relationship between CSA and sexual revictimization during childhood or adolescence (Boney-McCoy & Finkelhor, 1995). This relationship also extends to late adolescence and young adulthood, with CSA victims being at least 2–3 times more likely to be revictimized as adolescents when compared to nonvictims (Arata, 2000; Barnes, Noll, Putnam, & Trickett, 2009; Gagne, Lavoie, & Hebert, 2005).

Risk Factors for Victimization and Revictimization

A number of factors have been studied in relation to risk for victimization and revictimization among children and adolescents. There is evidence that family of origin dysfunction is a potential risk factor for

CSA (Drauker, 1996; Manseau, Fernet, Hebert, Collin-Vezina, & Blais, 2008). More specifically, victims of sexual abuse tend to report less emotional bonding among family members, decreased flexibility in family-member roles and structure during times of stress, and less parent-child involvement when compared to non-victims (Drauker, 1996). Similarly, difficulties that prevent parents from supervising children appropriately, such as being a single parent and parental alcohol and drug problems, have been linked to increased risk for child sexual abuse (Arellano, Kuhn, & Chavez, 1997). Parents of sexually abused children also report greater marital dissatisfaction (Paveza, 1988), poorer parent-child relationships (Boney-McCoy & Finkelhor, 1995), and less perceived emotional support (Pianta & Castaldi, 1989). Parents whose children are sexually abused are also more likely to have their own sexual abuse histories (Finkelhor, 1994). Although these familial variables have been associated with CSA, many studies utilized cross-sectional methodologies to examine caregiver or familial characteristics of identified sexual abuse victims. Thus, with the exception of the parents' own history of sexual abuse, it is unclear whether many of these factors preceded the sexual abuse or resulted from learning about their child's sexual abuse.

Beyond familial factors, social and environmental characteristics also may contribute to increased risk for abuse or assault. For instance, data from nationally representative samples of children and adolescents reveal that living in more dangerous communities is a risk factor for increased rates of sexual abuse (Boney-McCoy & Finkelhor, 1995), as is low socioeconomic status (Rowland, Zabin, & Emerson, 2000), which is associated with more dangerous conditions and with less supervision and protective resources to buffer against contact with potential perpetrators. Further, poorer children who have little parental or guardian supervision may be perceived by perpetrators as more vulnerable than children whose parents hold them accountable for family activities and provide consistent supervision.

Although the responsibility for an assault lies entirely with a perpetrator, there are some individual characteristics that may increase the likelihood of victimization. In terms of demographic characteristics, victims of sexual abuse are more likely to be Black and female (for a review, see Black, Heyman, & Slep, 2001). Child victims of sexual abuse also tend to have more academic problems and physical and intellectual disabilities (Sullivan & Knutson, 2000), as well as more behavior problems at home and school (for review, see Black et al., 2001). Although common in adolescence more generally, engagement in high-risk behaviors has been found to be a robust risk factor for adolescent victimization (Howard, Wang, & Yan, 2007). In particular, greater levels of alcohol and drug use may heighten risk for sexual victimization by lowering inhibitions, decreasing the ability to perceive risk, and increasing problems with engaging in active defensive behavior. Furthermore, adolescents who engage in consensual sexual behavior with a greater number of partners and those who have more frequent sexual encounters with persons they do not know well may be at higher risk for victimization when compared to adolescents who do not engage in such behaviors (for a review, see Lalor & McElvaney, 2010). Finally, risky sexual behavior and substance abuse may interact to predict increased risk for victimization. For example, adolescents who abuse substances prior to sex may be at heightened risk for victimization (McCauley et al., 2009; Young, Grey, Abbey, Boyd, & McCabe, 2008).

In addition to being implicated in the risk for initial victimization, a number of these risk factors also have been shown to increase risk for subsequent assault. Longitudinal studies of adolescents reveal that alcohol use, particularly heavy episodic drinking, and risky sexual behaviors increase the risk for revictimization (e.g., Testa, Hoffman, Livingston, & Turrisi, 2010). More specifically, adolescents who engage in risky sexual behavior, including intercourse with a greater number of sexual partners, are more likely to experience revictimization (Lalor & McElvaney, 2010), perhaps due to increased exposure to potential perpetrators (Orcutt, Cooper, & Garcia, 2005). Alcohol use, another commonly reported correlate among sexually abused adolescents (Danielson et al., 2009), is an independent risk factor for sexual victimization (e.g., Abbey, Zawacki, Buck, Clinton, & McAuslan, 2004; Testa & Parks, 1996). However, alcohol use may occur simultaneously with sexual risk taking and compound risk for revictimization by reducing perceptions of risk and effective defensive behaviors (Testa & Livingston, 1999).

Theories of Risk Factors for Victimization and Revictimization

A number of theories have been proposed to explain risk for sexual victimization and revictimization (Gold, Sinclair, & Balge, 1999; Macy, 2007; Marx, Gold, & Heidt, 2005). One of the most widely cited theoretical models incorporates risk factors occurring at multiple ecological levels (Messman-Moore & Long, 2003). This theory posits that victim-level variables (e.g., characteristics of the initial abuse and its psychological sequelae) can contribute to risk for victimization by increasing distress and maladaptive coping responses, such as impulsive behavior and substance use. In turn, these problems may increase difficulties in identifying risky situations. Further, microsystem factors involving the context of the abuse, such as the perpetrator's perception of the victim as an easy target, may increase the risk for victimization. In the case of CSA and ASA, older perpetrators may isolate children or adolescents, coerce or force them into abusive experiences, and then threaten them not to disclose the activity. Among adolescents, engagement in behaviors like drinking or risky sex also may increase contact with potential perpetrators and decrease the ability to engage in effective defense behaviors (Messman-Moore & Long, 2003). Exosystem factors, such as low socioeconomic resources and living in a risky neighborhood, may increase the likelihood of experiencing victimization due to exposure to potential perpetrators and limited safety resources. As noted, in single-parent, low-income families, caregivers may have difficulty providing an adequate level of supervision while simultaneously working to feed, clothe, and house the family. These children also may spend more unsupervised time in the community, which might increase exposure to perpetrators (Boney-McCoy & Finkelhor, 1995). Finally, macrosystem factors reflecting cultural and social forces (e.g., rape myth acceptance, victim blaming, patriarchal views) all likely contribute to sexual abuse, assault, and revictimization by increasing the acceptance of abuse and mistreatment of victims.

Outcomes of Child or Adolescent Sexual Abuse

Although not all children and adolescents who have been sexually victimized experience negative sequelae, a substantial proportion of victims do experience a wide range of negative outcomes, including physical, psychological, and behavioral problems (Kendall-Tackett, Williams, & Finkelhor, 1993; Noll & Shenk, 2010). In the immediate aftermath of sexual abuse, genital injuries and sexually transmitted diseases are unfortunately common (Anderson, 1995; Boyle, McCann, Miyamoto, & Rogers, 2008; Heger, Ticson, Velasquez, & Bernier, 2002). A recent meta-analysis revealed that CSA is also associated with longer-term physical health problems in the areas of general health, gastrointestinal (GI) health, gynecologic or reproductive health, pain, cardiopulmonary symptoms, and obesity (Irish, Kobayashi, & Delahanty, 2010). Characteristics of the victimization experience itself may impact in the degree of adverse outcomes. For instance, more severe abuse has been associated with greater genital injury (Heger et al., 2002), and children and adolescents reporting intrafamilial abuse tend to have greater emotional and physical injury (Fischer & McDonald, 1998). Further, adolescents victimized in the context of a long-term relationship may sustain more severe physical injury than those who were victimized in the context of a more casual dating relationship (Gagne et al., 2005).

In addition to physical outcomes, children and adolescents who have been abused often endure a number of psychological difficulties. For example, 37% to 53% of sexually abused children eventually develop post-traumatic stress disorder (PTSD) (e.g., Kendall-Tackett et al., 1993; McLeer, Deblinger, Atkins, Foa, & Ralphe, 1988; McLeer et al., 1998), and the large majority of sexually abused children referred to treatment have been shown to experience partial PTSD symptoms (McLeer, Deblinger, Henry, & Orvaschel, 1992). A large body of research also details links between sexual abuse during childhood or adolescence and the development of internalizing symptomatology. Specifically, 43% to 67% of children and adolescents meet diagnostic criteria for depression following sexual abuse (e.g., Koverola, Pound, Heger, & Lytle, 1993; Tebbutt, Swanston, Oates, & O'Toole, 1997). Further, the prevalence of anxiety disorders (e.g., phobias, separation anxiety disorder, and obsessive-compulsive disorder) is significantly higher in sexually abused children and adolescents than in nonabused comparisons (12% vs. 3%; Spataro, Mullen, Burgess, Wells, & Moss, 2004). Child and adolescent sexual abuse victims also tend to report self-blame, low self-esteem, and stigmatization related to the abuse (Feiring, Taska, & Lewis, 1996, 1998). Perhaps as a consequence of developing a negative self-concept, abused children and adolescents also report more social isolation than do their nonabused peers (Arellano et al., 1997).

In response to significant emotional distress stemming from the abuse, victims also may engage in a number of externalizing behaviors. More specifically, approximately 28% of sexually abused children exhibit highly sexualized behavior (Kendall-Tackett et al., 1993). Attention deficit/hyperactivity disorder (ADHD) (Ford et al., 2000), opposition defiant disorder (ODD) (Ford et al., 2000), and conduct disorder (CD) (Dubowitz, Black, Harrington, & Verschoore, 1993; Lynskey & Fergusson, 1997; Romano, Zoccolillo, & Paquette, 2006) also are commonly diagnosed among sexually abused children. Beyond diagnoses of ADHD, ODD, and CD, studies have shown that sexually abused children and adolescents are significantly more hyperactive, impulsive, and aggressive than are non-maltreated children (e.g., Dubowitz et al., 1993; Ford et al., 2000; Swanston et al., 2003). Further, sexually abused children and adolescents tend to lack skills to self-regulate angry and aggressive tendencies (Ford et al., 2000), which can lead to repercussions in the form of criminal justice involvement. For example, among adolescents entering the juvenile justice system, 25% report a history of sexual abuse (Dembo, Schmeidler, & Childs, 2007). The externalizing problems also can manifest in educational or school-related difficulties for children and adolescents. For instance, sexual abuse has been linked to poorer school adjustment (Caffaro-Rouget, Lang, & Van

Santem, 1989; Daignault & Hebert, 2009) and greater likelihood of school dropout (Dunlap, Golub, & Johnson, 2003).

Lack of coping resources can lead to increased reliance on substance abuse and other tension-reduction behaviors (e.g., sexual risk taking) to regulate negative abuse-related emotions (Arellano et al., 1997; Buckle, Lancaster, Powell, & Higgins, 2005; Caffaro-Rouget et al., 1989; Daignault & Hebert, 2009; for a review, see Danielson et al., 2006). For example, sexually abused adolescents report increased use of alcohol, marijuana, and other illicit substances, including crack cocaine (Freeman, Collier, & Parillo, 2002; Harrison, Fulkerson, & Beebe, 1997). Unfortunately, substance use by the victim or perpetrator has been linked to adolescent sexual assault risk (Seifert, 1999). Sexually abused adolescents also report greater engagement in sexual risk behaviors, including earlier age of first consensual sexual intercourse, higher frequency of sexual encounters with new acquaintances, decreased use of contraception or STD prevention methods, and a greater overall number of sexual partners (for a review, see Senn, Carey, & Vanable, 2008; Steel & Herlitz, 2005). Related to involvement with these high-risk behaviors, sexually abused youths are more likely to run away from home (Freeman et al., 2002) and become involved with prostitution, sex trading, and teenage pregnancy/parenting (Dunlap et al., 2003; Herrenkohl, Herrenkohl, Egolf, & Russo, 1998; Senn et al., 2008; Wilson & Widom, 2010).

Sexual revictimization is another unfortunate interpersonal outcome associated with early sexual abuse (Arata, 2002; Krahé, Scheinberger-Olwig, Waizenhöffer, & Kolpin, 1999). Revictimization itself is associated with heightened difficulties across multiple arenas of functioning (Casey & Nurius, 2005; Gagne et al., 2005), and revictimized adolescents and young adults tend to report greater self-blame, more severe trauma symptoms, and heightened substance abuse when compared to those reporting single victimizations (Arata, 2002; Filipas & Ullman, 2006; Follette, Polusny, Bechtle, & Naugle, 1996; Kilpatrick, Acierno, Resnick, Saunders, & Best, 1997). Adolescents and adults reporting revictimization also endure more nonsexual trauma exposure, greater health problems, and longer latency to recover from the most recent sexually assaultive experience (Arata, 1999; Gibson & Leitenberg, 2001).

Theories Explaining the Effects of Sexual Abuse and Revictimization

Various theories has emphasized different factors in explaining links between victimization and the development of short- and long-term negative outcomes. For example, developmental psychopathologists have posited an ecological transactional model suggesting that early abuse shapes neurodevelopment to result in chronic distress and other negative outcomes (Cicchetti & Valentino, 2006). Trauma theorists have postulated that emotional avoidance contributes to the development and maintenance of difficulties among sexually abused individuals. Perhaps the most prominent theory relating sexual abuse to negative outcomes is Finkelhor and Browne's (1985) traumagenic dynamics model, which suggests that the impact of childhood trauma can be accounted for by the dynamics of betrayal, traumatic sexualization, stigmatization, and powerlessness, which are said to "alter children's cognitive and emotional orientation to the world, and create trauma by distorting children's self-concept, world view, and affective capacities" (Finkelhor & Browne, 1985, p. 531). The dynamic of betrayal may come into play following abuse when victims come to realize that an adult (often a trusted adult or family member) has violated the tacit but fundamental trust that normally exists between children and adults. Older adolescent women who have experienced childhood trauma (sexual, physical, or psychological abuse) that engendered feelings of betrayal have been shown to experience revictimization during adolescence that involves similar feelings of betrayal (Gobin & Freyd, 2009). Traumatic sexualization, which refers to developmentally inappropriate and dysfunctional sexual behavior stemming from sexual abuse, may manifest in a variety of lasting difficulties, including increased vulnerability to subsequent sexual assault (Finkelhor & Browne, 1985). The third process, stigmatization, refers to internalized feelings of shame, guilt, and self-blame that arise from experiencing maltreatment. In the case of sexual abuse, stigmatization may evolve from direct threats and comments from the perpetrator as well as negative reactions by caregivers and family members upon disclosure of the abuse. Studies have found that even nonoffending parents who are typically supportive may exhibit negative or ambivalent responses to disclosure, which may increase the child's adjustment difficulties and stigmatization following abuse (Elliott & Carnes, 2001). Finally, the dynamic of powerlessness refers to a lack of self-efficacy that emanates from the uncontrollable and repeated physical boundary violations that accompany child and adolescent sexual abuse. Powerlessness engendered by early sexual abuse may undermine victims' sense of control in later dating relationships, rendering them less effective in asserting their needs during risky interpersonal encounters and increasing risk for additional victimizations. Indeed, among adolescent sexual abuse victims, low sexual assertiveness has been shown to increase risk for date rape (Vogel & Himelein, 1995).

Prevention and Treatment

A variety of prevention and treatment efforts have been developed in response to the prevalence and consequences of sexual abuse noted above. To create minimum standards for prevention programs, the Centers for Disease Control (CDC) has developed guidelines to aid in the prevention of CSA ranging from the selection of employees who work with children to ways of monitoring behavior and ensuring a safe environment to ways of responding appropriately to allegations of abuse (Saul & Audage, 2007). The CDC also has identified goals for training caregivers and youths to recognize risk factors for sexual abuse and identify potential solutions. Although mass media campaigns have been launched to prevent sexual abuse, evaluation of these efforts suggests that, alone, such methods of prevention are not sufficient to improve the primary prevention of sexual abuse (e.g., Rheingold et al., 2007). School-based educational prevention efforts have been shown to increase knowledge and awareness of sexual abuse, but they tend to have minimal impact on actual rates of sexual abuse. For example, one study that employed teacher training to prevent sexual abuse found that teachers who participated in a six-hour training on sexual abuse had greater knowledge of sexual abuse, behavioral indicators of sexual abuse, and appropriate intervention in suspected abuse cases (Randolph & Gold, 1994). However, the direct impact of school-based trainings on actual sexual abuse prevention is unclear. One evaluation of a psychoeducation group program designed to prevent sexual abuse found that children's knowledge about sexual abuse and ability to discriminate safe and unsafe scenarios increased significantly with improvements maintained over a one-year follow-up. Another study using a retrospective design to assess college women's experiences with prevention programs and sexual abuse found that 8% of respondents who had participated in "good touch/bad touch" school-based prevention programs reported experiencing sexual abuse compared to 14% of respondents who did not participate in such a program (Gibson & Leitenberg, 2000).

Secondary prevention programs also have been tailored to youths with specific risk characteristics. For instance, due to the increased risk of sexual abuse among children and adolescents with disabilities, clinicians and researchers have proposed a prevention model for work with this population that includes behavioral-skills training at the microsystem level, communication between appropriate agencies at the mesosystem level, federally mandated training for teachers working with developmentally disabled students at the exosystem level, and paradigm shifts at the macrosystem level (Skarbek, Hahn, & Parrish, 2009). Specific prevention efforts have also been suggested to reduce the risk of date rape among adolescents in dating relationships. In particular, these programs promote educating potential perpetrators about date rape and teaching active resistance strategies (e.g., verbal resistance, physical resistance, and fleeing) to potential date rape victims (Page, 1997).

In addition to school- and agency-based prevention programs, researchers have suggested designing prevention efforts to educate parents about the risk for sexual abuse in order to create safer environments in which children will be less vulnerable to sexual victimization (Wurtele & Kenny, 2010). For instance, among adolescents with a history of sexual victimization, risk reduction through family therapy, a multicomponent treatment that integrates components of existing evidence-based treatments, has been shown to be effective in reducing risk factors for sexual revictimization, including substance use, PTSD, and depression symptoms (Danielson et al., 2010). Further, these treatment gains were maintained at six-month follow-up. In another innovative study, mothers of graduating high school senior girls participated in a parent-based intervention. When compared to controls, girls in the intervention condition evidenced increased mother-daughter communication, decreased first-semester heavy episodic drinking, and had lower rates of alcohol-related sexual victimization in the first year of college (Testa et al., 2010). These family-based prevention approaches are promising; however, more research is necessary to examine whether these results are maintained throughout college.

Although prevention efforts are greatly needed, enhancing treatment for children in the aftermath of abusive experiences is also incredibly important in ameliorating negative outcomes associated with sexual abuse and preventing the occurrence of additional victimizations. To this end, meta-analyses reveal that cognitive behavioral treatments delivered either in an individual or a group format effectively reduce sequelae associated with sexual abuse, including PTSD symptoms, internalizing, and such externalizing problems as sexualized behaviors (Trask, Walsh, & DiLillo, in press). Further, to address the issue of possible revictimization among adolescents, multisession, manual-based treatment programs that focus on changing attitudes and behaviors that increase risk for sexual victimization and developing skills to ward off sexual victimization have been shown to be effective (Weisz & Black, 2009).

Summary and Conclusions

Child and adolescent sexual abuse are prevalent societal problems that result in a host of intra- and interpersonal negative outcomes, including PTSD, depression, dissociation, low self-esteem, and sexual revictimization. Several theories have been hypothesized to account for the risk for and outcomes of sexual abuse and revictimization; however, no single theory appears to fully explain these processes. Recent prevention efforts have demonstrated promise for the reduction of risk for victimization and revictimization among adolescents. More research is needed to evaluate interactions between risk characteristics known to co-occur (e.g., lack of parental supervision and poor family environment, sexual risk taking, and alcohol use) and the contexts in which victimization often occurs in order to further improve prevention efforts.

References

Abbey, A., Zawacki, T., Buck., P. O., Clinton, A. M., & McAuslan, P. (2004). Sexual assault and alcohol consumption: What do we know about their relationship and what types of research are still needed? *Aggression and Violent Behavior, 9,* 271–303.

Anderson, C. (1995). Childhood sexually transmitted diseases: One consequence of sexual abuse. *Public Health Nursing, 12,* 41–46.

Arata, C. M. (1999). Repeated sexual victimization and mental disorders in women. *Journal of Child Sexual Abuse, 7,* 1–17.

Arata, C. M. (2000). From child victim to adult victim: A model for predicting sexual revictimization. *Child Maltreatment, 5,* 28–38.

Arata, C. M. (2002). Child sexual abuse and sexual revictimization. *Clinical Psychology: Science and Practice, 9,* 135–164.

Arellano, C. M., Kuhn, J. A., & Chavez, E. L. (1997). Psychosocial correlates of sexual assault among Mexican American and White non-Hispanic adolescent females. *Hispanic Journal of Behavioral Sciences, 19,* 446–460.

Barnes, J. E., Noll, J. G., Putnam, F. W., & Trickett, P. K. (2009). Sexual and physical revictimization among victims of severe childhood sexual abuse. *Child Abuse and Neglect, 33,* 412–420.

Black, D. A., Heyman, R. E., & Slep, A. M. (2001). Risk factors for child sexual abuse. *Aggression and Violent Behavior, 6,* 203–229.

Boney-McCoy, S., & Finkelhor, D. (1995). Prior victimization: A risk factor for child sexual abuse and for PTSD-related symptomatology among sexually abused youth. *Child Abuse and Neglect, 19,* 1401–1421.

Boyle, C., McCann, J., Miyamoto, S., & Rogers, K. (2008). Comparison of examination methods used in the evaluation of prepubertal and pubertal female genitalia: A descriptive study. *Child Abuse and Neglect, 32,* 229–243.

Brener, N. D., McMahon, P. M., Warren, C. W., & Douglas, K. A. (2003). Forced sexual intercourse and associated health-risk behaviors among female college students in the United States. *Journal of Consulting and Clinical Psychology, 67,* 252–259.

Browne, A., & Finkelhor, D. (1986). Impact of child sexual abuse: A review of the research. *Psychological Bulletin, 99,* 66–77.

Buckle, S. K., Lancaster, S., Powell, M. B. & Higgins, D. L. (2005). The relationship between child sexual abuse and academic achievement in a sample of adolescent psychiatric inpatients. *Child Abuse and Neglect, 29,* 1031–1047.

Caffaro-Rouget, A., Lang, R. A., & Van Santem, V. (1989). The impact of child sexual abuse on victims' adjustment. *Annals of Sex Research, 2,* 29–47.

Casey, E. A., & Nurius, P. S. (2005). Trauma exposure and sexual revictimization risk: Comparisons across single, multiple incident, and multiple perpetrator victimizations. *Violence Against Women, 11,* 505–530.

Cicchetti, D., & Valentino, K. (2006). An ecological-transactional perspective on child maltreatment: Failure of the average expectable environment and its influence on child development. In D. Cicchetti & D. J. Cohen (Eds.), *Developmental Psychopathology: Vol. 3. Risk, Disorder, and Adaptation* (pp. 129–201). Hoboken, NJ: Wiley.

Daigle, L. E., Fisher, B. S., & Cullen, F. T. (2008). The violent and sexual victimization of college women: Is repeat victimization a problem? *Journal of Interpersonal Violence, 23,* 1296–1313.

Daignault, I. V., & Hebert, M. (2009). Profiles of school adaptation: Social, behavioral, and academic functioning in sexually abused girls. *Child Abuse and Neglect, 33,* 102–115.

Danielson, C. K., Amstadter, A. B., Dangelmaier, R. E., Resnick, H. S., Saunders, B. E., Kilpatrick, D. G. (2009). Trauma-related risk factors for substance abuse among male versus female young adults. *Addictive Behaviors, 34,* 395–399.

Danielson, C. K., de Arellano, M. A., Ehrenreich, J. Y., Suarez, L. M., Bennett, S. M., Cheron, D. M., et al. (2006). Identification of high-risk behaviors among victimized adolescents and implications for empirically supported psychosocial treatment. *Journal of Psychiatric Practice, 12,* 364–383.

Danielson, C. K., McCart, M. R., de Arellano, M. A., MacDonald, A., Doherty, L. S., & Resnick, H. S. (2010). Risk reduction for substance use and trauma-related psychopathology in adolescent sexual assault victims: Findings from an open trial. *Child Maltreatment, 15,* 261–268.

Dembo, R., Schmeidler, J., & Childs, K. (2007). Correlates of male and female juvenile offender abuse experiences. *Journal of Child Sexual Abuse, 16,* 75–94.

DiLillo, D., Hayes, S., Fortier, M., Perry, A., Evans, S., Messman-Moore, T., et al. (2010). Development and initial psychometric properties of the Computer Assisted Maltreatment Inventory (CAMI): A comprehensive self-report questionnaire of child maltreatment history. *Child Abuse and Neglect, 34,* 305–317.

Drauker, C. B. (1996). Family-of-origin variables and adult female survivors of childhood sexual abuse: A review of the research. *Journal of Child Sexual Abuse, 5,* 35–63.

Dubowitz, H., Black, M., Harrington, D., & Verschoore, A. (1993). A follow-up study of behavior problems associated with child sexual abuse. *Child Abuse and Neglect, 17,* 743–754.

Dunlap, E., Golub, A., & Johnson, B. D. (2003). Girls' sexual development in the inner city: From compelled childhood sexual contact to sex-for-things exchanged. *Journal of Child Sexual Abuse, 12,* 73–96.

Elliott, A. E., & Carnes, C. N. (2001). Reactions of non-offending parents to the sexual abuse of their child: A review of the literature. *Child Maltreatment, 6,* 314–331.

Feiring, C., Taska, L. S., & Lewis, M. (1996). A process model for understanding adaptation to sexual abuse: The role of shame in defining stigmatization. *Child Abuse and Neglect, 8,* 767–782.

Feiring, C., Taska, L. S., & Lewis, M. (1998). The role of shame and attribution style in children's and adolescents' adaptation to sexual abuse. *Child Maltreatment, 3,* 129–142.

Filipas, H. H., & Ullman, S. E. (2006). Child sexual abuse, coping responses, self-blame, posttraumatic stress disorder, and adult sexual revictimization. *Journal of Interpersonal Violence, 21,* 652–672.

Finkelhor, D. (1994). The international epidemiology of child sexual abuse. *Child Abuse and Neglect, 18,* 409–417.

Finkelhor, D., and Browne, A. (1985). The traumatic impact of child sexual abuse: A conceptualization. *American Journal of Orthopsychiatry, 55,* 530–541.

Finkelhor, D., Hammer, H., & Sedlak, A. J. (2004). Sexually assaulted children: National estimates and characteristics. *Juvenile Justice Bulletin,* U.S. Department of Justice.

Fischer, D. G., & McDonald, W. L. (1998). Characteristics of intrafamilial and extrafamilial child sexual abuse. *Child Abuse and Neglect, 22,* 916–929.

Follette, V. M., Polusny, M. M., Bechtle, A. E., & Naugle, A. E. (1996). Cumulative trauma effects: The impact of child sexual abuse, adult sexual assault, and spouse abuse. *Journal of Traumatic Stress, 9,* 25–36.

Ford, J. D., Racusin, R., Ellis, C. G., Davis, W. B., Reiser, J., Fleischer, A., et al. (2000). Child maltreatment, other trauma exposure, and posttraumatic symptomology among children with oppositional defiant and attention deficit hyperactivity disorders. *Child Maltreatment, 5,* 205–217.

Freeman, R. C., Collier, K., & Parillo, K. M. (2002). Early life sexual abuse as a risk factor for crack cocaine use in a sample of community recruited women at high risk for illicit drug use. *American Journal of Drug and Alcohol Abuse, 28,* 109–131.

Gagne, M., Lavoie, F., & Hebert, M. (2005). Victimization during childhood and revictimization in dating relationships in adolescent girls. *Child Abuse and Neglect, 29,* 1155–1172.

Gibson, L. E., & Leitenberg, H. (2000). Child sexual abuse prevention programs: Do they decrease the occurrence of child sexual abuse? *Child Abuse and Neglect, 24,* 1115–1125.

Gibson, L. E., & Leitenberg, H. (2001). Methods of coping with sexual aggression in a sample of young women: The roles of prior sexual abuse and stigma. *Child Abuse and Neglect, 25,* 1343–1361.

Gobin, R. L., & Freyd, J. J. (2009). Betrayal and revictimization: Preliminary findings. *Psychological Trauma: Theory, Research, Practice, and Policy, 1,* 242–257.

Gold, S. R., Sinclair, B. B., & Balge, K. A. (1999). Risk of sexual revictimization: A theoretical model. *Aggression and Violent Behavior, 4,* 457–470.

Harrison, P. A., Fulkerson, J. A., & Beebe, T. J. (1997). Multiple substance use among adolescent physical and sexual abuse victims. *Child Abuse and Neglect, 21,* 529–539.

Heger, A., Ticson, L., Velasquez, O., & Bernier, R. (2002). Children referred for possible sexual abuse: Medical findings in 2,384 children. *Child Abuse and Neglect, 26,* 645–659.

Herrenkohl, E. C., Herrenkohl, R. C., Egolf, B. P., & Russo, M. J. (1998). The relationship between early maltreatment and teenage parenthood. *Journal of Adolescence, 21,* 291–303.

Howard, D. E., & Wang, M. (2005). Psychosocial correlates of U.S. adolescents who report a history of forced sexual intercourse. *Journal of Adolescent Health, 36,* 372–379.

Howard, D. E., Wang, M., & Yan, F. (2007). Prevalence and psychosocial correlates of forced sexual intercourse among U.S. high school adolescents. *Adolescence, 42,* 629–643.

Irish, L., Kobayashi, I., Delahanty, D. L. (2010). Long-term physical health consequences of childhood sexual abuse: A meta-analytic review. *Journal of Pediatric Psychology, 35,* 450–461.

Kendall-Tackett, K., Williams, L., & Finkelhor, D. (1993). Impact of sexual abuse on children: A review and synthesis of recent empirical studies. *Psychological Bulletin, 113,* 164–180.

Kilpatrick, D. G., Acierno, R., Resnick, H. S., Saunders, B. E., & Best, C. L. (1997). A 2-year longitudinal analysis of the relationships between violent assault and substance use in women. *Journal of Consulting and Clinical Psychology, 65,* 834–847.

Koverola, C., Pound, J., Heger, A., & Lytle, C. (1993). Relationship of child sexual abuse to depression. *Child Abuse and Neglect, 17,* 393–400.

Krahé, B., Scheinberger-Olwig, R., Waizenhöfer, E., & Kolpin, S. (1999). Childhood sexual abuse and revictimization in adolescence. *Child Abuse and Neglect, 23,* 383–394.

Lalor, K., & McElvaney, R. (2010). Child sexual abuse, links to later sexual exploitation/high-risk sexual behavior, and prevention/treatment programs. *Trauma, Violence, and Abuse, 11,* 159–177.

Lee, S., & Tolman, R. M. (2006). Childhood sexual abuse and adult work outcomes. *Social Work Research, 30,* 83–92.

Lynskey, M. T., & Fergusson, D. M. (1997). Factors protecting against the development of adjustment difficulties in young adults exposed to childhood sexual abuse. *Child Abuse and Neglect, 21,* 1177–1190.

Macy, R. J. (2007). A coping theory framework toward preventing sexual revictimization. *Aggression and Violent Behavior, 12,* 177–192.

Manseau, H., Fernet, M., Hebert, M., Collin-Vezina, D., Blais, M. (2008). Risk factors for dating violence among teenage girls under child protective services. *International Journal of Social Welfare, 17,* 236–242.

Marx, B. P., Gold, S. D., & Heidt, J. M. (2005). Perceived uncontrollability and unpredictability, self-regulation, and sexual revictimization. *Review of General Psychology, 9,* 67–90.

McCauley, J., Ruggiero, K. J., Resnick, H. S., Conoscenti, L. M., & Kilpatrick, D. G. (2009). Forcible, drug-facilitated, and incapacitated rape in relation to substance abuse problems: Results from a national sample of college women. *Addictive Behaviors, 34,* 458–462.

McLeer, S. V., Deblinger, E., Atkins, M. S., Foa, E. B., & Ralphe, D. (1988). Posttraumatic stress disorder in sexually abused children. *Journal of the American Academy of Child and Adolescent Psychiatry, 27,* 650–654.

McLeer, S. V., Deblinger, E., Henry, D., & Orvaschel, H. (1992). Sexually abused children at high risk for PTSD. *Journal of the American Academy of Child and Adolescent Psychiatry, 31,* 875–879.

McLeer, S. V., Dixon, J. F., Henry, D., Ruggiero, K., Escovitz, K., Niedda, T., et al. (1998). Psychopathology in non-clinically referred sexually abused children. *Journal of the American Academy of Child and Adolescent Psychiatry, 37,* 1326–1333.

Messman-Moore, T. L., & Long, P. J. (2003). The role of childhood sexual abuse sequelae in the sexual revictimization of women: An empirical review and theoretical reformulation. *Clinical Psychology Review, 23,* 537–571.

Moore, S., & Rosenthal, D. (2006). *Sexuality in adolescence: Current trends.* London: Taylor and Francis.

Muram, D., Hostetler, B. R., Jones, C. E., & Speck, P. M. (1995). Adolescent victims of sexual assault. *Journal of Adolescent Health, 17,* 372–375.

Noll, J. G., & Shenk, C. E. (2010). Introduction to the special issue: The physical health consequences of childhood maltreatment—Implications for public health. *Journal of Pediatric Psychology, 35,* 447–449.

Orcutt, H. K., Cooper, M. L., & Garcia, M. (2005). Use of sexual intercourse to reduce negative affect as a prospective mediator of sexual revictimization. *Journal of Traumatic Stress, 18,* 729–739.

Page, R. M. (1997). Helping adolescents avoid date rape: The role of secondary education. *High School Journal, 80,* 75–80.

Paveza, G. J. (1988). Risk factors in father-daughter child sexual abuse: A case-control study. *Journal of Interpersonal Violence, 3,* 290–306.

Pianta, R. C., & Castaldi, J. (1989). Stability of internalizing symptoms from kindergarten to first grade and factors related to instability. *Development and Psychopathology, 1,* 305–316.

Randolph, M. K., & Gold, C. A. (1994). Child sexual abuse prevention: Evaluation of a teacher training program. *School Psychology Review, 23,* 485–495.

Rheingold, A. A., Campbell, C., Self-Brown, S., de Arellano, M., Resnick, H., & Kilpatrick, D. G. (2007). Prevention of child sexual abuse: Evaluation of a community media campaign. *Child Maltreatment, 12,* 352–363.

Rind, B., Tromovitch, P., & Bauserman, R. (1998). A meta-analytic examination of assumed properties of child sexual abuse using college samples. *Psychological Bulletin, 124,* 22–53.

Romano, E., Zoccolillo, M., & Paquette, D. (2006). Histories of child maltreatment and psychiatric disorder in pregnant adolescents. *Journal of the American Academy of Child and Adolescent Psychiatry, 45,* 329–336.

Rowland, D. L., Zabin, L. S., & Emerson, M. (2000). Household risk and child sexual abuse in a low income, urban sample of women. *Adolescent and Family Health, 1,* 29–39.

Saul, J., & Audage, N. C. (2007). *Preventing child sexual abuse within youth-serving organizations: Getting started on policies and procedures.* Atlanta, GA: Centers for Disease Control and Prevention, National Center for Injury Prevention and Control.

Seifert, S. A. (1999). Substance use and sexual assault. *Substance Use and Misuse, 34,* 935–945.

Senn, T. E., Carey, M. P., & Vanable, P. A. (2008). Childhood and adolescent sexual abuse and subsequent sexual risk behavior: Evidence from controlled studies, methodological critique, and suggestions for research. *Clinical Psychology Review, 28,* 711–735.

Skarbek, D., Hahn, K., & Parrish, P. (2009). Stop sexual abuse in special education: An ecological model of prevention and intervention strategies for sexual abuse in special education. *Sexuality and Disability, 27,* 155–164.

Spataro, J., Mullen, P. E., Burgess, P. M., Wells, D. L., & Moss, S. A. (2004). Impact of child sexual abuse on mental health: Prospective study in males and females. *British Journal of Psychiatry, 184,* 416–421.

Steel, J. L., & Herlitz, C. A. (2005). The association between childhood and adolescent sexual abuse and proxies for sexual risk behavior: A random sample of the general population of Sweden. *Child Abuse and Neglect, 29,* 1141–1153.

Sullivan, P. M., & Knutson, J. F. (2000). Maltreatment and disabilities: A population-based epidemiological study. *Child Abuse and Neglect, 24,* 1257–1273.

Swanston, H. Y., Plunkett, A. M., O'Toole, B. I., Shrimpton, S., Parkinson, P. N., & Oates, R. K. (2003). Nine years after child sexual abuse. *Child Abuse and Neglect, 27,* 967–984.

Tebbutt, J., Swanston, H., Oates, R. K., & O'Toole, B. I. (1997). Five years after child sexual abuse: Persisting dysfunction and problems of prediction. *Journal of the American Academy of Child and Adolescent Psychiatry, 36,* 330–339.

Testa, M., Hoffman, J. H., Livingston, J. A., & Turrisi, R. (2010). Preventing college women's sexual victimization through parent based intervention: A randomized controlled trial. *Prevention Science, 11,* 308–318.

Testa, M., & Livingston, J. A. (1999). Qualitative analysis of women's experiences of sexual aggression: Focus on the role of alcohol. *Psychology of Women Quarterly, 23,* 573–589.

Testa, M., & Parks, K. A. (1996). The role of women's alcohol consumption in sexual victimization. *Aggression and Violent Behavior, 1,* 217–234.

Trask, E., Walsh, K., & DiLillo, D. (in press). Efficacy of treatments for sexually abused children: A meta-analysis. *Aggression and Violent Behavior.*

Ullman, S. E. (2007). Relationship to perpetrator, disclosure, social reactions, and PTSD symptoms in child sexual abuse survivors. *Journal of Child Sexual Abuse, 16,* 19–36.

Vogel, R. E., & Himelein, M. J. (1995). Dating and sexual victimization: An analysis of risk factors among precollege women. *Journal of Criminal Justice, 23,* 153–162.

Weisz, A. N., & Black, B. M. (2009). *Programs to reduce teen dating violence and sexual assault: Perspectives on what works.* New York: Columbia University Press.

Wilson, H. W., & Widom, C. S. (2010). The role of youth problem behaviors in the path from child abuse and neglect to prostitution: A prospective examination. *Journal of Research on Adolescence, 20,* 210–236.

Wolitzky-Taylor, K. B., Ruggiero, K. J., McCart, M. R., Smoth, D. W., Hanson, R. F., Resnick, H. R., et al. (2008). Has adolescent suicidality decreased in the United States? Data from two national samples of adolescents interviewed in 1995 and 2005. *Journal of Clinical Child and Adolescent Psychology, 39,* 64–76.

Wurtele, S. K., & Kenny, M. C. (2010). Partnering with parents to prevent childhood sexual abuse. *Child Abuse Review, 19,* 130–152.

Young, A., Grey, M., Abbey, A., Boyd, C. J., & McCabe, S. E. (2008). Alcohol-related sexual assault victimization among adolescents: Prevalence, characteristics, and correlates. *Journal of Studies on Alcohol and Drugs, 69,* 39–48.

CHAPTER ELEVEN

Developing Teen Relationships: The Role of Violence

Andrea Poet, Catherine R. Swiderski, and Maureen C. McHugh

As parents and members of communities, we try to protect our youths from threats to their safety and to protect their health and well-being. Despite our efforts, their health and safety may be at risk from an unrecognized source, their intimate/romantic partners. Dating violence threatens the health and well-being of adolescents; engaging in dating and sexual relationships places adolescents at risk for becoming victims of violence (Teten, Ball, Valle, Noonan, & Rosenbluth, 2009). Experts have called teen relationship violence a major health crisis, a societal problem, and even a silent epidemic (Weingartner, 2008). Dating violence is not only a serious problem for teens but is also a predictor for intimate partner violence through adulthood.

The term "teen relationship violence" (TRV) acknowledges the existence of violence in the relationships of teens, and also suggests that there are some distinct aspects of violence in teen dating relationships. Teen relationship violence is a particular form of intimate partner violence (IPV). This broader term was coined when we realized that relationship violence was not limited to marital or heterosexual couples. IPV has been documented in marital, cohabitating, dating, and gay and lesbian couples (McHugh, Livingston, & Frieze, 2008). In this chapter, we examine the specific findings regarding teen relationship violence, but we also discuss teen relationship violence in the context of what we understand about intimate partner violence.

What Is Teen Relationship Violence?

Although definitions of TRV vary, it typically is used as a broader term to refer to three specific forms of abusive behavior that can occur in the context of a dating relationship (Teten et al., 2009). Teen dating violence may involve physical, sexual, and/or emotional/psychological abuse (Teten et al., 2009). Some also include the intent of the aggressive behavior in the definition (e.g., control or domination) (Werkerle & Wolfe, 1999). According to the Youth Risk Survey of female adolescents who experience dating violence, 57% have been victims of physical violence, 43% of sexual victimization, and up to 65% of psychological abuse (Maas, Fleming, Herrenkohl, & Catalano, 2010). Physical aggression is typically defined as acts intended to harm or kill and may involve such behaviors as hitting, slapping, strangling, and using weapons. Sexual violence entails completed or attempted penetration, unwanted nonpenetrative sexual contact, or verbal sexual harassment and includes incidents in which the victim is unable to consent (e.g., because of age) or unable to refuse (e.g., threatened with physical harm to self or others). Psychological abuse refers to aggressive acts, such as verbal intimidation, derogation and insults, social humiliation, constant surveillance, or threatened acts of violence that may cause emotional trauma. This type of abuse can be more subtle and often involves attempts to control, dominate, or isolate. Although much of the media and the professional literature is focused on instances of physical violence, verbal and emotional abuse may be the key component of teen dating violence. Emotional or psychological abuse has been found to precede and predict physical violence (Cano, Avery-Leaf, Cascardi, & O'Leary, 1998). Much of the harm to the victim, in the form of low self-esteem and depression, may actually be a reaction to the verbal and emotional abuse. Although Molidor (1995) reported low levels of psychological abuse for his high school sample, others have concluded that there are more psychological abuses than physical attacks in adolescent relationships (Jezl, Molidor, & Wright, 1996). Our understanding of teen dating violence now also includes stalking behaviors (Coker, Sanderson, Cantu, Huerta, & Fadden, 2008) and relational aggression (Linder, Crick, & Collins, 2002). Relational aggression refers to actions designed to hurt individuals via their relationships; an example might be deliberately flirting with another to make one's partner angry.

Technology has proven to have a significant impact on teen romantic relationships and the perpetrations of TRV (Ulloa, Castaneda, & Hokoda, 2010). Youths are more connected to technology and thus technology sometimes has a role in relational abuse in teen relationships. Cell phones, social-networking websites, and instant messaging are all ways in which teens maintain relationships and even enact abuse (Ulloa et al., 2010). Threatening and/or degrading messages can be sent through text, email, or social-networking sites and may be visible to more than just the dating partner. Stalking or spying may occur through logging onto the partner's email or social-networking account and by checking calls and texts on a partner's cell phone. In one survey, 30% of teens indicated that they received up to 30 text messages in an hour from a partner asking what they were doing and whom they were with (Picard, 2007). Texts and cell phones are also used by teens to engage in harassment and name calling. Twenty-five percent of the teens in a survey reported they had experienced this form of abuse. Teens may also feel pressure to engage in sexual behavior over the phone and/or Internet, as did 22% of this sample of teens. For example, one form of sexual behavior that can be used in coercive and abusive ways is sexting, the delivery of sexual material and images through texting.

Prevalence

Contrary to what adults, professionals, and the general population may believe, teen dating violence occurs quite frequently. Research studies indicate that teen dating violence occurs in anywhere from 9% to 57% of teen relationships (Herrman, 2009). In one of the first studies to document teen violence, Henton & Cate (1983) reported that 12% of their respondents had experienced relationship abuse. Other early research on dating violence indicated that about 1 in 5 dating couples experiences some form of violence in their relationship (Makepeace, 1981). Similarly, a more recent study of high school students (Silverman, Raj, Mucci, & Hathaway, 2001) found that 1 out of every 5 teens was a victim of some form of relationship violence. Other researchers reported that 46% of high school students experienced physical aggression from a dating partner (Watson, Cascardi, Avery-Leaf, & O'Leary, 2001).

It is important to realize that many teens do not report their experience of violence, and others who do discount the seriousness of their situation. One study of 11- to 14-year-old adolescents indicated that about 62% of the teens claimed they knew of someone who had been a victim of verbal abuse during their relationship (Teten et al., 2009). These numbers are frightening. Further, there are some indications that the incidence of dating violence may be increasing with each cohort. The more violence that teens observe, the more violence and abuse appears to be normative to them.

Gender

The most publicized cases of TRV are those involving serious injury or even death. These cases typically involve a male abuser and a female victim. There are documented cases of TRV involving this pattern of unilateral and serious violence perpetrated by the male toward a female victim. However, much of the research on teen relationship violence suggests that physical violence and psychological abuse are also perpetrated by girls and young women against their boyfriends. Some research finds that girls and boys are equally likely to use violence against their partners. Two different meta-analyses, examining the research from many studies, indicated that girls/women are as likely to perpetrate physical violence in their relationships as are boys/men (Archer, 2000).

Even in the early studies, respondents indicated that teen dating violence was reciprocal (Henton & Cate, 1983; O'Keefe, Brockopp, & Chew, 1986). Similar results of bidirectional or reciprocal dating violence was reported in more recent research (Renner & Whitney, 2010) using data from the National Longitudinal Study of Adolescent Health (Add Health). Other research also confirms that violence in teen relationships is often bidirectional, that is that both partners are engaging in and receiving violence (Gray & Foshee, 1997).

Other researchers report that female adolescents perpetrate more physical abuse in dating relationships than do male adolescents (e.g., Foshee, 1996; Wolfe, Scott, Wekerle, & Pittman, 2001). However, some research contradicts these conclusions. In a study of rural youths, Marquart, Nannini, Edwards, Stanley, and Wayman (2007) reported that girls were 3.5 times more likely to report being hit, pushed, or threatened by their partner than were their male counterparts. Other research suggests that girls are more likely to push, slap, or bite their partners, but boys are more likely to punch their girlfriends or threaten them with a gun (Schwartz, Magee, Griffin, & Dupuis, 2004). West and Rose (2000) report that girls in their study reported slapping and pushing their partners, whereas boys were more likely to use sexual aggression. Girls are more likely to experience more severe forms of physical violence, and male-to-female violence results in more injury than female-perpetrated physical aggression (Archer, 2000; Molidar, Tolman, & Kober, 2000). A review of studies of sexual violence indicated that while young men and women were equally likely to pressure partners to engage in sexual activities, female respondents were four times more likely to have experienced rape (Spitzberg, 1999). Similarly, in their study of Latino/a adolescents, Hickman, Jaycox, and Aronoff (2004) found that girls perpetrated more physical and psychological violence, whereas boys were more likely to perpetrate sexual violence and to cause more injuries. Further, girls are more likely to be killed by a partner than are boys (U.S. Department of Justice, 1998).

Young men and women may use and experience abuse and/or violence differently. Males reported experiencing higher amounts of psychological abuse than did females (Molidor, 1995), including being sworn at, given the silent treating fewer positive and more psychologically abusive behaviors than did their female counterparts. Molidor suggests that young women learn how to implement psychological abuse earlier than males, and that such strategies work as a defense against male entitlement and sexual coercion.

Inconsistencies in the research record on who (men or women) uses more violence in intimate relationships has been tied to the methods employed to measure violence and to the respondents who were surveyed (Johnson, 1995; McHugh, Livingston, & Ford, 2005). Elsewhere, McHugh and Frieze (Frieze, 2005; McHugh et al., 2005; McHugh & Frieze, 2006; McHugh et al., 2008) have argued for recognition that women use various forms of violence in their intimate relationships. Refusal to recognize women's use of violence undermines our understanding of relationship violence and the effectiveness of our interventions. However, we should be careful not to label young men's and young women's use of violence as equal, equivalent, or symmetrical. Evidence suggests that men's violence and women's violence differ in terms of force, severity, injury, intent, and perception.

Johnson (1995), Frieze (2005), and others have argued that there are multiple patterns of relationship violence, including male battering, mutual reciprocal violence, and female-initiated unilateral violence. A similar approach appears to be warranted in our study of TRV. Research is needed to discern multiple forms and patterns of teen dating violence and to assess the consequences of each pattern. We may need to examine the relation of gender to relationship violence using more complex ideas about gender. For example, teens' conceptualizations of dating violence appear to differ according to gender. Sears, Byers, Whelan, and Saint-Pierre (2006) found that while girls tended to perceive violence as a means of control, boys tended to view violence as the result of being provoked. Girls viewed their violence as less serious than that of boys; they viewed their use of violence more lightly or jokingly. Boys, however, viewed their infliction of harm more seriously and tended to define acts of dating violence according to whether or not it was intended to result in pain or harm. While boys tended to focus on the physical aspects of dating violence, girls' definitions were broader and included the negative emotional impact of dating violence. The research suggests that both male and female teenagers use and experience violence in their relationships, but the forms, patterns, and perceptions of violence are different for young men and women.

Help Seeking

Recognizing the signs of teen dating violence is important, particularly as teens are much less likely to report relationship violence than adults. Approximately 1 in 11 incidents of teen dating violence is reported, and 60% of victims and 79% of perpetrators do not seek help (Ashley & Foshee, 2005). There are numerous reasons why teens do not seek help for violent relationships. When teens are asked about unreported dating violence, they cite reasons such as fear of retaliation or escalation of the violence, denial, self-blame, emotional ties to the perpetrator, and feelings of helplessness (Seimer, 2004). Embarrassment, or potential for embarrassment, also plays a role in why teens are reluctant to report abuse. Both male and female teen victims of relationship violence report concealing their abusive relationships due to feelings of embarrassment (Sears et al., 2006). Self-blame may also contribute to teens' reluctance to report violence. Some common myths among teenagers are that the victim is to blame for the victimization: "Even if I am hit, I am nothing without my partner," and "If I told people I was abused, they would think it was my fault" (Herrman, 2009). Some relationship violence may also be seen as normative and may even be reinforced by one's family or culture (O'Keefe, 2005).

Even when teens are aware of appropriate resources, they feel that these resources will only let them down. When Gallopin and Leigh (2009) questioned teens as to why they felt that they could not tell their parents about a violent relationship, most teens strongly felt that their parents would not believe them. Research by Sears and colleagues (2006) also indicates that a lack of reporting may be due in part to teens' gender-role beliefs. Females reported believing that abuse by males will not be taken seriously by adults because it is seen as normal, whereas males reported that abuse by females will not be taken seriously because it is less likely to lead to injury.

Ashely and Foshee (2005) found that teens reported being willing to report relationship violence to friends, family members, teachers, and counselors. The authors found there to be a gender difference in which teens were more willing to report. Girls, if they were to confide in someone, reported being more likely to tell friends, siblings, and parents, whereas boys indicated that they would be more likely to go to nonfamily members and professional adults. In the research by Gallopin and Leigh (2009), teens felt that police officers were prejudiced and stereotyped these behaviors, making them less willing to take this matter seriously. It is common for teens to seek the advice of their peers when faced with these situations. However, the problem with this is that their peers are inexperienced in this area and often lack the knowledge and maturity to deal with this situation (Ruiz, Exposito, & Bonache, 2010).

Lesbian, gay, bisexual, and transgender (LGBT) teens express more serious concerns when it comes to help-seeking behaviors. In a study done by Gallopin and Leigh (2009), LGBT participants claimed that dating violence was an everyday occurrence in their lives. According to the National Coalition of Anti-Violence Programs, 50% of LGBT teens experience dating violence. In terms of help-seeking, these teens feel even more isolated. One teen stated that police officers often dismissed dating violence cases as soon as they discovered an LGBT teen's sexual orientation. When asked who they would feel comfortable seeking help with, LGBT teens said that they would not seek a therapist or service provider, but rather a close friend, another survivor, or an LGBT youth organization (Gallopin and Leigh, 2009).

Signs of Distress

Since teen victims of relationship violence are especially unlikely to seek help, it is important for parents, teachers, and others who interact with teens to recognize any signs of dating distress. Some generally recognized signs of distress in teens include changes in activities and activity levels, such as interacting with friends and clubs less often and/or becoming socially isolated. Often the teen may discontinue confiding in or disclosing to parents, and they may develop a resistance or oppositional stance toward parents. While this may be difficult to distinguish from adolescent behavior in general, in teens as in adult relationships an abuser may discourage the victim from interacting with friends and family members. Social isolation makes individuals more vulnerable to abuse and more dependent on the abusive partner. Teens in abusive relationships may also display irritability, mood shifts, and depression. Depression is characterized by withdrawal, lack of motivation, irritability, sleep and eating disruptions, and sadness. Repeated bruising, black eyes, or other injuries may signal violence. Teens experiencing physical violence may wear inappropriate clothing to cover bruises, such as wearing long sleeves in hot weather. Teens may avoid contact with parents and friends to avoid detection of injuries.

A number of resources online seek to educate parents about the warning signs of teen dating violence. For example, www.4parents.gov urges parents to be mindful of a decline in grades, increased emotional outbursts and isolation, and any signs of physical injury. The Parents Guide to Teen Dating Violence, from the Crime and Violence Prevention Center at the California Attorney General's Office, also encourages parents to be aware of teens withdrawing from friendships or school activities, displaying hostility or shame, being increasingly secretive, or apologizing for their boyfriend or girlfriend's behavior. Other warning signs that a teen may be involved in an abusive relationship include physical injuries or bruises (although these may not be easily visible) as well as alcohol or drug use, which is often used as a coping mechanism. The Parents Guide also provides warning signs of teens who are abusive, including jealousy or possessiveness, uncontrollable anger or bursts of hostility, blaming others when angry, and criticizing, demeaning, or belittling the teen's boyfriend or girlfriend. The Parents Guide to Teen Dating Violence is available at http://new.vawnet.org/category/Documents.php?docid=2219&category_id=995.

Outcome/Impact

Teen dating violence has a number of serious potential consequences, both short and long term. Teens involved in abusive relationships are at higher risk for physical injuries, ranging from minor to fatal (Banyard & Cross, 2008; Simonelli & Ingram, 1998). Foshee and colleagues (1998) found that 8% of teens sought medical attention for injuries due to a violent incident in the context of a dating relationship. The most serious outcome of teen dating violence is death. According to the Supplementary Homicide Reports, 10% of murdered girls between the ages of 12 and 15 were killed by an intimate partner. The percentage of homicides by partner in girls aged 16 to 19 is even higher (22%).

As dating violence can involve other types of abuse (e.g., psychological or sexual), the impact of this abuse takes forms other than the physical. There are a number of mental health consequences for teens involved in violent relationships (Herrman, 2009). These teens are at increased risk for depression, post-traumatic stress disorder, disordered eating, and suicidal behavior (Bossarte, Martinez, & Blustein, 2008; Seimer, 2004; Teten et al., 2009). Victims may also struggle with low self-esteem, feelings of guilt and shame, loss of trust, and social isolation or withdrawal (Bossarte et al., 2008; Herrman, 2009; Teten et al., 2009). Teens involved in abusive dating relationships may also turn to substance use/abuse to help cope with the physical and psychological impact of such abuse (Champion, Foley, Sigmon-Smith, Sutfin, & DuRant, 2008).

Dating violence also appears to have an impact on sexual health, particularly for female victims. Female victims are 2.6 times more likely to test positive for sexually transmitted diseases than those without abusive partners (Decker, Silverman, & Raj, 2005). Teens involved in abusive relationships are more likely in general to practice risky sexual behaviors, and these relationships are also more likely to result in unplanned pregnancy (O'Keefe, 2005; Silverman et al., 2001; Ulloa et al., 2010).

Abuse in high school dating relationships may establish a pattern of relationship violence that persists for a long time, even a lifetime (Roscoe & Callahan, 1985). Some research has found that involvement in an abusive dating relationship during the teenage years may establish a pattern of future dating and relationship behavior (Herrman, 2009; O'Keefe, 2005; Ulloa et al., 2010). In a sample of college students, dating violence was found to predict future violence in dating relationships (Rich, Gidyca, Warkentin, Loh, & Weiland, 2005). Dating violence during the teen years may even predict marital violence (Perry, 2002). Thus, not only does teen dating violence put teens at risk for numerous and potentially lethal outcomes, teen dating violence may play an important role in the experience and perpetration of future violence in adulthood.

Explanations for Teen Dating Violence

As McHugh and colleagues (McHugh & Frieze, 2006; McHugh et al., 2005; McHugh et al., 2008) indicated, our labels for violence typically reflect our theories and may limit our conceptualizations of intimate partner violence(IPV). For example, early recognition of wife abuse resulted in theories that explained serious forms of violence in terms of marital roles and expectations. The realization of violence in cohabiting relationships forced new understandings, as did awareness of gay and lesbian couple violence and dating violence. The increasing recognition of TRV similarly argues for new explanatory approaches. Existing models of relationship violence (see e.g., McHugh & Swiderski, 2010; McHugh et al., 2008) might not explain TRV. Teens differ from adult victims. Typically teens do not share financial or other dyadic responsibilities. Teens do not have the same stresses and frustrations that have been offered as explanations for adult relationship violence. Parents and other adult authorities do not encourage the violent couple to stay together. Understanding or explaining the use of physical, psychological, and/or sexual abuse in teen dating relationships requires us to adopt new approaches and a developmental model. The developmental tasks, maturational levels, relationship skills, and stressors are different for teens than for emerging adults.

Teen Perceptions of Causes

Despite their awareness of dating violence, teens do not perceive these issues as serious or detrimental to themselves or the relationship. Some research with teens indicated that many of them view dating violence as acceptable behavior in a relationship. Although not considered a major issue, teens seem confused and undecided about the causes of dating violence. Some teens feel that violence is an aggressive way to solve an argument. Other causes teens came up with were rushing into a relationship, lack of relationship experience, being confused about the difference between love and lust, and lack of parental guidance and appropriate relationship figures (Gallopin and Leigh, 2009).

Individual Variables

Research has attempted to identify cognitions and characteristics of individuals who are likely to perpetrate violence with their partners. Some evidence supports the idea that acceptance of violence is correlated with using violence with a partner (Gray & Foshee, 1997); other studies have not validated a connection between acceptance of violence with perpetration of IPV (Bookwala, Frieze, Smith, & Ryan, 1992). However, externalizing behavioral problems (that is acting out against others) was a salient predictor of teen dating violence for boys (Maas et al., 2010); the authors concluded that aggressive boys were more likely to become involved in high-conflict relationships and subsequently engage in (and experience) reciprocal dating violence. Lack of empathy has been investigated as a characteristic of perpetrators, and some evidence has linked a lack of empathy to TRV (Wolfe, Wekerle, Scott, & Grasley, 2004). Other research has focused on the anger-expression styles of teen partners, demonstrating that this individual approach mediates teen violence in complex ways (Wolfe, Wekerle, Reitzel-Jaffe, & Lefebvre, 1998). Generally, we have not been able to provide a personality profile for perpetrators of IPV (McHugh & Swiderski, 2010), and similarly we cannot identify the teen that will hurt his (or her) dating partner.

Teen Relationships

An important element in teen dating violence may be that teens lack experience in intimate relationships. They may lack the skills to communicate their anger, to negotiate conflict, to express their feelings, and to deal with rejection. These are skills that are being developed and practiced in early dating situations. Repeated breaking up and making up is frequently observed. During the teen years, individuals attempt to develop serious intimate relationships and the skills to maintain relationships, but the learning process is often a painful one. The nature of dating relationships varies as individuals age; relationships in early adolescence are particularly short term, less well defined, and more fluid than the relationships of young adults (Furman & Hand, 2006).

Teens have poor conflict-resolution skills. Inability to resolve conflicts has been identified as an issue in adult relationships that involve violence. Generally, as a culture, we do not provide individuals with extensive conflict-resolution skills. In many contexts we reward individuals for resolving conflict by using verbal intimidation, bullying, and force. Peaceful and nonconfrontational strategies are not always admired, especially for boys and men.

Teens in relationships may be influenced by romantic notions of how love is expressed. Love may be associated with acts of devotion, high levels of passion and emotionality, and jealousy and possessiveness; the absence of such behavior is sometimes seen as the absence of love (Johnson et al., 2005). Other authors have similarly suggested that teens' behavior in relationships is the result of their perceptions about what it is to be "romantic" in a relationship (Ulloa et al., 2010). Jealousy in particular has been associated with relationship violence at multiple developmental stages. Male batterers demonstrate more jealousy than do happily married and nonviolent men (Barnett, Martinez, & Blustein, 1995; Pagelow, 1981). For teens, however, jealousy, possessiveness, and acts of control may be thought to demonstrate devotion and passion.

In the early teen years, many girls and boys develop an interest in the other sex. Sometimes girls report changing their appearance and their interests in order to attract the attention of boys, or of a particular boy. Having a boyfriend is one way to achieve status and popularity for girls in some schools. The importance placed on having a boyfriend leaves girls vulnerable to dating violence. Some girls would rather endure physical or psychological violence than not to have a boyfriend. The pressure to demonstrate one's heterosexuality and one's ability to attract a boyfriend has been referred to as "compulsory heterosexuality" (Rich, 1994). Rich argues that regardless of women's own sexual desires, girls and women may experience heterosexuality as imposed or managed by society in the form of the messages they receive every day that promote heterosexuality in the form of myths and norms. Some women are encouraged to adopt the goal of making themselves attractive to men. The pressure to have a date, and to maintain a relationship with a boyfriend, encourages young women to put up with unacceptable behavior from men.

Family Factors

Family interactions have been shown to predict relationship quality in adolescents (Conger, Cui, Bryant, & Elder, 2000). Teens who come from families in which IPV occurs are at higher risk for involvement in TRV (Maas et al., 2010; O'Keefe, 1997). Teens may model the violent and abusive behaviors they witnessed at home. Teens who grew up in violent homes may find relationship violence normative or acceptable (O'Keefe, 1997). They may have developed their parents' anger-expression styles and/or have poor models for conflict resolution. They may be reactant to others' attempts to control or dominate them.

Other research suggests that young people who have experienced neglect, abandonment, or maltreatment are especially at risk for having relationship problems (Maas et al., 2010); bonding with parents is a documented protection against becoming a victim of teen dating violence. The degree of parental involvement and monitoring of children has been identified as a correlate of adolescent behavioral problems and TRV (Straus & Savage, 2005). Sibling violence, including emotional, sexual, and physical types of violence, is linked to later perpetration of violence in dating relationships (Simonelli, Mullis, Elliott, & Pierce, 2002).

Peer Influence

Even if an adolescent is not experiencing dating violence personally, most teens know of someone who is experiencing violence in a relationship. However, intervening in another's relationship may not be seen as acceptable. Most teens feel that it is none of their business what goes on in another person's relationship and claim that they would not report something if they saw it happen (Gallopin and Leigh, 2009). The context of the violent act also seems to be important to a teen's perception of dating violence. Some indicate that in certain circumstances, it is okay to use violence, such as in self-defense (Gallopin and Leigh, 2009).

A study done by O'Keefe, Brockopp, and Chew (1986) examined teens' views on dating violence. The researchers found shocking results. Thirty percent of the time, teens felt that violence had no effect on the victim. They felt that it had no effect on the perpetrator only 37% of the time. Students also indicated that teens felt that violence hurt the relationship 33% of the time and improved the relationship 21% of the time. Violence was grounds for termination of a relationship only 12% of the time. From these results, it can be assumed that teens do not feel that violence in a relationship is an adequate reason to end their commitment to each other.

Alternatively, psychological, relational, or physical aggression against a boyfriend or girlfriend in junior high or middle school might be comparable

Developing Teen Relationships

to other forms of aggression perpetrated and experienced at this age, including bullying, teasing, and gender harassment (Teten et al., 2009).

Community/Culture of Violence

Some researchers have suggested that the acceptability of violence within one's culture or subculture is a predictor and a causal factor in relationship violence. Sanday (1981) examined violence against women across 186 societies and identified cultural characteristics that supported violence against women, including cultural ideologies that support male dominance and gender roles for men and women. Examining subcultures or regions within the United States, Sugarman and Hotaling (1989) found a regional pattern in violence in dating relationships; IPV was especially prevalent in the southern United States. A similar finding was reported by Marquart and her colleagues (2007); dating violence was substantially higher in the southern region. Others have noted a connection between levels of violence in the community and teens' experience of relationship violence (O'Keefe et al., 1986). One study found that violence in the community was the highest predictor for later dating violence (Malik, Sorenson, & Aneshensel, 1997). This research suggests that effective intervention efforts may involve modifying the acceptability of violence for the entire community rather than intervening at the individual or couple level.

Interventions

TRV is increasingly recognized as a serious and prevalent problem, and there are a number of interventions designed to reduce or prevent dating violence. There are two types of interventions: primary and secondary. Primary interventions attempt to prevent teen dating violence from ever occurring, while secondary interventions help to fix the problem once it has already occurred. Although most teens expressed that they do not seek help when involved in a violent relationship, it is important for resources to be available. Most schools do not have any programs or even rules addressing teen dating violence; however, some schools and other programs have taken on an active role in order to prevent this issue.

Primary Interventions

Several national organizations have taken on the task of bringing adolescent dating issues to the attention of parents, teachers, and teens. During high school, students are taught about abstinence, drug use, and even fire safety. But most schools do not provide any type of education on dating relationships. However, some schools have already set in place curriculum that covers interpersonal relationship skills, warning signs of abuse, and help-seeking behaviors. One of these campaigns is the Choose Respect program. This organization uses public service announcements, websites, interactive teaching methods, bathroom literature, and advertising materials in order to bring out the issues of teen dating (Herrman, 2009). The goal of this program is to promote positive dating relationships among teens (Herrman, 2009). Schools have also taken these issues seriously and created health classes that focus on dating violence, interpersonal skills, and healthy relationships. Two programs, Safe Dates and Healthy Relationships, have been nationally recognized in the school system as being effective for preventing teen violence (Herrman, 2009).

Safe Dates involves an interactive, dramatic play put on by the students, a 10-session curriculum, and a poster contest that is aimed at addressing teen dating violence. These activities help improve conflict-management skills and change teens' perceptions of dating violence (Herrman, 2009). Healthy Relationships consists of similar content that is aimed toward preventing teen dating violence. This program helps increase teens' self-esteem and teaches them appropriate relationship skills (Herrman, 2009). Take Back the Halls: Ending Violence in Relationships and Schools is a program created at DePaul University for application with poor and minority adolescents in urban areas.

Educational programs are likely to become increasingly common as several states legally mandate the inclusion of dating violence in the curriculum. For instance, the state of Rhode Island requires that all high schools implement this material into their curriculum (Weingartner, 2008). This mandate, the Lindsay Ann Burke Act, was created after the tragic death of Lindsay Ann Burke. This young woman was found dead in her ex-boyfriend's bathtub after suffering years of violence in her relationship (MSNBC, 2008). Since then, other states, like Texas, have also required high schools to teach these important life skills (Weingartner, 2008). Parents of victims of dating violence are similarly lobbying for legally mandated education in other states.

Secondary Interventions

Secondary intervention is directed at helping teens deal with a violent relationship. Although few programs exist in this area, it is the responsibility of the people involved in a teen's life to recognize and help the teen deal with his or her situation. It is important for parents, teachers, doctors, and school nurses to be able to identify the signs of violence and take an active role in that teen's life. Teens do not seek help from a person based on a professional title; rather, the relationship they hold with a person is the most important factor in help-seeking behaviors. Therefore, it is important for anyone involved in a teen's life to be aware of the warning signs and to be willing to reach out and support that individual.

Although several professions provide training with domestic violence, this training may not be adequate for teen dating violence. For instance, therapists who work with domestic violence in adults may not even think to look for these signs in young teens. The idea of providing couple's counseling for young teens is uncommon and seen as irrelevant due to their age and maturity. However, these teens are possibly young enough to modify their behaviors or learn new skills. This is why interventions and prevention programs are so important at this young age. Providing training for proper communication skills, interpersonal skills, and anger management techniques may help prevent future violence in a teen relationship.

Studies have shown that intervention programs improve knowledge and skills related to dating violence prevention (Ulloa et al., 2010). Intervention programs also increase the likelihood that these teens will seek help when faced with violence in their relationship (Ulloa et al., 2010). Future research for intervention programs should focus on more long-term studies. One of the issues with current research on teen dating violence is that many studies are short-term and lack follow-up with participants (Ulloa et al., 2010).

Conclusion

TRV is prevalent and may have long-term serious consequences for young men and women. Sometimes TRV is even lethal; teenage girls are more likely to sustain serious injury or to be killed than are boys. However, teen relationship violence can be perpetrated by both boys and girls and may often be reciprocal. Parents should be alert to the possibility that their son or daughter who is involved in dating may be the victim or agent of violence. Although both boys/young men and girls/young women perpetrate violence in dating relationships, TRV is not necessarily gender symmetrical or gender neutral. Gender impacts the type of violence perpetrated, the strategy and motive for the violence, the perception of the violence by both actor and recipient, and the short- and long-term impact of the violence. As in the study of adult IPV, we do not have a comprehensive understanding of how gender impacts the expression of violence in teen dating relationships. We need to continue to examine the impact of gender and gender roles on the use of violence in relationships, and to develop more complex models of gender and violence.

Currently, we have limited understanding of why physical aggression, psychological abuse, and/or sexual violence are prevalent in teen relationships. Many of our theories about (adult) IPV do not seem to apply to teen relationships. We need to develop more developmentally based models of dating violence. For example, we proposed that, in the teen years, the pressure and/or desire to have a boyfriend and the acceptance or even romanticization of violence in relationships contribute to TRV. Further, teens may be especially inexperienced in relationship problem solving and unable to express anger or resolve conflict. Research documents a connection between violence in teen relationships and violence in adult relationships. The patterns of conflict and violence that teens observe in parental and peer relationships appear to influence their own relationship patterns. Moreover, the patterns of physical, psychological, and sexual abuse experienced in teen relationships may be repeated in later adult relationships unless effective interventions are implemented.

Recognition of the potential for harm had led to increasing efforts to intervene in TRV. Interventions are based on the recognition that teens are unlikely to seek help and that adults have often been oblivious to the signs that relationship violence is occurring. Current interventions are often school based and focus on the identification of TRV, and on developing healthy relationships and interpersonal and communication skills. Additional research on TRV that advances our understanding of why TRV occurs may result in more effective interventions.

References

Archer, J. (2000). Sex differences in physical, verbal, and indirect aggression between heterosexual partners: A meta analytic review. *Psychological Bulletin, 126,* 651–680.

Ashley, O. S., & Foshee, V. A. (2005). Adolescent help-seeking for dating violence: Prevalence, socio-demographic correlates, and sources of help. *Journal of Adolescent Health, 36,* 25–31.

Banyard, V. L., & Cross, C. (2008). Consequences of teen dating violence: Understanding intervening variables in ecological context. *Violence Against Women, 14,* 998–1013.

Barnett, O. W., Martinez, T. E., & Blustein, B. W. (1995). Jealousy and romantic attachment in martially violent and nonviolent men. *Journal of Interpersonal Violence, 10,* 473–486.

Bookwala, J., Frieze, I. H., Smith, C., & Ryan, K. (1992). Predictors of dating violence: A multivariate analysis. *Violence and Victims, 7,* 297–311.

Bossarte, R. M., Simon, T. R., & Swahn, M. H. (2008). Clustering of adolescent dating violence, peer violence, and suicidal behavior. *Journal of Interpersonal Violence, 23,* 815–834.

Cano, A., Avery-Leaf, S., Cascardi, M., & O'Leary, K. (1998). Dating violence in two high school samples: Discriminating variables. *Journal of Primary Prevention, 18,* 431–446.

Champion, H., Foley, K. L., Sigmon-Smith, K., Sutfin, E. L., & DuRant, R. H. (2008). Contextual factors and health risk behaviors associated with date fighting among high school students. *Women and Health, 7,* 1–22.

Coker, A. L., Sanderson, M., Cantu, E., Huerta, D., & Fadden, M. K. (2008). Frequency and types of partner violence among Mexican American college women. *Journal of American College Health, 56,* 665–673.

Conger, R. D., Cui, M., Bryant, C. M., & Elder, G. H. (2000). Competence in early adult romantic relationships: A developmental perspective on family influences. *Journal of Personality and Social Psychology, 79,* 224–237.

Decker, M. R., Silverman, J. G., & Raj, A. (2005). Dating violence and sexually transmitted disease/HIV testing and diagnosis among adolescent females. *Pediatrics, 116,* 272–276.

Forbes, G. B., Jobe, R. L., White, K. B., Bloesch, E., & Adams-Curtis, L. E. (2005). Perceptions of dating violence following a sexual or nonsexual betrayal of trust: Effects of gender, sexism, acceptance of rape myths, and vengeance motivation. *Sex Roles, 52,* 165–173.

Foshee, V. (1996). Gender differences in adolescent dating abuse prevalence, types, and injuries. *Health Education Research, 11,* 275–286.

Foshee, V. A., Bauman, K. E., Arriaga, X. B., Helms, R. W., Koch, G. G., & Linder, G. F. (1998). An evaluation of Safe Dates, an adolescent dating prevention program. *American Journal of Public Health, 88,* 44–49.

Frieze, I. H. (2005). *Hurting the one you love: Violence in relationships.* Belmont, CA: Thompson Wadsworth.

Furman, W., & Hand, L. S. (2006). Romance and sex in adolescence and emerging adulthood: Risks and opportunities. In A. Crouter & A. Booth (Eds.), *The slippery nature of romantic relationships: Issues in definition and differentiation* (pp. 171–178). Mahwah, NJ: Lawrence Erlbaum Associates.

Gallopin, C., & Leigh, L. (2009). Teen perceptions of dating violence, help-seeking, and the role of schools. *The Prevention Researcher, 16,* 17–20.

Gray, H. M., & Foshee, V. (1997). Adolescent dating violence: Differences between one-sided and mutually violent profiles. *Journal of Youth and Adolescents, 12,* 126–141.

Henton, J., & Cate, R. (1983). Romance and violence in dating relationships. *Journal of Family Issues, 4,* 467–481.

Herrman, J. W. (2009). There's a fine line . . . adolescent dating violence and prevention. *Pediatric Nursing, 35,* 164–170.

Hickman, L. J., Jaycox, L. H., & Aronoff, J. (2004). Dating violence among adolescents: Prevalence, gender distribution, and prevention program effectiveness. *Trauma, Violence, and Abuse, 5,* 123–142.

Jezl, D., Molidor, C., & Wright, T. (1996). Physical, sexual, and psychological abuse in high school dating relationships: Prevalence rates and self-esteem issues. *Child and Adolescent Social Work Journal, 13,* 69–87.

Johnson, M. P. (1995). Patriarchal terrorism and common couple violence: Two forms of violence against women. *Journal of Marriage and the Family, 57,* 283–294.

Johnson, S. B., Frattaroli, S., Campbell, J., Wright, J., Pearson-Fields, A. S., & Cheng, T. L. (2005). "I know what love means": Gender-based violence in the lives of urban adolescents. *Journal of Women's Health, 14,* 172–179.

Kasian, M., & Painter, M. A. (1992). Frequency and severity of psychological abuse in a dating population. *Journal of Interpersonal Violence, 7,* 350–364.

Linder, J. R., Crick, N. R., & Collins, W. A. (2002). Relational aggression and victimization in young adults' romantic relationships: Associations with perceptions of parent, peer, and romantic relationship quality. *Social Development, 11,* 69–86.

Maas, C. D., Fleming, C. B., Herrenkohl, T. I., & Catalano, R. F. (2010). Childhood predictors of teen dating violence victimization. *Violence and Victims, 25,* 131–149.

Makepeace, J. (1981). Courting violence among college students. *Family Relations, 30,* 97–102.

Malik, S., Sorenson, S. B., & Aneshensel, C. S. (1997). Community and dating violence among adolescents: Perpetration and victimization. *Journal of Adolescent Health, 21,* 291–302.

Marquart, B. S., Nannini, D. K., Edwards, R. W., Stanley, L. R., & Wayman, J. C. (2007). Prevalence of dating violence and victimization: Regional and gender differences. *Adolescence, 42,* 645–657.

McHugh, M. C. (2005). Understanding gender and intimate partner abuse. *Sex Roles, 52,* 717–724.

McHugh, M. C., & Frieze, I. H. (2006). Intimate partner violence: New directions. In F. Denmark, H. Krauss, E. Halpern, & J. Sechzer (Eds.), *Violence and exploitation against women and girls. Annals of the New York Academy of Sciences* (pp. 121–141). New York: Blackwell.

McHugh, M. C., Livingston, N. A., & Ford, A. (2005). A postmodern approach to women's use of violence: Developing multiple and complex conceptualizations. *Psychology of Women Quarterly, 29,* 323–336.

McHugh, M. C., Livingston, N., & Frieze, I. H. (2008). Intimate partner violence: Perspectives on research and intervention. In F. Denmark & M. Paludi (Eds.), *Psychology of women: A handbook of issues and theories* (pp. 555–589). Westport, CT: Praeger.

McHugh, M. C., & Swiderski, C. R. (2010). From battered women to intimate partner violence: (Re)conceptualizing relationship violence. In M. Paludi and F. Denmark (Eds.), *Victims of sexual assault and abuse: Resources and responses for individuals and families* (pp. 241–279). Westport, CT: Praeger.

Molidor, C. E. (1995). Gender differences in psychological abuse in high school dating relationships. *Child and Adolescent Social Work Journal, 12,* 119–134.

Molidar, C., Tolman, R., & Kober, J. (2000). Gender and contextual factors in adolescent dating violence. *Prevention Researcher, 7,* 11–14.

MSNBC. (2008, October). R.I. schools must teach about dating violence. Retrieved from www.msnbc.msn.com/id/27035312/ns/us_news-e.

Oberlin, C. (2006, August). *Teen dating violence.* Paper presented at the annual meeting of the American Sociological Association, Montreal, Quebec, Canada. Retrieved from http://www.alacademic.com/meta/p104340_index.html.

O'Keefe, M. (1997). Predictors of dating violence among high school students. *Journal of Interpersonal Violence, 12,* 546–568.

O'Keefe, M. (2005). *Teen dating violence: A review of risk factors and prevention efforts.* Retrieved from http://new.vawnet.org/Assoc_Files_VAWnet/AR_TeenDatingViolence.pdf.

O'Keeffe, N. K., Brockopp, K., & Chew, E. (1986). Teen dating violence. *Social Work, 31,* 465–468.

Pagelow, M. D. (1981). *Woman battering: Victims and their experiences.* Beverly Hills, CA: Sage Publications.

Parents Guide to Teen Dating Violence. Retrieved from http://new.vawnet.org/category/Documents.php?docid=2219&category_id=995.

Perry, K. B. (2002). *Physical aggression in dating relationships: A typology of male perpetrators.* Retrieved from Dissertation Abstracts International: Section B: The Sciences and Engineering. U.S., ProQuest Information & Learning (62, 3386).

Picard, P. (2007). *Abuse in teen relationships study.* Retrieved from http://www.loveisrespect.org/wp-content/uploads/2009/03/liz-claiborne-2007-tech-relationship-abuse.pdf.

Renner, L. M., & Whitney, S. D. (2010). Examining symmetry in intimate partner violence among young adults using socio-demographic characteristics. *Journal of Family Violence, 25,* 91–106.

Rich, A. (1994). Compulsory heterosexuality and lesbian existence. *Blood, bread, and poetry.* New York: Norton.

Rich, C. L., Gidyca, C. A., Warkentin, J. B., Loh, C., & Weiland, P. (2005). Child and adolescent abuse and subsequent victimization: A prospective study. *Child Abuse and Neglect, 29,* 1373–1394.

Roscoe, B. U., & Callahan, J. E. (1985). Adolescents' self report of violence in families and dating relationships. *Adolescence, 20,* 545–553.

Ruiz, J., Exposito, F., & Bonache, H. (2010). Adolescent witnesses in cases of teen dating violence: An analysis of peer responses. *European Journal of Psychology Applied to Legal Context, 2,* 37–53.

Sanday, P. (1981). The socio-cultural context of rape: A cross cultural study. *Journal of Social Issues, 37,* 5–27.

Schwartz, J. P., Magee, M. M., Griffin, L. D., & Dupuis, C. W. (2004). Effects of a group preventive intervention on risk and protective factors related to dating violence. *Group Dynamics: Theory, Research and Practice, 8,* 221–231.

Sears, H. A., Byers, E. S., Whelan, J. J., Saint-Pierre, M. (2006). "If it hurts you, then it is not a joke": Adolescents' ideas about girls' and boys' use and experience of abusive behavior in dating relationships. *Journal of Interpersonal Violence, 21,* 1191–1207.

Seimer, B. S. (2004). Intimate violence in adolescent relationships: Recognizing and intervening. *MCN: The American Journal of Maternal Child Nursing, 29,* 117–121.

Silverman, J. G., Raj, A., Mucci, L. A., & Hathaway, J. E. (2001). Dating violence against adolescent girls and associated substance abuse, unhealthy weight control, sexual risk behavior, pregnancy, and suicidality. *Journal of the American Medical Association, 286,* 573–579.

Simonelli, C. J., & Ingram, K. M. (1998). Psychological distress among men experiencing physical and emotional abuse in heterosexual dating relationships. *Journal of Interpersonal Violence, 13,* 667–681.

Simonelli, C. J., Mullis, T., Elliot, A. N., & Pierce, T. W. (2002). Abuse by siblings and subsequent experiences of violence within the dating relationship. *Journal of Interpersonal Violence, 17,* 667–681.

Spitzberg, B. H. (1999). An analysis of empirical estimates of sexual aggression victimization and perpetration. *Violence and Victims, 14,* 241–290.

Straus, M. A., & Savage, S. A. (2005). Neglectful behavior by parents in the life history of university students in 17 countries and its relation to violence against dating partners. *Child Maltreatment, 10,* 124–135.

Sugarman, D. B., & Hotaling, G. T. (1989). Dating violence: Prevalence, context, and risk markers. In M. Pirog-Good & J. Stets (Eds.), *Violence in dating relationships: Emerging social issues* (pp. 3–32). New York: Praeger.

Teten, A. L., Ball, B., Valle, L. A., Noonan, R., & Rosenbluth, B. (2009). Considerations for the definition, measurement, consequences, and prevention of dating violence victimization among adolescent girls. *Journal of Women's Health, 18,* 923–927.

Ulloa, E., Castaneda, D., & Hokoda, A. (2010). Teen relationship violence. In M. A. Paludi & F. L. Denmark (Eds.), *Victims of sexual assault and abuse: Resources and responses for individuals and families: Vol. 1. Incidence and psychological dimensions* (pp. 111–135). Westport, CT: Praeger.

U.S. Department of Justice. (1998). Bureau of Justice statistics factbook (NCJ Publication No. 167237). Washington, DC: Author.

Watson, J. M., Cascardi, M., Avery-Leaf, S., & O'Leary, K. D. (2001). High school students' responses to dating aggression. *Violence and Victims, 16,* 339–348.

Weingartner, N. (2008, October). Rhode Island and Texas: The teen dating violence duo with public education mandates. *Digital Journal.* Retrieved from www.digitaljournal.com/article/260905.

Wekerle, C., & Wolfe, D. A. (1999). Dating violence in mid-adolescence: Theory, significance, and emerging prevention initiatives. *Clinical Psychology Review, 19,* 435–456.

West, C., & Rose, S. (2000). Dating aggression among low income African American youth: An examination of gender differences and antagonistic beliefs. *Violence Against Women, 6,* 470–494.

Wolfe, D., Scott, K., Wekerle, C., & Pittman, A. (2001). Child maltreatment: Risk for adjustment problems and dating violence in adolescence. *Journal of the American Academy for Child and Adolescent Psychiatry, 40,* 282–289.

Wolfe, D. A., Wekerle, C., Reitzel-Jaffe, D., & Lefebvre, L. (1998). Factors associated with abusive relationships among maltreated and non-maltreated youth. *Development and Psychopathology, 10,* 61–85.

Wolfe, D. A., Wekerle, C., Scott, K., & Grasley, C. (2004). Predicting abuse in adolescent dating relationships over 1 year: The role of child maltreatment and trauma. *Journal of Abnormal Psychology, 113,* 406–415.

Wolfe, D. A., Wekerle, C., Scott, K., Straatman, A. L., Grasley, C., & Reitzel-Jaffe, D. (2003). Dating violence prevention with at risk youth: A controlled outcome evaluation. *Journal of Consulting and Clinical Psychology, 71,* 279–291.

CHAPTER TWELVE

Stalking of Adolescents

Thomas M. Evans and Todd Hendrix

Stalking can best be viewed as an attempted, forced, and unwanted relationship. No stalking laws existed until the death of actress Rebecca Schaeffer, who was stalked and eventually murdered by an obsessed fan. California became the first to pass such a law in 1990, and since then all 50 states have followed suit (Tjaden & Thoennes, 1997). Research was scant prior to this period of time but has exploded since laws were passed. Various typologies exist (Mohandie, 2006) but are limited to adults.

What Is Juvenile Stalking?

While the developmental period of adolescence is marked by impulsivity, emotional reactivity, shortened time perspective, and risk-taking behaviors (Steinberg, 2005), juvenile stalking is a behavior that is out of the norm for typical postbreakup or rejection behavior. Stalking involves a pattern of behaviors that are frequently exhibited for a period of time and can consume a youth's thoughts to a degree that most conversations with friends are focused on this topic. Their preoccupation is likely to cause their friends to become concerned. Further, the youth spends an inordinate amount of time planning and preparing his next encounter with the intended target. The juvenile stalker is likely to decrease in participation of other activities and become more socially isolated as he plans his next advance and becomes so singularly focused that there is a drop in grades or failure to meet other obligations.

The intensity of the anger and duration of the pursuit, harassment, and terrorizing is distinguished from typical adolescence in scope, breadth, and duration. While typical postbreakup behaviors from a jilted partner can include name calling, spreading rumors, or sending hate-filled emails and text messages, these incidents tend to be short-lived, and soon this individual regains his emotional equilibrium and moves on to the next relationship. He or she will seek consolation from friends and after a few days seek to become involved with more social activities. The juvenile stalker, however, will continue to engage in behaviors intended to frighten, humiliate, or terrorize the intended target. These persist for an extended period of time and increase in frequency and intensity, including escalating into violence. They have a need to "even the score," but there is no defined goal to achieve or timeframe to achieve this objective so that they can ultimately move on. These behaviors will endure even as a new relationship is established.

Research on Juvenile Stalking

Currently, there is very limited research on juveniles who engage in stalking behaviors. McCann (1998) was one of the first to examine the behavior of stalking in the adolescent population. Due to the almost complete absence of empirical literature on juvenile stalking, he provided three cases studies to illustrate how these behaviors can be displayed by teenagers. He used a now-outdated typology to categorize these three cases: Erotomanic, Love Obsessional, and Simple Obsessional. This study highlighted that adolescent stalking is a course of behavior that does occur during adolescence and that many psychodynamic factors that are present in adult stalkers were also present in the three youths presented, such as attachment pathology and disturbances in identity.

Purcell, Moller, Flower, and Mullen (2009) provided the first empirical study of juvenile stalkers. They identified a group of 299 juvenile stalkers after completing a review of court records from the juvenile and civil court in which a protective order was granted against a juvenile under the age of 18. Interestingly, the majority of the cases came from the civil court, not juvenile court. Six categories emerged from the underlying motivation for stalking: stalking as an extension of bullying, retaliating stalkers, rejected stalkers, disorganized and disturbed stalkers, predatory stalkers, and intimacy-seeking stalkers.

Overall, threats were made in 75% of the cases, and 54% of the cases involved both physical and sexual violence. Sixty-four percent of the perpetrators were male, and the victim was previously known to the perpetrator in 98% of the cases. From a risk-assessment perspective, the high level of threats made will make assessment difficult, as threats in the absence of any other data are poor predictors of violence.

However, the classifications of stalking as an extension of bullying, retaliating stalkers, disorganized and disturbed stalkers, and predatory stalkers do not represent pure stalking behaviors, as their motivation is not to form a relationship with another individual or to torment the individual after the termination of the relationship. These four classifications water down the term stalking and would be better classified as bullying subtypes. Their categories of rejected stalkers and intimacy-seeking stalkers are more reflective of pure stalking behaviors, as the motivations are based solely on a dyadic relationship and are very personal and carry a high degree of emotional valence. These two categories are similar to the typology proposed by Evans and Meloy (in press). These include only behaviors that are fueled by the desire to form an intimate relationship or seek retribution after the termination of the relationship.

A significant limitation of using data solely from file review is the inability to delve into the individual psychology of the perpetrators. Thus, we do not know the reasons why those in the rejected group sought to terrorize their former partners. We do not know if those in the intimacy-seeking group have diagnosable mental illness. Questions regarding parental attachments or family system functioning cannot be answered, nor can questions regarding substance abuse or previous histories of violence. We only know that a large group from this sample engaged in various forms of stalking behavior, the frequency of such behavior, and other descriptive information. We have no insight or understanding of the motivation to engage in this behavior. Without specific case data, we know almost nothing about the psychology of the juvenile stalker.

Evans and Meloy (in press) further describe the current state of juvenile stalking, in which they also state that it is largely an unrecognized behavior that has not been viewed as such by the juvenile courts. National juvenile stalking statistics do not exist, and there is no established protocol for how to best evaluate these youths. In an attempt to understand the psychology of the juvenile stalker, Evans and Meloy (in press) provide two separate case studies and offer a preliminary typology. The typology is based not only on the two stalking cases presented but also on the first author's data from numerous court-ordered psychological evaluations of youths who had engaged in stalking behaviors yet were not officially charged as such. For example, relational violence was charged as assault, while what was actually stalking, which resulted in the youth being arrested at midnight on the victim's residence, was charged as trespassing.

The following is a preliminary typology based upon approximately 100 juvenile cases over a 10-year period that could be classified as stalking:

Type I

Socially Awkward
Desires relations with others.
Socially awkward due to poor social skills and/or poor intimacy skills.
Lonely; has few interpersonal relationships.
Low-level depression possible.
Parental relations distant and unfulfilling.
Unpopular or feels "irrelevant" or "lost." Not part of any particular clique; rather is on the fringe and does not fit into any particular group.

Object Relations
Has preoccupied attachment style.
Has negative view of self and overly positive view of others.
Mirroring self-objects needed for idealizing and twinship experience (or dependency needs) not experienced during infancy.

Motivation for Stalking
Establishing a relationship the main motivating factor.
Limited or no prior relationship with object of pursuit.
Likely an acquaintance, coworker, or neighbor.
Targeted person more annoyed than frightened.

Stalking Modality
Obsessive following; peeping/spying; repeated phone calls, letter writing, emails, or text messaging.
Actual face-to-face contact may be limited due to extreme feelings of inadequacy.

Risk for Violence
Low.
No history of violence or aggression and does not threaten or aggress against targeted individual.

Type II

Angry/Disgruntled
Perpetrator is relatively popular youth.
Unrealistic (or unwarranted) high level of self-regard.

Has anger issues and is overly sensitive to criticism.

Engages in bullying activities.

Parental relationships appear good to the casual observer, but closer inspections reveals a narcissistic family pattern, and parents are distant yet overly indulgent.

Object Relations
Has a dismissing quality.

Overly inflated self-esteem; views others as inferior, yet overly sensitive to criticism and reacts with anger to slight narcissistic insults.

Victims viewed as part-objects to be used for own needs until no longer fulfills usefulness.

Motivation for Stalking
Anger and revenge fuels this behavior, which is a cover for feelings of humiliation.

Had previous relationship with targeted object.

Utilized threats, intimidation, or violence to control other person or dictate the terms of the relationship.

Stalking Modality
Attempts to enlist others in his campaign of public denigration of ex-partner while concomitantly and covertly trying to "win back" ex-partner. This is done to show her that if she is not with him, then she is "a nobody" and will be very unpopular.

Engages in stalking behaviors while also publically demeaning pursuit object.

Threatens or attempts to intimidate the other's new partner.

Refuses to accept that other person terminated relationship.

Will not take "no" for an answer.

Stalking behaviors include threats to self, pursuit object, or object's new partner.

Risk for Violence
Moderate to high.

Violence and/or aggression likely present in that relationship, possibly including forced sexual activity. There likely has been at least one incident of violence within the relationship.

Violence can be both predatory and affective.

These two classifications of adolescent stalking are similar to the subjects in Purcell and colleagues (2009) rejected and intimacy-seeking classification. Similar to what was found in research of adult stalkers, threats and actual violence were significantly higher in the rejected group.

Stalking Tactics

Purcell and colleagues (2009) found that the juvenile stalker is likely to engage in multiple methods of pursuit behaviors and harassment. These include threatening and unwanted emails, phone calls, and text messages; unwanted approaches; and following. Surveillance of the victim's home is another tactic that the adolescent stalker will employ in order to keep tabs on the victim. Threats to secondary victims, such as a new boyfriend or a relative, can occur when access to the primary victim is blocked. This multimodal approach is utilized when one form of stalking becomes ineffective in making contact at a particular time; the stalker will improvise and attempt to make contact using an alternate form.

Assessment of the Juvenile Stalker

Traditional assessments can provide good information regarding the psychological makeup of the offender but offer no information for risk assessment and management. When conducting a psychological evaluation on a youth who has been charged with stalking, it is imperative to conduct an evaluation that is comprehensive in nature, including a clinical interview with the youth and the youth's caregivers. Besides evaluating for psychological impairment of the youth, an assessment of the family unit must also be conducted. As discussed earlier, the roots of stalking behaviors can be traced back to faulty attachment patterns. Parental abuse or neglect is a particular area to address. This is an important area because treatment with a juvenile offender should include the family.

Psychological testing that provides information regarding cognitive functioning is also important. Many times learning disabilities are present that have not been discovered. The youth may also have an underlying mood disorder or emerging personality disorder. Psychological testing could provide further information in addition to data obtained from the youth and parent interviews.

It is also imperative that information be obtained from the victim. There is likely to be a discrepancy between what the youth reports and what the victim reports. The youth accused of stalking has a vested interest in minimizing the behavior. Thus, an interview with the victim provides a clearer understanding of the relationship between the two of them, the form the stalking took, how long it persisted, and what forms it took. Collateral reports, such as police reports and probation reports, also must be reviewed, as they are likely to have information that the youth will not provide.

As the one empirical study by Purcell and colleagues (2009) illustrated, violence in juvenile stalking cases exceeds 50%. Thus, a history of violent behavior needs to be obtained. This history can be from self-report, parent report, school records, juvenile court records (if there has been previous court involvement), and victim testimony. Once this information is obtained, two instruments that can assist the evaluator in determining risk for future violence are the Psychopathy Checklist: Youth Version (Forth, Kosson, & Hare, 2003) and the Structured Assessment of Violence Risk in Youth (Borum, Bartel, & Forth, 2003). These instruments, while not stalking-specific, will provide the evaluator with information regarding callousness, a lack of empathy for others, and manipulation of others. It also assists the evaluator by ensuring that all clinically relevant factors associated with youth violence have been addressed in the interview.

In addition to conducting a comprehensive psychological evaluation and assessing for general risk for violence, the evaluator who is conducting a psychological evaluation on a youth referred for stalking should have working knowledge of teen dating violence, cyberbullying, and, as mentioned before, attachment pathology. This information, combined with data from the psychological evaluation, will enable the evaluator to assess these concepts in this particular context and thus offer an informed opinion on the nature of the youth's stalking behavior and the risk for violence, as well as to develop the risk management plan to keep the victim safe and identify treatment needs of the offender.

Teen Dating Violence

Teen dating violence, a form of intimate partner violence, is defined by the Centers for Disease Control and Prevention (CDC) as "ever being hit, slapped, or physically struck on purpose by a boyfriend or girlfriend." Teen dating violence is considered by the CDC as a significant risk factor to an adolescent's health and well-being in the United States. The CDC estimates that of the 72% of 8th and 9th graders who reportedly "date," 25% report verbal, physical, emotional, or sexual abuse from a dating partner each year. About 10% of adolescents nationwide report being physically hurt by a dating partner in the last 12 months, with little differences in the rates for boys and girls or grade level (Centers for Disease Control and Prevention, 2009). The prevalence of dating violence among early teens is even higher. In a study of more than 2,000 ethnically diverse sixth-grade students who acknowledged having a recent "boyfriend/girlfriend," 29% reported perpetrating physical aggression against the boyfriend or girlfriend (Miller, Gorman-Smith, Sullivan, Orpinas, & Simon, 2009).

Teen dating violence appears to have become an accepted part of the social landscape for early teens. In a national sample of more than 5,000 sixth-grade students, almost 60% of the boys and 45% of the girls reported having begun to "date." However, all of the respondents, whether involved with dating or not, were asked their perceptions of the acceptability of relational violence. More than half of the respondents reported that a girl hitting her boyfriend was acceptable under certain circumstances, such as being angry or jealous, and more than 1 in 4 sixth graders reported acceptance of boys hitting their girlfriends under similar circumstances (Simon, Miller, Gorman-Smith, Orpinas, & Sullivan, 2010).

The etiology of teen dating violence remains as unclear as does the etiology of any violent behavior. However, like most forms of teen violence, some key factors remain consistent. Exposure to peer and family violence is a well-documented risk factor for dating violence perpetration (Spriggs, Halpern, & Martin, 2009). Additionally, research has also shown that witnessing violent crime in childhood and adolescence is a risk factor for ongoing victimization in teen dating violence and intimate partner violence in adulthood (Spriggs et al., 2009). The literature also indicates that teen dating violence remains stable across time and partners, implying that victims of teen dating violence appear to remain in abusive relationships or may involve themselves in a series of abusive relationships (Timmons Fritz, & Smith Slep, 2009).

Early-adolescent males who perceived close parental monitoring were reported to have lower levels of perpetration of dating violence, and girls who perceived their parents as being more supportive of nonaggressive solutions toward relationship conflict reported lower levels of teen dating violence. However, when parents were perceived as being supportive of aggressive solutions toward relationship conflicts, and an environment of negative or delinquent peers existed, higher levels of teen dating violence existed. Additionally, when an environment of negative or delinquent peers existed, close parental monitoring was not a protective factor for boys' likelihood to perpetrate relationship violence (Miller et al., 2009). The influence of a negative peer group was further explored in a study of more than 300,000 adolescent males. This study found that adolescent males involved with close-knit peer groups that were primarily small, dense, and mostly male with higher rates of delinquent behavior reported higher rates of teen dating violence than did adolescent males whose peer groups were more loosely grouped, reported less delinquent behavior, and were populated with both males and females (Casey & Beadwell, 2011).

The impact of teen dating violence, beyond its potential gateway to adult intimate partner violence, is varied and problematic. Teen dating violence, for both victims and perpetrators, has been positively correlated with lower academic achievement, ongoing sexual activity, suicidality, drug and alcohol abuse, and physical aggression (Centers for Disease Control and Prevention, 2009). Teen dating violence victimization was also positively correlated with poorer psychosocial functioning, substance abuse and dependence, and greater Axis I diagnosis (Brown et al., 2009). These psychological symptoms were prevalent at both the time of initial referral to community mental health agencies and also at six-month follow-up. These results indicate that along with the initial trauma, teen dating violence can result in extensive and long-enduring psychological symptoms (Brown et al., 2009).

Dating violence, however, is not the only form of sexual aggression that exists in the adolescent environment. In a qualitative study of 72 Australian youths aged 14–15, the vast majority reported that sexual harassment of adolescent girls by adolescent males was a common occurrence. This harassment was focused on verbal and indirect victimization, was almost entirely sexual in nature, and was school based. The authors felt that the term "sexual bullying" appropriately captured the gendered power structure underlying these behaviors (Shute, Owens, & Slee, 2008). Other researchers believe that sexual bullying appears to be the antecedent to more severe forms of relationship violence and provides the conceptual link between bullying and more advanced forms of sexualized violence (Fredland, 2008). However, because the school represents the epicenter of an adolescent's social life, it does not appear to be a coincidence that the majority of these aggressive behaviors originate and occur in the school setting. Among youths involved with teen dating violence, 35–40% report that physical violence occurred in school buildings or on school grounds (Theriot, 2008).

Cyberbullying

Bullying does not remain at school when the school day ends. With the advent of cell phones, the Internet, and online social communities, the opportunities to continue to victimize and bully have continued to expand beyond the school environment and into the relative safety of the adolescent's home. Recent reports indicate that more than 97% of all youths in the United States are connected to the Internet in some way, and 66%

of all fourth to ninth graders are able to go online from their bedrooms (Tokunga, 2010). While this almost limitless access to information and networking provides opportunities for learning and connectivity that is unprecedented, it also opens the door to almost as many opportunities for aggression and abuse. The media has presented numerous anecdotal reports of "cyberbullying," including those leading to suicide or violence. Approximately 20–40% of all youths in the United States report having experienced cyberbullying at least once in their lives (Tokunga, 2010). Contrary to the literature on traditional bullying, both boys and girls appear to be equally victimized in cyberbullying, whereas in traditional bullying boys are overrepresented as both victims and perpetrators (Tokunga, 2010).

The term "cyberstalking" has become part of the media's lexicon but has never been operationally defined. Behaviors associated with cyberstalking include seeking and compiling information online about the victim for the purpose of threatening, harming, or harassing the victim, either online or offline; repeated unsolicited and unwanted emails and instant messaging; electronic sabotage, such as spamming and sending viruses; identity theft; subscribing the victim to unwanted services; purchasing goods and services in the victim's name; impersonating another online; sending or posting hostile material, misinformation, and false messages; and tricking other Internet users into threatening or harassing the victim (Sheridan & Grant, 2007). In a large sample of more than 4,000 female undergraduates, more than 13% reported having been "stalked," and of those reporting having been stalked, more than 24% reported receiving unwanted emails from the stalker (Fisher & Wallace, 2000). In a 2002 study completed by Spitzberg and Hoobler (2002), almost one-third of 232 undergraduates polled reported some form of cyberharassment, and sexually harassing messages had been received by 18% of those polled. While still very little is known about cyberstalking, some generalities have emerged. Overall, women were significantly more likely to be stalked. When compared to conventional stalking victims, cyberstalked victims were more likely to have received threats, had the perpetrator threaten suicide, and had personal items taken, and they were less likely to have contacted the police (Sheridan & Grant, 2007).

Attachment

Attachment style plays an extremely important role in the assessment of the juvenile stalker, and stalking is best understood as a form of attachment pathology. Attachment theory assumes that all humans are born with an innate need to form close emotional bonds with others. This theory posits that if an infant is regularly blocked from forming nurturing bonds with primary caregivers, and that if this blockage continues through childhood, the child has significant difficulty forming positive, reciprocal, and enduring relationships with others that are gratifying and provide a sense of self-worth.

The juvenile who engages in stalking behaviors is likely to display one of two maladaptive attachment patterns: dismissing or preoccupied. The adolescent with dismissing attachment has an overly inflated view of himself and a negative view of others (Rosenstein & Horowitz, 1996). This interpersonal style provides cover for individuals who are quite emotionally vulnerable, and who protect themselves against threats to their brittle self-esteem by maintaining a sense of aloofness in interpersonal relationships. Because their early upbringing has led them to have little faith in others who are supposed to care about them, they see others as untrustworthy and are skeptical in their interpersonal relationships.

In stalking situations, the adolescent with this attachment style is likely to respond to a narcissistic wound with anger and thoughts of vengeance, as another person whom they had presumed cared for them ultimately betrayed them. Instead of internalizing their distress, they most often act out, including harming others.

Persons with a preoccupied attachment style feel very unworthy of another person's love or affection and view others in an overly idealistic manner. They can only feel good about themselves through their relationships and can be very submissive and fearful that their only source of psychological well-being will abandon them at any time (Rosenstein & Horowitz, 1996). They feel anxious when they are not around their partner. They can become excessively clingy, demanding of the other's time, and even harbor constant thoughts of infidelity. They are so afraid that their partner will leave them that they can never enjoy the relationship.

This has implications for stalking because they can become fixated on the partner who ended the relationship. Because the termination of the relationship has caused a significant amount of psychological distress, the adolescent becomes preoccupied with repairing the relationship, thereby restoring their psychological well-being. This attempt to restore emotional equilibrium may then result in stalking behaviors, such as following and spying.

Narcissistic families, domestic violence, parental substance use, neglect, and emotional abuse all serve as major obstacles to developing secure attachment bonds. Since this sets the template for future relationships, insecure, dismissing, or fearful attachment styles can make developing and maintaining interpersonal relationships difficult, and thus, upon termination of the relationship or outright rejection when attempting to form a relationship, these youths may respond with deep feeling or humiliation, which is then transferred into rage, followed by revenge-stalking behaviors. Thus, when assessing the juvenile stalker, it is crucial that the early parental or primary caregiver relationships be thoroughly examined, as well as other family-system dysfunction.

Risk Assessment/Management

The purpose of completing a comprehensive psychological evaluation on the youth who has engaged in stalking is not only to determine if he has a diagnosable psychiatric disorder, but also to determine the risk for violence toward the intended victim and if the stalking is likely to continue. Once the opinion is formulated (typically expressed as low, moderate, or high risk), the next step is to devise a management plan to reduce this behavior. The plan will target the key findings from the assessment and focus on changeable factors, such as family-systems pathology, substance abuse, etc.

Another critical area to address if the juvenile stalker has perpetrated any form of physical violence toward the victim is the mode of violence displayed. In other words, did the youth strike the victim immediately after becoming enraged or rejected, or was the violence preplanned and perpetrated after a period time has passed? This is a very important distinction in risk management, as the latter type has been referred to as predatory violence (Meloy, 1988). This type of violence would indicate that the juvenile stalker has planned his violent act much earlier than it occurred. The youth may plan his revenge over a period of time and do so in a very tactical manner that takes the victim by surprise. For example, if the juvenile stalker had been served with a restraining order and had no contact with the victim for an extended period of time, this lulls the victim into a false sense of security. She lets her guard down and believes that the problem is behind her. Unbeknownst to her, the youth who had stalked her had planned his attack well beforehand and then attacks according to plan, which is when she is alone and unable to summon help. As opposed to a juvenile stalker who engages in a reactive form of violence (directly after a threat or perceived slight) where the violence is immediate, the victim does not see this coming.

A key component in risk management will involve the school system, since it is quite likely that the stalker and victim will attend the same school. Managing a restraining order may be difficult if the two persons are in the same class or eat lunch at the same time. However, schools are responsible for the safety of the pupils and thus must be made aware of the situation so that they can plan accordingly. The school also serves as an excellent vehicle with which to identify stalking situations and thus make appropriate referrals to mental health professionals and juvenile justice authorities if need be.

Future Directions

The scientific study of the adolescent who engages in stalking behaviors is in its infancy. Currently, stalking is going on largely unrecognized by the juvenile justice system. Youths who engage in stalking behaviors are more likely to be charged with unruliness or assault when these situations involve violence. Thus, there is no way to study this population in a systematic fashion.

Very little is known about these youths at this time. Questions regarding this population remain unanswered, such as the prevalence of juvenile stalking. Or is it normative for this age group? If it is, when should it become classified as stalking? How long does the youth who engages in stalking persist in this behavior? What is the best way to assess and treat youths accused of stalking? How should schools handle restraining orders? However, the most salient question is if this behavior persists into adulthood. These questions will remain unanswered until youths who stalk others are charged in the juvenile justice system with stalking. This will then provide behavioral science researchers the opportunity to collect data and advance the knowledge of this population.

References

Borum, R., Bartel, P., & Forth, A. (2003). *Manual for the Structured Assessment of Violence Risk in Youth* (Version 1.1). Tampa: University of South Florida.

Brown, A., Cosgrove, E., Killackey, E., Purcell, R., Buckby, J., & Yung, A. R. (2009). The longitudinal association of adolescent dating violence with psychiatric disorders and functioning. *Journal of Interpersonal Violence, 24,* 1964–1979.

Casey, E. A., & Beadwell, B. (2009). The structure of male adolescent peer networks and risk for intimate partner violence perpetration: Findings from a national sample. *Journal of Youth and Adolescence, 39,* 620–633.

Centers for Disease Control and Prevention. (2009). *Understanding teen dating violence.* Retrieved from http://www.cdc.gov/violenceprevention.

Erdur-Centers for Disease Control and Prevention. (2006, May). *Physical dating violence among high school students—United States, 2003.* Retrieved from http://www.cdc.gov/mmwr/perview/mmwrhtml/mm5519a3.htm.

Evans, T. M., & Meloy, R. J. (in press). Identifying and classifying juvenile stalking behavior. *Journal of Forensic Sciences.*

Fisher, C. B., & Wallace, S. A. (2000). Through the looking glass: Reevaluating the ethical and policy implications of research on adolescent risk and psychopathology. *Ethics and Behavior, 10,* 99–118.

Forth, A. E., Kosson, D. S., & Hare, R. D. (2003). *Hare psychopathy checklist: Youth version.* Toronto, Ontario, Canada: Multi-Health Systems.

Fredland, N. M. (2008). Sexual bullying: Addressing the gap between bullying and dating violence. *Advances in Nursing Science, 31,* 95–105.

McCann, J. T. (1998). Subtypes of stalking (obsessional following) in adolescents. *Journal of Adolescence, 21,* 667–675.

Meloy, J. R. (1988). *The psychopathic mind: Origins, dynamics, and treatment.* Northvale, NJ: Jason Aronson.

Miller, S., Gorman-Smith, D., Sullivan, T., Orpinas, P., & Simon, T. R. (2009). Parent and peer predictors of physical dating violence perpetration in early adolescence: Tests of moderation and gender differences. *Journal of Clinical Child and Adolescent Psychiatry, 38,* 538–550.

Mohandie, K. (2006). The RECON typology of stalking: Reliability and validity based upon a large sample of North American stalkers. *Journal of Forensic Sciences, 51,* 147–155.

Purcell, R., Moller, B., Flower, T., & Mullen, P. E. (2009). Stalking among juveniles. *British Journal of Psychiatry, 194,* 451–455.

Rosenstein, D. S., & Horowitz, H. A. (1996). Adolescent attachment and psychopathology. *Journal of Consulting and Clinical Psychology, 64,* 244–253.

Sheridan, L. P., & Grant, T. (2007). Is cyberstalking different? *Psychology, Crime and Law, 13,* 627–640.

Shute, R., Owens, L., & Slee, P. (2008). Everyday victimization of adolescent girls by boys: Sexual harassment, bullying or aggression? *Sex Roles, 58,* 477–489.

Simon, T. R., Miller, S., Gorman-Smith, D., Orpinas, P., & Sullivan, T. (2010). Physical dating violence norms and behavior among sixth-grade students from four U.S. sites. *Journal of Early Adolescence, 30,* 395–409.

Spitzberg, B. H., & Hoobler, G. (2002). Cyberstalking and the technologies of interpersonal terrorism. *New Media and Society, 4,* 71–92.

Spriggs, A. L., Halpern, C. T., & Martin, S. L. (2009). Continuity of adolescent and early adult partner violence victimization: Association with witnessing violent crime in adolescence. *Journal of Epidemiology and Community Health, 63,* 741–748.

Steinberg, L. (2005). Cognitive and affective development in adolescence. *Trends in Cognitive Science, 9,* 69–74.

Theriot, M. T. (2008). Conceptual and methodological considerations for assessment and prevention of adolescent dating violence and stalking at school. *Children and Schools, 30,* 223–233.

Timmons Fritz, P. A., & Smith Slep, A. M. (2009). Stability of physical and psychological adolescent dating aggression across time and partners. *Journal of Clinical Child and Adolescent Psychiatry, 38,* 303–314.

Tjaden, P., & Thoennes, N. (1997). *Stalking in America: Findings from the National Violence Against Women Survey.* Denver, CO: Center for Policy Research.

Tokunga, R. S. (2010). Following you home from school: A critical review and synthesis of research on cyberbullying victimization. *Computers in Human Behavior, 26,* 277–287.

APPENDIX

Organizations Concerned with Teen Violence and Victimization

Michele A. Paludi

The following is a list of resources dealing with teen violence and victimization. This list serves as a good starting point for parents, adolescents, teachers, counselors, and administrators seeking additional information about teen violence. This list is neither complete nor exhaustive. These resources are not to be viewed as substitutes for counseling and/or legal advice.

Internet Safety Sites for Parents

www.wiredsafety.org
www.cybertipline.com
www.missingkids.com

Internet Safety Sites for Adolescents

www.safeteens.com
www.kidshealth.org
www.kidshealth.org/teen/safety

Organizations

Adults and Children Together Against Violence
   http://actagainstviolence.apa.org/
Advocates for Youth
   http://www.advocatesforyouth.org/about/ywoclc.htm
American Association of University Women
   www.aauw.org
American Psychological Association
   www.apa.org
Antistalking Website
   www.antistalking.com
Anti-Violence Project
   http://gayteens.about.com
Anti-Violence Resource Guide
   http://www.feminist.com/antiviolence/online.html
Break the Cycle
   http://www.breakthecycle.org
Business and Professional Women's Organization
   www.bpwusa.org
California Coalition Against Sexual Assault
   http://calcasa.org
Center for the Study and Prevention of Violence
   http://www.colorado.edu/cspv/
Centers for Disease Control and Prevention
   http://www.cdc.gov
Child Find of America
   http://www.childfindofamerica.org
Children of the Night
   http://www.childrenofthenight.org/
Choose Respect
   www.chooserespect.org
Common Sense about Kids and Guns
   http://www.kidsandguns.org
Empower Program
   www.empowered.org

Equal Employment Opportunity Commission
   www.eeoc.gov
Equal Rights Advocates
   www.equalrights.org
Family Violence Prevention Fund
   www.endabuse.org
Feminist Majority Foundation
   www.feminist.org
Flirting or Hurting?
   http://www.wgby.org/edu/flirt/fhmain.html
Focus Adolescent Services
   http://www.focusas.com/Violence.html
Gay, Lesbian and Straight Education Network
   www.glsen.org
Girls Inc.
   http://www.girlsinc.org/index.html
GLBT National Youth Talkline
   http://www.ginh.org/talkline/index.html
HOPE
   http://www.breakthecycle.org/join-us-nat-hope.html
KidsHealth
   http://www.kidshealth.org/teen/your_mind/relationships/abuse.html
Liz Claiborne: Love Is Not Abuse
   http://www.loveisnotabuse.com
Love Doesn't Have to Hurt
   http://www.apa.org/pl/pii/teen
Love Is Respect, National Teen Dating Abuse Helpline
   http://www.loveisrespect.org
MADE (Moms and Dads for Education to Stop Teen Dating Abuse)
   www.loveisnotabuse.com/made/
Men Can Stop Rape
   www.mencanstoprape.org
Mothers Against Teen Violence
   http://www.matvinc.org
Ms. Foundation for Women
   www.ms.foundation.org

National Alliance of Gang Investigators' Associations
    http://www. nagia.org
National Center for Missing and Exploited Children
    www.missingkids.com
National Center for Prosecution of Child Abuse
    http://www.ndaa.org/ncpca_home.html
National Center for Victims of Crime
    http://www.ncyc.org
National Center for Violence Prevention
    www.netam.net
National Center on Domestic and Sexual Violence
    www.ncsv.org
National Coalition Against Domestic Violence
    www.ncadv.org
National Coalition Against Violent Athletes
    http://www.ncava.org/
National Domestic Violence Hotline
    http://www.ndvh.org
National Hopeline Network
    http://www.hopeline.com
National Organization for Men Against Sexism
    www.nomas.org
National Organization for Women
    www.now.org
National Runaway Hotline
    http://www.nrscrisisline.org
National Sexual Violence Resource Center
    www.nsvrc.org
National Teen Dating Abuse Helpline
    http://www.loveisrespect.org
National Women's Law Center
    www.nwic.org
National Youth Violence Prevention Resources Center
    www.safeyouth.org

Office of Violence Against Women, U.S. Department of Justice
www.ojp.usdoj.gov/vawo

Polly Klaas Foundation
http://www.pollyklaas.org

Prevent Cyberbullying and Internet Harassment
www.cyberbully411.com

Preventing Violence in our Schools
www.extension.umn.edu

Promote Truth
www.promotetruth.org

Rape, Abuse and Incest National Network
www.rainn.org

Security on Campus
www.securityoncampus.org

Stalking Resource Center
www.ncvc.org/src/Main.aspx

Striving to Reduce Youth Violence Everywhere
http://www.safeyouth.gov/Pages/Home.aspx

Students Against Violence Everywhere
www.nationalsave.org

Teen Dating Violence
http://www.coolnurse.com/teen_dating_violence.html

Teen Relationships
http://www.teenrelationships.org

Teens Against Gang Violence
http://www.manta.com/c/mmft8gm/teens-against-gang-violence

That's Not Cool
http://www.thatsnotcool.com

Trust Betrayed
www.wvdhhr.org

U.S. Department of Education, Office for Civil Rights
www.ed.gov

Womenslaw
http://www.womenslaw.org

About the Editor and Contributors

The Editor

Michele A. Paludi, PhD, is the series editor for Women's Psychology and for Women and Careers in Management for Praeger. She is the author/editor of 38 college textbooks and of more than 170 scholarly articles and conference presentations on sexual harassment, campus violence, psychology of women, gender, and discrimination. Her book *Ivory Power: Sexual Harassment on Campus* (SUNY Press, 1990) received the 1992 Myers Center Award for Outstanding Book on Human Rights in the United States. Dr. Paludi served as chair of the U.S. Department of Education's Subpanel on the Prevention of Violence, Sexual Harassment, and Alcohol and Other Drug Problems in Higher Education. She was one of six scholars in the United States to be selected for this subpanel. She also was a consultant to and a member of former New York State governor Mario Cuomo's Task Force on Sexual Harassment. Dr. Paludi serves as an expert witness for court proceedings and administrative hearings on sexual harassment. She has had extensive experience in conducting training programs and investigations of sexual harassment and other Equal Employment Opportunity issues for businesses and educational institutions. In addition, Dr. Paludi has held faculty positions at Franklin & Marshall College, Kent State University, Hunter College, Union College, and Union Graduate College, where she directs the human resource management certificate program. She is on the faculty in the School of Management. She was recently named "Woman of the Year" by the Business and Professional Women in Schenectady, New York. She is currently the Elihu Root Peace Fund Professor in Women's Studies at Hamilton College.

The Contributors

Stuart C. Aitken is Professor and Chair of Geography at San Diego State University and Director of the Center for Interdisciplinary Studies of Young People and Space (ISYS). His research interests include film and media, critical social theory, qualitative methods, children, families, and communities. Stuart's recent and forthcoming books include *Young People: Border Spaces and Revolutionary Imaginations* (Routledge, 2011), *Qualitative Geographies* (Sage, 2010), *The Awkward Spaces of Fathering* (Ashgate, 2009), *Global Childhoods* (Routledge, 2008), *Philosophies, People, Places and Practices* (Sage, 2004), *Geographies of Young People: The Morally Contested Spaces of Identity* (Routledge, 2001), *Family Fantasies and Community Space* (Rutgers University Press, 1998), *Place, Space, Situation and Spectacle: A Geography of Film* (Rowman and Littlefield, 1994), and *Putting Children in Their Place* (Association of American Geographers, 1994). He has published more than 150 articles in academic journals, including the *Annals of the AAG, Geographical Review, Antipode, Transactions of the IBG, CaGIS, Society and Space, The Journal of Geography,* and *Environment and Planning A,* as well as in various edited book collections and encyclopedias. Aitken is past coeditor of *The Professional Geographer* and is current North American editor of *Children's Geographies*. He has worked for the United Nations on issues of children's rights, migration, and dislocation.

Donald E. Colley III is a second-year PhD student in the Joint Doctoral Program in Geography at San Diego State University and is currently in residence at the University of California–Santa Barbara. His dissertation research is broadly focused on violence, health, masculinity, and youths. Colley received an MA in geography from Kent State University in Kent, Ohio, and a BA in geography from Concord University in Athens, West Virginia. Previous research has explored the dimensions of belonging and exclusion in the context of sports and fitness. He has also presented on the sociospatial aspects of fraternity hazing, the importance of considering geography in fat studies research, and the resolution of violence in the writings of Robert Frost.

David DiLillo received a BA from Rhodes College and a PhD in clinical psychology from Oklahoma State University. He is currently an associate professor and director of clinical training at the University of Nebraska–Lincoln. His primary research interests lie in the area of family violence, including child maltreatment and marital and relationship violence. Recent projects have focused on the long-term adjustment of adults who have experienced various forms of childhood trauma and maltreatment (e.g., sexual, physical, and psychological abuse, and neglect). His work has explored several aspects of this issue, including the interpersonal functioning of adult survivors in both couple and parent-child relationships. His research has been funded by NIMH and NICHD. His most recent project is a longitudinal study of sexual revictimization.

Rukudzo Amanda Dzwairo is a transfer undergraduate student in psychology at the University of South Africa. She is a coauthor of published research conducted during her studies at the University of Evansville. This research won a Psi Chi award at the Midwestern Psychological Association Conference in 2009. She studies social psychological factors that shape perceptions of juvenile offenders and victims within the justice and legal system.

Thomas M. Evans, PhD, is a clinical and forensic psychologist. For 12 years he served as the clinical director of the Cuyahoga County Juvenile Court Diagnostic Clinic. He is currently in independent practice and devotes his time to forensic assessment of juveniles and adults. His research interests include stalking by juveniles, stalking in the workplace, and threat assessment.

Katlyn M. Sorenson Farnum, BS, is a doctoral student in the joint social psychology and law program at the University of Nebraska–Lincoln. Her research focuses primarily on understanding the causes and effects of discrimination and stigma within the legal system. She also studies juror perceptions of offenders and their victims. She is an Othmer Fellow and works closely with the Weibling Project on the psycholegal study and treatment of discrimination.

Ann Flynn, NTBSc (Hons), is a primary school teacher and was an education officer with the Cool School antibullying program for nine years. She has extensive experience in working with students, parents, and teachers. She was involved in the development of the program, training of teachers and parents, and research associated with the program. She is coauthor of Cool School publications and research papers.

Joanna L. Goodwin is a graduate student in psychology at the University of Texas at Tyler. Her undergraduate degree is in psychology. She worked as a case manager for children at a community mental health and mental retardation facility for 2 and a half years. She also worked as a case manager in a residential treatment center for 2 and a half years. Goodwin is currently a foster care and adoption case manager for a nonprofit organization. She has been a member of the Air National Guard for 18 years, 14 of which have been in Texas. As an enlisted member for 15 years, she maintained aircraft, and she has been deployed to the Middle East, serving in Operations Enduring Freedom and Iraqi Freedom. She received her commission as an officer and is now a captain, serving as the executive officer in charge of the administrative personnel for the 136th Maintenance Group, Texas Air National Guard.

Katie E. Griffin received her master's degree in forensic psychology at City University of New York's John Jay College of Criminal Justice. Her research interests include microaggressions and mental health, as well as hate crimes and associated legislation.

Todd Hendrix, PC, PhD, currently serves as the director of the Cuyahoga County Juvenile Court Diagnostic Clinic in Ohio and is also an adjunct professor at Cleveland State University.

Britney Hilbun is a graduate student in the general clinical psychology program at the University of Texas at Tyler (UTT). She received her undergraduate degree in psychology from UTT as well. She has worked as a research assistant in the psychology department for several years and has done volunteer work with the local crisis center for women and children who have been victims of domestic violence or sexual abuse.

Deborah James, PhD, BS (Hons), is a research psychologist with the Meath Child and Adolescent Mental Health Services. She has extensive research experience in mental health settings from childhood to old age. Her research interests include bullying, relational aggression, and epidemiology of mental health problems. She has been involved with the Cool School antibullying program for more than 13 years. Her roles included the development of the program, training of teachers, and evaluation of the program. She is author of journal articles and coauthor of a number of Cool School publications. She is currently training as an integrative psychotherapist.

Eric G. Jamison II is currently a third-year doctoral student at the University of Maryland, School of Public Health, and also holds a Master of Science degree in applied chemistry from Delaware State University. His current research interests include intervention and health promotion as it relates to underserved populations, using a community-based participatory research approach. He is particularly interested in adolescent violence, aggression, gang violence, and the associated risk and resilience factors.

About the Editor and Contributors

Ashley Kravitz is originally from Buffalo, New York. She earned a bachelor's degree in business management from St. John Fisher College and graduated from Union Graduate College in June 2011 with a master's in business administration. Ashley currently works for the New York State Office of Mental Health in Albany as a budget analyst. She enjoys running, reading, and collecting beach glass.

Jeanette Krenek has spent most of her life living overseas in various countries. She graduated from Le Tourneau University in Longview, Texas, with a BS in psychology in 2007. Krenek then provided intensive case management services to individuals with chronic mental illness for Community Healthcore from 2007 to 2010. She is currently a full-time graduate student in the clinical psychology program at the University of Texas at Tyler.

Maria Lawlor, MD, MRCPsych, is director of the Cool School antibullying program and consultant child and adolescent psychiatrist with Meath Child and Adolescent Mental Health Services. She has extensive experience in working with young people with psychiatric/psychological difficulties. She is founder of the Stay Safe program, which is a school-based program aimed at empowering children to recognize and resist abuse/victimization. This program has been implemented nationally within Ireland and in the United States. She is also involved in research projects examining bullying, epidemiology of mental health, child sexual abuse prevention, and Asperger's syndrome. She is author of books and journal articles.

Paula K. Lundberg-Love is a professor of psychology at the University of Texas at Tyler (UTT) and the Ben R. Fisch Endowed Professor in Humanitarian Affairs for 2001–2004. Her undergraduate degree is in chemistry, and she worked as a chemist at a pharmaceutical company for five years prior to earning her doctorate in physiological psychology, with an emphasis in psychopharmacology. After a three-year postdoctoral fellowship in nutrition and behavior in the Department of Preventive Medicine at Washington University School of Medicine in St. Louis, she assumed her academic position at UTT, where she teaches classes in psychopharmacology, behavioral neuroscience, physiological psychology, sexual victimization, and family violence. Subsequent to her academic appointment, Lundberg-Love pursued postgraduate training and is a licensed professional counselor. She is a member of Tyler Counseling and Assessment Center, where she provides therapeutic services for victims of sexual assault, child sexual abuse, and domestic violence. She has conducted a long-term research study on women who were victims of childhood incestuous abuse, constructed a therapeutic program for their recovery, and documented its effectiveness upon their recovery. She is the author of nearly 100 publications and presentations and is coeditor of *Violence and Sexual Abuse at Home: Current Issues in Spousal Battering and Child Maltreatment,* as well as *Intimate Violence Against Women: When Spouses, Partners, or Lovers Attack.* As a result of her training in psychopharmacology and child maltreatment, her expertise has been sought as a consultant on various death penalty appellate cases in the state of Texas.

Carol MacKinnon-Lewis is a professor in the Department of Child and Family Studies, University of South Florida. She received her PhD in child development from the University of Georgia. For 25 years, her research focus has been on the identification of family processes as they contribute to children's social emotional competence and how variations in youths' experiences within their families influence their relationships in other contexts, with a particular interest in their aggressive behavior with peers. More recently, her research has included the use of technology as a vehicle for the dissemination and implementation of preventive interventions and practices to the field. Funded by NSF, U.S. Department of Education, NIMH, NICHD, and the William T. Grant Foundation, MacKinnon-Lewis's work has been published in a number of professional journals, including *Developmental Psychology, Child Development, Development and Psychopathology, Journal of Family Psychology,* and *Social Development.*

Robert F. Marcus, PhD, is an associate professor of human development at the University of Maryland, College Park. Since joining the faculty in the Department of Human Development in 1973, Marcus has balanced his academic duties with his clinical work in the community. Marcus holds a PhD in human development and family studies from Pennsylvania State University. He has published or presented more than 100 papers, and for the past 20 years, he has focused his work entirely on violence in adolescence and emerging adulthood, the causes of dating violence, and personality and situational correlates of aggression and violence. Currently, Marcus is a licensed and practicing psychologist at Sheppard Pratt of Howard County, in Columbia, Maryland.

Jennifer L. Martin, PhD, has worked in public education for 15 years, 13 of those as the department head of English at an alternative high school for at-risk students in the Detroit metropolitan area. She is also a special lecturer at Oakland University, where she teaches in the Education Specialist

Degree Program and in the women and gender studies department. As an educational leader, Martin has been an advocate for at-risk students, and she has received several district, state, and national awards and recognitions for her advocacy, mentorship, and research. She has served as a mentor to high school, undergraduate, and graduate students, as well as to new teachers in a variety of areas, such as writing and publishing, career and leadership development, and advocacy. Martin is the editor of the two-volume *Women as Leaders in Education* (Praeger, in press). She has conducted research and published numerous peer-reviewed articles and book chapters on bullying and harassment, peer sexual harassment, educational equity, mentoring, issues of social justice, service learning, and teaching at-risk students. Martin is often an invited speaker at universities and nonprofit organizations on the aforementioned topics. As action vice president of Michigan NOW, she engages in volunteer Title IX education and legal advocacy work. Through this work she has been asked to comment on proposed Michigan legislation on National Public Radio.

Maureen C. McHugh, PhD, is a professor of psychology at Indiana University of Pennsylvania, where she teaches graduate and undergraduate courses in gender and in diversity. She has been teaching courses in the psychology of women and psychology of human sexuality since 1975. She has published journal articles and chapters in the areas of methods, violence against women, and gender differences, including chapters in many texts and handbooks. In 2005, she collaborated with Irene Frieze to edit two special issues on gender and intimate partner violence in *Psychology of Women Quarterly* and in *Sex Roles*. McHugh was awarded the Christine Ladd Franklin Award, for her contributions to feminist psychology, and the Florence Denmark Distinguished Mentoring Award, for feminist mentoring, from the Association for Women in Psychology.

Niamh Murphy, NDC BA (Hons), is a group therapist with the Meath Child and Adolescent Mental Health Services. She has worked with the program for eight years. In addition to working with the development and evaluation team, she has devised and implemented school-based interventions for dealing with victims and bullies. She has extensive experience in working with young people with emotional and behavioral difficulties. She is coauthor of a number of Cool School publications.

Kevin L. Nadal, PhD, is an assistant professor of psychology and mental health counseling at John Jay College of Criminal Justice at the City

University of New York. He earned his doctorate in counseling psychology from Columbia University. He has published several works focusing on Filipino American, ethnic minority, and LGBTQ issues in the fields of psychology and education. He is a fellow of the Robert Wood Johnson Foundation and is the author of the books *Filipino American Psychology: A Handbook of Theory, Research, and Clinical Practice* and *Filipino American Psychology: A Collection of Personal Narratives*.

Lindsay Marie Pantlin is a master's student at the University of Texas at Tyler (UTT) in the general clinical psychology program. She graduated with her bachelor's degree in psychology from UTT. During her undergraduate program she was a member of Psi Chi and Alpha Chi. She also collaborated on research projects with two professors at UTT. She is a volunteer at the East Texas Crisis Center and acts as an advocate for victims of domestic abuse and sexual assault who go to hospitals in Tyler. Lindsay is an early intervention specialist with the Early Childhood Intervention program at the Andrews Center in Tyler. She works with children who have developmental delays or atypical development.

Andrea Poet is a graduate student in the doctoral program in clinical psychology at Indiana University of Pennsylvania. She is currently involved with research on gender and aggression, including intimate partner violence and the sexual derogation of women.

Allison L. Skinner, MA, is an adjunct faculty member of the psychology department at the University of Southern Indiana and lab manager of Margaret Stevenson's Psychology and the Law Laboratory at the University of Evansville. Her research focuses on the impact of prejudice, stereotypes, and social biases in the legal system.

Margaret C. Stevenson, PhD, is assistant professor of psychology at the University of Evansville. She received her doctorate in social psychology from the University of Illinois at Chicago in 2008. Her dissertation was awarded the 2008 American Psychological Association (APA) Division 37 Dissertation Award; APA Division 37's Section on Child Maltreatment honorary mention; and the 2008 APA Division 41, American Psychology and Law Society (AP-LS) First Place dissertation award, and she is currently published in *Psychology, Public Policy, and Law*. She was also the 2010 recipient of the APA Division 37's Early Career Award in Child Maltreatment. Stevenson studies various issues at the intersection of children, psychology, and the law. Specifically, she examines social psychological factors that shape perceptions of child offenders and victims. Stevenson also serves on the editorial board for two professional journals and was appointed as a committee member of APA Division 41's (AP-LS) Dissertation Awards Committee.

Catherine R. Swiderski is a doctoral candidate in clinical psychology at Indiana University of Pennsylvania (IUP). Her dissertation research focuses on the experience of psychological abuse as a form of intimate partner violence experienced by men. Swiderski is a contributor to an ongoing viole-nce prevention program involving the integration of scholarship on violence against women into the psychology curriculum. She published a chapter on intimate partner violence and presented a poster at the American Psychological Association National Summit on Interpersonal Violence and Abuse (Dallas, 2010). Currently, Swiderski conducts crisis intervention counseling at a domestic violence shelter, and she counsels students at the Counseling Center at IUP. Her previous experience includes counseling clients with issues of trauma and violence at a community mental health center and volunteering with a sexual assault prevention program and at a residential treatment facility for abused adolescent girls.

Christine M. Wienke Totura, PhD, is a senior policy researcher with the Morrison Institute for Public Policy at Arizona State University. Totura's work focuses on examining the implications of behavioral health and educational policies and practices for communities, youths, and families both in Arizona and nationwide. Totura is specifically involved in research on the assessment of adolescent aggression and social development, as well as systemic factors impacting implementation of public health programming in schools and communities. She has published and presented extensively in these areas and has obtained numerous federal and local grants and contracts. Totura earned her Bachelor of Science degree in psychology and criminal justice from Loyola University in Chicago and her Master of Arts and Doctor of Philosophy degrees in clinical psychology from the University of South Florida. Additionally, Totura is a licensed clinical psychologist in Arizona.

Kate Walsh received a BA from Boston University and is a PhD candidate in clinical psychology at the University of Nebraska–Lincoln. She is currently a predoctoral clinical intern at the Medical University of South Carolina. Her research interests lie primarily in uncovering risk factors for adolescent and adult sexual revictimization. Recent projects, including her NIMH-funded dissertation study, have focused on laboratory examinations of emotion regulation and established risk factors (e.g., sexual risk taking, post-traumatic stress disorder) for sexual revictimization.

Index

Abdul-Kabir, S., 117
acquaintance rape, 205
adolescent employment and sexual harassment, 166–168
adolescent girls: cognitive maturity of, 181–184; mental health of, 168. *See also* sexual harassment of adolescent girls
adolescent sexual assault (ASA), 204
adolescents: metal health impact of sexual harassment, 168–170; workplace sexual harassment, 156–157
aggression: peer aggression, 112; physical aggression, 111, 222; prevalence of types by gender, 110–111; relational aggression, 42, 108, 222; verbal aggression, 111. *See also* microaggressions
aggressive girls, 48–49
Aitken, S. C., 91
Allen, M., 156
alternative dispute methods, 177
American Association of University Women (AAUW), 40, 155
American Association of University Women (AAUW) study, 161, 168, 183
anger as source of power, 50
Anger Coping program, 117
anti-bullying program elements, 118
Antonishak, J., 62
Aronoff, J., 224
Arriaga, X. B., 228
Ashbaker, B., 156
Ashley, O. S., 226
attachment bond obstacles, 253

attachment psychology, 249
attachment theory, 252–253
attention deficit/hyperactivity disorder (ADHD), 209
Austin, B., 11
aversive racial theory, 61–62, 68

bad reputation, 46
Barickman, R., 169, 172, 174, 179
Barnes, A., 133
Baron, R. M., 71
Barron, C., 48, 49
Basow, S. A., 40–41, 43, 46–47, 53
Bauman, K. E., 228
Bearinger, L. H., 11, 12
behavior change intervention program, 119
behavioral response of LGBT people, 8
Berson, L., 166
Berson, M., 166
betrayal feelings, 211
black juvenile sex offenders, 57
black women: physical strength, 69; stereotypes of sexual activity and dominance, 68
Blueprints Bullying Prevention Program, 107
Bogart, K., 163
books on mean girls, 42
Bottoms, B. L., 57, 63, 69, 70
Brain, P., 131
BrainPower program, 117
Brockopp, K., 232

Brown, C., 182–183
Brown, L. M., 42, 43, 50, 53
Browne, A., 211
Brumberg, J. J., 40, 41, 45, 47, 48
Bucceri, J. M., 5, 6
bulimia, 199
Bulimic Investigatory Test, 199
bullies: classifications of, 106; ethnic identification, 111; female, 42; gender differences of, 110, 113; hypotheses of, 4; motivations, 4; parents of, 114; prevalence of, 180; profiles of, 110, 112–113; research on, 118; response to, 96; social behavior of, 108–109; stereotypes of, 42; teacher response to, 128; zero-tolerance policies impact, 117
bullying: acknowledgement of, 15; as microassaults, 8; as microinsults, 8; as microinvalidations, 8; by girls, 39; from peers, 11; gender differences of, 110–111; geography of, 95; group discussion about, 15; long-term impact of, 112; microaggressions leading to, 16; programs to combat, 127; psychological consequences of, 16; vs. sexual harassment in schools, 179–184; vs. stalking, 245; vs. teacher discipline, 129–130
bullying, steps to take regarding: about, 140–146; denial, dealing with, 144–146; intervention, 141; interviews, 141; relational aggression management, 146–149; restorative justice approach, 142; what not to do, 142–144
bullying and victimization: as normative behavior, 131–132; by race and ethnicity, 111; genetic precursors of, 113; school climate and, 114–115
bullying in middle school: about, 105–106; bullying roles, 108–110; consequences for bullies, victims, and bully/victims, 111–113; cultural differences in expressions of, 110–111; definition of, 107; environmental impacts, 114–115; future research directions, 118–119; prevention and intervention, 115–118; risk factors for bullying and victimization, 113; statistics of, 106–107; types of, 107–108
Bullying Prevention Program, 117
bullying roles: about, 108; bully/victims, 109–110; defenders, 110; henchmen/contributors, 110; peer group-observers, 110; victims, 109
bullying sociogram: implementation steps, 138–140; preventative steps, 137–138; procedural steps, 138; reactive steps, 138; sociogram use, 138–140
bully/victims: behavior problems, 109–110; characteristics of, 113; dynamic of, 41, 92; future of, 111; normative problems, 131
Butler, J., 99
Byers, E. S., 225, 226

Cao, Y. H., 52
Capodilupo, C. M., 5, 6
Carter, Jimmy, 59
Cate, R., 223
Centers for Disease Control and Prevention (CDC), 24, 212, 249
Chesler, P., 41–42
Chew, E., 232
child abuse, 193
child or adolescent sexual abuse (CASA): described, 204; physical health impact of, 208; post-traumatic stress disorder (PTSD) and, 209
child sexual abuse and adolescent sexual assault and revictimization: about, 203; definitions of, 204; outcomes of child or adolescent sexual abuse, 208–210; prevalence of childhood and adolescent victimization and revictimization, 205; prevention and treatment, 212–213; risk factors for victimization and revictimization, 205–207; socioemotional context of victimization, 204–205; theories explaining the effects of sexual abuse and revictimization, 210–211; theories of risk factors for victimization and revictimization, 207–208; conclusions, 213–214

Index

child sexual abuse (CSA): and sexual victimization, 205; described, 204
children, education process for, 88
Choose Respect program, 234
chronic groups, trajectory of violence for, 26
Civil Rights Act Title VII, 158–159
class observation, 136–137
Clement, Tyler, 3
cognitive maturity of adolescent girls, 181–184
Collins, R., 95
Columbine High School, 105
compulsory hetero sexuality, 231
conceptual model for managing bullying: about, 134–135; bullying sociogram, 137–140; class observation, 136–137; confidential questionnaires, 135–136
conduct disorder (CD), 209
Connolly, J., 11, 12
Cormier, S., 43
Coronado v. State of Texas, 73
Corpus, M. J. H., 6, 7
Courtois, C. A, 194
Craig, W., 11, 12
Cresswell, T., 98
culture of fear, 84
cyberabuse, 222–223
cyberbullying, 3, 108
cyberstalking, 252
cyberstalking vs. sexual harassment, 166–168
Cyr, M., 198

Daly, M., 33
date rape, 205
dating skills, 230–231
dating violence, 221; metal health impact of, 228; sexual health impacts of, 229; teens' views on, 232
DeBlase, G., 50
Dedman, B., 102n4
defenders, 110
DeGennaro, J. T., 62
developmental criminology, 30, 31
Dewey, L., 165
direct bullying, 107

discrimination, 183
dismissing attachment, 253
Dixon, Marcus, 58–59
Dohrn, B., 49
Donnella, A. G., 63
Dovidio, J. F., 63
Drobac, J., 157
DSM-IV-TR, 198
Duffy, J., 169
Dupper, D. R., 89–90
dynamic of powerlessness, 211
Dzwairo, R. A., 65, 70

early desisters, trajectory of violence for, 26
eating disorders, 40
Education Act of 1972 Title IX, 158–159
Edwards, R. W., 224, 233
Elkind, D., 181, 182
Elliot, William, 58–59
Ellsworth, P. C., 61, 62, 63
embarrassment, 226
emerging adulthood: and romantic involvement, 24, 31; defined, 24; described, 31; personality evolving during, 30–31; prevalence rates of violence, 23
emerging adulthood theory, 23, 30
Émile (Rousseau), 87
environmental impacts: family context, 114; school climate, 114–115
Equal Employment Opportunity Commission (EEOC), 157, 159, 166–168, 176, 177–179
Erikson, E., 38
erotomanic behavior, 244
Ertesvag, S., 180
Espelage, D., 180
Espeland, P., 164, 168
Esqueda, C. W., 65
Etherington, K., 197
Evans, T. M., 245
evolutionary prospect theory, 30
evolutionary theory, 23, 32, 33
exclusionary bullying, 99
exclusionary violence, 98, 99
exosystem factors, 208
explicit discrimination, 5

family of origin dysfunction, 205–206
Faragher v. Boca Raton, 170
female adolescents, physical abuse by and of, 224
female aggression, 42
female friendships, 42–43
female sexuality, 46
females: policing of other females, 49; self-sensorship of, 38–39. *See also* black women; girls
feminine norms of sexual behavior, 46
feminine sexist stereotypes, 42
feminism, 182–183
Ferron, J., 166
Filipas, H. H., 198
Fine, M., 45, 47
Fineran, S., 156, 168, 169, 171
Finkelhor, D., 211
Flower, T., 244, 247–248, 249
forced-rape case, 69
Ford, A., 229
Foshee, V. A., 226, 228
Foucauldian perspective, 93
Foucault, M., 50
Freed, L. H., 11
Freedner, N., 11
Friend to Friend program, 117
Frieze, I. H., 225, 229

Gaertner, S. L., 63
Gallopin, C., 226, 227
Galloway, D., 133
gender conformity, 11
gender microaggression towards LGBT people, 8
genetic precursors of bullying and victimization, 113
Gilligan, C., 39–40, 42, 43
Girl Scouts, 155
Girl Scouts of America study, 165, 181
girls: adolescent girls, 168, 181–184; aggressive girls, 48–49; bullying by, 39; incarceration of, 49; mean girls, 42; self-esteem of, 50–51; suicide by, 37; suicide risk of, 40; violence physical assault by, 37. *See also* sexual harassment of adolescent girls

girls and women: anger as source of power for, 50; sexual desire of, 45–46
Giroux, H. A., 52
Glassner, B., 84
grievance procedures, 176–177
Grossman, M., 117
Gruber, J., 156, 168, 169, 171
Gullan, R. L., 117
Gunn, Sakia, 13

Haegerich, T. M., 70
Hall, G. Stanley, 88
Hamit, S., 15
Haney, C., 73
Hanmer, T. J., 42
Harmon, T., 46, 47
Harris, A., 41
Harris, Eric, 105
Harrison, L. A., 65
Haw, R. M., 62
Healthy Relationships program, 234
Heaton, E., 156
Helms, R. W., 228
Henton, J., 223
Hickman, L. J., 224
Hill, C., 163
Hispanic juvenile sex offenders and victims, 73
Holder, A. M. B., 5, 6
Holt, M., 180
homicides: among urban males, 26; at schools vs. homes, 85; bully/victims cycle and, 85; by intimate partners of girls, 228; decline in, 33; in urban America, 33; statistics, 24
Homma, Y., 11, 12
hostile attribution bias, 115
hostile environment sexual harassment, 158–159
Hotaling, G. T., 233
How the Other Half Lives (Riis), 88
Hunter, Tyra, 13

identity politics, 100
Iglesias, E., 43
In a Different Voice (Gilligan), 39
incarceration of girls, 49

incest: age and risk of, 197–198; developmental effects of, 197–198; dissociation and post-traumatic stress disorder (PTSD), 198; obesity and eating disorders, 199; psychological effects, 199–200
inclusionary bullying, 99
inclusionary violence, 97
Incredible Years program, 116
indirect bullying, 107–108
in-group biases, 63–64
inner-city school violence, 91
internalized sexism, 42
interracial relationships, 64–65
Interventions: primary interventions, 233–234; secondary interventions, 234–235; conclusions, 235–236
intimacy-seeking stalkers, 245
intimate partner violence (IPV), 85, 221
Irving, L. M., 199
Is Your Daughter Safe at Work (PBS program), 166
Issa, M. A., 15

Jackson, H., 68
Jawad, A. F., 117
Jaycox, L. H., 224
Johnson, B., 198
Johnson, M. P., 225
juries: race salience in, 61–62; racial bias by, 60–61
juvenile sex offenders: of racial minority groups, 73; perception of, 57; recidivism, 58; registration support and, 71; registration support and race of, 71
juvenile stalking: about, 243–244; assessment of juvenile stalkers, 248–249; attachment, 252–254; cyberbullying, 251–252; future study, 255; physical violence by, 254; prevalence of violence in, 249; research on, 244–247; risk assessment and management, 254–255; socially awkward stalking types, 246; socially popular stalking types, 246–247; stalking tactics, 248; studies on, 245; teen dating violence, 249–251

Kalodner, C. R., 40
Kenkel, M., 198
Kenny, D. A., 71
Klebold, Dylan, 105
Koch, G. G., 228
Kowalski, R., 49, 92

Lacombe, D., 48, 49
Larkin, J., 169
late desisters, trajectory of violence for, 26
Laub, J., 31
Leaper, C., 182–183
Leary, M. R., 92
LeFebvre, H., 93, 101
Leff, S. S., 117
Leigh, L., 226, 227
Lera, M. J., 132
lesbian, gay, bisexual, and transgender (LGBT) adolescents, 9–10
lesbian, gay, bisexual, and transgender (LGBT) children, 4
lesbian, gay, bisexual, and transgender (LGBT) people: behavioral response of, 8; cognitive response of, 8; emotional response of, 8; help seeking behavior, 227; microaggression towards, 6; microinsults, 6; murders of, 13; physical and mental health problems, 14; rights of, 6; stereotypical image of, 17
lesbian, gay, bisexual, and transgender (LGBT) teens: microaggressions from peers, 11; microaggressions within schools/educational systems, 10; microaggressions within the family, 12; of color, 12–13; protective factors, 12
lesbian, gay, bisexual, and transgender (LGBT) youths: depression in, 14; suicide attempts by, 14
Levy, A., 175, 179
Lewis-Charp, H., 52
Linder, G. F., 228
Lindsay Ann Burke Act, 234
Livingston, N. A., 229
love and romantic notions, 231
love obsessional behavior, 244
Loveless, Tom, 87
Lowery, Joseph, 58

Lund, I., 180
Lynch, M., 73
Lyons, N. P., 42

macrosystem factors, 208
Males, Mike, 101n1
Marchant, R., 91
marital commitment, 32
Marquart, B. S., 224, 233
Martin, J., 183
mass schoolyard shooting, 91
Massey, D., 94
Mather, Cotton, 87
McCann, J. T., 244
McCluskey-Fawcett, K., 199
McDuff, P., 198
McHugh, M. C., 229
mean girls, 42
media image of femininity, 37
media messages, damage from, 41
media's influence on teen violence and victimization: about, 37–39; alienation and body image, 39–41; alienation through social space, 41–44; anger and the "bad" girl, 48–50; hope of education, 50–53; sexuality, desire, and the bad reputation, 44–48; conclusion, 53–54
Meissner, C. A., 62
Meloy, R. J., 245
mental health: bullying impact on, 15; dating violence impact on, 228; gender microaggression, 8; impact responses on, 169; Internet and video games use, 119; of adolescent girls, 168; of LBGT teens, 9, 13–14; of LBGT youths, 17; sexual harassment and, 168, 189; sexual harassment of adolescents impact on, 168–170; teacher social support and, 128; violent relationship impacts, 228
Meyer-Adams, N., 89–90
microaggressions: about, 3–4; affect on emotional and physical health, 8; based on intersectional identities, 12–13; described, 4; from student and teacher interactions, 10; impact of, 4; impacts of, on LGBT adolescents' mental health, 13–14; leading to bullying, 16; on marginalized groups, 7; preventing or dealing with, 15; racial microaggression taxonomy, 5–6, 7; recommendations for addressing teen bullying and microaggressions, 14–18; review of microaggression literature, 5–9; sexual orientation, 7, 9–10; systemic change to decrease, 16; teen bullying as, 9; towards LGBT people, 6, 7, 8, 10, 11, 12; victims of, 5
microassaults, 6, 8
microinsults, 6, 8
microinvalidations, 6, 8
Miller, D. A., 199
Mitchel, T. L., 62
Modern Racism Scale, 63
Molidor, C. E., 222, 225
Moller, B., 244, 247–248, 249
Morrow, K., 200
Mortimer, J., 168
mother-child sexual abuse, 196–197
Mullen, P. E., 244, 247–248, 249
Munro, M. A., 117
murder, 228
murder rate, 101n1
Murnen, S., 169

Nadal, K. L., 5, 6, 7, 8, 15
Najdowski, C. J., 57, 69, 70
Nannini, D. K., 224, 233
National Center for Missing and Exploited Children, 165
National Incident Base Report System (NIBRS), 195
National Longitudinal Study of Adolescent Health, 23
National Youth Survey, 23, 24, 25
No Child Left Behind Act of 2001 (NCLB), 51
Noguera, P. A., 93, 94
Nuttall, R., 68

O'Brien. M., 196
Office of Civil Rights (OCR), 171–172
Office of Juvenile Justice and Delinquency Prevention, 195
O'Keeffe, N. K., 232

Olweus, D., 107, 117
opposition defiant disorder (ODD), 209
Ortega, R., 132
out-group biases, 63–64, 67
Owen, Robert, 86–87

Paludi, C., 170, 176, 179, 183
Paludi, M., 169, 170, 172, 174, 175, 176, 179, 183
parental education on sexual abuse, 213
parental monitoring: involvement and, 232; of teen dating, 250
parent-child relationship, 206
Parents Guide to Teen Dating Violence (CVPC), 228
Parkinson, M., 156
Paskewich, B. S., 117
passive victims, 109
peer aggression, 112
peer harassment impacts, 38
peer mediation, 117
Pepler, D., 11, 12
Perron, A., 198
Pfeifer, J. E., 62
Phillips, S., 92
Phinney, G., 163
physical aggression, 111, 222
physical bullying, 107
physical health impact: of child or adolescent sexual abuse (CASA), 208; psychological difficulties of, 209
Pimental, P. S., 57, 69, 70
Pittsburgh Youth Study, 25
playground violence, 85
playgrounds, 89
police officers, 227
Polly Klass Foundation, 165
post-traumatic stress, 169
post-traumatic stress disorder (PTSD): child or adolescent sexual abuse (CASA) and, 209; dissociation and, 198; violent relationship impacts, 228
power, 113
Power, T. J., 117
Precious (movie), 193
prejudice in history, 5
preoccupied attachment style, 253

prevalence rates: age related, for serious violent offenders (SVOs), 25; decline of, in serious violence, 23; of emerging adulthood, 23; of violence by age, 27; of violence by age and type, 28
prevention and intervention: about, 115–116; lessons learned, 118; what works and what doesn't, 116–117
primary schools, 132
profiling, 102n4
protective factors for decreased violence probability, 29
psychcopathology, risk of, 197
psychological abuse, 222, 225
psychological maltreatment, 129
Psychopathic Checklist: Youth Version, 249
Purcell, R., 244, 247–248, 249
Push (Sapphire), 193

quid pro quo sexual harassment, 158–159

race impact on perceptions of adolescent sex offenders: about, 57–60; conclusions and directions for future research, 72–74; effects of defendant and victim race, 60–61; effects of juvenile defendant and victim race, 62–64; effects of juvenile defendant and victim race on registration support for forced rape, 68–69; effects of juvenile defendant and victim race on registration support for statutory rape, 65–68; perceptions of interracial domestic violence, 64–65; social psychological theory explaining effects of race, 61–62
race of juvenile defendant and victim on impact of registration support for forced rape, 68–72; discussion of preliminary findings, 71–72; method, 69–70; preliminary results, 70–71
race salience in juries, 61–62
racial bias by juries, 60–61
racial microaggression taxonomy, 5–6, 7
rape: acquaintance rape, 205; date rape, 205; forced-rape case, 69; registration support for forced rape, 68–69;

registration support for statutory rape, 65–68; reporting of, 224; reports of, 205; stranger rape cases, 64
reactive victims, 109
registered sex offenders, suicide risk by, 58–60
registration support: gender and victim race, 67; juvenile sex offenders' race and, 71; victim race and, 72
Reis, E., 11, 12
rejected stalkers, 245
relational aggression, 42, 108, 222
relational bullying, 108
Reppucci, N. D., 62
Resnick, M. D., 11, 12
restorative justice, 134, 148
restraining orders, 254–255
retaliation fear, 226
retributive goals of punishment, 66
retributive justice, 134
Rich, A., 231
Rigby, K., 133
Riis, Jacob, 88
risk: assessment and management, 254–255; of incest, 197–198; of psychopathology, 197; perception vs. reality, 85. *See also* suicide risk
risk factors: bullying and victimization, 113; increased violence probability, 29; victimization and revictimization, 205–207; victimization and revictimization theories, 207–208
risky sexual behavior, 207, 210
Rivera, D. P., 6, 7
Roland, E., 133, 180
romantic involvement and emerging adulthood, 24
Roots of Empathy program, 116
Roscoe, B., 161
Rose, S., 224
Rousseau, Jean-Jacques, 87
Rubin, L. R., 40–41, 43, 46–47, 53

Saewyc, E. M., 11, 12
Safe Dates program, 234
Sagrestano, L., 177
Saint-Pierre, M., 225, 226
Salerno, J. M., 57, 69, 70
Saltzburg, S., 12
Sampson, R., 31
Sanday, P., 233
Sandler, B., 171, 180
Sapphire (formerly Ramona Lofton), 193
Schaeffer, Rebecca, 243
school interventions, 118
school systems, physical and psychological safety of LGBT in, 17–18
school violence, structural nature of, 93
school-based educational prevention of sexual abuse, 212
schools: bullying vs. sexual harassment in, 179–184; incidence of sexual harassment in, 156; single-sex, 51–52; standardization focus, 52
schools and workplaces responsibilities on sexual harassment: aggression tolerance, 117; characteristics of investigators, 175–176; confidentiality, 178; educational programs, 174–175; impartiality, 178; investigator gender, 176; investigatory procedures, 173; mediation, 176–177; Office of Civil Rights, 179; promptness, 177; reactive measures, 175–176; responsibilities of schools and workplaces regarding, 170–177; retaliation, 178–179; sexual harassment complaints, 179; sexual harassment policy, 171–173
schoolyard bullying, 96
schoolyard segregation, 99
schoolyard violence: about, 83–86; as a relational event, 94–97; as cultural, 92; as implicit, 90–92; as structural, 93–94; complex schoolyard geographies of violent events, 97–100; groupings of, 90; rethinking spaces of violence, 89–90; schoolyards as moral spaces, 86–89; conclusions, 100–101
schoolyards as moral spaces, 101
Scott, E. S., 62
Sears, H. A., 225, 226
Second Step Violence program, 116–117
secondary schools discrimination training, 183
Sekely, A., 65, 70
self-blame, 226

self-esteem of girls, 50–51
serious violent offenders (SVOs) age related prevalence rates, 25
Seventeen (magazine), 162
sex offender registration policies, 57
sexual abuse: parental education of, 213; race and gender of victims, 206; school-based educational prevention of, 212
sexual abuse of teens by family members: about, 193; effects of, 197–199; incest, defined, 194; incest, statistics regarding, 194–195; sibling incest, 195–197; conclusion, 200
sexual agency, 44, 46
sexual assault: ages most susceptible to, 47–48; in dating relationships, 205
sexual bullying, 251
sexual desire of girls and women, 45–46
sexual harassment, 45; and adolescent employment, 166–168; behavioral examples of, 159; by gender, 161; by race, 160–161; complaints, 157; in schools, 161–162; incidence of, in schools, 156; investigation of, 177; legal definition of, 157–159; metal health impact to adolescents, 168–170; post-traumatic stress and, 169; vs. cyberstalking, 166–168
sexual harassment of adolescent girls: by peers and teachers, 159–163; by teachers, 163–164; epidemic proportions, 155–157; legal definition of, 157–159; on Internet, 164–166; peer sexual harassment, 160–162; reasonable care in preventing and dealing with, 170–174
sexual harassment of adolescents, metal health impact of, 168–170
sexual harassment vs. bullying in schools, 179–184
sexual orientation, 109
sexual orientation microaggressions: LGBT adolescents, 9–10; taxonomy of, 7
sexual victimization, 205, 210
sexual violence, 222
Sheffield, C., 169
Shepard, Matthew, 13

Sibley, D., 97
sibling incest: definition of, 195; in context, 195–197
sibling violence, 232
silence and speaking out implications, 42
Silva, E., 163
similarity-leniency bias, 62
Simmons, S., 163
simple obsessional behavior, 244
single-sex schools, 51–52
Skay, C. L., 11, 12
Skolnik, A., 8
Small, M., 85
Smith, A. C., 65, 70
Smith, J. K., 63
Smith, L., 92
Smith, P. K., 131
Smolak, L., 169
social control theory, 31
social manipulation, 41
social stature, 113
social-information processing theory, 115
socioeconomic status (SES), 74n2, 206
sociograms, 137
Sommers, S. R., 61, 62, 63
Sorenson, K. M., 65, 70
Soukamneuth, S., 52
stalking: juvenile stalking, 243–255; motivation for, 244; vs. bullying, 245
stalking behaviors, 244, 248
stalking typology, 246
Stanley, L. R., 224, 233
Starzynski, L. L., 198
Stein, N., 162, 163, 169, 170, 171, 180, 181
Stein, S., 163
stereotypes: of black women, 68; of bullies, 42; of feminine sexists, 42; of LGBT people, 17; of self-sacrificing females, 38
Stern, S. R., 39
Stevenson, M. C., 57, 63, 65, 69, 70
stigmatization, 211
Stockdale, M., 177
Stonehill, H., 171, 180
stranger rape cases, 64
Strauss, S., 164, 168
Striepe, M. I., 46, 47

Structured Assessment of Violence Risk on Youth, 249
substance abuse, 206–207
subtle discrimination, 5
Sue, D. W., 5, 6
Sugarman, D. B., 233
suicidal thoughts, 112
suicide risk: body image and, 37, 40; by LGBT youths, 14; by registered sex offenders, 58–60; of adolescent incest survivors, 198; of girls, 40; of registered sex offenders, 59; peer aggression and, 112
suicides: by girls, 37; by LGBT youths, 18; from bullying, 112; from cyberbulling, 252; from teen bullying, 3–4, 15; sexual harassment and, 169
Supplementary Homicide Reports, 228

Take Back the Halls program, 234
teachers: intervention of bullying, 133; sexual harassment of adolescent girls by, 163–164
teachers and teen bullying: about, 127; bullying eradication, 131–133; managing bullying conceptual model, 134–140; managing bullying in schools, 133–134; schools, levels of bullying in, 127–128; steps to take regarding bullying, 140–146; students bullying teachers, 130–131; teacher attitudes toward bullying, 128–129; teachers bullying students, 129–130; teachers managing bullying, 131; telling about bullying, 133; conclusions, 149
technological approaches for therapeutic purposes, 119
teen bullying: as microaggression, 9; suicide from, 3–4
teen dating, parental monitoring of, 250
teen dating violence, 223; etiology of, 250; explanations for, 229; impact of, 251
teen relationship violence (TRV): about, 221; cases of, 224; community/culture of violence, 233; definition of, 222; described, 222–223; explanations for teen dating violence, 229; family factors, 232; gender, 224–226; gender impacts of, 235; help seeking behavior, 226–227; individual variables, 230; interventions, 233–235; lack of empathy to, 230; outcome/impact, 228–229; peer influence, 232–233; prevalence, 223; teen perceptions of causes, 230; teen relationships, 230–231; warning signs, 227–228
Tetrick, K., 85
"The Net Effect: Girls and New Media," 155
Thomas, M., 99, 100
Thomson, S., 89, 93
Timmerman, G., 156, 169
Title IX, 51, 158–159, 171, 179
Tolman, D. L., 46, 47
Tomaszewski, E., 163
Torino, G. C., 5, 6
Townsend, S. M., 198
traumatic sexualization, 211
Tuan, Y. F., 98
turning points, 30
Tyner, J., 85, 88, 97

Ueno, K., 11
Ullman, S. E., 198
universal education goals, 87–88
U.S. Department of Education, 156, 164, 181
utilitarian goals to protect society, 66

Vaca, R., Jr., 57, 69, 70
van Roosmalen, E., 45
verbal aggression, 111
verbal and emotional abuse, 222
verbal bullying, 107
victimization: genetic precursors of, 113; long-term consequences, 112; risk factors for, 113, 205–207; sexual victimization, 112, 205; theories, 207–208. *See also* bullying and victimization; child sexual abuse and adolescent sexual assault and revictimization; media's influence on teen violence and victimization

victims: behavior problems, 109; race effect of, 74n1; registration support and race of, 72; social economic status (SES) of defendant and, 74n2

violence: exclusionary violence, 98, 99; interracial domestic violence perceptions, 64–65; levels of, 90; metal health impact of, 228; prevalence rates, 23, 27, 28; protective factors, 29; sexual violence, 222; sibling violence, 232; teen dating violence, 223, 250, 251; trajectory of, for chronic groups, 26; trajectory of, for early desisters, 26; use of by gender, 225. *See also* media's influence on teen violence and victimization; schoolyard violence; teen relationship violence (TRV)

violence in emerging adulthood: National Longitudinal Study of Adolescent Health (Add Health), 26–29; prevalence rates reduction of, 23; sources of violence in the late teens and early 20s, 29–30; theoretical explanations for risk and protective influences on violence, 30–33; violence in the late teens to mid-20s, 24–26; conclusion, 33

violent behavior: developmental course of, 24–25; trajectory for, 25–26

Walkerdine, V., 88
Walsh, M., 169
Wareham, S., 169
Wave I of Add Health, 28
Wave III of Add Health, 26, 29
Wayman, J. C., 224, 233
West, C., 224
Whelan, J. J., 225, 226
White, J., 49
whole school approach, 127, 129
Wiley, T. R. A., 57, 69, 70
Williams, T., 11, 12
Willis, C. E., 69, 72
Wilson, Genarlow, 57–58, 64
Wilson, M., 33
Wilson v. State of Georgia, 65
Winfrey, Oprah, 58
Wishnietsky, D., 164
Wong, Y., 8
workplace sexual harassment, 156–157
Worling, J. R., 196
Wright, J., 198

Yang, Y. W., 11
Young, E., 156
Younger, B., 40
Youth Risk Survey, 222

zero-tolerance policies, 92, 94, 96, 117

FOR REFERENCE ONLY
NOT TO BE TAKEN FROM THIS ROOM